D1274141

RED,
BLACK,
BLOND AND
OLIVE

BOOKS BY EDMUND WILSON

RED, BLACK, BLOND AND OLIVE

Studies in Four Civilizations:
Zuñi, Haiti, Soviet Russia, Israel

EDMUND WILSON

New York

OXFORD UNIVERSITY PRESS

1956

© Edmund Wilson, 1956
Library of Congress Catalogue Card Number: 56–5162
Printed in the United States of America

Second printing, 1956

GALLAUDET UNIVERSITY LIBRARY
WASHINGTON, D.C. 20002

CONTENTS

POSTSCRIPT

ACKNOWLEDGMENTS are due the *New Yorker,* in which a part of the material in the Zuñi section of this book originally appeared; and the *Reporter,* in which a part of the Haitian material appeared. Some passages from the discussion of Haitian literature were used in an introduction to the English translation of *The Pencil of God,* a novel by Pierre Marcelin and Philippe Thoby-Marcelin. Parts of the Russian diary originally appeared in the *New Republic,* the *New Yorker* and *Travel* magazine, and it was afterwards included, in a version considerably different from this one, in a book called *Travels in Two Democracies,* published by Harcourt, Brace in 1936. The two Hebraic pieces originally appeared in the *New Yorker.* The poem by Emile Roumer, with the translation by John Peale Bishop, are reprinted by permission from *An Anthology of Contemporary Latin-American Poetry,* copyright 1947 by New Directions; the passages from *Strange Altars,* copyright 1952, by permission of the Bobbs-Merrill Company, Inc.; and those from *The Divine Horseman,* copyright by Maya Deren, by permission of Thames & Hudson, Ltd.

In the case of the first two sections—those on Zuñi and Haiti—I have indicated by putting them in brackets passages written at a later date than the original accounts of my travels; in the case of the section on the Soviet Union, I have bracketed both passages written later and

vii

passages included in my diary but not published in 1936.

I have marked the accentuation of Zuñi, Russian and Hebrew words and names of places and people, except in the case of the more familiar and obvious Russian names such as Pushkin, Dostoevsky and Gorki, Lenin and Trotsky and Stalin, of which I assume that the reader knows which syllable to stress, and of such Hebrew words as *yeshiva* and *Rosh Ha-Shanah,* which are common to the whole Jewish world, but which are accented differently in the Ashkenazi pronunciation and in the Sephardic, which is official in Israel. To certain of the Russian names—such as Chaíkovsky, Músorgsky, Nizhínsky—I have restored their proper spelling. The German and French versions that we have got into the habit of using make no sense whatever in English, and—as in the case of Nizhínsky, where the letter j has a different sound in English from in French—have sometimes led to mispronunciations.

ZUÑI
1947

THE PUEBLO: Ever since reading, some years ago, a book called *Dancing Gods,* by Miss Erna Fergusson, which describes the ceremonials of the Pueblo Indians in New Mexico and Arizona, I had had an ambition to attend what seemed from her account the most spectacular of them: the Zuñi festival called Shálako. But this takes place under what are, for an Easterner, rather inconvenient conditions: in midwinter, at a date which varies and which may be set only a few days in advance; and at a place, in northwestern New Mexico, which is off the tourist route and not very easily accessible. When I did finally get a chance to visit the Shálako festival, I discovered certain other difficulties.

The little pueblo of Zuñi is one of the Indian communities that have survived, since the arrival of the whites, most successfully as a social organism. Its strength and cohesion it seems mainly to owe to the extraordinary tribal religion: a complicated system of priesthoods, fraternities and clans which not only performs the usual functions of religions but also supplies it with a medical service, a judiciary machinery and year-long entertainment. This cult includes the whole community, distributing and rotating offices, and organizing it so tightly that it is completely self-contained in a way that perhaps no white community is, and equipped to resist the pressures that have disintegrated other Indian groups. The ceremonies are partly in the nature of the enactment of a national

3

myth, and they present a sort of sacred drama whose cycle runs through the entire year. The legends show a
good deal of imagination and the impersonations a good
deal of art, and the cast is so enormous that a very considerable proportion of the little town of twenty-six hundred has, at one time or another, a chance to play some
role. With this, the Zuñi religion imposes an effective discipline, involving periods of continence and fasting, and
insisting on truthfulness—"speaking with one tongue"—
and on civility and gentleness in personal relations. The
Zuñis as a group are extremely self-controlled, industri-
ous and self-reliant.

The Spanish explorer Coronado first discovered the
Zuñi region in 1540 in his search for the reported treasures of "the Seven Cities of Cibola." The Spaniards were
disappointed to find a cluster of seven little Indian villages
possessing nothing more valuable than a few ornaments
made of turquoise. Coronado thought these Indians intelligent, and exceptionally skilled in building and in the
domestic arts. He captured one of their towns, to which
he gave the name of Granada, whereupon the inhabitants
of all of them took refuge on a large mesa, where they
resolutely fortified themselves and held out against the
invaders. Thereafter, though they were sometimes driven,
in the course of the two centuries that followed, to pro-
fessing allegiance to Spain or submitting to Christian
baptism, they continued to stand up to the Spaniards with
remarkable unanimity and courage. Twice they murdered
the resident missionary and transported the whole community to the top of their impregnable mesa, where they
remained, the first time for three years, the second time
for twelve. In the meantime, the seven villages had been
forced to amalgamate, and there was finally only one; but
the size of the population seems never to have been permanently reduced. There were twenty-five hundred Zuñis

in 1680, about as many as there are today—and the estimates made by members of the Coronado expedition
seem to give about the same number.

Against the Yankees, too, the Zuñis have held their
own. They have not been deprived of their lands as have
so many of the other pueblos, and, in spite of the presence
in Zuñi of a Catholic school and a Christian Reform mission, they have never been influenced by the white man's
religion. Nor, on the other hand—although John Collier
has recently reversed the policy of the Indian Bureau in
the direction of encouraging the Indians in their native
way of life—have the Zuñis been at all eager to accept
any favors from it. The Reorganization Act of 1934,
intended to benefit the Indians by offering them local
self-government and the opportunity to organize in fed-
eral corporations, was formally accepted by the Zuñis, but
no advantage was taken of it. They feel that they do not
need it. According to the estimate of the Indian Bureau,
they made, during 1945, when there were several army
posts in the region, at least a million dollars out of their
silverwork, beadwork and other products, and in peace-
time they also prosper. They do not like their status as
"wards of the government," which involves, among other
things, the imposition of stock reduction and of a ban on
buying liquor; but they have survived, with their well-
ordered society, as a completely autonomous unit. They
have managed in a most curious way to incorporate modern conveniences—radios, phonographs, cars, gas ovens,
Delco plants—in their traditional tribal life without being affected by modern ideas, and they strive to relax not a
strand of the web that holds them together. This is really
the Indians' domain: and it is run by interlocking religious
orders, with a board of priests at the top. The Zuñis cannot vote as citizens; a bill to give them the franchise has
encountered much opposition in the New Mexico legisla-

ture, where some local politician has recently referred to them as "aliens"—to the sardonic amusement of the Zuñis, who thought it was just the other way. They certainly succeed in making it so for the visitor and even for the resident officials. The white Indian Agent in residence has no powers except in the matter of limiting the grazing of the Indians' flocks so that their pastures may not be destroyed: his office is merely to supervise the government services provided and to coöperate with the Zuñi civil governor; and the authority of the governor himself is limited to the relations of the Zuñis with the whites and to such problems as caring for the livestock and cleaning up the village.

Yet the weight of the outside world must be making itself felt in Zuñi. Relations seem very much strained between Indians and whites this year. Though the Zuñis sixty years ago were made the object of intimate ethnographic studies, they are today determined that the whites shall never again photograph their ceremonies or take down their chants and prayers—regarding such records, apparently, as leaks which will detract from the efficiency of their ritual. (They regard with amused contempt the indiscriminate publicizing of the Christian missionaries, saying, "They throw their religion away as if it weren't worth anything and expect us to believe it.") This may be a sign that the return to the pueblo of young Zuñis who have been in the services has lately been challenging the old ideas as they have never been challenged before. Last summer, a description of the Shálako appeared in a local paper, and a young anthropologist who now lives in the pueblo was wrongly suspected of having written it. An attempt was made to expel him, as had been done with one of his predecessors, on the charge that he was practicing witchcraft, and he was only allowed to remain as a result of the intervention of the Indian Agent. An-

other resident anthropologist had been put out not long
before, and all his notes destroyed. The rumor has just
reached the Zuñis that the wife of a California judge, who
has visited the pueblo often and regards its inhabitants
as her special pets, is coming to Shálako this year to take
down the prayers in shorthand. As for Spanish-speaking
Americans—in revenge for the cruelties of Coronado—
the Zuñis do not allow them to come near the festival: if
any is recognized, he is immediately arrested and imprisoned. There is a feeling that the resentment of the Zuñis
may come to a head this year, and that no whites may in
future be allowed to attend. I was told that I must not take
notes or sketch or ask questions about the cult, and that I
ought not to leave around too casually the anthropological
works I had brought, which had photographs of the dances
and plates of the masks—though they were mostly Smithsonian reports, one of them published sixty years ago. It
was as if they had been contraband political tracts under a
totalitarian dictatorship; and it was surprising to me to find
myself out here, in the midst of the United States, in an
atmosphere that reminded me of Moscow on the eve of
the purges or of a steel town in Pennsylvania at the climax of a serious strike.

There is even, I understand, some revival of antagonism
toward the Navahos. These traditional enemies of the
Zuñis have long been on more amiable terms with them
and have for decades been flocking to Shálako, but today
the flourishing Zuñis are saying that the impoverished
Navahos only want to take advantage of the Zuñi hospitality to eat a square meal at their banquets.

The town of Gallup in northwestern New Mexico is
one of the most forbidding stops on the Santa Fe railroad.
It is a trading post and coal-mining town of the dismal
and grimy kind, and the place to which the Indians resort

to buy the liquor they are not supposed to have. They get drunk, have their wallets stolen, and come to in the morning in jail.

The government headquarters in the Zuñi reservation is forty miles away, at Black Rock. There are a guest-house, where the Indian agent put me up, a handful of other houses and a good little one-story hospital. The latter and the pueblo schoolhouse are the two gifts of the New Deal Indian Bureau that the Zuñis have made most use of. It is estimated that about two-thirds of the cases which need attention turn up in the hospital for medical treatment; but this does not mean that the Zuñis do not, also, practice their own therapeutics. Among their innumerable groups are a set of medical guilds, each of which specializes in a different kind of ailment: bullet wounds, delayed childbirth, epilepsy, coughs, etc. Their cures involve much incantation and a certain amount of sleight of hand, as the doctors pretend to extract from the patients various foreign bodies—feathers, stones, bits of fur or calico—which are supposed to have been conjured into them by witchcraft.

Zuñi proper lies four miles below Black Rock and is surrounded by little farms and agricultural villages to which the Indians go in summer to raise corn and tend their flocks. On the way down the slope to the pueblo you get a good view of Corn Mountain, the great mesa to which the Zuñis were in the habit of resorting, in early times, to defend themselves against the Spaniards. This dominates the Zuñi landscape and plays a considerable role in their myths, and they still maintain altars there. The first time I saw it in daylight, it was colored a deep brick red and well salted with the night's fall of snow, but its tints are always changing with the light, and it sometimes seems pink or purple or dry yellow or even striped green. It is studded here and there with those statuelike stones that are carved out by erosion of the tufa: there is one pillar standing halfway down the cliff that looks like a long-necked mountain lion, and certain others along the top are supposed to be Zuñi maidens, who were for some reason thrown from the cliff when the Indians were living on the mesa. In general, however, these shapes are regarded as the remains of monsters that were blasted into petrifaction by the thunderbolts of a legendary cataclysm. There is also a modern structure that offers no stimulus to fancy: an automatic beacon for planes. The pueblo itself is situated in a kind of amphitheater of mesas, the nearer ones red, the more distant dark. When one sees it, one understands why the Zuñis at last settled here, believing that they had come to the middle of the world.

Walking down a red bridle path, I passed a Zuñi woman on horseback, who had stopped in the Zuñi River to allow her horse to drink, and I was passed by a Zuñi boy showing off on a pony. You cross the river on a crude little wooden bridge which will not bear heavy traffic, and come to the governor's house, marginal to the community, like his functions, and a garage run by a Zuñi, which, it seems, is an audacious venture, a departure from the habits of the tribe. It does not engage in business but sells all its products through non-Indian traders. In Zuñi, even the trading posts, where all the supplies are bought, are run not by Zuñis but by whites.

Coming down into the village proper—among one-story adobe houses and the beehive-shaped outdoor ovens that are both the same purplish pink as the bare grassless earth they are made of—is a descent into a foreign country. The air is full of piñon smoke that has a smell as rich and fragrant as roast chestnuts. The dogs come out everywhere to bark at you—half-wild and rather horrid mongrels: some look like degenerate huskies, others as if they were crossed with coyotes. I saw one family of half-grown pups in which every one was different. I was reminded for a moment by the earth and the smell, the women wearing gay shawls and carrying baskets or jars on their heads, of the towns in southern Europe. But this is something remote from Europe, at once newer and older: a piece of prehistoric America that has absorbed some of the customs of the United States.

There are great preparations in evidence: everywhere men chopping wood and women baking loaves in the ovens; outside the houses hang sheepskins, fresh from the dozens of sheep that will be barbecued or stewed for the feasts. Against the monotonous background, the blankets are bright green or red. The people have an Eskimo Mongoloid look: stout, compact, and not very tall, with round black eyes that shine. Some of the men have frank friendly faces, but all look as if they had been cut out of some very hard substance, and they are in general reserved and solemn, talking little among themselves and not even glancing at visitors. The women have bulky swathed bodies on feet and legs made enormous by a kind of wound puttees, and their wrapped and wadded bodies go along on legs that seem spindling. There are many small primitive corrals, mere rows of rough stakes, with sheep, burros, cattle and horses. Here and there is a domesticated wild turkey or an eagle in a wooden cage, both kept to furnish feathers for costumes. Beyond rises Corn Mountain, which belongs to the Zuñis and to which they belong, now transformed by the setting sun: the upper part of the mesa is for a moment vividly reddened, and its markings and outlines become distinct, then suddenly it is all left in shadow. On the other side of the sky, the clouds are a dull brickish red that corresponds with the color of the mesa and harmonizes with that of the soil. The little Zuñi River shines palely as twilight falls.

The town is no longer the anthill (the Zuñis themselves called it the Middle Anthill of the World) that the travelers of the eighteen-eighties found and that the Taos pueblo still is—with the houses piled up in terraces and scaled by outside ladders. There is a nucleus of these old buildings left that encloses the little plaza, but the Zuñis have prospered so much that they have built themselves capacious houses, which now cover a relatively large area. They seem to put them wherever they like, at various distances from and angles to one another, and there is scarcely in the whole pueblo anything that can be called a street. The typical Zuñi house has only a single story and not more than three or four rooms. These rooms are hung with shawls and blankets, and one of the more pretentious houses is decorated with maps. I saw none that showed any signs of squalor—though the Zuñis' ideas about bedding are not so nice as ours—and none that did not smell clean. In spite of the generally high standard of living, there are different degrees of wealth, and the families I visited were pretty well off. Yet, even with their chairs and beds, these houses, to a non-Indian, seem rather bare, because they are still the dwellings of people who have for millennia been used to sitting and sleeping on the ground and have not yet had the time to acquire the sense of furniture. The pieces are set around without system, often at great distances from one another, just as the conversations that take place when a white visitor calls are full of immense silences that are the product not of embarrassment but of the natural taciturnity of the Indian. There are two or three houses with a second floor, but this is merely "conspicuous waste," as the owners do not live in the upper part but use it, if at all, to store corn. Lately, the Zuñis have shifted from round to square beams, because the women have found that the latter are easier to dust—a motivation of a kind which, as a visiting

anthropologist says, could hardly be guessed in the ruins
of the past by a student of archaeology.

Some of these houses have curious features that are the
result of their having been built to receive the Shálako
gods, or Shálakos. There are six of these gods, and tradition demands that each of them be received in a house
especially built for the purpose. There have also in the
past been two houses to entertain other groups of divinities. Now, the building of these eight houses and the banquets, on a medieval scale, with which the gods are welcomed have in some cases ruined for the whole of the year
the families that have undertaken them. So the Zuñis
sometimes cheat on the expense and merely replaster old
houses or build on a new room or two or entertain two
Shálakos in one house. Even so, this means that every
year there are several new houses, equipped for the re-
quirements of the Shálako dance. They must have each a
long room, which sometimes runs to sixty feet, and a ceiling at least twelve feet high to accommodate the enormous masks. Each must also have a row of windows that
opens on the Shálako room from another large chamber
next to it and from which certain special groups have
the privilege of watching the performance, as if from
theater boxes. These windows, which have regular sashes
and panes, with little paper stickers on them to advertise
the company that makes them, are one of the queerest examples of the mixture in Zuñi of the old and the new.
When the celebration is over, and a family comes to live
in the house, the windows become a nuisance and are usually walled up.

Contrasting with these modern houses stands the old,
sordid, roofless shell of embrowned mud and beams that
is all that is left of the first Christian church built by
the Spaniards in Zuñi. Beside it is a little plot of ground
with a plain wooden cross in the middle, and everybody

who dies in Zuñi is buried in this narrow yard. Burial among the Zuñis is accomplished with a minimum of ceremony. The Zuñis are collective-minded. Their religion is concerned with the life of the tribe, and it takes very little account of the life of the individual. The rites for birth, marriage and death are relatively perfunctory and simple; and in this cemetery of bare earth that has no grass and no flowers, they separate the men and the women, burying them on different sides, but they do not mark the graves: they simply dig another hole and put in another body, with the result that the place is a jumble of unidentifiable bones. One remembers the little churches in the Spanish-speaking part of New Mexico, with their death's-heads and their throned skeletons that are paraded in religious processions. The Spanish had a cult of mortality, but the Zuñis are not interested in death. They are healthy themselves, and their chief concern is to procure, in their arid country, enough rain to insure fertility. Their dead do not lie with their bones in this boneyard but are supposed to be alive and merry in a delightful village not far away, and constantly to revisit their people in order to keep up their morale. The early Catholic missionaries found Zuñi so tough a nut that they abandoned it for a hundred years. The present Catholic priest in the pueblo is said to feel that he has made some progress, now that the Zuñis, after a quarter of a century, when they meet him out of doors, do not spit at him.

The only other remaining relic of the Spanish proselytizing is a small wooden image, a *"santo,"* which is kept by a certain family and which they show at the price of a coin which you drop into a bag around its neck. Once a year this image is taken out and made the object of a ceremonial dance performed by young girls and boys, which is the only dance of the cycle that "Mexicans" are allowed to attend. The figure is dressed in blue and must once have represented the Virgin. The Zuñi legend about it was thus recited to Miss Erna Fergusson and is reported by her in her book *Dancing Gods*: "They said that a long time ago Mexicans brought the doll to Zuñi. She was a queen and she was in the family way. She was not married, but the sun gave her a baby. They brought her to the old church which was used then, and there she had a baby. Her baby was a doll, too. When she got up, after four days, the Acoma Indians came to Zuñi to dance, and the mother liked their dance so much that she wanted to go to Acoma. So she asked her daughter: 'Do you want to go to Acoma or do you want to stay in Zuñi?' The daughter wanted to stay in Zuñi. So the mother went to Acoma, and the daughter stayed in Zuñi, and the Zuñis were so grateful because she liked Zuñi better that every year they have a dance for her." The Zuñis, preoccupied with weather, believe that the *santo* presages rain by breaking out in beads of sweat.

When I left the little town, it was dark, and the new moon, which had been a thin sliver in the clear sky of previous nights, was bulged out like a segment of orange and blurred to subdued light by a large darkish soft gray cloud, while the sky behind it was fading to a paler but still limpid gray, and below hung a lemonish dying light. The whole thing reminded me, in its delicacy, of the coloring of certain butterflies that have yellow below black on their wings—an idea perhaps suggested by my just having read of the sacred black butterflies which one of the orders of priests is supposed to put into their drums and which are said to drive the hearers to frenzy.

The people in the village went to and fro, their activity was now intense, yet everything was utterly quiet. The three or four general stores, which are always called "trading posts," were crowded with men, women and children buying things for the Shálako festival, but these, too, were very quiet and appeared to pay so little attention that one ceased to remember how observant they were and to realize that one was being intently watched. It is a queer thing to go from a community where people depend on print to a community in which everyone's relations with Nature and with his neighbor depend on direct perception, and in which the handing on of history and the transmission of technical skills, as well as the spreading of news, are all oral and very limited. The world they inhabit is different from ours: it is confined to a much smaller area but it must be much more searchingly seen and heard. Their language has no printed literature, and, though most Zuñis can more or less read English, they usually get little farther than popular weeklies and the Gallup paper.

The Anthropologists: It is difficult, even, to tell whether any but an exceptional Zuñi has any idea to what extent his people have been studied and written about.

When the Bureau of Ethnology was founded in 1879, an expedition was sent out the same year, of which one of the principal objects was to make a detailed inquiry into the life of the pueblo of Zuñi. The adventures of this party were remarkable and the reports that they produced brilliant. The expedition included one man of genius, a youth of twenty-two named Frank Hamilton Cushing, who had begun collecting arrowheads at the age of nine and was now an authority on Indian handicrafts. Cushing's history had been a strange one. As a child, he had been so weakly that he had passed his first three years on a pillow, and, since it was thought impossible to send him to school, he grew up, in central New York, without the companionship of other children, spending much of his time in the woods, where he exercised his remarkable faculties in a very unusual way. Finding him-

self alone with the forest, he invented a special language
for his relations with the birds and the animals, and he
acquired an extraordinary sense of the lives of the departed Indians, discovering remains of their passage where
no one else would have been able to recognize them,
identifying artifacts that no one had understood, and
teaching himself to chip flints and weave baskets in such
a way as to reproduce the Indians' work. He had indeed,
through his own unusual habits, in some sense reproduced
the experience of the Indian, and he had always an alternate world in which he was more at home than in that
of Anglo-Saxon America. Once arrived in the Zuñi
pueblo, he first imposed himself on the Indians, taking up
his abode among them, thoroughly learning their language and walking in on their sacred ceremonies. Finding
that they could not get rid of him by pointed suggestions
or threats, they ended by being impressed by his manual
skill, his sang-froid and by a sympathy with their way of
life that must have been quite unexpected after their
previous relations with the white man, and they finally
set out to assimilate him, to acquire him for their tribe.
They stole all his white-man's clothes and made him wear
the Zuñi costume; they instructed him in their customs
and tried to get him to marry a Zuñi girl—which he
firmly declined to do. They came at last to value him so
highly that they made him a Priest of the Bow, one of the
highest offices in Zuñi, which enabled him to sit in on the
councils and take part in the most esoteric rites.

Frank Cushing spent almost four years in Zuñi, sharing
the life of the natives, before he went back to the East
and married a girl of his own race. But he soon returned
to the pueblo, bringing his wife and a colored cook, and
set up a more comfortable household. Yet his position
was still a queer one, and he signed himself in his official letters "1st War Chief of Zuñi, U.S. Asst. Ethnolo-

gist." His defense of the interests of the Indians soon brought about his recall. The boundaries of the Zuñi reservation had, it turned out, been carelessly described in the order which assigned it to them, and, taking advantage of this, an attempt was made by local whites to get a part of it away from them for ranching. This was countered by Cushing, who carried on, in the Boston and Chicago papers, such a vigorous agitation that the President at last intervened and obtained a correction of the boundary. The career in Zuñi of Cushing was, however, soon brought to an end by Senator Logan of Illinois, the father-in-law of one of the land-grabbers. He had been implicated in the newspaper controversy, and his political enemies had seized on this. Logan was furious with Cushing, and accused him of having had scandalous reasons for his intimate relations with the Zuñis (John Collier, more recently, met the same sort of slander when he was trying to get money for the Indian Bureau). The Senator threatened to see to it that the Bureau of Ethnology should not go on unless Cushing were removed from Zuñi, and Cushing was obliged to resign by superiors who found themselves helpless.

In the meantime, he had published in the *Century Magazine*—where a piece of his once appeared side by side with a study by Henry James of *Du Maurier and London Society*—a series of fascinating articles under the title *My Adventures in Zuñi*. One learns from these articles and from others of his writings that the America of Chester A. Arthur inevitably suspected the adventurer scholar of lying about what he had seen and done. Unfortunately, he did not live to write a full-length study of Zuñi; but he did publish a series of monographs on various phases of Zuñi life, and a volume of *Zuñi Folk Tales* that belongs with *Uncle Remus* as one of the few first-rate things of the kind that have been produced in the United States. For

Cushing was an admirable writer—almost as much a literary man as he was a technical expert; and, if the historians of American literature had seriously done their work, he would be recognized not merely as a classic in the anthropological field but as an artist who had something in common with a figure like Doughty of Arabia. A good deal of Cushing's work has an autobiographical element, and his account of his queer dual life is a unique literary document on the struggle between white man and red man, not in the forest or on the plains, but in one dislocated human spirit. The actual adaptation to Indian life, when he had had to face its customs and conditions, had not been easy for Cushing. He had never become really strong, and the Zuñis, observing his frailness, had determined, as they told him, "to harden his meat." He was taken upon winter journeys, involving much exposure and little food; and he was subjected to the ordeals of his cult, which sometimes involved the swallowing of great bowls of revolting messes. In Cushing's book called *Zuñi Breadstuff,* though he praises the Zuñi cuisine—which, it seems, is as various as their ritual and, like it, has a purely aesthetic side—he shudders at the memory of his first attempts to emulate their eating habits. It is curious to see the repugnance revived by these Indian memories persistently contending with his pride at having recreated himself as a Zuñi. He couldn't bear their cruel punishment of hanging people up by the wrists to make them confess to charges of witchcraft, and did his best to prevent them from carrying it out. Yet it is always, in Cushing's writings, the boy that grew up as an Indian who gets in the last word. He speaks appreciatively, for example, of a greenish paste, with a flavor of aromatic plants, made from boiled and mashed-up wood-rats. But his four years in Zuñi had shortened his life. He died prematurely at forty-two, having previously destroyed his notes on the secrets that he had learned in his capacity as priest, and that he felt he ought not to divulge.

The head of the Smithsonian expedition of 1879 was an ethnologist named James Stevenson. His wife was also an ethnologist, and they worked together on Zuñi till Stevenson died in 1888. Mrs. Stevenson published, in 1905, as a report of the Bureau of Ethnography, a comprehensive volume called *The Zuñi Indians,* which deals professedly with "their mythology, esoteric fraternities and ceremonies," but which actually gives an all-around picture of the life of the Zuñi pueblo. The book is elaborately illustrated with drawings and photographs, and contains a fine series of colored plates of the ceremonial masks and altars. Mrs. Stevenson, by her own methods, different from Cushing's, got to know in the course of the years a great deal about the Zuñis, and the story of her relations with the pueblo is almost as strange as Cushing's. She had made, at an early stage, the acquaintance of a Zuñi whose name was Wéwha and whom she believed for years to be an able and exceptionally intelligent squaw. Wéwha was an authority on the Zuñi religion and, becoming very friendly with the white woman, supplied her with much information. Then it turned out, to Mrs. Stevenson's astonishment, that Wéwha was not a woman but a man who dressed and lived like a woman. The custom of the Zuñis, it seemed, in cases of borderline sex, was to put it up to the males at puberty whether they wanted to assume women's dress. The men in the family remonstrated with them, but, once the decision was made, they were accepted in the role they had chosen. It seems likely that Wéwha, an orphan, had identified himself from childhood with a beloved and admired aunt who had taken him into her house. He was far from being completely effeminate. Mrs. Stevenson describes Wéwha as "perhaps the tallest person in Zuñi; certainly the strongest, both mentally and physically"; and "his strong character," she says, "made his word law among both the men and women with whom he associated." His feminine role did not prevent him from begetting at least one child and being credited with several more. Matilda Coxe Stevenson was an aggressive intellectual woman, and she took a great liking to Wéwha and developed with him a close alliance. He was, she declares, unquestionably the most remarkable member of his tribe. At one time she brought him to Washington for a visit of six months, during which he rapidly learned to speak English, called on President Cleveland and came to be on very friendly terms with the Speaker of the House and his wife. When he returned to the pueblo, he assured his compatriots that the white women were mostly frauds, for he had seen them, in the ladies' rooms, taking out their false teeth and the "rats" from their hair.

Mrs. Stevenson's account, in her book, of Wéwha's death in 1896 is one of her most eloquent passages. Wéwha had a bad heart and strained it that winter in preparing his house—he had laid the stone dance-floor himself—for the reception of a Shálako god. He died a few days after the festival, with Mrs. Stevenson at his side; and his family, which included the devoted aunt, were somewhat offended that Wéwha's last words should have been for the intruding white woman: "Tell all my friends in Washington good-by. Tell President Cleveland, my friend, good-by. Mother, love all my people; protect them; they are your children; you are their mother." All the gifts from these friends were then destroyed, according to Zuñi custom, as well as the photographs they had given him, with the exception of those of the Stevensons and of Speaker and Mrs. Carlisle, which the foster-mother could not bear to lose. Now the question arose on which side of the cemetery—with the men or the women—to bury him, and it was answered by slipping his legs into a pair of white trousers.

Mrs. Stevenson's friendship with Wéwha had been her single really close link with Zuñi. She had otherwise been anything but well received. It had been only by threatening to call out the troops when the Zuñis showed serious opposition that she had forced them to allow her to come and go; and they got to dislike her so bitterly that she was driven to post a bodyguard outside the tent in which she slept. (In another pueblo she studied, the people who answered her questions were murdered.) Her inquiries were finally halted when the Zuñis took a positive stand against admitting her to one of their ceremonies, and defied her to produce her troops. The government, she found, would not back her, and her activities came to an end. She had owed her knowledge of Zuñi to an individual as much out of the ordinary and as much a departure from the norm of his tribe as Frank Cushing had been among his own people; and as Cushing had burned his notes, destroying his data on Zuñi, so Wéwha's connections with the white man's world were symbolically annihilated when his Washington mementoes were burned.

Since then, the pueblo has been visited by a number of other investigators. Miss Ruth Benedict's *Patterns of Culture* contains a good popular account of the peculiar society of the Zuñis; but the pueblo has been studied more thoroughly by another trained anthropologist, Miss Ruth L. Bunzel, who came to Zuñi in 1928 and remained there for five years. Miss Bunzel told the natives that the purpose of her visit was to learn to make Zuñi pottery, and she actually became proficient in this art, but she also mastered the Zuñi language so completely that she was later able to write a grammar of it, and she managed to learn so much about the Zuñi religion that she could com-

pile a kind of encyclopedia of the Zuñi sacred personages
called "katchinas." She also published, with literal translations, the texts of the Zuñi creation myth and of much
of their ritual poetry. When the report of this got back
to the pueblo, the Indians seem to have felt that Miss
Bunzel had imposed upon them, and they have become
more suspicious of whites, alleging any purpose whatever, who seek to live in their village. But the attitude of
the visitors themselves, as well as that of the Zuñis, has
undoubtedly somewhat changed. This is apparent in Miss
Bunzel's monographs. Her work is of the same order of
importance as that of Mrs. Stevenson and Cushing; her
contribution to the subject is most valuable. But her
studies are less personal, more technical, than those of
her predecessors. In Miss Benedict's case, though she
warns us herself of the danger the anthropologist must
run of forcing the complexity of life into a too self-
consistent pattern, she has not quite escaped that temptation; and one is struck, if one comes to her book after
reading these other authors, by the discrepancies between
her picture, all made up of round generalizations, and
certain specific instances reported by firsthand observers
who had no interest in establishing a pattern. It is the aim
of Miss Benedict to present the pueblo as an example of
the "Apollonian" culture, moderate, smooth and restrained, which is contrasted, by Spengler's distinction,
with the "Dionysian" kind; and, not knowing the Zuñis
intimately, she has managed to keep out of sight their
truculence toward the outside world and the harshness of
their methods of repression. For Miss Benedict's didactic
purpose, the Zuñis must be calmer and more consistent
than the people of any human community, no matter how
well "integrated," can possibly ever be: she needs a speci-
men for a demonstration.

The ideal of these later students is, however, an objective one. Where the explorers of 1879 approached the Indians as human beings, the contemporary anthropologist, who has first studied his subject in college and is working for some sort of degree, applies to them a technique of scientific notation, and transposes all that he sees into an anthropological jargon—of "institutionalizations," "acculturations," "patterned gestures"—which, although it may have its uses, must also, to some extent, impede realistic perception. This new academic approach is probably the very last thing that the Zuñis can understand. They conclude that the aloof intruder is curious about their secrets for no good reason, and they bring charges of witchcraft against him. They are ashamed of their lapses in the past in letting such people in, and are resolved that no more shall occur. "Our priests aren't soft like they were in Stevenson's time," said the Governor to the young anthropological field-worker at present living in Zuñi; and the young man could only wonder, with envy and almost with incredulity, at the days when it was possible for Cushing to sit in on the highest councils and for Mathilda Coxe Stevenson to get duplicates made—by Zuñis—of all the most sacred masks.

Shálako: I started for the first night of the Shálako festival (December 16 this year), with a small party of other visitors, at about four in the afternoon. All cars going down the hill were stopped by the police and searched for liquor. This, I was later told, failed almost completely in its purpose, since the Zuñis, by way of their grapevine, would send the word back to Gallup for their bootleggers to come in around the hills.

We arrived at the pueblo just in time for the advent of the Council of the Gods, a group in which the Shálakos are not included. A fording place of mud and stones had been built across the Zuñi River, and the gods, coming down from a stone formation known as the White Rocks, made their entrance over it into the town. The young Fire God comes first—a boy in his early teens, his nude body painted black and spotted with red, yellow, white and blue, wearing a black spotted mask, like a helmet, that covers the whole of his head, and carrying a smoldering brand. We missed his arrival, however, and did not see him till later. The main procession, which was now approaching, produced an uncanny impression. First comes the high god of the festival, Sáyatasha, the Rain God of the North; and behind him his deputy, Hútutu, the Rain God of the South. Sáyatasha, in his mask, has what looks from a distance like a blank black-and-white pierrot face, between a black banged wig and a black-and-white striped ruff, and he is dressed in a white gown. He stalks pompously in a long slow stride, accompanied by a short sharp rattle, made by shaking a cluster of deer scapulae every time he puts down his foot. It is the rhythm of authority and dignity which is reserved for him alone and—like the music for Wotan in the *Ring*—accompanies him all through the ceremonies. As he comes closer, we make out his accoutrements. A long flat horn, in place of an ear, sticks out from the right side of his mask, like an upcurved turquoise pennon; it has a heavy black fringe on its underside and a white feather dangling at the end. This horn presages long life for the Zuñi people; and the left eye, a long black streak prolonged through an outstanding wooden ear, also heavily fringed, invokes a special long life for the "people of one heart." The right eye, not extended beyond the face, is intended to threaten short life to those who practice witchcraft. Sáyatasha has a bow and arrows, and "prayer plumes"—that is, sticks with feathers attached that are supposed to give wings to the prayers. His follower Hútutu is much the same, except that he has two ears and no horn, and that his eyes are set in a single black stripe which stretches across his mask, and from the tip of one ear to that of the other. Each is followed by a Yámuhakto, or Wood Carrier, who comes to pray for the trees, so that the people may have firewood and beams for their houses. The masks of the Yámuhakto are turquoise and bell-glass-shaped, with expressionless holes for the eyes and mouth, and each of these masks is surmounted with an untrimmed black wig, a tuft of yellow macaw feathers, and a kind of long green wand, from which hang down toward the shoulders long tassels of many-colored yarns. The Yámuhakto are wearing white buckskin skirts, and the naked upper parts of their bodies are painted a kind of purple and festooned with great garlands of beads. They carry deer antlers and bunches of feathers. All four of these principal divinities are wearing enormous round collars—shaped like life preservers and striped black-on-white like peppermints—that extend far beyond their faces and conceal the joint made by the mask. The two whippers, the Sálimopiya, come last, carrying yucca switches. Both have bell-glass-shaped masks, noses like long pipes, eyeholes that are connected like spectacles, yellow topknots of feathers that stick out behind like weather vanes, and huge ruffs of black raven feathers. Both are nude except for a loincloth and wear spruce wreaths on wrists and ankles; but they are decorated in different ways: one, the Warrior of the Zenith, has a mask that is checkered in bright squares of color, with much yellow and red, which represents a spectrum of the midday sun, and red sunbursts where the ears would be. The other, the Warrior of the Nadir, is wearing a black mask with blue eyes and a blue snout.

All these figures proceed at a rhythm that is set by Sáyatasha's rattle, but involves at least three different gaits. Hútutu paces at a shorter stride than Sáyatasha, and the

Sálimopiyas move with a quicker, a running step. All the time one hears a soft lively whistling that resembles the calling of birds. One cannot tell which of the figures is making these sounds, because one cannot see their faces; and, arising from no visible human source, scanning no human chant, yet filling the quiet air, the song seems the genuine voice of deities that are part of Nature. So they pass, while the people wait in silence, across the little dwindled river, where a dead dog lies on the bank and old tin cans and paper boxes have been caught here and there on the mud flats; they march up between the rude corrals, in one of which a big sow is grunting.

The Council now blesses the village, proceeding to six different points, where small holes have been dug in the ground. The people come out of the houses and sprinkle the divinities with sacred meal, and the Council, at every excavation, plants prayer plumes and sprinkles meal and performs some solemn maneuvers. Sáyatasha and Hútutu, each with his Yámuhakto, make two units that parade back and forth, while the Sálimopiya mark time, never slackening their running pace but turning around in one spot. The climax of the ceremony comes when Sáyatasha and Hútutu walk up to one another and stop. Sáyatasha cries "Hu-u-u," and his vis-à-vis answers "Hu-tu-tu. Hu-tu-tu." The livelier calls, one decides, must be made by the Sálimopiya, since they seem to match the brisker tempo. It is evident that all these calls have been imitated directly from bird-cries—one remembers the expertness at this of Fenimore Cooper's Indians—bird-cries, perhaps, heard at dusk or at night and attributed to elemental beings. Though owls, with the Indians, have a bad reputation, being usually connected with witchcraft, Hútutu is obviously an owl. I assumed at first that the voices were whistles in the snouts of the Sálimopiyas, but learned that they were produced by the throat and lips. I was told of a conversation in English in which one Zuñi had said to another, "Gee, you make that noise good!" At one year's Shálako, Miss Bunzel says, the Sálimopiyas were severely criticized for not being sufficiently handsome, for not showing sufficient animation, and for not giving loud enough calls. Yet the whistling is never shrill, it is always under perfect control; and the confrontation of Sáyatasha and Hútutu is performed with an unearthly impressiveness. At last, with much ceremonial, they enter the house prepared for them—it has a cozy, brand-new, suburban look. Though we whites have been behaving with discretion, the Indians are afraid we may go too close and warn us to keep our distance.

In the meantime, the six Shálakos, the guests of honor, have been sitting out in front of a cabin, in which the actors put on their costumes, in a field back of one of the trading posts. These creatures are gigantic birds, the messengers of the rain gods, which, erect, stand ten or twelve feet tall. They have cylindrical turquoise faces with protruding eyes that roll up and down, long wooden beaks that snap, and upcurving tapering turquoise horns on either side of their heads. They wear big ruffs of raven feathers, black banged wigs and towering fan-shaped crests of black-and-white eagle tail-feathers. But their entrance into the village is arranged to take place just at the moment when twilight is falling, and one can now see them only dimly as, proceeding in single file and escorted by men in black blankets, they make their way to the river and, with a rhythmic jingle of bells fastened around their ankles, come slowly across the ford. The dark is blotting them out at the moment they arrive on the hither side; they squat in a row of six on the road by which the Council came. Now, with night, it grows very cold. The visitors hang around for a time— there is a group of young men and women, anthropolog-

ical students from the University of New Mexico—
afraid to ask the Zuñis what is going to happen next or
when it is going to happen. We lean on the egg-shaped
ovens, and one of the girls gets a present of a loaf of
white Zuñi bread, made from sour dough, which she
breaks up and offers around: it is still warm and tastes
delicious. But the last orange-yellow light has faded out
of the sky to our left, and still the birds do not move. The
Zuñis have gone indoors, and the whites drift away, too.
Only the Indian Agent and I remain.

An hour and a half pass. We walk up and down to un-
freeze our feet. The Shálakos utter from time to time a
single reiterated bird-note, which sounds as if it came, not
from close at hand, but from the other side of the river;
and at invervals they clack their beaks—which we can
hear with remarkable distinctness—not at random, but
one at a time, like counting-off in the Army. At one point,
while they are making this sound, the bell in one of
the churches, with a strange irrelevance, begins to ring.
The men, wrapped in black blankets, go back and forth
silently with flashlights, which are never allowed to play
on the birds. They are only revealed now and then for a
second by the swerve of an occasional Zuñi car. An air-
plane passes above us, winking green and red. The Indians begin to emerge and line up along the road; we assume that the show is starting, but we still have a long
time to wait. At last, with other blanket-swathed figures, a
group of twelve men arrives, jingling bells on their ankles; surprisingly, they seem costumed like characters in a
production of *Romeo and Juliet*. These are the Shálako impersonators. (The birds, during the interval of waiting,
have apparently been worked by "managers," who accompany and supervise them.) For each bird there are two
dancers, who will alternate through the night. These
twelve dancers, appointed a year ago, have been in train-

ing for their work ever since. Their roles, which bring much prestige, are exacting and responsible ones. Besides learning the difficult dances and memorizing endless speeches, they have had to build the Shálako houses. Though they begin by impersonating the gods, these latter, the night of the festival, will actually enter into them, and the men, with their masks, become sacred objects. If anyone touches a Shálako, or if the Shálako stumbles or falls—as it seems one of them did last year—the dancer is supposed to be struck dead by the god. A mistake on the part of the impersonator means either that someone has seen his mask while it was still in the dressing room and has not been whipped for impiety or that he himself has been making love to somebody else's wife and is unworthy to play the role. When a disaster of this kind occurs, the crowd must at once go away: the Sálimopiya drive them off with whips. The dancer, of course, does not actually die, but his family go into mourning and behave as if he had. And though the Shálako actor must pull the cords that control the beak and the eyes, he is never—on pain of instant death—allowed to look up toward the top of the mask to watch the mystery in operation. Nobody except the manager may understand the Shálako's mechanics. These, then, were the dancers whom we now heard returning from six different points of the pueblo. We counted the jingling groups till the sixth had disappeared in the shadow where the birds were sitting.

Then suddenly, at some signal, a chorus of voices was raised. The Shálakos were on their feet. They came up from the road to the river and filed past us with their escort and choir; and the effect of this was thrilling and lovely in a way that it would be hard to imagine. The great birds, not rigidly erect but bent forward with the dignity of their kingly crests and their beardlike feathery ruffs, as if they were intent on their errand and knew each its destination, did not, in the frosty night, the pale moonlight and the window lamplight, appear in the least comic, as they had in the pictures that one had seen; they hardly seemed even grotesque. And the welcoming hymns that accompanied them, in a harmony one did not understand but with the voices intertangled and singing against one another, had a beauty one could not have expected— not wild but both solemn and joyful—not entirely unlike our own anthems. Each of the Shálako birds is brought to the house prepared for it, and when it has come, it kneels down in front of the door, while prayer meal is sprinkled before it. The warm yellow light from inside gives comfort and life in the winter dark. The chants of reception are sung, and the bird, curt and proud in acceptance, snaps its beak in response to the welcome. Then the Shálako goes into the house and takes its seat before a turquoise altar. The impersonator comes out from inside, while a blanket is held up to screen him, and he and his alternate make offerings of seeds. Then they take seats beside the host, who hands them a cigarette, which he and they pass back and forth as they smoke it. The host addresses as "Father!" that one of the impersonators who is supposed to speak for the Shálako, and the latter replies, "Son!" They exchange other terms of relationship; then the host asks it, "How have you prayed for us? If you will tell us that, we shall be very glad to know it."

"I have come," says the Shálako, "from the sacred lake, and I have come by all the springs." He enumerates all the springs that the Zuñis in their wanderings passed, when they were looking for a site for their town. "I have come to see my people. For many years I have heard of my people living here at Ítiwana [the Middle], and for long I have wanted to come. I want them to be happy, and I have been praying for them; and especially I want the women to be fortunate with their babies. I bring my people all kinds of seeds, all the different kinds of corn, and all the different kinds of fruit and wild green things. I have been praying for my people to have long life; and whoever has an evil heart should stand up in the daylight. I have been praying that my people may have all different kinds of seeds and that their rooms may be full of corn of all colors and beans of all colors and pumpkins and water gourds, and that they may have plenty of fresh water, so that they may look well and be healthy because of the pumpkins and the beans and the corn. I want to see them healthy. . . . Yes, I have worked hard and prayed for all my people. I do not want any of the roots to rot. I do not want anyone to sicken and die, but I want everyone to stand up firmly on his feet all year. This is how I have prayed for you."

I did not myself follow the bird into the house, knowing that I should be ejected, and I am indebted to one of Miss Bunzel's monographs for my report of what happens inside. I walked away and soon got lost as I was trying to find my way to the house of the young anthropologist, my base of operations for the evening. There are no streets, as I have said, in Zuñi, and no public lighting of any kind. The houses all face in different directions, and you are continually landing in the *culs de sac* of partially enclosed backyards, where you are challenged by hyena-like dogs. You step into mysterious pits and break your shins over unexpected obstacles. Everything was silent and dark except in the sacred houses, of whose music and lights, dim and distant, widely scattered through the whole pueblo, I occasionally became aware. I fell in with a Navaho couple who had also lost their way, and the young man, a little tight, assumed, with an expansiveness quite foreign to the Zuñis, that we were both in search of the same house. The Navahos, I was told, were deeply impressed by the Zuñis. They had borrowed their own meager rites from the ritual of the pueblos, but the richness and complexity and splendor of the Zuñi ceremonial baffled them, and remained for them an object of admiration. They were always rather apprehensive of falling foul of the Zuñi witches, who were also more sophisticated, and consequently more dangerous, than theirs.

When I finally got back to the house, I found a party of people cooking some excellent meat—a gift from the abundance of Shálako—and drinking quantities of coffee from a pot that never left the stove till morning. You have to sit up all night, and the occasion resolves itself for visitors into a series of expeditions from a warm and crowded interior, where people are eating and sleeping and talking comparative anthropology, through an outdoors that, as midnight approaches and passes, gets steadily colder and colder, to the intense life and brilliance of the sacred houses. My first foray was in company with a man who talked to me, while we stumbled through the dark, of his experience during the war as a psychiatric worker in an army hospital. This, he said, had so filled him with horror that it had taken him months to get over it. The doctors had used their position of practically unlimited power to indulge in sadistic orgies of crude experimentation at the expense of the helpless GI's, who, arriving with all the varieties of neurotic and psychotic derangement, were subjected more or less indiscriminately to the agony of electrical and insulin treatments—exploits which seem almost to have rivaled the experiments by German doctors on men from concentration camps. Such savagery as the Zuñis exhibit seems almost, by comparison, gentle. They are sometimes cruel to animals, and they had a few very harsh punishments such as that against which Cushing protested. This latter has been discontinued at the instance of our government; but a couple of years ago they turned up with a scalp for a scalp-dance—a feature of the Zuñi repertoire which they have little occasion nowadays to perform. I found that the white authorities were rather non-committal about this, suggesting that the hide of a dog may have been used or that the Zuñis may have dug up a dead Navaho. Originally, witchcraft and cowardice in battle were the only capital crimes. Cushing says that he came to the conclusion that the Zuñis' judiciary system worked out, on the whole, pretty well, since the death penalty was rarely inflicted, and then—although invariably for witchcraft—only in the case of persons who had shown themselves as permanently dangerous. Such an offender was tried by the priests and executed in secret, and the body was never seen.

The dances do not begin till midnight, for the ceremonies connected with the reception of the gods are affairs of tremendous length. The speech made by Sáyatasha alone—which the actor has had to learn by heart—takes him six hours to deliver. I did not try to visit the house where this god was being entertained. The old lady from California who was suspected of sinister designs, had walked in and sat down in front, and immediately been asked to leave. The Agent himself with his wife had been moved on from there by an officious visiting Navaho. The whole atmosphere was quietly hostile. Elsewhere a discourteous visitor was invited "kindly" to remove his hat; and another, who was standing at the door, was ordered not to come in by a boy of about twelve, who fixed him with a hateful eye. When the visitor tried to explain that his intention had been merely to look on from there, the boy grimly told him, "Don't look!" I did not, therefore, go into the house, but simply peered through the misted windows—where some of the Indians had also gathered—casually walking away

and then walking up again. One cannot in the least blame
the Zuñis for wanting to keep strangers out of these ceremonies, for they are services of the most solemn kind, comparable in dignity and devotion to any that I have ever
seen.

Besides the six houses prepared for the reception and
the dances of the Shálakos, there are supposed to be one
for the Council of the Gods and one for another group,
called the Kóyemshi, or Old Dance Men; but just as two
pairs of Shálakos had doubled up this year, so the
Kóyemshi and the Council have combined. As I gazed in
through the panes at these latter, the Council were beyond my vision, but I got a good view of the Kóyemshi.
These are a group of ten clown-priests, familiarly known
as the Mudheads, who play roles of the first importance,
being threaded in and out of ceremonies which continue
through the whole year. When the Zuñis, according to
their legend, were wandering in search of a home, they
sent out a brother and sister on a prospecting expedition.
But the boy raped the girl in her sleep, and she gave
birth to a brood of nine idiots. These are the Mudheads,
who stand as a warning of the danger of incestuous
unions. Largely naked and painted pink, they wear masks
that are pink and bald and knobbed with enormous
warts, and have imbecile round pop-eyes, gaping mouths
like tadpoles or frogs, and fleshy topknots or catfish
antennae. Each of these masks differs slightly from the
others, and the roles of the Mudheads differ. One tries to
repeat sacred rituals and always breaks down into gib-
berish; one is a coward, who hides under ladders and
hangs back behind the rest; another is called the Bat and
is supposed to be blind, so that he is always stumbling
about and bumping into things; another believes himself
invisible and hides his head like an ostrich; another can
only laugh; another is glum, etc. When they are in char-

acter and wearing their masks, they pass in and out of the houses, performing all sorts of antics or—in infantile simpleton voices that seem to whimper and wheedle, to bubble and ooze from their masks—entertaining the spectators with ribald jokes that often probe into their private affairs. When the festival was announced by them eight days before, it was in such terms as these: "In eight days my people come. You must look around for nice girls and stay with them. . . . I come to tell you that in eight days everyone will be happy and have a good time. Men should trade wives." But they, too, are sacred beings, venerated as well as loved. During the year of their impersonation, the actors in the mythical dramas partly lose their own identities and become for the people of the pueblo the personages they represent. In the case of Sáyatasha, the actor even loses his own name and is known by the name of the god. The affection and reverence felt for the mythical role that a man is playing is said sometimes to contrast sharply with the opinion his neighbors have had of him.

It is strange now to see these ten men (the incestuous Father makes the tenth), their masks pushed up on the tops of their heads, here dedicating themselves with prayer, after days of retreat and fasting, to the impish and ridiculous parts it is their duty to resume at midnight. Some of them are rather old, and have arms of skin-and-bone and aquiline Dantesque profiles. The audience sits on one side of the room, with a space between it and the celebrants. The Kóyemshi, by themselves in a row, sit against the opposite wall; the man of the house sits facing them, flanked with five men of his own clan, the Dogwood, and four men of the Frog clan, his wife's, each drawn up so close to his vis-à-vis that their knees are almost touching. Long cigarettes made of reeds have been lighted from burning coals and are being

passed back and forth between the Mudhead and the man
who is receiving him, each taking six whiffs and waving
the cigarette in the direction of the six Zuñi points of
the compass—North, South, East, West, Up and Down.
The Father recites a long speech like that of Sáyatasha,
while the others answer, "*Áthlu*" (Amen). Says the Father of the Kóyemshi to his hosts, "I leave my children
with you for five days. They will dance in your houses;
they will then go to the home of the gods in the East. . . .
Give us food that we may eat, and next year we will
bring you all kinds of seeds." They have little packets of
seeds concealed under their black neckcloths, and the
knobs on their heads are filled with seeds.

The young people came and went, looking in for a time
through the windows or lingering on the porch. This part
of the evening's ceremonies did not interest them much. A
boy who had been in the war greeted two others boys with
a *"Come sta, signori?"* and they showed off with Italian
conversation. A boy and a girl had a moment of necking
as they sat on the rail of the porch. He enveloped her
plump round figure, dressed in poinsettia red, with a
wing of his black blanket-cloak, and for a moment they
rubbed their cheeks. Then he carried her off as she softly
laughed, still with his cloak about her.

The monotonous chanting of the ritual went on without
pause for hours: an unvarying repetition of six beats that
ended in a kind of short wail.

The first Shálako house I visited, when, later, the dancing began, made upon me a tremendous impression. The
rooms where the dances are held are dazzling with electric light and blazing with decorations. The walls are
completely covered with brilliant blankets and shawls,
pale buckskins and queer blue or green hangings, made
by the Navahos, on which square-headed elongated fig-

ures represent the Navaho gods. At one end of the room is a turquoise altar, ornamented with eagle feathers. A group of fetishistic animals, carved from stone, is set out in a row before it. In the audience, most of the men, having discarded their modern clothes, are wrapped in their best black blankets, and the women wear over their heads their best green or red or flowered shawls, and sometimes a kind of black apron, made of silk with fancy designs.

Against this background and before this audience, a Shálako and his alternate are dancing, balancing one another in a bizarre moving composition that seems to fill and charge the whole room. The unmasked dancer here is putting on such an extraordinary performance that he distracts attention from the bird. His costume has a suggestion of the Renaissance that may have been derived from the Spaniards. He wears a tight-fitting white buckskin cap with a curtain that hangs down behind, like the headwear of Giotto's Dante, and a fillet of red ribbon with silver bells. His black shirt is trimmed at the shoulders and sleeves with ribbons of many colors; his black kilts are embroidered in blue and circled with embroidered sashes. His knees are painted red, and the lower part of his legs is yellow, and he has tassels of blue yarn tied below the knees. With his brown bare feet he treads up and down—at a rate, as one observer has calculated, of about four times as many steps a minute as a marathon runner takes—in a quick, sharp, unflagging rhythm. This rhythm is also marked with a pointed yucca wand held before him in the right hand at an unwavering phallic angle. His eyelids are dropped, his eyes seem closed; the firm line of his mouth is drawn down—as if, in dedicating himself to his role, he has achieved a solemn sublimation and is shut off from the rest of the world. His whole demeanor is perfectly disciplined as he slowly moves thus back and forth from one end of the room to the other. And the Shálako, towering above him, actually seems lighter than he and dancing to an easier rhythm, as it turns in place or marks time or—astonishing in its swiftness and grace—swoops the length of the floor in a birdlike flight, never butting into the wall or ceiling and never so much as brushing the spectators, who sit close on either side.

These spectators rarely move, they are receptive, quiet and calm; and the white visitor, too, becomes rapt. He, too, feels the thrill and the awe at the elemental power summoned. It seems as if the dancer, by his pounding, were really generating energy for the Zuñis; by his discipline, strengthening their fortitude; by his endurance, guaranteeing their permanence. These people who sit here in silence, without ever applauding or commenting, are sustained and invigorated by watching this. It makes the high point of their year, at which the moral standard is set. If the Zuñis can still perform the Shálako dances, keeping it up all night, with one or other of the performers always dancing and sometimes both dancing at once, they know that their honor and their stamina, their favor with the gods, are unimpaired. The whole complicated society of Zuñi in some sense depends on this dance. Our ideas of energy and power have tended to become, in the modern world, identified with the natural forces—electricity, combustion, etc.—which we manipulate mechanically for our benefit, and it is startling to see human energy invoked and adored as a force that is at once conceived as a loan from the non-human natural forces and as a rival pitted against them; or rather, to put it in terms that are closer to the Zuñi point of view, to see all the life of the animal world and the power of the natural elements made continuous with human vitality and endowed with semi-human form.

Here, too, one finds theater and worship before they have become dissociated, and the spectacle suggests comparisons in the fields of both religion and art. In the theatrical connection, it seems curious at first to be reminded of the Russian Ballet, but the reason soon becomes quite plain. It must have been true that Dyághilev brought into the conventional ballet, with its formal routines and patterns, something that was genuinely primitive. He had really opened the way for an infusion of old Russia—by giving new life to the music of Rimsky and Borodín, who had already returned to folk material; through the Mongolian wildness of Nizhínsky; through the barbaric splendors of Bakst; through the atavistic stridencies and iterative beat of the Stravinsky of *Le Sacre du Printemps*. The kind of thing one sees in the Shálako dance must be something like the kind of thing that was revived by the Russian Ballet—not brought to the point of refinement to which Dyághilev was able to carry it, but, in its color and variety and style, in the thoroughness of the training involved and the scrupulous care for detail, a great deal more accomplished and calculated than one could easily conceive without seeing it. In the other, the religious, connection, one comes quite to understand the student of comparative religions quoted by Erna Fergusson, who said that it was "no wonder missionaries have had no luck in converting these people to Christianity. It will never be done. The essential mental rhythm of the two races is too far apart. You could imagine reducing that Shálako figure two feet or even four; you could not possibly turn it into Christ on the Cross." The difficulty, one sees, would be to induce the flourishing Zuñis—who have maintained their community for centuries, as sound and as tough as a nut, by a religion that is also a festive art—to interest themselves in a religion that has its origin in poverty and anguish. The Zuñis, moreover, have

no sense of sin; they do not feel that they need to be
pardoned. What the Shálako bird brings is not pardon,
but good cheer and fecundity. It is formidable; the children hide from it the day it comes into town, and if anybody falls asleep, it leans over and wakes him by snap-
ping its beak. But the great bird loves the people, and
the people love the bird. They build a house for it and
spread it a feast, and it dances before them all night to
show them its satisfaction.

In each of the other two Shálako houses, two Shálakos
were dancing together, occasionally assisted by Mudheads. At one place, where I looked in through a window,
I saw people holding a blanket while the Shálako sat
down in a corner. and the alternate changed places with
the weary man who had just been performing his role. In
the house of Sáyatasha, the Council of the Gods, with
their masks off, were performing stately evolutions, accompanied by the adolescent Fire God, who—slim and
handsome in his speckled nudity—danced with the
dropped eyelids and resolute lips of the Shálako impersonator. But the great success of the evening was a
Shálako who danced alone. It was marvelous what this
dancer could do, as he balanced his huge bird-body. He
would slowly pavane across the floor; he would pirou-
ette and teeter; he would glide in one flight the whole
length of the room as smoothly as a bird alighting. The
masks are constructed like crinolines; there are hoops
sewn inside a long cylinder that diminishes toward the
top; and the whole thing hangs from a slender pole attached to the dancer's belt. So the movements are never
stiff. The Shálakos, ungainly though they may seem at
first when one watches them from afar by daylight, are
created in the dance as live beings; and this one was animated from top to toe, vibrating as if with excitement—
gleaming with its turquoise face, flashing its white em-

broidered skirt, while its foxskins flapped like wings at the shoulders. The dance conveyed both delicacy and ecstasy, and the music—produced by a small group of men who sat, as if in a huddle, facing one another, as they chanted, beat a drum and shook rattles—exercised a peculiar enchantment. There are many different songs for the dances, and they vary in mood and pace; but each consists of a single theme repeated over and over, with a rest after so many bars and occasional changes in tempo, which momentarily relieve the dancer. In this case, the recurrent lapses—during which the Shálako, poised for flight, marked time and snapped his beak at the end of his room-long runway—would be followed by brisk pickings-up, when the bird would skim across the floor; and this reprise always had about it an element of the miraculous, of the miracle of the inexhaustible energy, leaping up after every subsidence with the same self-assertive joy. Carried along by the rhythm yourself, alternately let down and lulled, then awakened and stimulated, in a sequence that never faltered, you were held by a kind of spell. The great blue-and-white creature irresistibly took on for you, too, an extra-human personality, became a thing you could not help watching, a principle of bounding and soaring life that you could not help venerating. A white woman who had once seen the dance told me that it had given her a shudder and thrill, in her chair at the end of the room, to feel the eaglelike bird swooping down on her. And I found that it was only with effort that I, too, could withstand its hypnotic effect. I had finally to take myself in hand in order to turn my attention and to direct myself out of the house. For something in me began to fight the Shálako, to reject and repulse its influence just at the moment when it was most compelling. One did not want to rejoin the Zuñis in their primitive Nature cult; and it was hardly worth while for

a Protestant to have stripped off the mummeries of Rome
in order to fall a victim to an agile young man in a ten-
foot mask.

Yet the effect of it lingered and haunted me even after
I was back in my guest-house. Kept wakeful as I was with
coffee, the monotonously repetitive music, the indefatigable glowing bird that had dominated the crowded room,
drawn toward it all upward-turned eyes, suspended in a
trance all wills, stayed with me and continued to trouble
me. I was glad to find a letter in my room which recalled me to my own urban world and which annoyed
me, when I read it, so much that I was distracted from
the vision of the Shálako.

The next morning, some of my friends who had spent
the night in Zuñi and had been present at the departure
of the Shálakos at dawn told me, as people so often do,
that I had missed one of the best parts of the show. By
morning, the dancers are groggy: they find it hard to
keep up their brisk tempo. They had amused themselves
on this occasion by chasing the Mudheads around, and
one had made a lunge at the Agent. But now, at the end
of their other exertions, they must put on an out-of-doors
"race." This is not an athletic contest but a running back
and forth to plant prayer-plumes, which represents the
function of the Shálakos in their role of Couriers of the
Rain Gods. The Council of the Gods have also appeared
and prayed "for rains from all quarters: that the rivers
may be great and come dashing through the canyons;
that the streams may swell like rivers, flooding the water-
courses; and that the lakes may grow large and the wells
be filled to overflowing, so that the earth may give to
them the fullness of her being." Those who had seen this
said that the Shálakos, clacking their beaks as they ran,
seemed—such was their lightness and grace—to float

back and forth across the field. When this ceremony is over, the Shálakos start back to their dressing quarters, stalking in single file; but after putting a certain distance between themselves and the watching crowd, they suddenly break into a run. The young men give chase, try to catch them. The moment a Shálako is captured, the actor throws his mask to the ground, and the pursuer cries out, "I have killed a deer!" He sprinkles the mask with sacred meal and prays to become a successful hunter. Catching the Shálako is supposed to bring him good luck.

In the old days, it seems, the whole crowd, Zuñis and Navahos both, rushed into the ceremonial field, and the day was given up to races, horseback and on foot. Mrs. Stevenson says that in her time the Zuñis beat the Navahos hollow and won from them all their fine blankets, their ponies, their silver and their coral beads.

Navaho Interlude: The next day, when I went down to the pueblo, I discovered that Zuñi indignation had been roused by a further scandal. The Gallup paper that morning had published a picture of the Shálako races, and this had at once led the Zuñis to assume that the paper had sent a reporter and had them photographed. I encountered in certain quarters an attitude that seemed definitely menacing, and I decided to skip the dances that night. The Shálako proper is only the first of six nights of ceremonial dancing, and I had been told by a man I met—that excessively rare phenomenon, a Zuñi of mixed blood, who had traveled and knew the world— that I "hadn't seen anything yet." "All you see on Shálako night," he declared in the tone of the connoisseur who tells you that Montmartre is a tourist-trap, "is just a lot of Navahos." But I thought that it might be a good thing not to be seen in the pueblo for a couple of days, so I accepted an invitation from another young

anthropologist to visit the Navahos, of whom there are
about six hundred living outside their own reservation,
just beyond the boundaries of Zuñi.

It was a relief to get away from the Zuñi domain and the
tension between whites and Indians, and it seemed to me
positively exhilarating to find myself back in an America
where the white man felt himself a native. There were
traces of snow on the ground, but the temperature was
mild, the day sparkling. Level plains and low hills, red
mesas with their queer formations—their "notches" and
their sentinel giants—that vague local mythology of
landmarks which somehow connects red man with white.
In the trees flashed the Southwestern blue-jays, with
their special metallic sheen; among the unenclosed wild
pastures, a lone lovely Navaho girl, wearing a long blue
skirt, was tending her flock on horseback. The little
Mormon town of Ramah seemed like home after a trip
abroad: one-story wooden houses; a small red Mormon
church, built of New Mexican sandstone; an avenue of
cottonwoods and poplars, dry and yellow but not
stripped by winter. In the trading post were tall men
with big-brimmed hats, straight wide mouths and narrow
Yankee eyes. This was simply an enormous village store
—a long room with a high ceiling, a towering iron stove
that heated the whole place, and infinite shelves of
canned goods and old-fashioned white pasteboard boxes.

My friend the anthropologist was born here, and he
took me to the ranch-house where his family lived: his
mother, his wife and their children, and his sister with
her children. It was cheerful to find oneself with a free-
spoken American family not enmeshed in a tribal religion. Outside, trees, sheds and cabins, horses, sheep and
goats were strewing on the dry bare ground light irregular dried-leaf-like shadows; and there was a large long-
haired black-and-tan dog sitting in the sun at the door,

who greeted us with friendly confidence. The one-story ranch-house was pleasant, with its atmosphere of comfort and ease—its long room with the fire at the further end, the Navaho rugs on the floor: patterns of white, gray and red; the shelf of Smithsonian reports; the guns and ears of corn on the walls; the not bad little local landscape painted by one of the family; and the low windows open to the country that always, in this part of the West, make indoors and outdoors continuous. The young man's mother laughed scornfully at the notion that the picture in the Gallup paper had been taken the day before, and, getting out Mrs. Stevenson's volume, soon identified it as one of the plates, made at least fifty years ago.

My guide was intelligent and lively and perfectly natural with the Indians. He had the immense advantage, as a student of anthropology, of having grown up with the Navahos as neighbors and acquired some command of their language. It seems to be generally true that the Navahos have a charm for the whites, and that we feel for them a kind of sympathy that we do not feel for the Zuñis, who so resolutely repel our advances. Though the Navahos are very independent and sometimes, I was told, rather arrogant, they are also, in their present phase, pathetic. Once nomads who preyed on the pueblos, they have become, since the early sixties, when Kit Carson rounded them up, an impoverished and peaceful race of sheep-farmers, who do silverwork and blanket-weaving, living mostly on their reservation of sixteen million acres. At the time that we subdued the Navahos, we signed with them a treaty, which we did not keep, promising to provide them with a schoolhouse for every thirty children. There were very few roads, to be sure, and it was difficult to get the children to the schoolhouses, and even when it was possible to do so, the parents some-

times kept them home to mind the sheep; but there is no
question at the present time that the Navahos want more
education than it is possible for them to get. Three or
four times as many children now apply for admission to
the fifty schools than these can accommodate, and the
students who live at a distance sometimes sleep in the
classrooms and washrooms. The result is that eighty per
cent of the Navahos still cannot speak English. Nor is the
medical situation better. The Navahos of recent years
have been ravaged by tuberculosis and venereal diseases;
yet the Navaho reservation possesses only six hospitals,
with a hundred beds for t.b. and three hundred and fifty
for other cases; half a dozen doctors, none of whom is free
to make calls; two field nurses and no field ambulances.
These problems have now become pressing, for the
Navahos have recently been multiplying at an apparently
unprecedented rate. Instead of the five or six thousand
that Kit Carson had to deal with, there are now some
sixty-two thousand, increasing at a constant rate of more
than two per cent a year. The Navaho headquarters at
Window Rock was equipped during the Collier regime
with a formidable staff of scholars—ethnographers, anthropologists, psychologists—living in the comfortable
quarters that were thought to be indispensable to induce
them to endure a long residence in that primitive part of
the world; but, beyond turning in their reports, they are
said to have accomplished little toward improving the
condition of the Navahos. The Indian Bureau has sometimes persuaded these, where the pastures were over-
grazed, to reduce the size of their flocks—but since Navaho blankets are woven of wool and since the Navahos
eat mainly mutton and sit on and dress in sheepskins—
the immediate result of this has been to bring them to the
direst privation; as well as, my friend tells me, to inflict
upon them a kind of trauma: it is as if, in being made to

destroy their sheep, they had had to slaughter members of the family.

The Navahos do not, however, in the least know what to do for themselves. Their organization is only of the loosest; and their governing body, their "Council," was set up by the whites in the twenties and plays little vital part in their lives. Their poverty and helplessness are touching—all the more because, unlike the Zuñis, they seem, with their slender build, their long fingers, their oval faces, somewhat physically akin to ourselves. This may perhaps be due, in part, to their admixture of Yankee and Spanish blood. One is sometimes, in any case, startled to see a Navaho whose straight pure profile and Mongoloid high cheekbones might well have been derived from New England.

It may be that there are other motives than those of humane feeling involved in the recent publicity that has been given by the Eastern press to the trials of the Navahos—that this group of destitute natives has been used to divert attention from the needs of European peasants. This is certainly not true, however, of the admirable series of articles contributed to the *Herald Tribune* by Mr. Kenneth W. Bilby, to which I owe part of my information; and the Christmas appeal for supplies comes from "friends of the Indian" in the West. Sent out through the papers and over the air, this has produced unexpected results. Truckloads and truckloads of food, from canned goods and packages of noodles to Smith Brothers' coughdrops and Coca-Cola, have been coming in from all kinds of sources: private individuals, wholesale grocers, manufacturers, clubs. The Navahos have been astounded: they think it all comes from "Washingdone," the Indian name for the power of the white man, and never in memory has Washingdone done anything like this for them before. They were laughing, I was told, with a lack of control

unusual for Navahos, when they went off with their loads
of supplies; and today, at the little schoolhouse where the
stuff is being handed out, an atmosphere of elation reigns.
The women are all wearing their gayest shawls—purple
plaids, red and yellow stripes, and are weighed down, having borrowed for this public appearance as much jewelry
as their neighbors would lend them, with pounds of turquoise and silver, bracelets, pendants and chains. They
stand around waiting their turns, very quiet and rather
shy.

The Navahos live in "hogans," little huts made of logs
and mud. These are either hexagonal or octagonal and
built up to a mud-plastered dome. In the center of this
vault is a hole, through which a stovepipe passes. The
hole is much larger than the pipe, but they depend on the
heat, it seems, to vaporize the rain and snow. They sleep
with their feet toward the stove, raying out like the
spokes of a wheel.

When you call on a Navaho, you wait for a moment
outside the door. Infallibly, he has heard you coming, and
this gives him a chance to get ready. These dwellings are
much cosier and cleaner than you could possibly expect
them to be. The ones that I saw were not cluttered, and
they never smelt badly or even close. Utensils and other
things are put away on a shelf that runs around the
whole wall. The people sit cross-legged on sheepskins on
the hard dry earthen floor. In the first of the hogans we
visited, a woman—very handsome, with her regular features, like so many of the Navaho women—was sitting
with a little girl, who promised also to be very good-
looking. On the floor, spread out on a paper, was a quan-
tity of hard candy that had just been brought home from
the schoolhouse. The woman put her hand to her mouth
as if she were screening a cough, in what my guide explained to me later was a conventional gesture of diffi-

dence. She told him, in answer to his questions, put to her in Navaho, that her husband was taking a sweat-bath —a ceremony, performed in a group, which involves throwing water on heated stones and is accompanied by ritual singing. My attention was called to an object lying under a blanket beside me, and the woman lifted off the blanket, revealing a baby on a "cradle-board." Wrapped up and strapped to this wooden back, the children can be laid down to sleep or stood up against the wall, so that they can see what is going on, or completely got out of the way by being hung from a nail higher up. They are nursed till the next baby is on the way, sometimes two years or more. It is said that the women will nurse, also, on occasion, young lambs that have lost their mothers. These children are, it seems, well brought up, gradually and gently trained. I noticed that the little girl made no attempt to grab the candy, having evidently been told she had had enough. Neither Navaho nor Zuñi children are ever corrected by whipping, and the Navahos are shocked by our brutal methods (though, in Zuñi, the punishment of certain offenses and the initiation of adolescents involve ceremonial whippings).

We visited the various households of another and more prosperous family, dominated, I was told, by the grandfather, a prominent medicine man, and his very strongminded daughter. The old man we found in a small log house, an advance on the primitive hogan and furnished with chairs and a bed; but he was sitting on the floor, where we joined him. He had cataracts on both eyes, one of which seemed completely blind, but otherwise—with a gray mustache—he was quite fine-looking; and he received us with a good deal of dignity, shaking hands without rising and smoking quietly as he talked. He spoke Spanish and had been to Washington, was relatively a man of the world. Later, children and grandchildren came in, and some general conversation took place, rather haltingly, between Navaho and English and Spanish. There was a big upright loom at one side, on the cords of which one of the women had started a red and white blanket, whose design of diagonal stripes was already constructing its angles. Rolls of wool lay ready for carding, and she was twisting carded wool into thread and winding it on a spindle. They all seem to keep little cats, for which they have a Spanish word, *mossi*.

They are more flexible than the Zuñis, unquestionably, in spite of their less modernized ways. My guide had been studying the effects of the war on the Navahos who had been in the services (many of them had been operating radio, for which they had the odd qualification of a language that the enemy could not decode); and it was easier to see changes in their habits of thought than in the case of the conservative Zuñis. Some, he told me, had broken in radical ways with Navaho tradition. It is one of the tribal conventions that, from the day when a man is married, he may not look at his mother-in-law or remain in a room where she is. If she even comes into the trading post before he has finished his business, he must quietly slip away. But one young man who has returned from the army has decided not to bother with this, thus outraging the mother-in-law, who feels that she is treated with disrespect. Another ex-soldier has declined to take part in either the ceremonies of the Navaho religion or the services at the Nazarene Mission, declaring that they are both "superstition"—which does not appear unnatural when one learns that the Christian priest has been putting his ministry on a level with the incantatory therapeutics of the Navahos by telling them that conversion to the cult of Christ will safeguard them from losing their sheep. On the other hand, some of those who are known to have killed Germans or Japs have submitted to the strenuous tribal rites for the exorcism of the ghosts of the slain, and one smiling young fellow I met, who had never been farther away than Texas, had managed, through boasting of overseas prowess, to get himself purified on false pretenses. It is a part of this defense against ghosts to smear the patient all over with charcoal. He is supposed to wear his black-up for many days; but one young man, who wanted to sleep with his girl, had flouted the spirit world by immediately washing his off. Another had tried on his girl a modern birth control device of which he had learned the use in the army—one way of meeting the population problem—and had provoked a spirited protest.

Shálako Continued: I went back after that to the dances.

Now that the prayers and sacred services of the opening night had no longer to be protected from the public, the strain seemed somewhat relieved; and one could sometimes get a seat in the houses, in one of the outside rooms, from which one could study the place and the people. There was a good deal of linoleum and oilcloth, and some of the kitchens were wonderfully equipped with the latest in sinks and ranges. Everybody was busy preparing for the feasts that take place every night. When the Spaniards first discovered the Zuñis, the latter did most of their eating with their fingers, and their only table implements were little earthen scoops; but for these banquets, at any rate, they have today knives and forks and spoons. In one place, we found the women cutting up carcasses of sheep into innumerable little chunks and carrying them out on trays to be cooked behind the house in huge caldrons. Here we were offered fried bread: large brown slabs that had the taste and consistency of the old-fashioned doughnuts called "fried cakes." In one of the kitchens, katchina dolls—all Zuñi sacred personages are called "katchinas"—had been hung on the opposite wall from a framed citation for the Purple Heart. The audience, even when waiting before the performance begins and through the sometimes long gaps between numbers, is perfectly calm and patient. Though everything gets done in order, it is never done, from our point of view, on time: the Zuñi has no sense of the clock. The children are incredibly well behaved; only babies in arms ever make a sound. Nothing is heard except the popping of bubble gum, which, no more than the Coca-Cola that the venerable elders sometimes drink, seems incongruous with the rest of the picture.

The performance has a good deal of variety. The katchinas are appearing here mainly in the capacity of entertainers. When the Zuñis were looking for a home, they are supposed to have lost some children as they were fording a certain lake. The children had been squirming in their mothers' arms and had thus dropped into the water, and were afterward mourned as drowned. But later on, after the Zuñis had founded their nation, when they were feeling despondent and dull, these children, in the form of katchinas, came to visit their people and explained that they were still alive at the bottom of the fatal lake, and that they had a town of their own there, where they were happy and danced all day. Periodically, after that, they would come in groups to the Zuñis and cheer them up with singing and dancing. But the drawback was that, when the dancing was over and the dancers went back to the lake, somebody always died, because the katchinas were souls of the dead and had to take toll of the living. So the Zuñis and the katchinas decided to manage things differently. The katchinas told the Zuñis to copy their masks. "You will make them," they said, "and give them life. When you dance with them, we shall come and stand before you. If we do thus, perhaps it will be all right, because if we take someone with us when we go, it is not right." The whole pantheon of real katchinas is residing at the bottom of the sacred lake (at the junction of the Zuñi with the Little Colorado, some eighty miles away in Arizona), in what is known as Katchína Village, and the souls of certain groups of Zuñis, persons of higher status, are supposed, when they die, to join them. The pueblo Indians, in their early days, must have suffered much from boredom and discouragement, because this legend has something in common with the legends of other tribes, among whom the orders of clowns called Kosháre owe their prestige and importance to the fact that they represent emissaries of the gods, sent to the people in their ancient trials to raise their morale by making them laugh. The amusement value of the Zuñi religion is unquestionably one of its greatest assets, for the people are kept always looking forward to something and are never, in the course of the year, given quite the same thing twice (and some of the ceremonies recur only once every four or eight years). Besides the winter dances of Shálako and a long series of summer dances out of doors, in which a great many more people take part; besides the clowning of the Mudheads and of another set of comedians, which involves new jokes and songs made up every year—special groups, at certain ceremonies, present sword-swallowing, fire-eating and conjuring, and in the season of dreary weather that corresponds to our February and March, when there is nothing for them to do for their crops, the Zuñis give themselves up to gambling games, with large prizes that make them worth while, which they justify by asserting that the gods had thus "whiled away the aeons of ancient times."

All the Zuñi boys at ten or twelve (only very rarely

girls) are initiated into the katchina cult and made eligi-
ble to take part in the dances. Younger children seem
more or less expected to believe that the katchinas are
real—one reason perhaps that they behave so well. The
boys, at initiation, are admonished by a hair-raising parable not to give the secret away. There was once a little
boy, they are told, who said to the other children, "See
that young man going by there? The other night he was a
katchina maiden. Perhaps the masked gods do not really
come." The impersonators, hearing of this, summoned
the real katchinas, who came straight to the pueblo and
searched for the boy. When they could not find him anywhere and were told by his parents he was not at home,
they went and stood on the four corners of the roof of
the house and turned around four times, uttering each
time the word, "Bu-ix!" The fourth time, the house
cracked apart and revealed the unfortunate boy in a back
room where his parents had hidden him. The katchinas
angrily beat him and finally cut off his head, which the
Mudheads then used to play football and finally dropped
on an ant-hill. So nothing must ever be said to damage
the children's belief that the katchinas actually come.

The diversity of the katchinas is extraordinary. They are
the characters of a rich mythology. Miss Bunzel, in her
monograph on the subject, lists a hundred and fifteen
figures—differing widely in costume, mask and role—
that she or some other observer has seen and been able
to describe. I give below some of the dances that I saw
performed, helping myself out, when possible, by reference to Miss Bunzel's book—though this does not provide the key to certain of the numbers that were done.
The symbolism of these dances is a language, at once
complex and precise, that the visitor can hardly read. He
is bewildered by the detail of the costumes, the objects
carried and worn, the ornamentation of the masks, the

gestures and maneuvers of the dancers; and it is difficult
for him to report them intelligently. For the audience,
every touch is important: a feather from the wrong part
of an eagle may produce immediate scandal; an innovation of any kind will give rise to a controversy, for getting
the desired result—procuring enough rain—depends on
carrying out a procedure that must always be exactly the
same. But even when one does not understand, the dramatic and aesthetic effect is often overwhelming and wonderful. Each act lasts about twenty minutes. Each team
has to perform every night at each of the sacred houses,
so if you stay in one place, you will see them all. Every
night the repertoire is different, though dances may be
repeated. I saw the same dance done twice on two suc-
cessive nights, but by different sets of men. The music is
more highly developed than any Indian music I have
heard before. Each chant is the same thing over and over,
but each dance seems to have its own chant. These are
melodies that one can hum and that are even sometimes
rather infectious. You hear young people singing them
out of doors, and I found that they would echo in my
head till their peculiar harmonies eluded me, and I
would find myself with something in a more familiar
scale that had substituted itself: in one case, Ravel's
Bolero, and in another a ritual theme from de Falla's
El Amor Brujo—from which I was led to conclude that
an element of Spanish folk music had got into the Zuñi
chants.

Here are some of the performances I saw on the two
evenings when I attended the dances:

1. A very handsome set of young men, unmasked, come
in, carrying prayer-plumes, bows and yucca wands. They
have eagle plumes down their backs and long black hair
that reaches to their waists. They wear fillets around their

temples and a feather of eagle's down—one pure white, one vivid red—at either side of the head. Their demeanor is very proud, and one feels that they enjoy being admired in their costumes. Their dance involves bending at intervals to the right and to the left, but not low enough to abase their dignity.

To them enters a blackfaced bugaboo, who gives low roars when he first appears. He has black bear feet like fur galoshes, and black white-speckled legs; a mask with a great black beard, a wide mouth that ferociously shows its teeth, and a long red tongue hanging out. He wears a coarse black bearskin-like wig, and his eyes are crescent moons, with the horns pointing down to suggest that the new month will bring rain, because the moon is pouring water. He makes his way to the end of the dancers' line, bowing, as they have been doing, first to one side, then to the other, and there he dances and dips by himself, out of line at one side of the column, while the young men, their beauty and elegance set off by his ugliness and roughness, continue in perfect unison, all turning from time to time to face in the opposite direction and keeping the beat with rattles. For this dance, there is no other orchestra: their singing is the only music.

This bugaboo belongs to a group which I shall describe in another connection. The Indian Agent told me later that he had been walking in the pueblo that afternoon, and that just as he was passing the Christian Reformed Mission, he was roused by a menacing roar, and, looking up, saw this blackfaced katchina, whom he had been just about to run into. He stifled an impulse to roar back at the monster, and stepped aside and let it pass.

2. The Mudheads dancing without their masks. They gave at intervals a kind of whoop and laughed as if they had sung something funny.

3. A file of unmasked men with bows, accompanied by

three katchinas of the common long-snouted kind that one sees represented in katchina dolls. They had vari-colored faces and wore fox-furs and many feathers. The rear was brought up by a man, unmasked but with his face painted gray, the whole upper part of his head en-cased in a tight white cap and surmounted by a top-knot of corn-husks. On his back was strapped a great bundle not unlike a soldier's pack, which might have been either a symbolical burden or one of their cloth drums.

This was the only example I saw of a member of the Néwekwe fraternity, another order of clowns, whose practices have been something of a stumbling-block to the amateurs of the Zuñi religion. The Néwekwes are a medical fraternity, whose principal business it is to deal with digestive disorders. They are supposed to possess the secret of an extremely potent medicine, and—appar-ently to demonstrate its efficacy—it is their custom to give public exhibitions at which they drink urine and eat ex-crement, chew up pieces of cloth and wood, swallow peb-bles and handfuls of ashes, bite the heads off live mice and devour the entrails of dogs, which they have just torn to pieces alive. Cushing says that, on one of these occasions, when they demanded of him to bring them more food and convention forbade him to refuse, he pro-duced a paper-bag of crackers, on which he had poured some molasses in the hope of giving them something more appetizing, and wrapped the whole thing in an army jacket, which he hoped would be an acceptable gift. The Néwekwe, after throwing these around in the dust, ate bag, molasses and crackers, and a considerable part of the jacket. These doctors are rarely called in, as the patient who survives their care is obliged to belong to their cult, and only in desperate cases can the sick man be brought to face this. Yet the Néwekwe are applauded and honored, and it is clear from both Cushing's account and that of Matilda Stevenson that even these white visitors got over their original horror and came to take the Néwekwe for granted. Matilda Stevenson, especially, appears to have been on the best of terms with them. The swallowing of a little excrement, the chewing-up of a few live mice—arrived at, it seems, by the most gradual training, often begun in childhood, and only performed on sacramental occasions—are practices imposed by profession and rank which ought not perhaps to seem more abhorrent than many that one gets used to on the part of one's friends. Another nineteenth-century observer, Captain John G. Bourke, was taken by Cushing to a Néwekwe ceremony, and this so stimulated his curiosity that he eventually wrote a whole book on these scatological rites, which he found were practiced also in many other primitive communities scattered all over the world. In the case of the Zuñis, he conjectured that, just as their clowning was a heritage from long-ago moods of despair in their period of pioneering, so the eating of filth was a memory of early days of privation when they had been driven to some such expedients. They were commemorating a practice that was hallowed on account of its having, as they thought, enabled them to survive their ordeal.

It was formerly, as Captain Burke tells us, a specialty of the Néwekwes to do a parody of a Catholic mass, with its congregation and priest. They have recently, I was told, been performing, with enormous success, a burlesque radio program and a take-off on the medical inspections held at the Black Rock Hospital in the days of the Indian Division of the New Deal's C.C.C.

4. This number was the most gorgeous I saw. The dancers were mostly unmasked and wore purple, blue and red velvet cloaks, with silk ribbons falling from their shoulders. They were decorated with turquoises and silver dollars, and carried poles with more long bright ribbons

hanging down from the ends. With them danced two charming katchinas that had long orange snouts, head-dresses like ladies' hats, full of pink and white artificial roses, and kilts of red and white beadwork. They wore great collars or beards of green spruce boughs, and had spruce sticking out from their armpits and belts. At the side and independent of the rest, a very special katchina performed. He was of the same general snouted genus but had two long purple ribbons depending from a pair of tall feathers sticking up in a V at the back of his head.

It is difficult, without seeing this type of katchina—the most familiar, from pictures and dolls, because the Hopis have something similar—to appreciate its extraordinary attractiveness. These are known as the "pretty katchinas," and their air of felicity and beneficence makes them appear indeed the bright visitors from another world. Distinctly not of human kind, it is perfectly easy to imagine them eternally happy and dancing in their palace at the bottom of the lake. Such beings, no longer subject to the conditions of the creatures of earth, could not look in the least like us. They are beautiful, but their beauty consists of features and dress quite different—combined in different proportions—from our human ones.

5. Five very broad stout men, who danced with their backs to the audience. The two at the ends wore masks with large butterflies painted on the backs—one black and white, the other red, white and green—which they thus displayed to the audience. At intervals, they would turn around uttering a kind of bird-cry and revealing their turquoise faces and their small bent beaks, orange with a streak of black on the bridge; but they would always keep on turning till they had made a full revolution and confronted us with the butterflies again.

6. A very queer dance, which included five of the so-called Old Tshákwena group, to which belonged the

blackfaced bugaboo described in connection with the first
dance above. Here each wears a different-colored beard:
black, white, gray, pepper-and-salt and brown. They have
black tongues instead of red, their masks are glossy instead of dull, as the earlier bugaboo's was, and their
teeth and eyes gleam more whitely. Two of them wear
ducks on their heads, tied up with red Christmas ribbon,
the bill pointing forward and two tail feathers behind
making prongs like the feather of an arrow. They enter
with gruff bugbear noises and sing a chant that has a
menacing sound. They are accompanied by a "pretty
katchina," with a blue face and small red ears and a big
fan-shaped crest like the Shálako's; and by a queer sort
of pseudo-Mudhead, with gray feathers as well as warts
sticking out of his face and head. This latter has a long
stuffed sack, like a bag of flour or salt; he lays it down
on the ground, kneels beside it and begins to wallop it
with what looks like a policeman's club. This, it seems,
is the drum for the dance—less effective, one would say,
than the ordinary kind, and a great deal more trouble to
perform on. I was sitting just behind the drummer and
was appalled at the effort he was making. He had to hit
the sack so hard to get out of it a loud enough sound—
working, also, under the handicap of the mask—that
concentration on keeping this up made it hard for him to
stick to the beat, and he was constantly getting at odds
with the chanting and steps of the dancers, so that a stage
manager would have to come up from time to time and
set him back on the rhythm. But this incompetence, as I
later found out, had, like everything, its special explanation.

Old Tshákwena, the head of this group, is a figure who
admonishes and threatens. He tells the young children
that they must mind their parents or the earth will crack
apart and the wild men come out and eat them; the little

girls that if they misbehave themselves with little boys they will immediately be turned into stones; the old people that they must wash their pots when they take them off the fire, so that their lips will not get sore. His chief lieutenant is the nastiest of the bugbears, who once used to come, as people are told, to eat babies and to crush them with his big bear feet. This may possibly have been the monster who appeared in the previous dance—though the Zuñis, who tone down extremes, explain that this super-bugaboo does not visit them much any more.

But the group that I saw in the later dance are a subspecies of Tshákwena dancers, who represent something different. It seems that the people of Zuñi have always been on particularly good terms with the people of the pueblo of Laguna, eighty-five miles away. Years ago they paid a visit to Laguna and performed the Old Tshákwena dance. They then exchanged songs with the Lagunas, each pueblo teaching some of its own to the other; and the Zuñis, when they got back home, arranged a special Laguna dance, which has been in their repertory ever since. In this, the Tshákwena figures appear with modified personalities: they stand upright instead of stooping, and they wear their hair short instead of long. In place of their own songs, they sing, in the Laguna language itself, the chants that the Lagunas taught them, which, it seems, are simple hunting songs. The blue-faced katchina with the crest had formerly figured in another dance, but now he has been assigned to the short-haired Tshákwena number. He is supposed to have a very sweet voice and gives calls which are signals for the dancers. The pseudo-Mudhead with the feathers on his face is a personage from the Laguna mythology, whom the Zuñis are said to have brought back with them, and he is supposed to make jokes in the Laguna language. He has no status, however, in Zuñi: the part may be acted by any young man who has for some reason not practiced a regular role but who wants to take part in the dancing; and his mask is not sacred and personal, as all the others are, but something that has been knocked together and that anyone can assume for the evening. Hence the amateurishness, tonight, of his drumming. Nor was he, so far as I heard, up to making any jokes in Laguna.

Someone noticed that one of the katchínas had the name of a U.S. destroyer tattooed on his bare arm.

7. The Bear Dance. This was the last performance I saw and brought the evening to a splendid climax. When the short-haired Tshákwena had filed away, a formidable snarling was heard. A visitor who had been standing by the door told me that it had given him quite a turn when he saw the monster now looming—a great hairy pair of arms with long claws—for whom he had to make way. The grizzly was the most ferocious of the animals that the Indians encountered, and to be possessed by the spirit of the bear has been one of the great objects of Indian cults. In Zuñi, the bear is regarded as one of the sources of the power to heal, and putting on the bear claws and "calling the bear" is the most serious of their medical rituals. But I have not been able to find any description of the bear dance that was now performed. The figure that appeared in the doorway, posing for effect a moment, was not dressed entirely in a bearskin but, avoiding literalness, seemed all the more convincing in his role. He wore the bear mitts halfway up his upper arms, and on his head a kind of rough black mane, through which were stuck two long skewers that protruded above his forehead and gave him a bristling look. The face had been made up with great skill, so that the eyes looked small and bestial, and the whole of the lower part, clothed with what looked like a heavy beard, was thickly coated with white. Improbable though it may seem, the bear as represented

in Zuñi is always partly white—in memory, apparently, of the days when the Indians came down through the Bering Strait and had intimate experience of polar bears. In this white part of the face, the nostrils showed black, like those of an animal's muzzle.

Behind the bear entered a chorus, unmasked and not conspicuous in costume, who carried a growling chant that was curiously reminiscent of some out-of-date popular song that I could not identify. But the bear was the whole thing here: the actor felt his part like an artist and was one of the high spots of the festival. He danced by himself outside the line, making the tour of the room and always face to face with the audience. His paws were always held up in front of him, like those of a bear erect, and he would raise first one, then the other, cumbrously and slowly advancing, like a bear on its hind legs. The effect of this was quite intimidating, for he everywhere stared into the audience with a look that was not that of a human being but of an animal, in a clearing in the forest, which has been alarmed by a sound and is trying to find out what is going on. It was as if he could not see the audience but had sensed that there was present some inimical thing, which he would plunge upon the moment he saw it. This illusion was maintained so successfully that it even made little difference when the buskin he was wearing became undone, and he had to stop for a moment to allow the stage manager to tie it up.

The ending of the act was superb. The chorus slouched out of the room and left the stage to the bear impersonator, who went on dancing without the music but still keeping the heavy beat and who made thus, alone in the silence, a final tour of the room—peering at the trees again to see what was lurking behind them, to be sure nothing hostile was there before he dropped back on all fours and returned to eating his honey. Now at last he may see us and make for us! But no: his little eyes cannot reach us. He backs away to the door and goes out.

One had an impulse to applaud this number: in our theater, a comparable performance would certainly have brought down the house. It seemed difficult, as someone said, to believe that the dancer of the bear had never seen Paul Draper. But he left his Zuñi audience—as if mesmerized—unstirring and mute.

I had to get back East on December 24 in order to be with my family for our Christian equivalent of the Shálako festival, so I missed the farewell to the Mudheads which was to be the great event of the following day. The Mudheads are paid off for their year's hard work with great piles of food and clothing that are heaped for them in the plaza. They also have presents thrown at them, and between the Néwekwe and the Mudheads a general roughhouse takes place involving a bean-bag game and some horseplay of a ribald character. But the Mudheads may not yet eat. The evening before I left, I had watched the dances at the Mudheads' house, and had seen how exhausted they were. They had been fasting and dancing for days, and they now sat against the wall, unmasked and wrapped in thin blankets, sound asleep, with their heads sunk forward. These elderly men, who for fourteen days have been following a severe regime and who have had nothing to eat or drink since supper the night before, must wait to break their fast till midnight, when each, at a final ceremony, will take a sip of water and with this lose his holy character. They will pray, and their Father will admonish them that, "Even though you have finished your year, you must still be kind to everyone, so that when our time comes again, we may not have a bad name." They will not have to serve for four years, when rotation will bring them into office again. And now they are at last brought a feast. The people feel grateful to them—and though they will still have the actors as neighbors—they are sad at the idea of the Kóyemshi's leaving.

Now the Zuñis must lose the sun, and a period of mourning ensues. The Sun Priest, unless incompetent, as has happened within recent memory, makes a correct calculation of the winter solstice, not by reference to the white man's calendar, but by standing outside the village on a certain petrified stump and watching for the sun to rise behind a certain point on Corn Mountain. This is a season that they feel to be dangerous. The sun must be summoned back. For ten days they hoard their fire: no fire or light may be made outside—they may not even drive their cars at night—and no ashes may be thrown out. For periods of various lengths they may not indulge in sexual intercourse, eat animal food or engage in trade. At the end, a ceremonial is held at which a new fire is kindled, and the cycle of the year begins anew.

Departure: I arrived in Gallup about three in the morning to take the train for Chicago and went into the lunchroom of the Harvey House, which is next door to the station. A tall Indian in soft hat and overcoat, his arms straight down at his sides and his hands plunged into his pockets, would come in from the platform from time to time, as if he were looking for something, but obviously stiff with drink: he did not seem to know where he was. In the lavatory, two Indian youths in Army uniform, also completely drunk, were holding a conversation that was infinitely slowed-up and repetitious. They evidently belonged to different tribes, so that they did not speak the same language, and they did not know very much English and were so thick-tongued they could hardly talk. While I was pacing back and forth in the lobby, the

woman clerk at the desk asked the bellboy, who was just
coming in, to carry down somebody's bags, and he replied that he would have to "get rid of this Indian first."
The Indian was lying outside in such a way as to obstruct the entrance, as inert as a felled tree. I remembered how, the morning after Shálako, the nephew of a
pueblo official, said to be drunk from the celebration, had
driven off the road into an arroyo, killing three and seriously injuring two of a mixed load of Navahos and
Zuñis.

This was my final impression of what the white man
had given the Indian; and of what the modern white man
had made of himself. I got an equally discouraging impression among the travelers on the Sante Fe Railroad. From
the moment that the whites of the American West have
not had to be hard and alert under pressure of rugged
conditions, they have been turning soft, fat and blank
to a degree that is disgusting and dismaying. What do
these puffy-faced doughbags do? Some, no doubt, are
commercial travelers; others, businessmen, well-off and
retired, who have bought themselves "homes" in Los
Angeles. The women, whether squashy or scrawny, are
equally charmless and sexless. If the Zuñis are human
beings, these must be something else.

I had at first expressed surprise, in Zuñi, that the Zuñis
of our own day should continue to believe that their village was exactly at the center of the world, that they were
in danger of losing the sun every year at the time when
the days grew short, and that their gods and deceased
relations were inhabiting a lovely village at the bottom
of a little lake in the State of Arizona. But I was reminded by the Zuñi Agent that the Zuñis saw a good
many more people who did believe all these things than
people who did not believe them—which is, of course,

usually the case with the believers of any religion. (It was only later on that I learned that the candles of the Jewish Hanukkah and the candles of the Christmas tree are survivals from similar rituals intended to recall the departed sun.)

My feelings about the Zuñis, as I left, were mixed. I was torn between admiration for their stoutness and self-consistency and impatience at their exclusiveness and bigotry in relation to the rest of the world. One had to admit that a highly developed and vividly imagined mythology was a great thing to hold a people together and to inspire them with confidence in themselves. But the effects on our own society of the mythologies which have influenced it lately are anything but reassuring. The Christian mythology is obsolete, almost as impracticable for the modern man as that of Sáyatasha and his colleagues. To revive it at the present time is to seek to conceal our real problems under fables that derived their original force from the belief in a superterrestrial world —a belief which, for grown-up minds, has become as inadmissible today as belief in the sublacustrine world of the Zuñis' Katchina Village. On the other hand, modern attempts to create a non-Christian mythology produce cults like that of Hitler and his hero-race of Germans, like that of the infallible Stalin and the grandiose historical drama of the working of the Dialectic.

But in the meantime we white Americans glance wistfully at moments toward the Indians, whom only a short time ago we were fighting tooth and nail. The idealist like John Collier, once a social worker in big cities, finds in Indian life a "wholeness" and a harmony with Nature that the specialized urban man, quite divorced from the earth for a century, is incapable even of imagining. An anthropologist like Ruth Benedict goes to the pueblos for evidence to prove to us that there are other human possibilities than our badly run industrial societies, with their murderous national phobias and their jarring individual neuroses. The aesthete in Santa Fe admires, even adores, the Indian for the vitality and the self-sufficiency that he has known how to sustain in his art. And the journalist like myself, who has reported many hateful and destructive events, wants to get a good look at the Shálako birds, bringers of happy abundance, before they shall have ceased to come, and before the bad liquor of the white man and the worship, perhaps, of some white Führer shall, even for the Zuñis, have taken their place.

The Zuñis, so far, however, have evidently given no ground. I heard, when I was back in the East, that the resident anthropologist, my host at the Shálako festival, who had already been threatened with expulsion, had been charged with stealing the war god from his shrine at the top of Corn Mountain. The pressure had become so unpleasant that, remembering the fate of his predecessor, my friend had decided to go. He had, of course, not stolen the image, the accusation had no doubt been a frame-up; but it had served the Zuñi priests, as they thought, to keep their society sound by maintaining its culture intact.

HAITI
1949

COTTON BLOSSOM EXPRESS: I went to sleep in the winter darkness, and wake up to a dazzle of golden light on green palms and low-growing pines that drip with Florida moss. An extraordinary pageant of bird-life presents itself outside the window: snowy egrets, several kinds of heron —some bluish, some beige—and other darker long-winged birds that I take to be buzzards—all looking as if they had flown right out of Audubon: how excited he must have been when he came here. There are also some smaller birds that fly in flocks with quick twinkling wing-beats, and one experiences a pleasure that has something in common with the pleasure derived from music in following the contrasts of tempo between these and the slower rhythms of the larger birds that hover. They all fly quite close to the train and not far from the endless pale swamps and plains. It is wonderful to watch an egret alighting and folding its wings, deliberately, with dignity and grace.

Miami: I have never been here before and am astounded and appalled by this place. It is not that it is particularly different from other American seaside resorts, from Asbury Park to Coronado Beach, but that here both the cheap and the expensive aspects have been developed on a scale that I have never elsewhere seen equalled. You have acres of nougat-like shops, mountain-ranges of vanilla ice-cream hotels. Miami Beach goes on for miles, with its monotonous lines of palms, its thousands of hotels and houses which seem to have had imposed on them, by the exigency of a city-planning board, a blanched and insipid uniformity. It even makes one feel more kindly toward Southern California, with its elements of lunatic fantasy. What draws people down to this vacuum? How do they amuse themselves here?

These vacationists look soft and vapid. You rarely see a really pretty girl, and the men do not give the impression of doing much fishing or swimming. You find them at the movies in the evening. The American ideal of luxury is in Miami carried to lengths that I have never encountered before. At my hotel, I had the annoyance of removing encasements of cellophane from the toilet-seat and the drinking tumbler. In the movie-house, the seats are the kind that swing noiselessly back and forth to let people get in and out, and their cushions melt beneath one like a featherbed. A subdued indirect lighting, like the sweet creamy liquid of an ice-cream soda, bathes a dove-gray and shrimp-pink interior, the walls of which are ornamented with large cameo-like white seashells framing naked mythological figures that seem to have been badly imitated from the bas-reliefs of Paul Manship in Rockefeller Center, and with branching white plaster exfoliations that remind one of the legs and defensive antennae of the crawfish in the Miami aquarium. The film—*Oh, You Beautiful Doll*—was a technicolor that covered the whole surface of a high and overpowering screen with a routine sentimental romance, trumped up to manufacture glamor from the career of an American song-writer whose songs were widely sung in my college days. They were commonplace enough then, and today they are simply sickly. These attempts on the part of Hollywood to exploit the immediate past—in which the fashions of the eighties and nineties are sometimes confused with those of the twenties —show the precipitous decline of the movies as purveyors of entertainment, since the producers, after wrecking such contemporary talent as their salaries have tempted to Hollywood, have now been obliged to fall back on the favorites, first, second or third rate, of the day before yesterday and yesterday, when it was possible for a producer or an actor, a composer or a dancer, to perfect an art of his own and create for himself a reputation. Yet this product has its steady customers: one finds oneself among them here. Comfortably padded in the muffled atmosphere that seems to smell of scented face-powder—one cannot tell whether the theater has been perfumed or the women are all using the same cosmetics—this inert and featureless drove that have been drifting through the bleached sunny streets now sit watching stereotyped characters that are made to appear impressive by being photographed in very bright colors and gigantically magnified. The three shorts that follow the first showing of the film all happen to deal with animals: a hunting number, an animated cartoon that gets some not ill-deserved laughs, and a picture about racing whippets. The commentator seems slightly embarrassed at the spectacle of the uniformed attendants who have a full-time job grooming the whippets. "You may think they work as hard as the dogs," he propounds, with his microphone emphasis that gropes through time and space and can never drive any nails. "Well, they work a lot *harder!*" The truth is that so many Americans, specialized in operating machines or in transacting long-distance business, have deteriorated as animal organisms, that we now have a special pleasure in watching almost any agile animal. What the audience gets out of these animal shorts is the same thing that I have been getting out of looking out the window at the birds and contrasting them with the Miami vacationers.

This is all the kind of thing, I realize, that strikes foreigners who visit this country, but that I have long ago

arranged my life in such a way as to avoid or ignore, so
that I am likely to be shocked by and to discount the un-
complimentary reports of visitors. Miami is a rude revelation: I had not really known this was going on. I read
uneasily of President Truman's recent arrival in Florida
for one of a long series of sunlit holidays. This is the place
where he seems most at home. It is only when I get to the
airfield that my national self-respect picks up. It is a feat
to have conceived, to have built and to navigate these passenger planes. We humans have contrived our wings by
deliberate calculations, out of inorganic materials, instead
of growing them out of our bodies, and this does leave us
less hardy than the buzzard, less graceful than the white
egret; but we have, after all, by our planes, in other ways
surpassed the birds, and there had been moments in Miami
when I was doubtful of that before I took off for Haiti.
And those disparate rhythms of flight that I found so delightful to watch, Walt Disney, in his film *Snow White,*
where deer and rabbits and other animals are shown running together at different speeds and gaits, has rendered
them for the first time in plastic art. The multiplied drawings of the studio that turns out the Disney cartoons are
as anonymous as the hundreds of parts that go to make
up a plane. I couldn't myself have invented the simplest
of these mechanisms or processes; but the current prestige
of the United States is partly derived from these, and I
cannot help feeling a pride in them.

Two West Indian Authors: On the train and on the
plane to Port-au-Prince, I read a book called *La Résistance Haïtienne* by a Haitian, Dantès Bellegarde, and a
long surrealist poem called *Cahier d'un Retour à Mon
Pays Natal,* by a Martinique writer, Aimé Césaire. Both
these books—in their very different ways—involve one in
painful conflicts that are quite out of key with Miami

and that perhaps heightened my sense of its fatuity. *La Résistance Haïtienne* is an account by a distinguished official, formerly ambassador to France, of the occupation of Haiti by the United States between 1915 and 1933. It is sober and documented, and it relies for its criticism of American policy mainly on quotations from American sources. It made me wonder anew at the capacity for self-deception of Woodrow Wilson, who, at the time when he was proclaiming the rights of small nations, had sent the United States Marines to invade and take over this country, with court-martial law and suppression of free speech, and at the expense of two thousand Haitian lives, in the interests of the National City Bank, which had bought up the French loan to Haiti. True, we wanted to keep the Germans, who also had a stake in Haiti, from taking the island over; but, when Germany had been defeated, we could no longer invoke that danger, and, disregarding our original pledges, we remained in Haiti eighteen years.

When, however, I knew more of the island, my bad conscience was somewhat quieted as I found evidence that, interested though our motives were and highhanded though our procedure became, we did accomplish something constructive in Haiti. M. Bellegarde, a former Minister of Public Education and an exponent of old-fashioned French culture, is scornful of the American technical and agricultural schools that were established under the occupation, and of our indifference to his own more humanistic ideals. He cites as a *reductio ad absurdum* of this our refusal of credit for the salaries of three professors from France at a time when we were importing, at the public expense and at salaries of two hundred dollars a month, two rat-catchers from the United States. But at that time we had been notified from New Orleans of the occurrence there of cases of bubonic plague, and there are moments when two hundred dollars may appear to be better spent on preventing the spread of disease than on disseminating Racine and Bossuet. In American accounts of Port-au-Prince at the time of the Marines' arrival, one reads of streets as filthy and stinking as in the towns of southern Italy. The Haitians depended on the rains for garbage and sewage disposal. Today Port-au-Prince is clean, and there is very little rubbish in the streets. But the drainage system, it seems, is our work. So are such roads as exist—though they were built by a forced labor system, administered with slave-driving methods, that proved one of our most serious blunders.

What is also lacking in this book, as in the author's larger work, *La Nation Haïtienne,* is any real admission of the scandalous state into which the Haitian government had got itself at the time when the United States intervened. When I met M. Bellegarde in Port-au-Prince—a very polished and upright old gentleman, a Mulatto almost white, with his stiff hair worn *en brosse* like a Frenchman—he said to me that it had never been difficult for the agents of imperialist skulduggery in Haiti to find *"des gens corrompus"* to coöperate with them. But from reading M. Bellegarde's books, conscientiously though he chronicles events, one would hardly get an adequate vision of the greediness and turbulence of the struggle for power which had gone on among Haitians themselves, during the first decade and a half of the century. Of the thirty chiefs of state—presidents or self-crowned emperors —that had ruled or governed Haiti since her declaration of independence in 1804, nineteen were deposed by revolutions, and seven were shot, poisoned, blown up or murdered in even more unpleasant ways. The recurrent attempts of the presidents to alter their constitutions in such a way as to make it possible for them to prolong their terms of office (constitutions in Haiti are almost as mortal as presidents), the inevitable armed opposition that eventually becomes successful and, in the event of his escaping death, the invariable flight to Jamaica of the superseded president, would be comic if, in view of the qualities displayed by the early Haitian patriots and the conspicuousness of Haiti as an instance of what the Negro can do, her self-misgovernment were not distressing. This does not, of course, excuse the stupidities and brutalities of the United States; but it has to be remembered that, when the Marines came in, there had been nine Haitian presidents in nineteen years; that under the last of these, Guillaume Sam, some hundred and sixty political prisoners, belonging to the best families, had been done to death in horrible ways, and that Guillaume Sam himself had been dragged out from under a bed in the French Legation by representatives of those first families and thrown to a boiling mob, who tore him to bits in the street. It is impossible to deal realistically with the primitive elements of Haitian life by means of such abstract formulas as those of M. Bellegarde. His excellent classical French is too pale and too rationalistic: it seems to screen from him as well as us a good deal that is of basic importance in the Haitian situation.

M. Aimé Césaire, a Negro, *has* faced his own situation in relation to the white world. He is a Communist, and has been sent to the French Chamber of Deputies as the member from Martinique, which was given the status of a French department in 1946, as the result of its having been exposed, as an outpost of Vichy in the last war, to the danger of being taken over by Germany or the United States. His *Cahier,* when I began to read it, seemed to me the best thing of its kind—the symbolist prose poem which is also a dramatic monologue—since Rimbaud's *Une Saison en Enfer.* If one rereads Rimbaud today, one is struck by his immense superiority to his imitators. The images and rhythms of *Une Saison en Enfer* were minted under pressure of a real desperation, where the deliriums of his surrealist followers are mostly a deliberate rhetoric that conforms to its own convention. Now, Césaire has not achieved a distinction that is comparable to the crystalline form of Rimbaud, but, here, too, the need to *say something* has charged his soliloquy with passion and power. In Césaire it is the impasses created by blood that give rise to the eruptive emotions. Yet the *Cahier* is not a tract: it is an expression of the shifts of feeling, of the savagery and the refinement, of the rage, the love of race, the frustration, of the Negro of first-rate abilities growing up in a non-Negro world. It goes on perhaps a little too long: I am not sure that the surrealist imagery, at its most confused and opaque, does not sometimes obstruct the poet's utterance. But on the whole it is a brilliant performance, which brings home the embittered will of the gifted and ambitious Negro contending against his difficult destiny with a force that seems as terrific as that of the acts and words of the heroes of the Haitian revolution. One thinks also of their tragic doom, the death of Toussaint L'Ouverture, the black leader of the slave revolt and one of the great men of his century, who has his place beside Bolivar and Washington, in the prison where Napoleon extinguished him by condemning him to cold and hunger, that prison the commandant of which reported that, although the prisoner was "naturally quick and passionate," he the commandant, in view of the fact that "the constitution of Negroes resembled in no respect that of Europeans," had "dispensed with giving [Toussaint] either physician or surgeon, who would not be of any use to him."

King Christophe's Citadel: Cap-Haïtien on the northern coast of the island gives a better idea than Port-au-

Prince of the days when Saint-Domingue, as the island
was earlier called, was the richest of the West Indian colo-
nies. You find there a colonial cathedral, handsome, severe
and solid (destroyed by an earthquake in 1842, but recently well restored), and a few old French manor houses,
reconstructed or still intact, turned into hotels or hospitals,
with the grounds now beautifully tended and red or purple
bougainvillea spilling over the walls. Where plantations
were, outside the town, empty old gateways stand, gaping
to the wild fields, yet suggesting still that life of abundance that the struggle with the Negroes wrecked. It is
only in Haiti, where the Negroes have written a chapter
themselves, that one grasps the importance and the violence of this episode of Western history: the accumulating
hatreds engendered by the centuries of the slave-trade; the
practical impossibility of a system enforced through fear,
which could only beget, by refraction, a blind panic on
the part of the planters; the contest of atrocities between
blacks and whites that could stimulate a French general
like Rochambeau to stage elaborate horrors that sound like
episodes in Sade's *Juliette;* the fight to the finish, with
victory won at the cost of total devastation. We are hardly
aware, in the United States, of this clear-cut drama of
Haiti. Our drama was a different one. Our planters of the
South were defeated yet the Negroes did not win their
freedom. The issue of our Civil War was between the
North and the South, so that the issue between whites
and blacks is never quite plainly seen. It is only since I
have been in Haiti that I have realized what "the colo-
nies" meant, and how the outrage and the impasse they
represented, from the eighteenth century on, bedeviled
the calculations of European and American politics—
cramping the Rights of Man of the French revolutionary
bourgeoisie by a very awkward reservation, balking the

designs of Napoleon in his projects for American conquest, and splitting the cohesion of the United States
eighty-five years after our own Revolution.

Breakfast in the early morning, looking out at the
bright gold light through the big green leaves of plants
on the window-sill and the lacelike leaves of shrubbery
outside the window. People always get up early in Haiti,
as they rarely do in Latin countries: the mornings are exhilarating, delicious. Setting out from the village of
Milot, twenty miles inland from Cap-Haïtien, one can
make the ascent on horseback to the Citadel of King
Christophe. On the summits of the stocky and assertive
hills that do not undulate like ordinary mountains but
have the look of illustrative peaks plucked up on a new-
laundered table-cloth, plushed with green though they
are by their varied plantations—on their summits the fresh
and strong morning light saturates the small white unmov-
ing clouds. By a path, stony, narrow, broken down by the
rains, you mount through a low rich forest, to enumerate
the features of which—mahogany, coconut, cocoa-bean,
pomegranate, custard-apple, breadfruit, mango, banana,
orange, avocado, calabash, bamboo and sugar-cane—may
suggest an overgrown jungle or the sorted and packed display of the goods of a grocery-store, but where everything
is green and free. Underfoot, frailer leaves of anise yield
their expected flavor, of citronella their expected fragrance; yams twine their vinelike tendrils. You climb
up into that light; you arrive at the top; it is as if you embraced the morning. But what rises before you suddenly,
revealed by a turn of the path, is the flat-iron "prow" of
the fortress, the great smooth wedge of lime and brick,
that looms sheer from the steep rock, on which it has been
grafted without foundations. From here the abrupt hills
take on a strategic look, an aspect of "mamelons and rave-

lins"; Cap-Haïtien rims the bay with a curving slice of white; the sea's blue is not so far off green that it much contrasts with the plain. The Citadel commands the whole expanse. Christophe was awaiting the return of the French, who had been first worn down, then driven out by himself and the other rebels, but they never gave him a chance to try his guns.

Here the cannon balls lie dull and inert, brimming immense bins; the cannon, so laboriously accumulated, point from their high slots at nothing. Down below, half hidden by vegetation, one gun lies partway up the path, where it was left at the death of Christophe, no one ever having cared enough to move it either up or down. These munitions are a little like the images of which the agglomeration bogs down Aimé Césaire's poem: a weighting of Negro strength, a brooding of Negro defiance, which has not been able to discharge itself because it has not found its target. Born on an English island, a tall straight-nosed Soudanese Negro, Christophe much admired the English; had Englishmen around him at court and made friends with the British admiral in command of the West Indian fleet. He was a model of administrative efficiency as well as a demon of energy. He organized the whole life of his kingdom, exacted from his peasant cultivators regular hours of work; he made his plantations productive and managed to put money away. King Christophe's was perhaps the only solvent government that has ever existed in Haiti. But the blacks whose revolt he had led were recalcitrant to the heavy corvée. In that period, the southern part of the island was a republic under the presidency of Pétion, who, a Mulatto and therefore suspect, could not press too hard on the blacks. In his domain there was no obligation to work, and this made Christophe's subjects envious. They found themselves enslaved by a Negro. Christophe is supposed to have sacrificed the lives of some thirty thousand men to the building of the La Ferrière citadel, and he was never to live to finish it. He had become, in his last years, a tyrant, who had resorted to enforcing discipline by commanding his workers to jump off the cliff and dropping them into oubliettes. He would scrutinize the country with a spy-glass, and if he found a man dozing in work hours, he would pick him off with a cannon. Thus oppressed, Christophe's subjects revolted. They burnt down the whole set of palaces that were his centers of cultivation. When, half-paralyzed by a recent stroke, he learned that his household guard had joined the rebellion against him, he shot himself with a golden bullet that he had kept for such an occasion.

Yet all Haiti takes pride in the Citadel. A falsetto-voiced one-eyed Mulatto, who had driven us from Port-au-Prince (I had made the trip north with Haitian friends) and who had never had a chance to see the Citadel, went up with the guide and me, and became very much excited. On the way, he told us gleefully the legend that Christophe—though nominally a Catholic—had retorted, when menaced with the wrath of God: "*He* is God of the Heavens, but *I* am God of the Earth!" And he repeated it, this driver, giggling again, when we looked down from the battlements of the Citadel. The black guide, too, it seemed to me, put into his routine patter a good deal more of genuine enthusiasm than such dodderers among ancient monuments as one usually finds in Europe. He would exclaim, "*C'est incroyable!*" as he showed us how the bricks for the citadel had been baked on the mountain itself, how they had been put together without mortar, how the guns had been dragged up one by one, how the structure had been poised on the ragged rock. "The foreigners who come up here all say that they can't understand it!" And there *is* something here for awe, the visiting stranger feels. It thrills, it brings to life the old

fight, to happen on the captured cannon lying harmless
in the Citadel courtyard: these dolphin-handled guns of
bronze, elegantly shaped and engraved, with the vapid
blazing mask of le Roi Soleil, the English *Dieu et Mon
Droit* and *Honni Soit Qui Mal y Pense,* and the arrogant
martial N; to remember how Christophe in his insurgent
days burnt the whole of Cap-Haïtien rather than receive
the French, how he compelled the respect of the British, and how he baffled and snubbed Napoleon. His
palace—Sans-Souci—at the foot of the mountain was
sacked in the peasant rebellion and has since been completely dismantled by the people of the countryside: there
is almost nothing left but a shell as hollow as a Roman
ruin, a staircase that spreads out from the entrance and
once sought to rival Versailles but is now scaled with
lichen and fuzzy with grass, the broken-off battered
head of a big female bust or statue, and the tree under
which Christophe, in the tradition of the older French
monarchs, liked to dispense justice out of doors. But the
Citadel itself stands unchastened as an affirmation of Negro power, a challenge to the non-Negro world. Even the
tomb of Christophe in the courtyard, thickset as these compact hills, has the look of a clenched fist.

My guide I found quite sympathetic, not only for his
capacity to rise to his subject, but also for a gentle politeness, of a kind characteristic of Haiti, that never seems
servile or insincere. When I asked him about a bird that I
had heard laughing harshly in the forest, he replied, *"C'est
le rossignol, monsieur."* I inquired whether this were the
bird that was celebrated in Europe for its song. *"C'est le
même oiseau, monsieur,"* he answered. I assumed that he
was graciously improvising, but learned later that the
mocking-bird is called *rossignol* in Haiti.

When we were back at the hotel, I asked him how

much I owed him for his services, and he answered in English, "Five bucks." This immediately provoked a scene. The lady who ran the hotel—whom I took to be a white Frenchwoman—overheard and scolded the man. I was told that I should pay him only two and a half, which was the regular rate per person; and she gave him a dressing-down: "*Pourquoi faîtes-vous des histoires comme ça?*" etc. But there had been, after all, *two* persons: the driver and myself—so I gave him his five bucks. I realized that in some way the driver wasn't supposed to count, and that the reasonable claims of the guide, as opposed to the convenience of tourists, were not supposed to count either. It is all too easy, of course, when looking in on a foreign community, to decide that someone or other is being unjustly treated and to exploit some superficial impression to the advantage of one's own finer feeling. This fellow may have been a rascal—I met several such who tried to swindle me; but the guide did not strike me as one, and he was here well within his rights. I was, in any case, heartily sorry that my most amiable relations with him—we had walked together part of the way while we were waiting for the car to pick us up, and had looked in on the preliminaries of a cockfight—should have ended with this painful scene. He had been so humiliated that he could now only hang his head, could not smile when I shook hands good-by.

This formidable lady, I learned—who has made of the Hostellerie du Roi Christophe probably one of the best small hotels in the world—is a Haitian of the highest stratum, a stratum of which the members have a minimum of Negro blood and do their best to breed that minimum out. The incident was the first of several that very soon made me see that only in a limited and peculiar sense can Haiti be called democratic; that the gap between the edu-

cated minority who carry on the business and the public
affairs and the illiterate peasantry who live on the land is
so wide that the country, in many respects, is more like
pre-Revolutionary Russia than it is like the United States.
Where the color-line prevails in the United States, we are,
of course, frankly un-democratic; but the distinction between black and white has also given rise in Haiti to a
principle of inequality—not in the form of Jim Crow restrictions, but through a complicated system of values that
is based on the varying proportions of white and Negro
blood. A contest between black and white, or rather a
swaying of the balance between them, has been going on
in Haiti ever since the San Domingan revolution, when
the conflict was so much confused by the wavering allegiance of the Mulattoes, who were—by the white planters,
their relatives—at one moment accepted and recruited, at
the next repulsed and persecuted, with the result that the
Mulattoes themselves oscillated between taking the side of
the slaves and supporting the status quo. The visitor from
the United States may not be prepared to grasp this feature of Haitian life. He is familiar, at home, with a discrimination which works against anybody whomever who
is known to have any black blood, and he may not at
first be aware of the complex internal strains of a society
where everybody has more or less. Here adjustments have
continually to be regulated between European traditions
and African ones, and these confront one another, not as
they do in the United States, in the shape of two groups
—black and white—clearly (if sometimes fraudulently)
defined, but in the contrariety of instincts in the nature of
a single individual; among differing members of a family;
in the vicissitudes of families of mixed blood in relation
to one another; or in the rises and declines of political
parties.

Color Politics: For the visitor, this issue of color is most clearly to be observed in politics. The Haitian ship of state has been heavily and recurrently rocked by it. Though the French-trained Mulatto "élite" have for long periods maintained their ascendency, keeping the blacks and near-blacks out of office, the latter have had their *revanches.* One of these has just occurred. The present administration, that of President Dumarsais Estimé, represents an accession to power of the pure Negro element in the educated class, after a long and unbroken period of Mulatto domination, for which the attitude toward color of the American authorities is said to have been largely responsible (we sent Southerners to Haiti, on the theory that they were "used to dealing with Negroes"!). The regime of Estimé was at the beginning outspokenly anti-white: there was talk about "non-Aryan" and "Aryan" and a certain amount of Mulatto-baiting. Last March, however, Estimé repudiated this uncompromising policy, and the campaign against white blood is supposed to have been somewhat relaxed—though I occasionally ran into traces of it when I visited the Rex Theater, which stands at the edge of the Champs-de-Mars and is haunted by young loafers, who sometimes try to stare you out of countenance. One boy, on seeing me, exclaimed *"Un blanc!",* crossed himself and muttered something about the President. And the Mulattoes have not ceased to be militant. They have provided one of the strongest elements in a rather strangely mixed opposition, which in the middle of November [I am writing as of December 1949] attempted a revolution. This was thwarted by Estimé, who imprisoned the opposition leaders and suppressed the opposition party.

One of the most effective figures in the recent pro-black campaign was a Negro named Daniel Fignolé. He has succeeded in organizing—what is difficult in Haiti—a Mouvement Ouvrier Populaire, familiarly known as

MOP, and he has had a big radio following. When Estimé became president, he made Fignolé Minister of Education; but the latter, continuing his broadcasts in office, began criticizing his colleagues with the utmost freedom, and his resignation was soon demanded. He then announced his disillusionment with the principle of black superiority, declaring that the darker-skinned public officials were not only no more reliable than their lighter-skinned predecessors, but actually a good deal worse. Daniel Fignolé is said to be a genuine idealist, quite sincere but not very intelligent, and with no program that differs from that of the administration he helped to put in. He became nevertheless the most influential leader of the parties attacking the government, and the MOP sufficiently formidable to provoke Estimé to repress it. Fignolé followed Haitian tradition by taking refuge in the Argentine Embassy and so escaped being put into jail. (The President, in a generous gesture, has pardoned the opposition leaders, and they are now theoretically, though probably not really, at liberty to publish their papers.)

The pro-Negro policy of Estimé has also aroused opposition in another and quite different quarter. To be pro-Negro may mean being pro-Voodoo, and the Catholics, who, in Haiti as elsewhere, have been going into action with new militancy in behalf of their own religion, have accused the officials of the present regime of practicing Voodoo rites. It is asserted that Estimé, who comes of peasant stock, has a near relative who is a Voodoo priest. At the beginning of last year, the principal Catholic paper published a series of articles by a Catholic priest, Père J. Foisset, who asserted that Voodoo was enjoying an unprecedented popularity in Port-au-Prince, that there were scores of new Voodoo temples, some of which had cost thousands of dollars, and that the candidates at the last election, in hope of insuring success, had spent a good deal

of money on petitions and sacrifices to the Voodoo gods.
This priest was soon compelled to leave Haiti, on the
ground that he was interfering in public affairs. The anti-
government Catholic paper, *L'Action Sociale,* which had
reprinted these articles with the heading IL FAUT ÉCRASER
LE VAUDOU, was suppressed in the recent crisis, and its
editor, Paul Cassagnol, organizer of a Parti Populaire Social Chrétien, was one of the political leaders imprisoned.

Add to these incongruous elements that of the Communist Party in its guise of Parti Socialiste Populaire,
under the leadership of Anthony Lespès. M. Lespès is a
serious and able man, who has specialized in the national
problems of water and soil conservation, and who at one
time acted as advisor to the Department of Agriculture.
He has also written a "documentary" novel, *Les Semences
de la Colère,* which shows an imaginative as well as a
practical grasp of the agrarian situation in Haiti. This
novel of Lespès' deals with the attempt to repatriate on
the Haitian land the survivors of the horrible massacre
of 1937, when the Dominicans, under their dictator
Trujillo, drove resident Haitian peasants out of the Dominican Republic. (The Haitians share their island uncomfortably with the Spanish-speaking Dominicans, who
occupy the western half.) Lespès had taken part in this
project. Later, he became a Communist, but a Communist
who—it seems to a visitor from the hunting-grounds of
hardshell Stalinism—of rather a peculiar kind. The Kremlin has its agents in the Caribbean, but these little island
countries are remote from Moscow and not just now of
importance to it. It is still possible here for persons of
sincere democratic sympathies to be sold on the Communist Party through the idealism of Marx and Lenin. I
visited Lespès on the farm to which he has been forced to
retire. Finding a portrait of Stalin on the wall along with
those of Lenin and Marx, I was surprised that he should

talk about current affairs with intelligence, freedom and
humor. He has studied in the United States, and he told
me that he liked and admired us, that the only thing he
had against us was the conditions we had insisted on
making in connection with a recent loan to Haiti for the
improvement of the Artibonite Valley. I read later, in a
back number of his paper (now suppressed with the rest),
a reply he had written to Trygve Lie on the occasion of his
having been invited to take part in a Scientific Conference held under the auspices of UNESCO. In explaining, along orthodox Communist lines, that the basi-
cally capitalist economy represented by the United Nations
was hopelessly inimical to the object—conservation of natural resources—proposed for discussion by the conference,
he made the point, no doubt sound, against this loan, that
it had been granted them only on condition it be used
for the production of goods which would not compete
with ours, and not for the building up of Haitian in-
dustries, which, however beneficial to Haiti, might take
away some of our trade—a suicidal policy, he goes on to
say, from the American point of view itself, since we
count also on selling our gadgets there, and the peasant,
in the position we impose on him, that of producer of
raw materials exclusively, would never be able to purchase
our refrigerators and television sets. This paper, however, I
was told, has also obediently to publish the party-line
boilerplate passed on to it, presumably, from Cuba, and
has sponsored a hair-raising story that the American health
mission to Puerto Rico have been "infecting" the natives
with cancer in order to kill them off—just as Communist
doctors in the Soviet purge were accused of having infected their patients with syphilis. It is a pity that a man
like Lespès, whose professional abilities are needed by his
country, should have been brought, by his very social
conscience and intellectual courage, to a state where he is

condemned to impotence by the ineptitudes of the Kremlin, on the one hand, and, on the other, by persecution at home. There is hardly, at the present time, even a labor movement in Haiti that a Marxist could hope to indoctrinate. The trade union movement there dates only from 1946, and total membership is no more than a thousand.

Let us also take into account that President Estimé, in his statements, has put the whole blame for the political crisis on a certain Colonel Astrel Roland, a former supporter of his, who he says, is conspiring against him from the hostile Dominican Republic, in the interests of the dictator Trujillo. Roland, who was military chief of the Department of Artibonite and "intervened" in the elections there in behalf of Estimé, was dissatisfied, after the election, when the latter sent him out of the country as military attaché to Washington. In Washington, Roland fell in with the Minister of the Interior of the Dominican Republic, and he eventually betook himself to San Domingo, from which he has been broadcasting attacks on the Estimé administration. There seems to be no question that Trujillo is ambitious to dominate Haiti. The President says that the dictator is trying to have him assassinated. When Estimé recently attended an evening party at the British Embassy, he had machine-guns at the back of the building, and he announced a few weeks later that the government, discovering weapons, had foiled a Trujillo plot.

But, aside from the Voodoo issue, what exactly are the opposition's charges? They are the same sort of charges, it seems, that have always been brought by oppositions in Haiti, and that leave experienced observers, both Haitian and foreign, cynical. Those who know Haiti's history say that the politicians out of office are always driven mad with envy at seeing the ones who are in enjoying conspicuous luxury, and that they always bring charges of corruption that are usually all too well-founded. The misapplication by officials of public funds to personal uses seems to have reached fantastic lengths in Haiti. There have been large foreign loans to meet urgent needs of which the public has seen scarcely a penny, and it has been partly as a brake on such scandals that the American occupation has been defended. You hear many circumstantial stories— such as the one about the barrels of concrete that are said to have been diverted from public works to a new villa then being built by one of the high officials. When the barrels were traced to his place, he is said to have announced frankly that the Mulattoes had had the spoils long enough and that now it was the Negroes' turn.

Suspicion has been lately directed at a sum of eighty-four million dollars which is supposed to have been expended on a giant Exposition. It is true that this Exposition, which commemorates the second centenary of the founding of the city of Port-au-Prince, has as yet very little to show. December 8 had been set for the opening, and in order not to disappoint the tourists, the ceremonies took place on that day. Bells boomed and choirs resounded; a salute of guns was heard; officials in top hats and frock coats were seen circulating in public places. Orations and masses took place on the Exposition grounds. The President pronounced a *discours* which he may well have written himself, given the literary proficiency of the Haitians, and which struck me as exhibiting a brilliance of style and a sweep of historical imagination well beyond the reach of any living white statesman known to me, not excluding Winston Churchill. But when one tried to visit the Exposition, one found almost nothing there. The Palace of Tourism as yet had nothing in it but murals, at which people were staring through locked glass doors. The aquarium housed no fishes and was not yet even equipped with tanks. There was an interesting ethnological exhibition but it had not yet been moved into its place and was still housed, as it had been for years, in the dark basement of the Hôtel de Ville. Many of the buildings were hardly begun. The only one that was open for business was a post office, in which people were staring, quietly and enigmatically, at some blood-curdling native woodcarvings of figures from Voodoo mythology that had evidently been stuck in there till their building was ready, and where the clerks were weighing the mail in their hands and guessing at the postage. The only items that were ready on time were a hideous series of murals which—a monument to the prestige for Haitians of almost any sort of reputation from France—a painter named Pierre Bourdelle, pathetically third-rate son of a fashionable but second-rate father, had been asked to contribute to the Exhibition: huge allegorical figures—the Negro breaking his chains, etc.—the effect of which might have been caricatural had they not, with their formless drawing and their messy blues, browns and reds, proved so featureless and two-dimensional as to suggest the small birds and animals that one sometimes finds on asphalt highways squashed out by passing cars. Almost any of the primitive native artists, working, as they often do, with a few pots of automobile paint, would have produced something more respectable. It was only at the far end of the grounds that one found, in the evening, a little life: some restaurants, an attractive night club out of doors in a grove of palms, and a small American "carnival," with merry-go-round, popcorn-vendor, ferris-wheel, cooch-show and freaks, which, due to the poverty of the populace, was not doing a very good business. A gambling casino was opened later, and gambling slot-machines installed all over Port-au-Prince. This house had official sanction, and the proprietor of it, from the United States, assured me that Haiti depended on him to raise funds for education.

The opposition has criticized the government for sinking so much money in the Exposition when it was needed for other things, and, at the moment of the threatened revolt, there are said to have been incitations, in the destructive Haitian tradition, to call attention to this waste of money by tearing the buildings down. Yet, aside from its value as publicity and for attracting the tourist trade, the Exposition will have left an asset in the considerable stretch of waterfront which has been reclaimed from swamp for its grounds. I felt in most quarters in Haiti, and even on the part of his opponents, a certain respect for M. Estimé. True, he locked these opponents up, but he soon let them out again, and one has to judge such acts, I suppose, in the light of President Sam, who dealt with his own opponents by slaughtering a hundred and sixty hostages. One discovers that Estimé has allotted funds to such good causes as the starved Bibliothèque Nationale and the UNESCO experiment at Marbial. He is now trying to get a forty million dollar loan for a comprehensive road-building program.

Yet the President has recently shown evidence of yielding to the same compulsion, apparently irresistible in Haiti, which has brought so many of his predecessors to violent or ignominious ends. A President of the Haitian Republic, according to the present constitution, is elected for a term of six years, and he cannot have a second term. Estimé is due to relinquish his office in 1952; but he is already, according to his opponents, maneuvering for an amendment to the constitution which will enable him to serve again. In August of last year, after declaring a "state of siege," Estimé took the unconstitutional but apparently classical step of dismissing the Conseil Communal, an

elected municipal body which is entrusted with the function of registering the votes and thus plays an important
role in the election of the deputies to the legislative Assembly. The elections were supposed to take place the
following January, and the parties of the opposition,
united by this common interest, had protested the dis-
missal of the Council and demanded a check on the polls.
They had recourse to the equally classical, if equally unconstitutional, step of provoking a student strike, which
involved political meetings and an attempt to call out the
shopkeepers. But no coup d'état ever took place. What
averted it was partly, it would seem, the general popularity of Estimé, partly the forethought of the United States,
which, before its official withdrawal, had disarmed the
population and subjected the police and the army to the
single control of the President. The government, as they
say in that part of the world, *mit main basse* on the
malcontents, and appears to have remained in a strong
position. When the January elections were held, they were
boycotted by the opposition.

[The position of Estimé was not so strong as it looked.
The Exposition was not a success; and the President could
not be discouraged from his efforts to succeed himself by
amending the constitution. He had thus roused against
him, by May, a movement so menacing that he was forced
to resign. He first fled to Jamaica in the usual way, and
later to the United States, where he recently died in New
York. The government was taken over by a junta of army
officers, one of whom, Colonel Paul Magloire, was later
elected President and still remains in power. He is said to
have undertaken a large program of public works and to
have pledged himself to maintain a balance between Mulattoes and Negroes.

I have left the account above of the political situation

in Haiti as of December, 1949, since the elements are always more or less the same, and such crises, as I have said, recurrent.]

Marbial: But this question of elections brings us to the fundamental problem in Haiti. In this country of three and a half million people (there has never been a satisfactory census, and the number has been variously estimated), only about ten per cent are literate. These are the urban "élite," who are likely to know two or three languages (as well as the local Creole) and who have never done manual work. The illiterate ninety per cent, in their primitive lath and mud huts, thatched with banana-leaves, inhabit an African jungle, dominated by Voodoo divinities, in which even the conception of a Haitian government is difficult for them to grasp. When one of these peasants comes in to the polls and indicates his choice of a candidate, it is no trouble for the official recording the votes to write down any name he pleases, and if the voter can read a little, it is almost as easy to get him drunk so that he will not notice what has been written. It is obvious that the political life of Haiti will never make very much sense so long as such conditions prevail; and wherever, in any field, in Haiti today, you encounter a serious person who wants to do something for his country and who is young enough not to be prisoned in the Francophile culture of the nineteenth century, you will almost certainly find him working to diminish the disabling differences between the illiterate and the educated classes, either by teaching the peasantry to read and write, by instructing them in agricultural methods, by extirpating the diseases that prey on them, or by studying their folk-lore and cults in order to understand them better.

A conspicuous example of this is the recent UNESCO

experiment, begun in August, 1948, which aims at all these kinds of improvement. This project was originally suggested by a young Haitian, M. Emmanuel Gabriel, a former school inspector in Port-au-Prince, who had gone to England on a British scholarship to study education and who had attended a Paris conference in October, 1946, at which plans were discussed by the United Nations Educational, Scientific and Cultural Organization for supplying technical assistance to governments who were members of the United Nations. M. Gabriel communicated with the Methodist Missionary in Port-au-Prince, Pastor H. Ormonde McConnell, an able and active man, who had become a leading figure in the educational field in Haiti. He suggested to Pastor McConnell that the Pastor go to President Estimé and propose to him that Haiti apply to get the benefit of UNESCO assistance. The application was granted, and the government was invited by UNESCO to choose a suitable place to conduct an educational experiment.

The locality selected was Marbial in the valley of the Gosseline River, which flows from the hills into the Bay of Jacmel (near the town of Jacmel on the south coast): a community of about thirty thousand, impoverished and peculiarly unfortunate in being alternately starved by protracted droughts and inundated by terrible floods. The only access to Marbial is by way of an abominable road, full of holes that recall the craters of a bomb-riddled highway in Europe. This runs along the Gosseline River, and river and road together make the main artery of Marbial life. In this river, walled by infertile mountains, where the whitish volcanic rock shows through the vegetation, you see the tall blue-black males bathing among the pale stones and pale mud of the sprawling and shallow stream; the swollen-bellied children playing; the women rinsing out their washing; and the horses and cattle being watered.

This is also the water the people drink. The roadside is sprinkled with their only commerce: edibles that are sometimes displayed on stands under roofs of dried palm or banana leaves, sometimes laid out on the ground, and that include ripe bananas, bottled syrups, queer phalliform loaves of white bread that suggest the primitive features of the Voodoo rites, and some brown and sticky confection that looks like peanut butter or pralines. The small children are holding on the tops of their heads—both hands clasped above them—single oranges or calabash gourds; the women balance great trays or baskets, with mixed loads of tinware and bottles, or a gruesome brown cow's head with one ear wagging. Little donkeys are their main beasts of burden; some of them have lost their ears, which have become diseased and had to be lopped (to call somebody a crop-eared donkey is one of the worst insults). These are likely to hold up passing cars by balking in the middle of the road, from which they may be gradually budged by the pulling of barefoot girls, in one-piece dresses and big flat straw hats, or by women puffing on pipes. The men do not do much toting, but men and women alike are often seen carrying the West Indian poultry that, as food, as sacrificial offerings and as contestants in the most popular sport, play a very large role in their lives. They tie the bird's legs together and carry it as if it were a parasol, with one hand clasping the legs and the rest tucked under the arm. These fowls are extremely beautiful, with an infinitely varied mixture of bronzy greens, yellows and reds which are often combined with white. They must be almost the only aesthetic objects that these drably clad peasants possess. The roosters are bred for fierceness, and they are very highly prized, since cock-fighting, with dancing and Voodoo rites, make the whole of their amusement, their drama. One especially handsome gamecock was being transported in a fancy basket. No machines, hardly any modern implements. I saw two men sawing a log on a high improvised sawhorse, one standing up on the horse and holding the top end of the saw, with the other man below on the ground, working the lower end. The people are accompanied by famelic dogs and by lean black pigs, which they lead on ropes.

The UNESCO headquarters—announced to us by signboards in phonetic Creole. "Sous Onesko" means UNESCO spring (*source*). The "Katié Général" includes a "Bibliotèk," a "Sinéma," a "Pépiniè," an "Atélie Tisaj," an "Atélie Séramik," and a "Sât (*centre*) Koopérativ." It is a little more difficult for the visitor who is not familiar with Creole to recognize in "Â non aprân li ak écri" "Let us learn to read and write," or to translate "Kay sa a sé pou habitâ Mabial la dâ yap aprân ton sa ki pou ba yo moyê pou viv tâkou moun dé bien" as "This building is for the people of Marbial. Here they teach you everything you need so that you may live like decent people." This Creole language is a mixture of the Negro tongues of West Africa, from which the slaves were brought, with the French provincial dialect that was spoken in the maritime regions involved in the colonial trade and which still preserves ancient locutions that were current in the seventeenth century. In the sentence above, for example, the words *yap aprân* mean *they are teaching*. *Yap* is a contraction for *yo ap*, *yo* being the Creole version of an African plural suffix that has come to be used for *they*, and *ap* being *après* in the antiquated usage— the dictionary of the Academy has an example from Bossuet—which gave *être après à* the same sense as *être en train de*. It was necessary for the slaves in the early days to improvise as quickly as possible some means of communicating with their masters, as well as some means of understanding each other when their African languages differed. The result was a tough little tongue, laconic and perfectly logical, worked out from lowest common denominators. The curious thing is that, fixed from this early period, it has become, with a few local variations, the popular language everywhere in the French-speaking West Indies as well as in Guiana and Louisiana. It is also much spoken by educated Haitians even when they are talking among themselves, though they are forced to fall back on French when they want to deal with abstract conceptions, which cannot be expressed in Creole. The broadcasts from Port-au-Prince are often made in this macaronic jargon of Creole helped out with French. On the one hand, in Haiti, you have classical French, the language *par excellence* of formulas, becoming continually staler as the destiny of the island in our hemisphere estranges it more and more from the nation that colonized it. "The French say we talk like books," M. Gabriel remarked to me; and it is true that the Haitian press becomes sometimes unintentionally comic through its dressing-up of petty events in an insipid ceremonious garb that suggests the high stocks and tight breeches of the era of the Dominican revolution. On the other hand, you have the reformers, who ask: "If the Creole-speaking Haitians are to be taught to read and write, why start them off with French, a language of which they have had no experience and which is certainly, in their present phase, beyond their intellectual grasp?" These advocates of Creole declare that the old-fashioned people who oppose them do not want to have the peasantry taught anything at all. In its present benighted state, they can exploit the black population, and they are afraid of its eventual recalcitrance if it should become better educated. To this fear has been also attributed the objection one sometimes hears that the phonetic method in use has been based on the values of English, so must disqualify the student from learning French.

This pro-Creole movement, in any case, is only just getting under way. One of the obstacles it has to contend with is the fewness of Creole texts. Creole folk-tales have sometimes been written down, but it has been always in some form of French spelling, and such original exercises in Creole as the amusing adaptation of La Fontaine by the poet Georges Sylvain have been meant for literate readers. Pastor McConnell, at the beginning of the forties, founded a Creole newspaper, and has had some Creole textbooks printed, but the paper, after two and a half years, was suspended for lack of funds, and the textbooks have not been reprinted. Today you will find at Port-au-Prince, in the basement of the Centre d'Art, an American UNESCO worker, a Negro girl from Massachusetts, a college graduate and former social worker, making a shorter, less sophisticated version than those in Sylvain's La Fontaine of *La Cigale et la Fourmi* (the moral of which is felt to be needed), with charming illustrations by the Haitian artist George Remponeau, and preparing a little tract to explain that the disease of yaws is not an affliction imposed by an angry and malignant spirit but a consequence of the depredations of a very small kind of animal, from whose attacks it is possible to protect oneself. Nor has the method of teaching Creole been definitely settled yet. The system worked out by McConnell begins by teaching sounds and syllables, which are later put together in words; but M. Gabriel, who has studied with I. A. Richards, is replacing this method at Marbial by one derived from Basic English, in which sentences are the primary units. It has already been found possible by the other method—unexpectedly to skeptical conservatives— to teach students to read and write in from two to three months.

Here, at any rate, in a little white building that is hardly more than a shelter are two schoolrooms hung with

charts and maps, on one of which the United States
figures as "Etazini." There are two hundred children now
in this largest of the UNESCO schools. In Marbial there
are altogether twenty-seven UNESCO schools and sixteen
others run by various volunteers, but these take care of
only from six to seven hundred children out of the three
thousand children of school age—that is, between seven
and fourteen. Many of them live in remote areas, where
UNESCO ultimately hopes to set up what it calls "feeder"
schools. The children are to be taught the rudiments of
reading and writing and arithmetic, along with "fundamental hygiene." Efforts to teach them French are likely
to become stalled in the mere memorizing of isolated
passages whose meaning they have never grasped. There
are ten teachers at this main center: four for the primary
school, one for adults, five for the crafts. These crafts
consist of basketweaving with sisal fibres, beautifully clean
and white, making combs out of cow-horn, moulding
pottery from the pallid mud and constructing simple
wooden furniture. There has as yet, though it is badly
needed, been little agricultural instruction. A nursery has
been begun with small plantings of tobacco, pistachio,
eggplant and a tree called divi-divi, the pods of which
are used for tanning. It is hoped, by the cultivation of
divi-divi, to avert the waste of mahogany trees, which have
been ravaged by the peasants for this purpose. There is
also a small dispensary, to which a doctor comes once a
week and where a nurse and a male assistant give the
patients injections and dressings when the doctor is not
there. Before the center existed, there was no way to get
medical attention except—what was rarely done—to pay a
doctor to come out from Jacmel. The local witch-doctors,
it seems, have some skill at setting fractures and know a
few effective herbs for minor ailments, but they are otherwise completely helpless. Of the patients who come to this

clinic twenty per cent have syphilis and sixty per cent the probably related and hardly less disastrous yaws. This latter disease, with its running sores, rapidly debilitates its victims: they become incapable of effort and a dead encumbrance to their relatives.

When the UNESCO people first came to Marbial, they found the peasants so undernourished that it was out of the question to teach them before they were adequately fed. So canteens were set up, and they were given work on the new buildings and roads, which would enable them to earn a little money. Some who have been watching the experiment have come to the gloomy conclusion that even such improved irrigation as the region is susceptible of would not raise the subsistence level to a point which would make it possible for the natives to improve themselves much. It is encouraging, however, that the people do seem to want education, have been eager in attendance at the center. In the interior of the island, however, along the Dominican border, such a project, it is said, would be hopeless, since the peasants there are quite incapable of imagining anything different from the life they have always led. And from the opposite side of the project, the side which is offering assistance, there are difficulties to be got over, too. First of all, there is a religious question. The natives of Marbial, though they actually practice Voodoo, are nominally divided about half and half between the Catholic Church and various Protestant sects. The representative of the government on the project has been a fanatical Free Methodist, M. Arthur Bonhomme, whose father founded in Port-au-Prince an independent Methodist church, not acknowledging the authority of the Methodist Mission. M. Bonhomme was sentenced to jail in 1937, for complicity in a plot to assassinate the Chef du Garde Présidentiel of President Vincent, and, while serving his term, read the Bible and experienced a revelation. He came out preaching a red-hot doctrine and possessed by a fervent mission to have the Gospels translated into Creole (a project that is now being carried out). In 1946, he was made head of the Comité Pour la Diffusion de l' Enseignement par le Créole, and so was assigned to the UNESCO experiment. But the Catholics took alarm at a project which, in the absence of the UNESCO director, was being supervised by a militant Protestant, and which was known to have been initiated by the resident Methodist missionary. To make matters worse, the UNESCO school, though its teaching was of course non-sectarian, was originally lodged in the Protestant church. As a result of all this, the local Catholic priest has obstructed UNESCO so determinedly that it has been necessary to move the school and to detach M. Bonhomme from the project.

It may be worth while at this point—as illustrating the difficulties encountered by the innovator in Haiti—to include an account of my return from Marbial with a party that included Pastor McConnell, M. Gabriel and a young man from the United States State Department. We had come to Jacmel by plane, and it had taken not much more than half an hour. Getting back was another matter. Every resource failed. They had told us at the airport in the morning that it would be possible for us to charter a plane, but now they said that the weather was unfavorable. Nor was it easy to find a car. When we arrived, we were supposed to be met by a command car which would take us to Marbial, but this unsatisfactory vehicle, which had half fallen over a precipice on the dangerous north-coast road and which had just been abandoned for several days—not having been able to cross it—in the bed of the bridgeless river, had turned out to be now in such very bad shape that we had had to borrow a truck from a hospital. We could not, however, drive this truck all the way back to Port-au-Prince, so an attempt was made to fix up the command car, under which six or seven men were seen lying for about two hours. The man who had met us and was supposed to look after us faded quietly away from time to time and finally disappeared altogether. Our attempts to hire a car at the town garage did not result in anything definite. The truth was, as we soon came to understand, that nobody wanted to make the trip. The proprietor of a little hotel in the café of which we were waiting invited us to look at his bedrooms, which were he said specially suited to Americans. The State Department man and I then learned from our Haitian companions that they had always had a certain suspicion that our trip was being sabotaged by the partisans of M. Bonhomme—of whom our greeter was one—men who had lost their jobs when Bonhomme had been taken off the project.

Later in the evening, however, the command car was made to run, and one of the garage mechanics consented to drive us to Port-au-Prince, though only after having us wait while he went home and changed his clothes in order to be dressed for the city. When we had started, and one saw what the road was like, one wasn't sure that the reluctance of the drivers had necessarily been sabotage. The wonder, one felt, in fact, was that anybody had been willing to embark at that hour in that old piece of rickety junk, which seemed ready to fall to pieces with every jolt of the much-jolting road. We broke down about every fifteen minutes, and had long waits among the nocturnal banana-groves, while the driver, who did not have a flashlight, tinkered by the flame of small flares which were held for him by boys from roadside farms. It was proposed to turn back to Jacmel, but the man from the State Department had some sort of engagement that evening, and Pastor McConnell, an Irishman, displayed a very British spirit in not wanting the Jacmel people to see that we had been defeated. The buses that came from the other direction would find us blocking the road, and the drivers would get out to help. We finally persuaded one of them, by offering him forty dollars, to drive us to Port-au-Prince after his passengers had been delivered. This bus was called La Sainte Famille: a colored print of its patrons had been pasted up to face the driver. The passengers, as is common in Haiti, sang in chorus to beguile the journey. The driver and the man who spelled him always called one another *"mon cher"* and showed everybody the quiet courtesy that is characteristic of Haiti. At one point this driver ran over a dog that was lying in the middle of the road, and uttered a short "ha ha" as he hurtled away from its howls of pain. The bus was jammed, inside and on top, with the passengers and their baggage and with great sacks of potatoes and yams, which gradually unloaded in the sleeping town. At last we headed back toward Port-au-Prince, and the true rigors of the trip were revealed to us. We had had bumpy enough going before, but we had not become involved with the Gosseline River. The road to Port-au-Prince from Jacmel crosses this, by our actual count, more than eighty times, and it sometimes runs along its bed, so that the bus must forge upstream like a ferryboat. These phases of navigation are alternated, at frequent intervals, with excursions into the mountains, where the bus must thread a narrow pass, on one side of which drops a precipice. When we emerged from the bed of the river, there were usually stones in the tires that could only be dislodged by long pounding. Yet the drive was exhilarating: the wild country in the moonlight; and the ups and downs of the road, like a roller-coaster, kept one alert. In the final stage of the journey—when the dangerous part was over—the driver several times went to sleep, with the result that the bus made some sudden swerves that might have smashed into a tree or a house, if the watchful Pastor McConnell, who was sitting beside the driver, had not waked him up in time. We arrived at about 3:30.

A few days later one read in the paper a long protest by M. Bonhomme, addressed to the Secretary of State of National Education. He was answering an announcement by the Secretary that, dating from December 31, all activities connected with the Marbial project were *pro tem* to be suspended. The man at Jacmel who had fallen down on the problem of our transportation had, I learned from another source, been relieved of his UNESCO duties. Bonhomme was indignantly complaining that the staff at Marbial center had not been paid for months and that he had been compelled to meet expenses out of his own pocket. In rebuttal, one heard it said—unjustly, it may very well be, but in Haiti, as one had learned, inevitably—that he had been handling the funds so recklessly that it was thought inadvisable to give him more. In any case, a new director, an Englishman from Mauritius, has now been installed at Marbial, with M. Gabriel as Assistant Director.

Between the rivalries of Haitian politics and the dissensions within the U.N. itself, the vagaries of the Gosseline River and the activities of the yaws bacilli, the struggles of the Christian churches and the prestige of the Voodoo divinities, it may seem that the experiment at Marbial is rather a precarious enterprise. The U.N. has recently published—editions in both English and French —a three-hundred-page report on the mission to Haiti of "a team of experts, set up," at the request of the Haitian government, "in a consultation with four specialized agencies, namely, the Food and Agricultural Organization, the International Monetary Fund, the United Nations Educational, Scientific and Cultural Organization, and the World Health Organization, which were requested to nominate experts in their service who could participate in the United Nations Mission as members conversant with the various problems in the field of agriculture, credit organization, education and health, having a bearing on the general problem of economic development of under-developed countries." This mission was undertaken "in implementation" of the following aims: "(1) to examine the problems of and the conditions affecting the economic development of Haiti primarily in the fields of agricultural industry and related activities, having regard to the inter-related economic and social problems bearing, in particular, on the improvement of health and education; (2) In the light of this examination and in taking cognizance of related government programs or plans, to formulate proposals as to practicable measures, including those of a public finance nature, designed to promote the economic development of the country; (3) To appraise the needs in terms of organizational arrangements and technical assistance implied by the measures proposed." The report is mostly written in this language. It goes on to say, for example, that, "as initially agreed with the Haitian Government, the Chief of the Mission made a two-weeks' preliminary visit to Haiti in the early part of August, 1948, for organizational arrangements, for exploratory examination of the general economic picture with a view to determining the main lines of the programme and the most expedient composition of the Mission, and for the assembly of pertinent documentation in preparation for the studies to be undertaken." (One is reminded of the Murphys' motif in *Finnegans Wake:* "—to them who are latecomers all the year's round by anticipation, are the porters of the passions in virtue of retroratiocination, and, contributing their conflingent controversions of differentia-

tion, unify their voxes in a vote of vaticination". . .) And
although one does find in this document a good deal of
useful data, the conditions of life in Haiti and the rem-
edies proposed by the mission are all more or less presented
in this pompous, polysyllabic and relentlessly abstract
style. In contrast to the massive *amoncellement* of three
hundred pages of this, the Marbial center seems tiny, and
the twenty-six hundred dollars that is all that the United
Nations combined with the Haitian government has so
far been able to raise for it, a meager enough expenditure.

There are, however, positive forces working for Marbial: on one side, the earnest desire of certain idealistic
young Haitians, who have been well trained in modern
techniques and who do not share the mentality of the
politicians, to see their people become something better
than a diseased undernourished peasantry, manipulated
by a spendthrift élite; and, on the other side, the interest of the United States, as emphasized by Truman's
Point Four, in providing new markets for its products by
raising the standards of backward countries. The mention
of "measures of public finance" in the survey quoted above
reminds us of the banking interests that, along with the
strategic ones, first brought the United States into Haiti.
But "capitalist" governments today, as well as educators
and engineers, are obliged to talk in terms of aims like
those of the Socialists and Communists with whom these
governments are now competing. The publicity put out
by UNESCO in connection with its Haitian Mission is
curiously reminiscent—by its blankly dehumanized style
as well as by its declared objectives, though the jargon is
a little different—of the literature of the Communist Party
in the days when it had so much at heart the welfare
of the "toiling masses."

It will be interesting, in any case, to see how far Marbial will get. Of the two other similar experiments that

UNESCO has undertaken, one in China and one in British East Africa, the first has been made impossible by the Communist successes in China, and the second given up, for reasons that are left obscure by the UNESCO reports on the subject.

Haitian Literature: This concern for the Negro population of Haiti, which is expressed by both the present black government and the Left opposition to it, which has stimulated the movement for Creole education and which inspires the various experts connected with the Marbial experiment, has also played lately a central role in all fields of Haitian culture. A volume of ethnographical studies, *Ainsi Parla l'Oncle,* by Dr. Price-Mars, published in 1928, seems clearly to mark the moment when the Haitian intelligentzia began to be interested in folk-lore and to worry about peasant problems. In 1931, the reading of folk-tales in the schools was advocated for the first time; on Flag Day, 1945, to the horror of the classically trained, folk dances were done in the Champ de Mars; and the next year, to the outrage of the Catholic priests, Voodoo dances and chants were performed at the Rex Theater at a *fête universitaire* presided over by the Sécretaire d'État de l'Éducation Nationale. In the meantime, there had been published two monographs on Voodoo, *Vaudou et Névrose,* by Dr. J. C. Dorsainvil and *Le Vaudou Haïtien* by Dr. Louis Maximilien, as well as the important anthropological novel, *Canapé-Vert,* by the brothers Marcelin; and the novelist and poet Jacques Roumain had founded the Bureau d'Éthnologie. The committee for the teaching of Creole had, as I have said, been founded in 1947; and the Port-au-Prince Centre d'Art, which encouraged peasant painters, was organized by an American, Mr. De Witt Peters, in 1944.

The Centre d'Art has already succeeded in discovering

or stimulating some remarkably brilliant work by wholly
untrained painters; it has not, however, as yet had time
to get any striking results from the educated students in
its school. Haitian painting is only beginning. The literature of Haiti, on the other hand, is highly sophisticated
and has a long and sound tradition behind it. It is surprising to learn that this island, since the revolution of
1804, has produced a greater number of books in proportion to the population than any other American country,
with the exception of the United States. Venezuela, it
seems, with about the same population as Haiti, has, exclusive of government documents, published less than two
thousand volumes to Haiti's five thousand; and neither
Argentina, with twenty million, nor Brazil, with forty-
five million, has, again with the exclusion of official pub-
lications, printed twenty thousand volumes. The public
library in Port-au-Prince, founded in 1812, is supposed
to have been the first in the Americas, though, like everything else in Haiti, it suffered from the vicissitudes of her
civil wars, and by 1843 was in total eclipse. But all
through the later nineteenth century and the first fifty
years of this, a good many of the upper class, ministers
and diplomats, doctors, professors and lawyers, have turned
their hands to poetry or novel-writing, historical or social
studies. William Seabrook, on his visit to Haiti, was astonished to hear, at a gathering of practicing politicians, an
animated discussion of poetry.

The first productions of the Haitian writers were rather
pale imitations of the French. Even when Haitian poets
wrote patriotic apostrophes, they declaimed in old-fashioned French rhetoric; even when they turned off little
pictures—those of Oswald Durand were charming—of native girls in native landscapes, they would fall back on
the intricate stanzas of Hugo's *Sara la Baigneuse*. The
chief Haitian novelist of the nineteenth century, Demes-

var Delorme, did not write about Haiti at all, but made
his stories all take place in Italy, France or Turkey. The
Haitians have had their Romanticism, their Naturalism,
their Parnassianism, their Symbolism, their Surrealism
and their lyrical radicalism. The period of romantic poetry,
which M. Duraciné Vaval, in his *Histoire de la Littérature
Haïtienne,* has indicated as lasting from 1835 to 1915,
produced an enormous output, much of it published in
France, and several reputations that have loomed rather
large in Haiti and that have sometimes been honored by
the French Academy. I am far from having mastered this
body of work, but, from the sampling of it I have made,
I am not sure it is much worth while for a foreigner.
The Haitians had their dimmer Victor Hugo, and their
dilution of the diluted Lamartine. They had even their
Haitian *Sonnet d'Arvers.* Yet one does find in these poets
some very nice things. Oswald Durand (1840-1906), who
wrote in Creole as well as in French, had a light and
naïve lyric humor that has little to do with Paris and
which even turns up rather quaintly in a classical poem
about the fall of Adam. A tame doe accompanies Adam
when he leaves the Garden of Eden with Eve,

"Qui suivait tous ses pas, qui lisait dans ses yeux
    Et s'égayait soudain quand il était joyeux.
    Alors Éve sentit que le froid d'une lame
    Lui passait dans le coeur et lui traversait l'âme:
    'Tu l'aimes plus que moi!' dit elle a son époux,
    En lui montrant du doigt la biche aux yeux si doux.
    C'est que le maître, aussi, pensait à l'étincelle
    Qu'ils venaient de ravir à la flamme éternelle.
        Alors, pour être sûr de la punition,
        A côté de l'amour, céleste passion,
    Dieu venait de placer, d'un mouvement rapide,
    La sombre jalousie, au teint pâle et livide."

And the vein of Charles Séguy Villevaleix (born in 1835), with its thin-drawn fineness and purity, its imagery which runs so much to pearls, drops of water, silver pebbles and bubbles, liquid crystal and lilies-of-the-valley, is something, so far as I know, quite his own, not an echo of anything French. A later poet than these, Edmond La Forest (1876-1915), composed a whole volume of *Sonnets-Médaillons du XIXème siècle*. These obviously derive from Heredia, but apply his technique to the portraiture of the celebrities of the nineteenth century, from Toussaint L'Ouverture to Tolstóy. At their best, they are not without merit; and they show an unusual range, not merely in cosmopolitanism—which is characteristic of Haiti—but in moral and historical imagination. It is curious to note how the Haitians seem to recognize a special affinity with French writers who are natives, like themselves, of faraway French-speaking islands and seem always a little alien to France. The cult of the Cuban Heredia has been, in our own day, succeeded by a cult of the Mauritian poet P.-J. Toulet.

The distinctively modern era in Haitian literature dates from the founding in 1927 of *La Revue Indigène* by a group of young men who were prepared to break with the traditional Francophile culture and who included three individuals of exceptional courage and talent: Émile Roumer, Jacques Roumain and Philippe Thoby-Marcelin. All three of these men had been living in Europe and all three, independently of one another and under the stimulus of foreign books, had come back to Haiti convinced that the day had arrived for their country to be given a literature that correctly represented its people. Their movement was a little belated, but not very much more so than ours in the days of Amy Lowell and Ezra Pound. They were fighting, as young writers had been doing elsewhere, for *vers libre* and symbolist literature, for the right to treat the past with irreverence. "There are in Haiti," they wrote, "whole library stocks to be destroyed." In the manifesto by Émile Roumer in which this challenge occurs (*Revue Indigène,* September 1927), one finds also a dissatisfaction with the tepidity of the patronage of Paris and an assertion of cultural self-confidence (the name of the magazine is significant): "Our writers are not known in the world. Who is to blame for that? The French anthologies are open to the Belgians, the Swiss and the Canadians. . . . The Haitians [themselves] cannot admit that a gentleman who drinks his beer on the terrace of the Eldorado may be a world poet." "Lafcadio Hearn," he adds, "passed more than three years at Port-au-Prince without anybody's ever having heard of him."

Roumer was himself a poet who would have stood up in any anthology and who has recently been included in two English ones: *An Anthology of Latin-American Poetry,* edited by Dudley Fitts, and *One Hundred Modern Poems,* edited by Selden Rodman. He is sometimes reminiscent of Toulet, but has nothing of Toulet's almost Landorlike dryness, and he has quite escaped the insipidity from which the surrealist dithyrambs of Haitian poets have sometimes suffered as much as from their old romantic strophes. Roumer's style is dense and rich; his language, both literary and local, is full of bold combinations. It is the poetry of a brilliant sensuality that could only be West Indian. In his single published collection, *Poèmes d'Haïti et de France* (1925, Éditions de la Revue Mondiale, Paris), the superiority of the Haitian poems to the European ones shows how right the indigenous movement was to take the line it did. A good example of Roumer at home—though not one of his very best pieces—

is the uncollected *Déclaration Paysanne* translated by John Peale Bishop in the Latin American Anthology mentioned above. I give it in Bishop's translation:

Déclaration Paysanne

Marabout de mon coeur, aux seins de mandarine,
tu m'es plus savoureux que crabe en aubergine,
tu es mon afiba dedans mon calalou,
le doumbreuil de mon pois, mon thé de zerbe à clou.
Tu es le boeuf salé dont mon coeur est la douane,
l'accasan au sirop qui coule en ma gargoine.
Tu es un plat fumant, diondion avec du riz,
des acras croustillants et des thazars bien frits . . .
Ma fringale d'amour te suit où que tu ailles.
Ta fesse est un boumba chargé de victuailles.

The Peasant Declares His Love

High-yellow of my heart, with breasts like tangerines,
you taste better to me than eggplant stuffed with crab,
you are the tripe in my pepper-pot,
the dumpling in my peas, my tea of aromatic herbs.
You are the corned beef whose customhouse is my heart,
my mush with syrup that trickles down the throat.
You are a steaming dish, mushroom cooked with rice,
crisp potato fries, and little fish fried brown . . .
My hankering for love follows you wherever you go.
Your bum is a gorgeous basket brimming with fruits and
    meat.

Jacques Roumain, who died in 1943 at the age of thirty-six, was an energetic and versatile figure: a novelist, a poet, a scholar, who eventually became active in politics. He was an authority on West Indian civilization of the precolumbian ages, who published archaeological and anthropological studies; founded, as I have already said, the

Bureau of Ethnology of Haiti; and engaged in what a biographer calls *"une retentissante polémique"* with Père J. Foisset, the exposer and the vilifier of Voodoo whose crusade I have mentioned above. This crusade itself had been provoked by a pamphlet in which Roumain had replied to a blast by the Papal Nuncio on the subject of Voodoo by pointing out that the peasants of Brittany, from which most of the Catholic priests in Haiti came, had many superstitions similar to those of the Haitian peasants; that Voodoo, since colonial times, had been inextricably mixed up with Catholicism; and that the only way to get rid of superstition was to educate the Voodoo-practicing peasantry—a process which ought to begin with the building of decent roads to make it possible for the teachers to reach them. Roumain founded, also, in 1934, the Communist Party of Haiti. He had already served a term in prison for his fight against the American occupation, and was now imprisoned again for three years. When he got out, he went to Europe, where he studied palaeontology and ethnology. He left Paris, on the arrival of the Germans, and came to the United States, where he worked for a time at Columbia. On the advent of a new government in Haiti, he was allowed to come home again, and then sent as chargé d'affaires to the Haitian Embassy in Mexico; but there, broken in health by his years in jail, he almost immediately died. I have read only four books of Roumain, two of them, posthumously published, belonging to his late Communist period. *Bois-d'Ebène* (1945) is a collection of poems, or rather, of declamations, which somewhat parallels Aimé Césaire's *Cahier,* but fails of the latter's effect of passionate and cruel veracity. Roumain here invokes for the Negro a self-vindication and self-liberation which are simply his own special version of that now too familiar apocalypse, the victory of the proletariat. Except for a few happy images, *Bois-*

d'Ebène seems to me unimportant as literature. So does his novel, *Gouverneurs de la Rosée* (1944), which—one assumes, through the efforts of the Communists—has been translated into English, under the title *Masters of the Dew*. This is simply the inevitable Communist novel that is turned out in every country in compliance with the Kremlin's prescription. You have the struggle against the bourgeoisie, the summons of the exploited to class solidarity, the martyr who dies for the cause—in this case, scientific irrigation. The Creole-speaking peasant hero is fired by a social idealism which he is supposed to have learned from a comrade on the sugar plantations of Cuba, but which he expounds with a *Daily Worker* eloquence that would scarcely have been possible in Creole. When one compares *Gouverneurs de la Rosée* with Lespès' *Les Semences de la Colère,* one sees that the experienced agronome (who has evidently been reading Malraux), though he, too, has allied himself with the Communists, has limited himself to observed fact and allowed himself only such sentiments as may be aroused in a sympathetic official by the spectacle of the trials of the peasants, whereas the radical man of letters, Roumain, has indulged himself in a Marxist fantasy. It is quite evident that Jacques Roumain did not know the black peasants well. But he did know the Mulatto bourgeoisie, to which he himself belonged, and his earlier novel, *Les Fantoches* (1931), which deals with the élite of Port-au-Prince, throws so much light on its subject that one regrets it should not have been projected on a more extensive scale. A blasé young man of society aroused to a rabid race-consciousness by the attentions of a visiting Frenchman to his beautiful fiancée—whom, however, he loves only half-heartedly—and her touching but useless attempt to restore his confidence in her by telling him in Creole that she loves him; the strange experience of one of the guests

at a big evening party in a splendid house, when he walks
by mistake into a sordid chamber, where the grandfather,
an aged general, is found setting up lead soldiers and mut-
tering about campaigns—these scenes have been lived
and felt. The attempt to make contact with the people—
one is often reminded in Haiti of pre-revolutionary Russia—is dramatized more convincingly by one of the episodes of this novel than by the author's own Marxist exploit in writing *Gouverneurs de la Rosée.* Here a black
girl who has put up a fight against the amorous son of
her Mulatto employers is rescued from the misery to
which they have consigned her by an upper-class intellectual, who demonstrates his exceptional nobility by taking
her to live with him without making her sleep with him.
Another earlier short novel of Roumain's, *La Montagne
Ensorcelée* (also published in 1931), is somewhat more
convincing than *Les Gouverneurs,* because it does take
account of the beliefs of the peasants and not merely of
their economic situation. I shall return to this tale in a
moment.

There has lately been a whole crop of these peasant
novels. The fashion is accounted for by the Port-au-Prince
poet, M. Léon Laleau, as so many other phenomena of
Haiti have been, as a result of the American occupation: "The young writers of my generation, with an un-
yielding passion of nationalism boiling in their hearts,
have been fleeing the world of the cities, so treacherous
and so snobbish, that welcomes the Yankee with open
arms." And it is true that there has been something in this
movement of the impulse which made writers like Yeats
and Synge, impatient of the English domination, look for
nourishment to the peasant life of Ireland. But the resistance to the occupying Yankee has been also a special
instance of the general reaction in our time, as the life-
span of capitalism closes, against the privileges and func-

tions of the bourgeoisie. In Haiti, this reaction directs
one, not to the problems of an industrial proletariat, but to
the mass of the black peasantry, and this confronts one
with the whole world of Voodoo, which the writers of
earlier periods have either ignored or glossed over. A brilliant result of this confrontation is the fiction of the
Marcelin brothers. The Marcelins are a distinguished family, who have already produced several writers. Frédéric
Marcelin (1850-1901) was the inventor of the modern
Haitian novel, the first writer of fiction on the island
who described local manners and types. His cousins of
a younger generation, Philippe Thoby-Marcelin and
Pierre Marcelin, have collaborated on three novels, *Canapé-Vert* (1944), *La Bête de Musseau* (1946) and *Le
Crayon de Dieu* (1951)—all now translated into English
—which deal with the influence on Haitians of three different milieux of the ancestral African religion. The point
of view of the Marcelins was quite different from that of
their ally Roumain. Investigating the lives of the peasantry, they had come upon a special situation not provided
for by Marxist theory. They had found people who were
not only not class-conscious, who were not only hopelessly
primitive in their economic life, but who were living in
imagination in a world of omnipresent myth. To treat
them as a rural proletariat, as Roumain had tried to do,
was to force them to play a false part. Roumain, in *La
Montagne Ensorcellée,* had probably first set the example
for the serious study in fiction of the superstitions of the
peasants; but even here he had not tackled Voodoo, he
is occupied with black magic, and the point of view is
that of the reformer. If the community in his story could
have understood what their government official was trying
to tell them: that they were suffering from an epidemic of
intestinal fever, they would never have murdered two innocent women, whom they imagined to have put a spell

on them. The Marcelins attempted, however, to get inside the peasant mind and to recreate the world in its terms.

They had begun by knowing little of Voodoo. Like most educated people in Haiti, they were Catholics; and they had lived much abroad. But Dr. Price-Mars was urging on the Haitians the importance of coming to terms with the culture of the black lower classes, pointing out that its superstitions played a much more considerable role in the psychology of the educated people than they were generally ready to admit; and the young writers were startled and fascinated when, in 1929, there came into their hands a new book from the United States— *The Magic Island,* by William Seabrook—which was full of amazing tales of zombies and charms and Voodoo rites that the author had picked up in Haiti. The young Marcelins—Pierre, Philippe and a third brother, Milo— set out to investigate the popular cults, and they have made themselves authorities on the subject. M. Milo Marcelin began collecting materials in a scholarly way—which meant winning the confidence of the peasants in order to be admitted to their ceremonies and memorizing—since notes were impossible—long rituals and incantations; and he has recently, at the suggestion of Dr. Alfred Métraux, the American anthropologist who was sent by UNESCO to Marbial, been working on a compendium of Voodoo mythology, the most ambitious thing in the field that has yet been undertaken, of which two volumes have now been published (*Mythologie Vodou*). This analysis of the rather complex and very curious Voodoo pantheon is at least as readable as Bulfinch, and it provides a sort of reference book for the novels of the other two brothers. Of these novels, the first, *Canapé-Vert,* which won the prize in a Latin-American fiction contest in 1942 and was translated into English so badly as to be almost unintelligible, is of great anthropological interest: it takes us straight into the Voodoo world and persuades us to accept its assumptions. This world, when we are first introduced to it, is somewhat difficult to get the hang of, and even when the foreign reader has come to understand what is going on, he may be inclined to suppose that the authors have brought together a collection of exceptional cases and exploited them for dramatic effect. A little further acquaintance with Haiti will, however, dispel these doubts. The strange doings described by the Marcelins are matters of common occurrence. I was told by the Episcopal Bishop of Haiti and the Dominican Republic (a white native of the United States), who has seen a good deal of back country, that, in dealing with the people of these regions, he has had to readjust himself to a conception of human life that turned our own upside down: with us, it was the real world that seemed the immediate thing and the supernatural world something above and beyond; but in Haiti the immediate thing was the supernatural world (for which, of course, *super*natural would be thus an inappropriate term) and what we call the real world no more than a symbolization of events in the world of religious myth. Thus we find in *Canapé-Vert* that a tree blown down on a drunkard or the bite of a mad dog is not considered a natural accident but appears as a deliberate move in a game of transgression and punishment, revenge and counter-revenge. M. Pierre Marcelin has said to me that the external meagerness of peasant life gives no clue to the richness of the life of myth which the peasants imagine themselves to be living; and it has been one of the interesting results of the recent encouragement of primitive painting that these peasants have put visually on record their conceptions of the beings that surround them. It is not merely that the Haitians, like the ancient Greeks, are in the habit of explaining everything in terms of the displeasure or the friendliness of one or other of their divinities, or that they act out a sacred drama, as the pueblo Indians do, only partially identifying themselves with the spirits whose roles they are playing. The central feature of the Voodoo religion is the *possession* of the worshipper by the spirit. He assumes the divinity's character, takes on its appearance and talks with its voice, must gratify its favorite appetites, is carried away by its peculiar passions. For his neighbors and even for his family, the man or woman who, as they say, is "mounted" by one of the *"loa," becomes* the god or the goddess. Whether or not the people about him have liked or respected the person whom the deity has superseded, they must now bring to this deity their tribute of whatever it is known to like: ornaments or food or drink. They must fear and propitiate the god of death; they must go to bed with the goddess of love (there has actually been preserved a contract drawn up for a marriage between this goddess and one of her preferred lovers); they must stand for the violence of a spirit who is given to terrible rages. They attribute to the possessed individual all the deity's indomitable power, and he himself feels and wields this power. A miserable servant-girl, as in the Marcelins' *La Bête de Musseau,* may even make herself a master who is free to command her own master by emerging from an hysterical seizure in the character of a formidable divinity known as Baron Samedi, talking in a deep voice which is recognizable at once as his, and demanding the cigars and liquor with which he must always be supplied. An old woman, in *Canapé-Vert,* who thinks it necessary to scold her children, arranges to augment her authority with that of a goddess called Grande Erzilie (*Grande,* in Creole, means grandmother); and a man works himself up to a murder by inducing in himself the delusion that he is ridden by a bloodthirsty spirit called

General Anglessou. These incarnations are often preceded
by paroxysms like epileptic fits, and, in the more serious
cases, these "mediums" appear to have retained no memory of what happened during their state of possession. Dr.
J. C. Dorsainvil, the author of *Vaudou et Névrose,* believes that this is a form of hysteria. He says that the
extent to which the Voodoo possessed succeed in trans-
forming their features and voice, and the consistency with
which the personality of any given *loa* may be reproduced
by different persons, from generation to generation, is
incredible unless one has seen it. Another Haitian psychologist is reported to have expressed regret that the
upper classes of Port-au-Prince do not go in for possession, too, since it would help them to relieve their neuroses. Through possession, the weak character may assert
himself, the neglected may claim attention, and the
woman who has been dropped by her lover may terrify
him into submission.

The peasants' life is further complicated by a general
belief in witchcraft, which is not necessarily a part of the
Voodoo religion proper. This is one of the most important
elements in the Marcelins' second novel, *La Bête de Musseau* (translated as *The Beast of the Haitian Hills*), as it
is in *Le Crayon de Dieu* (English title *The Pencil of God*).
La Bête de Musseau is a much better story than *Canapé-
Vert,* for it creates the suspense of a thriller that hangs on
a crisis of conscience. A bourgeois of Port-au-Prince, who
has just lost his wife, decides to satisfy a lifelong ambition
by moving to the country and becoming a planter. Never
having had to deal with the peasants, he makes the fatal
mistake of antagonizing the local people by trying to fence
off a spring on his property, and he incurs the ill-will of
the local boss (a figure quite distinct from the Voodoo
priest), who is supposed to practice black magic and has
succeeded in reducing the community to such a state of

intimidation that he can murder and rape with impunity. By arousing the African atavism of the Mulatto from Port-au-Prince and playing on his superstition, this wizard breaks down his morale and forces him to go back to the city.

It may perhaps be supposed, from my accounts of these books, that they could be only of special interest as glimpses of an odd civilization. But the notable achievement of the Marcelins has been to make of them something more. Both these stories have a larger significance. The situation of the inhabitants of *Canapé-Vert,* confused between the workings of Nature, the mythology they have been taught, and the instincts about good and evil that seem more or less to be felt by human beings everywhere, is made to throw a good deal of light on the situation of any social group in relation to its religion. In tracing the contagion of myth and the real motivations it masks through the whole life of this little community, the Marcelins stimulate us to think about the role of myth in any community. Is it really very much more fantastic to screw oneself up for a speech or a crime by imagining oneself Grande Erzilie or General Anglessou than by managing to identify oneself with the Will of the German People or the Sword of the Proletariat? So, in *La Bête de Musseau,* the beast is something more than a bugaboo with which the witch-doctor scares the planter: it is the bad conscience of the man he scares. This ex-grocer has been worried by a feeling of guilt in connection with the death of his wife. She had died giving birth to a child which he had known she was incapable of having, murmuring in her last moments, *"Je t'aimais . . . beaucoup . . . tu sais . . . ,"* and she had appeared to him at night in dreams, telling him that he had killed her. But he cannot get away from this guilt by leaving Port-au-Prince: a retribution from the African forests awaits at Musseau the free-thinker in

whom has been inculcated in childhood the Catholic
doctrine of sin. When he comes back to Port-au-Prince,
he learns from a friend of his wife's that she had felt that
he no longer loved her and that she had wanted to win
him back by giving him, at last, a child. This is the real
beast, and in the end it will track him down.

These books of the Marcelins are distinguished performances. They deal with difficult subjects—material
that is controversial in Haiti and unfamiliar abroad; and,
presenting them, without sentimentality or political melo-
drama and with no explicit comment, they bring out in
them a human poignancy that is communicated to readers
anywhere. Their importance is not unlike that of the novels of Ignazio Silone. In returning to the meager conditions of the backward Abruzzi villages, Silone produced
work that turned out to be of international interest, for
he had brought to them a knowledge of the world acquired through years of experience in the international
labor movement. The cultivated Haitian at his best, standing between four continents: the two Americas and Europe and Africa, yet rooted in his sun-bright island, has
the advantage of a critical judgment stimulated by diverse
impressions yet canny, independent, detached. With Roumer, Roumain and the Marcelins, he claims the attention
of the larger world by which he has hardly been heard.
Even at home, the audience of the Haitian writer has
been very much restricted. If he publishes a book in
Haiti, he is likely to have to do it at his own expense, and
his edition may not run to more than two or three hundred copies—just enough for the other Haitians with a liking for literature. Even the best books are rarely reprinted
—so that it soon becomes impossible to find them outside
public or private libraries. One can gauge the situation
through the fact that, since the days of such writers as
Frédéric Marcelin, whose books were published in Paris,

it has been usual for Haitian novelists to make their
Creole-speaking characters speak Creole. *Canapé-Vert* was
first written in this way, but the dialogue was transposed
into French when it was submitted for the Latin-
American contest.

[*Voodoo Converts:*   It has been one of the curious features of this period of religious revival that Voodoo should
have had its white converts. There have appeared, since
the above was written, two interesting books by non-
Haitians who have come to feel sympathy or admiration
for this ancient African cult. *Strange Altars,* by Marcus
Bach (1952), is the work of a medium-weight journalist
who has been interested in minority religious groups. In
this connection, he visited Haiti, where he found the
Voodoo ceremonies difficult of access, but made the acquaintance of Mr. Stanley Reser, the "Doc" Reser of
whom, inevitably, every visitor to Haiti hears as the white
man who knows most about Voodoo. Mr. Reser, a Scandi-
navian American, first came to Haiti twenty-five years ago
with the medical corps of the Marines, and he remained
when the Marines left. He seems sincerely to have
adopted the Voodoo faith, and to occupy a position of
authority not far removed from that of a native priest. His
situation has thus rather resembled that of Frank H. Cushing among the Zuñis, and he has hitherto been very dis-
creet, refusing to write anything about Haitian religion.
He has now, however, authorized the publication of Mr.
Bach's book, which is mainly a record of conversations
with Reser and ceremonies to which Reser took him. The
theology of Voodoo is here explained in terms that appear to bring it into the same theological world with the
more familiar religions:

"I only know," the author quotes Reser as telling him,
"that when I first set foot on Haitian soil, I knew that I

had found it, the pearl of great price. When I breathed the air of Haiti, something whispered to me, 'you are home.' When I went to my first Voodoo service, I had only one desire. I asked God to help me shake off my sophistication—begged heaven to give me the trusting soul of a peasant." . . . "Aristotle was right when he said that the dance is a spiritually imitative act. This is liturgy as we see it and feel it. It is nothing new or strange or exclusive in Voodoo to believe that our motion sets the gods in motion. Every true faith has believed that. . . . What I am saying is that Voodoo has its relationship with other religions at every point and draws together all the basic motivations in primitive and modern faiths." "He never allowed this opinion to slip from my mind," Mr. Bach, the reporter, adds: "Voodoo was the synthesis of the old with the new. It stood midway between religion as an obedience to forms and religion as an individual psychological experience. That is why he found in Voodoo form and spirit, something cosmic, yet personal, something interwoven with the whole of mankind even as the *asson* [a gourd covered with beads that is rattled in the Voodoo ceremonies] was interwoven with modern beads and the vertebrae of the snake. Those who missed this universal all-encompassing meaning saw Voodoo only as escape and superstition." . . . "The outward ceremony is the visible form of the inner reality. There is a baptism of fire that spectators do not see. That is the real thing. Putting one's hands in the fire is only the symbol of putting one's life into harmony with the unseen. Always look for the secret of Voodoo *within*." . . . "Extrasensory perception and precognition are elementary in Voodoo, but they accomplish a function which is highly important in the realm of faith. In your so-called civilized communities, church doctrines are purely academic. A person is taught to believe without evidence. In Voodoo one expects and finds proof of the things he is taught. If faith is believing in things unseen, then Voodoo goes beyond faith. It believes and then demonstrates that the belief is true." . . . "There is but one God, but He has infinite ways of expression. He is the Grand Maît [Grand Maître], immanent and transcendent. He is in the universe and behind the universe. By Him all things are made and in Him all things exist. He is primal cause and ultimate effect. One never gets very close to Him in this life, but there is always the *loa* who help us in our relationship with Him." "Are all the *loa* good?" asks the interviewer. "There are good *loa* and evil, just as there are good people and bad. They are like sparks from the divine anvil, broken off when the Grand Maît fashioned the universe. A man can choose the good or bad *loa*, just as he can choose good or bad companions." . . . Speaking of an insane asylum: "Many people who are brought here have offended the *loa*. Or would you rather call it sin or psychological error? . . . The more a person's character is in opposition to the *loa*, the more violently he fights them. There comes a time when something has to *give*. Either a person goes down to frenzy or up to ecstasy. . . . Some day men who deal in these cases will learn what every Voodoo priest knows instinctively. The obsessing personality is a distinct personality, and can be talked to, reasoned with, influenced and understood." . . . "There is something here that cannot be seen with the eyes or understood with the mind. I'll tell you what it is. I'll tell you the great secret of the Haitian peasant. Each soul knows and feels itself to be immortal. It feels and knows that the entire universe with all its goodness and greatness and beauty is for it and belongs to it forever."

Miss Maya Deren, a Russian-born American, went to Haiti as a Guggenheim Fellow in 1947 to make films and wire-recordings of the native life, and she fell under the spell of Voodoo, participated in its rituals and finally experienced possession. Her incandescently written account of this, in a book called *Divine Horseman: The Living Gods of Haiti* (the horseman is the *loa,* who "mounts" the worshipper), published in the same year as the Reser book, is, so far as I know, the only detailed record of this psychological transformation by one who has actually been through it. Miss Deren was possessed by Erzilie. She describes dancing to the drums till she felt herself on the verge of collapse: "The air seems heavy and wet, and, gasping, I feel that it brings no refreshment into my laboring lungs. My heart pounds in the pulse at my temple. My legs are heavy beyond belief, the muscles contracted into an enormous ache which digs deeper with every movement. My entire being focuses on one single thought: that I must endure." But she loses her sense of fatigue. "As sometimes in dreams, so here I can observe myself, can note with pleasure how the full hem of my white skirt plays with the rhythms, can watch, as if in a mirror, how the smile begins with a softening of the lips, spreads imperceptibly into a radiance which, surely, is lovelier than any I have ever seen. It is when I turn, as if to a neighbor, to say, 'Look! see how lovely that is!' and see that the others are removed to a distance, withdrawn to a circle which is already watching, that I realize, like a shaft of terror struck through me, that it is no longer myself whom I watch. Yet it *is* myself, for as that terror strikes, we two are made one again, joined by and upon the point of the left leg which is as if rooted to the earth. Now there is only terror. 'This is it!' Resting upon that leg I feel a strange numbness enter it from the earth itself and mount, within the very marrow of the bone, as slowly and richly as sap might mount the trunk of a tree. I say numbness, but that is inaccurate. To be precise, I must

say what, even to me, is pure recollection, but not otherwise conceivable: I must call it a white darkness, its white-
ness a glory and its darkness, terror. It is the terror which
has the greater force, and with a supreme effort I wrench
the leg loose—I must keep moving! and pick up the dancing rhythm of the drums as something to grasp at, something to keep my feet from resting upon the dangerous
earth. No sooner do I settle into the succor of this support
than my sense of self doubles again, as in a mirror, separates to both sides of an invisible threshold, except that
now the vision of the one who watches flickers, the lids
flutter, the gaps between moments of sight growing
greater, wider. I see the dancing one here, and next in a
different place, facing another direction, and whatever lay
between these moments is lost, utterly lost. I feel that the
gaps will spread and widen and that I will, myself, be altogether lost in that dead space and that dead time. With
a great blow the drum unites us once more upon the
point of that left leg. The white darkness starts to shoot
up! I wrench my foot free but the effort catapults me
across what seems a vast, vast distance, and I come to rest
upon a firmness of arms and bodies which would hold me
up. But these have voices—great, insistent, singing voices
—whose sound would smother me. With every muscle I
pull loose and again plunge across a vast space and once
more am no sooner poised in balance than my leg roots.
So it goes: the leg is fixed, then wrenched loose, the long
fall across space, the rooting of the leg again—for how
long, how many times I cannot know. My skull is a drum;
each great beat drives that leg, like the point of a stake,
into the ground. The singing is at my very ear, inside my
head. This sound will drown me! 'Why don't they stop!
Why don't they stop!' I cannot wrench the leg free. I am
caught in this cylinder, this well of sound. There is nothing anywhere except this. There is no way out. The white

darkness moves up the veins of my leg like a swift tide rising, rising; is a great force which I cannot sustain or contain, which, surely, will burst my skin. It is too much, too bright, too white for me; this is its darkness. 'Mercy!' I scream within me. I hear it echoed by the voices, shrill and unearthly: 'Erzilie!' The bright darkness floods up through my body, reaches my head, engulfs me. I am sucked down and exploded upward at once. That is all."

She loses consciousness for about four hours. The possession was considered authentic. On another occasion she was told that, possessed by Erzilie, she had correctly performed a whole drum routine for a ceremony of which she had no previous knowledge.

There remains, at last, Miss Deren says, "the question which has been posed, and would, I presume, be posed again. Since the *loa* mounted my head, is this to say that I believe in Voodoo and in Erzilie? In the context of Voodoo, such a question did not occur to me. I would say that, as a metaphysical and ritualistic structure, Voodoo *is a fact,* and does exist, and that, as such, it incorporates values with which I am in personal agreement, displays an organizational, psychic and practical skill which I admire, and accomplishes results of which I approve. I would say, further, that I believe that the principles which Ghede and other *loa* represent are real and true, in the sense that it is true, for instance, that nature follows a life-death-life cycle; and the possessions which I have witnessed have seemed to me to be exemplary and absolute personifications of these principles."

I have quoted from these authors at length in order to do justice to the religion of Haiti, which I did not observe at first hand.]

Pastor McConnell: I saw something of Pastor McConnell, who has taken such an active part in the move-

ment to teach Creole and with whom I had made the trip
to Marbial; who had sat beside the driver of the bus and
prevented him from going to sleep, who had asked us all
in for hot soup at half past three in the morning, and who
had himself driven us home through the empty streets
with the demoniac speed of absolute self-confidence. He
asked me, afterwards, to dinner at his house—he lived
with his family in austere comfort—and I had a long
interview with him on the subject of education in Haiti.
You had only to ask a question to elicit accurate facts: persons, statistics, dates. One couldn't but admire his handling of his work, so practically planned and direct. He had
lived in Haiti for years and was very realistic about it. But
what interested me most about him was what I learned
from him about Methodism in action. I had never before
encountered a serious Methodist pastor.

McConnell had been born in County Cork, but he did
not in the least resemble any other Irishman I had ever
known. I tried to talk to him about the role of the Protestants in Ireland, but found him surprisingly blank, not
only about Yeats but even about Wolfe Tone and Parnell.
When I said that Bernard Shaw's mentality was essentially
a Protestant one, he replied, "But Shaw is a free-thinker,
isn't he?" He saw everything in terms of his Wesleyan vo-
cation, which had occupied his whole life. This missionary work in the Antilles, begun during the lifetime of
Wesley, has always been a specialty of the Methodists,
from the time when, in 1786, eleven hundred Negroes of
Antigua were converted to Methodism. Pastor McConnell has had no such luck. He avoids and distrusts evangel-
ism. It is the practical side of Protestantism that he so
vigorously represents, and the distance between him and
the converted Bonhomme, of whom McConnell says that
he emerged from prison under the delusion that he had
been called to be the Haitian John Wesley, seems to be

almost as wide as his distance from the Catholic priests. These latter in Haiti, from all accounts, have been always on a pretty low level. The French Church has had the habit, very annoying to the Haitians, of referring to Haiti as "La Bretagne Noire," and sending them priests from Brittany who are nearly as ignorant as the Haitian peasants. These priests have been presiding immemorially— with only an occasional protest, such as that of the Nuncio mentioned above—over a very curious system of "syncretism," an amalgamation of Voodoo with Catholicism. Each of the principal Catholic saints has, for purposes of worship, been identified with one of the less maleficent of the principal Voodoo deities, and the Madonna in her various aspects with the various aspects of Erzilie. In the museum, you see Voodoo altars that have Catholic chromolithographs on them as well as Voodoo fetishes. But nothing could be more different from this than Pastor McConnell's approach to Voodoo. He can allow no compromise with it, so, from the point of view of proselytizing, he has had to resign himself to meager results. In all the years he has spent in Haiti, he has made only one real convert. This was a man in Cap-Haïtien, whose wife had for a long time been ill, and who was persuaded that one of the *loa* had put a curse upon the household. When the natives get into this state of mind—I gathered from Pastor McConnell—they become completely neurotic. The Pastor tried to rescue him from despair. "Do you tell them," I asked, "that the *loa* do not really exist?" There would be no use telling them that, he said: the *loa* are just as real to them as anything else in their lives. He told them that the *loa* were evil spirits. They had already been taught by the priests to refer to the bad ones as "Satan." He would ask which they thought was stronger: the *loa* or Jesus Christ; and he had ended by inducing this man to burn up all his religious paraphernalia, which he had brought

out from hiding places in the ceiling and in the floor—
fetishes, bottles, gowns. His wife had recovered then, and
the whole atmosphere of the household cleared up. Pastor
McConnell did not think it proper for him to go to Voodoo ceremonials, even to find out what they were, and he
had seen only one case of possession, when a woman had
been brought into the Mission "raving," but had presently
returned to her right mind. He did not share the tolerance of people who took the position that Voodoo was a
religion like any other and might as well be let alone. It
had a side that was positively bad: the imposition of spells
and curses, which, by force of psychological suggestion,
may have almost as serious results as if the powers of evil
had really sent them. The attitude of Pastor McConnell
was always commonsense and humane. A man who had
had a child by one woman but had been living for some
time with another had asked him what he ought to do.
The Pastor had replied to this that he would have to ask
God to show him, but added that it would hardly be possible for him to abandon either of the women—since he
also had an obligation to the one without the child, who
would have been "counting on him for affection." What
the man did was give some land to the woman who had
the child and marry the other woman.

In all this, the fundamental difference between the
Protestant point of view and the Catholic was brought
out for me very plainly. The uniqueness, the relative isolation of Pastor McConnell in Haiti—where there are
very few Protestant ministers and where his doctrine is
not very congenial to the natural temper of the natives—
threw him into clear-cut relief. In the case of the Catholic
priest, his function is to represent the Church, and to perform its prescribed rituals, and this means inducing the
natives to accept the faith and its rites by meeting them
on their own level. To the Methodist pastor, for whom

faith means works, it is quite evident that the Voodoo-worshipping peasant can never understand or share the convictions that the pastor has derived from the Gospels, that he cannot learn Christian morality till his cultural level has been improved. In order to accomplish this, one must teach him to read and write the language which he speaks and in which he thinks. The task of the missionary, then, is primarily education. He must himself master Creole and French. He must work out a method of teaching; he must even supply texts. And it is one of the striking proofs of McConnell's magnanimity and sense that he will not mix religion with his teaching—though he does impart a bit of morality through Creole texts of the Gospel stories and is opposed to their studying La Fontaine, some of whose fables, he thinks, are too lenient to certain forms of rascality. The only real way, in the meantime, in which positive proof may be offered for the value of the Gospel teaching is by setting a good example, by illustrating this teaching in one's own conduct. Where the priest, submissive to his Church, is personally of no importance, the Protestant must leave his mark, he must count as an individual. I did not hear the Pastor preach, so do not know how much of this he is in the habit of putting into his sermons; but one cannot watch him teaching school, with so much precision and patience, without being made aware of his moral ideal and his purpose. The Protestant must demonstrate virtue, and this demonstration, of course, if it exceeds the man's real resources, may amount to an odious fraud, and be infinitely less sympathetic than the humble routine of a simple priest; but—since my own tradition is Protestant—a really fine example of Protestant practice is to me a good deal more impressive than the giving oneself up to God of either the Voodoo-worshipper or the Catholic.

Port-au-Prince, the capital of Haiti, follows the curve of a lovely little harbor that may recall southern Italy, but only to lead you to note certain essential differences. The landscape of Italy is always solid, the color is likely to be laid on thick; but Port-au-Prince is insubstantial, with no sharp brightness or sudden contrasts.

Looking out from my second-floor verandah, over the railing of white wooden lace, I see below, in mid-afternoon, the shadowed green tree-tops and roofs of the loose-knit tropical town, and—beyond the rare sprinkling of spires and domes, the low bulks of public buildings, picked out, amid greenery, vivid white, and the warm red-and-blue of the Haitian flag that is flying from a wireless spindle—there stretches the blue of the water, varying as if with the shades of a sheet of *taffetas changeant,* pulled taut to the south in greenish shallows, to the north in a surface of a blue so tender that, though floating a white sail or two, it seems nothing so dense as salt-water but some element sheerly aesthetic, the discovery of a delicate water-colorist. Strips of cloud, not too heavily charged with rain, hang low over the bare coastal hills, which, though not far away, suggest mysteries. Then, even during the brief time I watch it, the dim blue of these mountains, darkening, begins to show faintly purple, the shallows on the left deepen to gradations of color that are never abrupt, the pure hue of that sensitive lap of the inmost part of the bay is imbued with a violet tinge.

An hour and a half later, as I sat at the Savoy Café with a lime-flavored lemonade, I gazed out again on the clouds, which were now a diluted gray canopying a sunset sky of a dull but soft diluted orange—all, again, less like natural phenomena than light tints laid on by a brush. To the south, over the nearer mountains, the rain clouds, still hardly inclement, were full of enchanting effects—these, too, the work of some master—of a fastidiously diluted inkiness. Sometimes these clouds were yellow—a pale yellow that was firmer than vapor but for which even the fluff of spun-sugar or some fine orange-flavored whip would provide too substantial a simile.

The gentleness and charm of this landscape seems reflected in the habits of the people. Combined with the tradition of French manners, it has made them restrained and quiet. In all matters of social relations, the taste of the Haitians is perfect. They criticize Negroes from the United States on the grounds that they are loud, that they are flashy, and that they like to play the clown. The Haitians rarely raise their voices, and they are usually soberly dressed and decorously behaved. It is odd to see an altercation between a taxi-driver and his passenger. If you want to be driven somewhere in Port-au-Prince, you simply stand on the side of the road, and somebody will pick you up, either a taxi or a private car which offers to do duty as a taxi. In the taxi you may find other fares, with whom you exchange polite greetings and to whom you say *au revoir* when you or they get out. On one occasion, I shared a car with a wispy Mulatto who stammered. When he had reached his destination, he refused to give the driver the two gourdes he asked, and, when the latter insisted, got back into the car and told the driver to take him to the police station. The man let him go for one gourde but was very bitter about it. Yet the argument had all been conducted in tones that would have sounded quite amiable to anyone who had not understood. On another occasion, a young girl got out and walked off without paying her fare. *"Vous n'avez pas payé, mademoiselle,"* the driver reminded her. The passenger expressed contrition. *"Ça arrive à tout le monde,"* said the driver.

The sea and the sky and the mountains are full of nuances at Port-au-Prince, but the harbor is self-contained, a little too much shut in on itself. It hardly seems to open on larger seas, and the great lozenge of the Île de la Gonave figures as a kind of stopper. No city I have ever visited has seemed to me so much a complete little world; and this has evidently its inconvenience if you have to live in Port-au-Prince. It is too hard to get away from home. Everyone knows everyone else. When you are going to see one of the élite, you do not need to have his address: you simply tell the driver his name. And everybody knows everybody else's business, as they do in all little old cities, where the families are mostly related. If the gossip based on actual happenings does not seem to be lively enough, they fabricate fantastic scandals. Yet for a stranger from the United States, after the vast uniformity of Miami or New York, a capital like Port-au-Prince exercises a strong attraction. Just as, swimming face-down with a mask of glass among the coral forests, there are revealed to you the bright mauves of sea-fans and the branching of madre-pores, the fishes, blue-and-yellow or silver-black, gliding by under your very nose, nothing of which from above was visible in apparently limpid depths—so, too, in the city of Port-au-Prince, which may seem at first drab and meager, you find yourself, on closer acquaintance, in a society which, though limited, is quite rich in interest, since it is all composed of individuals. This is an eight-eenth-century city like Dublin, where everybody is faced with an audience. Almost everybody figures as a "char-acter," and these characters must put on a play. Though the foreigner who is used to the freedom of the anony-mous American cities might in the long run find Port-au-Prince cramping, it will afford a certain gratification to the visitor who still has a memory of the older kind of American community, where everybody was somebody or something.

Not that Haiti is much like the United States—though

there are moments when one thinks of Louisiana; nor is it very much like Western Europe. The country that it reminded me of most was Greece. Greece and Haiti are both special cases; but, besides their peculiarity, they have several things in common. You find in Haiti, as you do in Greece, a history of heroic freedom alternating with foreign oppression, a tradition of a kind of democracy that is dependent on an inferior class and of a kind of individualism that has produced the insatiable tyrant as well as the tyrannicide; and you find, derived from all this, an intense and jealous nationalism in a country too small in the modern world not to be preyed upon and not to require protection at the hands of the larger powers. You will find also similar problems of reviving a deteriorated soil, rendered arid by deforestation; of an educated, if not up to date, minority confronted by an unschooled peasantry, resigned to conditions of living perhaps hundreds of centuries old; and of a literary language—in Haiti French, in Greece the so-called *katharévoussa* based on classical Greek—competing with a popular dialect—Creole, *demotiké*. Haiti has, of course, no background that is comparable to the ancient Greek civilization; yet the civilization of France does supply it with a cultural tradition.

The contrast between the classical and the popular cultures was illustrated in a striking way by two theatrical entertainments at which I "assisted." One of these was an excellent performance at the Rex of Jean Anouilh's *Antigone*. The manager and principal actor—M. Charles de Catalogne—has had a professional training in Paris, and was impressively brassy as Creon. A young amateur, Mlle. Adrienne Déjoie, was both statuesque and passionate as Antigone. This modernized classic of the forties, full of contemporary allusions, runs to tirades that, though written in prose, recall the alexandrines of the Comédie Française, and these scenes were sustained with great dignity by M. de Catalogne and Mlle. Déjoie. The whole long single act of the play held silent, from beginning to end, an audience that had earlier become quite rowdy in expressing its dissatisfaction when the curtain did not go up on time.

The other performance was an evening of brilliant musical entertainment at the open-air theater of the Exposition. The producer and chief dancer, M. Léon Destiné, has been working with Katherine Dunham in New York, and has brought back with him one of her women dancers, Mlle. Jeanne Raymond. He has combined, for the Exposition, with much taste and imagination, examples of the various forms of popular Haitian music. One has a chance to hear Mlle. Lumaine Casimir, the Creole Yvette Guilbert, and Ti Ro-Ro, the top Haitian drummer; to see gay-costumed colonial folk-dances that queerly combine Negro spells with eighteenth-century minuets; Voodoo ceremonies that, even theatricalized, become compelling, enthralling, with their stooping evolutions of white-gowned figures, their writhings along the ground and their crises of possession and sacrifice; and a whole suite of current *méringues,* a kind of dance-music peculiar to Haiti, for which the bare orchestra of drums is reinforced by a loud row of trumpets.

These drums are omnipresent in Port-au-Prince. They look primitive and are played with the hands, but the drummers have acquired great skill and are capable of complex rhythms. One of the most curious of the drumming numbers was a "conversation" between two drums, performed by Ti Ro-Ro and another man. The people in the hills, it seems, communicate with one another by a telegraphic code of drumming, and the audience laughed delightedly at what seemed to be a spirited repartee, but whether they were able to interpret something definite

that was being said or were simply amused as one is by
the interchanges of "Samuel Goldenburg and Schmuyle"
in Músorgsky's *Pictures at an Exhibition,* the foreigner
could not know. From the opening of the Exposition, the
drumming in Port-au-Prince became all-pervasive, inescap-
able. One could hear it going on all night in cabarets
and bars and probably in Voodoo rituals, sometimes so far
away one could hardly catch the rhythm, yet vibrant like
a taut thread of wire that interpenetrated the barking of
vagrant dogs, the nocturnal crowing of fighting-cocks and
the deep somber booming of bells that summoned the
pious to four o'clock mass. One day I met a boy bootblack
who was beating out a rhythm with his hands on the
shoeshining box he carried.

Between the open-air theater and the Rex, there is a
striking discrepancy of taste in everything but the acting
art. At the former, the décor and the costuming—pinks
and yellows and blues against a tropical green—had the
freshness of West Indian nature. At the latter, the lighting of Antigone was so very clumsily handled that the
actors cast shadows on each other's faces; and at a benefit
performance I attended, where *jeunes filles* played *mor-
ceaux* by Chopin and where a young man recited a
speech from *Chantecler,* the backdrop was punctured and
gashed, and the setting for a little play of Géraldy was a
rough job of squiggly brown curtains, painted-on yellow
doorways, department store furniture of wicker and wood,
and a single small picture which figured in the action but
was hung so high on the wall that the characters could
not possibly look at it. The theater itself is a barn; from
beginning to end of the intermissions, a metallic and
hoarse loud-speaker coughed out what must once have
been a Strauss waltz sung by a female voice. The houses
and the dress of the bourgeoisie, even in the case of the
rich, were, so far as I could see, in general, no more

decorative than the Rex. Amid the purples and scarlets and greens of the flowers and foliage of Haiti, the costuming and setting of human life has been allowed to remain strangely dull.

Not the women themselves, however. You see them at their best at the Rex or in the nightclub at the Exposition. They are very often beautiful, and beautiful in a variety of ways. There is the merry-eyed and lively black Negro girl, who has evidently been picked out for her prettiness to sell programs at the Rex and raise money for future productions; the trim little slender Mulatto, of a pale olive that verges on lemon, who blends with her French refinement something of Negro warmth; the French matron, charmingly coffee-stained, with straight nose and oval face, who sits sedate by her husband or children; and the woman with bronze-tinged hair and skin of a mat white, yet rose-flushed and faintly toasted, as to whose histrionic brown eyes and plump gesticulatory hands it would be hard to tell whether they were Negro or simply *méridional*. I sat, at one Rex performance, behind a group of good-looking young girls, all evidently well-to-do and on an equal social footing, whose complexions ranged from white to almost black and who presented me with a row of coiffures that included quite straight brown hair, worn in the white woman's way; hair that was reddish but crinkly; and abundant black hair that was straight. Another girl sitting near me had a prodigious head of dense black crêpe; and I saw, also, an old brown-skinned lady with white hair that was not that of a Negro, and a man who was even darker but had black glossy hair slicked back.

In no such cosmopolitan gathering as one might find in New York or Paris, could the differences in nationality, differences in social origin, be read on the flesh so plainly;

for here the mixtures of blood appear literally in black and white, in hair that is knotted or loose. Yet these textures and shades that declare the race make also a reduction to absurdity, since the people, so variously tinted, are inextricably bound together by the ties of a common blood. The absurdity is all the greater since, of any two sisters or brothers, one may be almost completely negroid, the other almost completely white. This upper-class society of Port-au-Prince involves, as I have already said, a complicated web of distinctions; but the snobbery of the Haitian élite is similarly a *reductio ad absurdum* of the theory and practice of snobbery. For in Haiti not only color but family is terribly important, very much as it is in our Southern States. You find not only Mulattos who—if one of Roumer's satirical poems is based on actuality—insist that they are quite free of Negro blood and ascribe their ineffaceable tan to the aboriginal San Domingan Indians whom the Spaniards exterminated (but who did, as a matter of fact, leave a certain admixture of genes to the peoples who superseded them). You find, also, in the hyphenated names that are adopted by many Haitians—as you do in the family middle names that are common in the United States—an eagerness to claim the prestige of a distinguished maternal line. I know one able and cultivated Haitian who has attached to his father's name the name of his mother's family, simply because it was originally borne by a Negro who escaped from his captors as soon as he reached San Domingo and, hiding out in the mountains for years, was able to leave to his descendants one of the very few Haitian names which have never had to pass through slavery.

Yet the conflict between cultures at different levels, the fluctuations between impulses in different directions, the confusion of passions and aims, seem to enter, for Haitians, into all relationships. It is this that makes Haiti interesting, and important out of proportion to her size. This and her unique situation of finding herself in a position to work out these black-and-white problems independently of the cramping and crippling inflicted by a white man's rule. So jealous of their freedom are the Haitians—and the spirit which finally succeeded in dislodging U.S. occupation was the same as that which vanquished the French—that they do not even care to know much of the affairs of the other West Indies, where the Negro is still kept in an inferior position. The stranger is surprised to find that—except, recently, for pleasure expeditions to Cuba—the Haitians do not visit their neighbors, and, though they are usually well up on the history of Haiti, may even seem oddly ignorant of events on the other islands in the period when San Domingo was winning its independence. They also seem rather indifferent toward the South American countries—with the exception, perhaps, of Brazil, where a similar mixture of blood prevails; and as for the United States, they cannot ignore us today but they ridicule us and belittle us, and are sometimes astonished, on coming here, to discover that we are actually a formidable nation.

On our side, for a native of the United States, a trip to Haiti is immensely instructive. If he has been depressed or discouraged by the Negro community in Harlem as well as by conditions in the South, he may be surprised to discover how stimulating Haiti is. He will note that, though the French were bad masters, they left the Haitians a sounder kind of education than most black Americans have had (though the Haitian Justin Lhérisson gives an example, in his satirical novelette La Famille des Pitite-Caille, of a Haitian oration which, for polysyllabic nonsense, sounds exactly like Father Divine). He will try to take account of the theory that the stock of the African tribes from which the Haitians came was superior to that of our Negroes. He may wonder whether the nuisance of segregation may not have kept him from knowing the best of American Negro life. He may decide that, however all this may be, our Negroes were particularly unfortunate in having had to share the defeat of the South, in the sense that they were fatally involved in its decadence and humiliation. In the Haitian revolution, the men of color won and were able to enjoy their independence; in our Civil War, they were freed but they had to go on living with their ruined masters.

In Haiti, in any case, for all their fiascos, they have made something out of their breed. It is something which is not provincial French, which is still less a reversion to Africa; it is a spirit and a point of view that are not likely to be easily malleable to either the South American or the North American mould. The Haitian—between the Americas, between the New World and Europe—is in a position particularly favorable to an international view of history; and he is not merely international, he is also interracial. In an epoch absolutely demented with trumped-up racisms and overdone nationalisms, it is possible for the Haitian to see the world in purely human terms. And these conditions all contribute, in Haiti, to produce, on the highest levels, a type of mind irreducibly first-rate. One finds it not only in the Marcelins' novels, with their clear intellect and their unashamed humanity; one meets it also in such a monograph as Dorsainville's inquiry into Voodoo, with its historical and psychological learning and its assurance in tackling directly and coming to his own conclusions about the outlawed native material that scientists abroad had not noticed; one finds it even in the more academic work of a writer like Dantès Bellegarde, which, in its French conventionalizing of history, still manages to be true to Haiti. One finds it today, especially, in those

few but earnest young men and women who, bored with
the bourgeois amenities and disgusted with the infantile
politics of their country, in touch with the great movements of contemporary thought and at home in the outside world, have applied themselves, as teachers, as physi-
cians, as engineers, as agricultural experts, to studying the
needs of Haiti and attempting to teach and to build. Such
people are comparable, it seems to me, to the best of their
kind in the world. There is a weakness of the Haitian intelligentzia of which one is often told. The varied elements
in their personalities make it hard for them to take a consistent stand, to see a project through. It is said that they
tend to agree sincerely with anyone who tries to convince
them, and then to be convinced sincerely by the opposite
point of view. One is certainly sometimes astonished to
find out that some champion of a cause, whom one knows
to be high-minded and intelligent, has been lately on the
other side. But there are also strong individuals who have
concentrated their disparate instincts and who have known
how to speak and to act with force. To distinguish oneself as a Haitian, one must prove oneself a man, and not
merely a patriotic nationalist or the member of a race or
class. There is a discord at the roots of the Haitian people
which is harsher even than that of race. Jacques Roumain has put it with bitterness in his novel *Les Fantoches:* "The Haitian aristocrat does indeed hold by deep
fibres to France. He has not forgotten that the cradle of
his birth was some dark hall of a colonial house, the night
when a white man, excited with drink, threw down the
Negro slave who was his grandmother." As a generalization, no doubt, this picture is somewhat misleading. There
were evidently white planters who lived quite happily
with Negro wives. Yet the situation was always precarious,
and it was headed for bloody disaster. Does this prove-
nance impose a handicap? Does it imply an unhappy fate?

It puts to the Haitian a challenge less easy for him to disregard than for the children of more uniform stock: the challenge to produce from the brutishness, the outrage of man against man, through which has passed the seed of all human life, from the discrepancies involved in all breeding, some assertion of the dignity of humankind. And this challenge, when the worst has been said, the Haitians have somehow met.

SOVIET RUSSIA
1935

The text of this record has been much revised since it was first published in 1936, but I have made no attempt to emend it in the light of later events or subsequently acquired knowledge. The tone and the point of view are a part of the original experience, which I could not reinterpret now. But I have here indicated by brackets, not merely, as in the case of the other studies, the passages more recently written, but also details and incidents which were noted at the time in my diary but omitted from the published account, in order either not to embarrass people and get them into trouble or not to put too much emphasis on absurdities which I regarded then as inessential.

I

OLD ENGLAND

I FOUND that I was not unmoved to see the shores of England again. The Isle of Wight, with its velvet fields, its great houses level with the water and its spreading symmetrical trees, softened and made rich by the moist air and under a troubled sky, reminded me of Tennyson and the greenwood tree and Victoria at Osborne Castle.

When I had last seen the Isle of Wight, we had been anchored in a troop-ship outside Southampton Harbor, waiting for a clear night to cross. When it got dark, the British soldiers would cluster together at the bow and sing a lugubrious convivial song:

> Here's to good old sherry—
>   Drink 'er down, drink 'er down!
> Here's to good old sherry—
>   Drink 'er down, drink 'er down!
> Here's to good old sherry,
>   For it makes you feel so merry!
> Here's to good old sherry—
>   Drink 'er down!
>
> Raolling 'aome, raolling 'aome,
> By the light of the silvery mune.
>   Ha-ha ha-ha ha!
>   And a ha-ha ha-ha ha!
> Here's to good old sherry—
>   Drink 'er down!

149

How abysmally that gaiety of soldiers getting shipped back to France seemed to have been swallowed up by time!

Yet there were the docks where we had waited. I had been trying to remember our embarkment, and now I had it again: the horrible blankness and boredom as we had sat on our packs at the pier. My memory had struck it out. At Southampton, we had slept on the ground, in a rest-camp which was deep in water. I had read in the English papers little scraps about more trouble in Russia, with men named Lenin and Trotsky coming to the top. Walking back and forth among the beech-woods, I had run into a man whom I had known at school and who was now a lieutenant in the Infantry. I had never seen him again because he was killed soon afterwards; and now I was returning to Europe with books about Lenin and a Russian grammar.

Nevertheless, as I went up to London in the little neat, green, fast boat-train, green England, all a park, all a garden—the patches of mosslike lawn, the trees planted long ago to grow in a certain way and kept carefully clipped by their masters, the little dark shining streams, which had been domesticated, too—seemed to me lovely, familiar and dear.

But London, when I got there, was a shock. I had not really seen it since 1914, and the city seemed now so changed that I could hardly find my way. London looked much like Chicago. I had found on the boat that I was oddly depressed to discover that the old English weeklies were full of pictures of Hollywood actresses; and now I was confronted in London with the same insipid neon signs, the same uniform yellows and reds that glow without seeming to burn, the same pretentious movie palaces

with gaudy decorations and people waiting outside in
long queues, the same tabloids, the same newspapers with
no news in them, the same cheap window displays in
drug stores and five-and-ten-cent stores, which I thought I
had left behind at home. And the different sections of
London—Leicester Square, Trafalgar Square, the Strand
—which I remembered as things quite distinct, now
seemed neon-lighted and submerged in one great amusement center and traffic nexus. I tried to find something I
recognized, but I had to ask my way to Regent Street and
I had to walk a long way before I remembered Liberty's.

I realized with some astonishment that it really was true
that I had grown up in one world and lived to inhabit
another. Except for a few hours in 1921, I had not been
here since the summer of 1914. I had been here on Bank
Holiday when war was declared and seen people riding
on top of taxis and gathering around Buckingham Palace and calling for the King and Queen. Now they were
celebrating the Jubilee of the same king and queen; but
in the meantime they had had the War, the dole, the
General Strike. The Jubilee seemed to me flat, mostly
neon signs.

I tried a musical show, 1066 *and All That,* and was
more let down than before. There was none of the old
coarse clowning of the music hall, and there was little
that was really satiric. The revue, to be sure, was made to
center about a character called "The Common Man,"
who was supposed to wander through history and always
to get the worst of it; but his misfortunes seemed to
have no upshot except that at the end of the evening he
sang "God Save the King" with the rest. There was a
sketch in which Guy Fawkes and Columbus were arraigned before a magistrate: Guy Fawkes for not blowing

up Parliament, Columbus for discovering America. Columbus, of course, chewed gum and was made to talk like a gangster, and one of the charges against him was that he had ruined the English language. Yet the show was full of gags based on American slang such as *"You're* telling *me!"* and "Oh, yeah!" The author had got hold of phrases which were stale and fading out at home, and had featured them as curtain lines, as if they were sure to be breathtaking. I had never seen anything quite like this in an English revue before, and the effect was queer and unpleasant. Where were the language and the humor of the English? Did they create no new idiom any more? Had they lost touch with their historical tradition till it no longer had enough reality even to provide subjects for jokes? Shakespeare seemed a long time ago.

As I came back through the streets at night, I saw men and women lying in doorways and digging in garbage-cans for food, just as I had left them in Chicago and New York.

II

LONDON TO LENINGRAD

When i boarded the Soviet boat the next morning, the sailor who carried my bags refused a tip.

It was strange to find the little broad white steamer flying the red flag, with its one yellow star and the yellow hammer and sickle, so close to the Tower of London. Unlike an English boat, it did not start on time; but the atmosphere of amiable informality was a relief after an English liner. And it was exhilarating to swim out of the Thames, with the radio playing Strauss waltzes and old Sousa marches. The great jaws of the turreted Tower Bridge unclamped to let us pass; and we shook off the dark old docks and all the river traffic: coal barges and trim little boats with dark-tarnished brick-red sails.

I went down to my cabin and found the three young Russians with whom I shared it huddled around the porthole, singing sad-sounding Russian songs. In the cabin next to ours, somebody was practicing the cornet.

There was a piano in the saloon, and somebody very soon sat down to it and began playing old banal airs, on which he would give out when he was halfway through. It was a sober but bright little room—quite different from the ship-shape comfort of the English—with gray walls and shiny woodwork. There was a series of inlaid panels depicting deer on Siberian wastes of snow, and wild lakes and rock formations like Canada and the American West.

One very uncomfortable feature: the chairs at the writing desks were straight-backed, absolutely hard and fastened tight to the floor.

The little blond stewardesses and kitchen girls were pretty though somewhat slatternly. They insisted on doing their work in high heels, which were badly worn down and pushed out; and while they worked, they smoked cigarettes, which dangled out of their mouths.

When we went into the dining-room for tea, we found caviare, jam, candy, sliced sausage and sardines and herring set out around flowerpots, petticoated in white paper, of little primrose-like purple flowers. A man with a kettle came around from time to time and asked you whether you would have some tea: no obsequious service as with the British. Here, too, the chairs were fixed to the floor so that you could not draw them up to the table. With all that is lax in Russia, there is, as I was afterwards to find, always something of which the severity is terribly overdone.

———————

A new smell on the boat, new soap, towels of a new size and shape, new people, new food, a new language. I walked around in a kind of elation.

———————

In the evening, a jazz-band of Jewish musicians, who had been forced to leave Nazi Germany and were going to try their luck in Russia, practiced in the saloon. Everybody came in to listen: the captain, the passengers, the purser, the crew, the little girls with their cigarettes and their handkerchiefs around their heads. When the jazz-band knocked off for the night, one of the sailors sang Russian songs; then the crew—one very handsome boy with a sullen adolescent's mouth—played some English

phonograph records, including, notably, *Got the Jitters!*
till the owners came and took them away; then they fell
back on their Russian records, which included a curious
Russian version of the old American darky song, *Po'
Monah*.

All this was very different from what I had expected: I
had been prepared for something rather grim.

As I sat up late reading, one of the girls came to put
away the phonograph. I tried to ask her whether she
wanted to turn out the lights; but she gestured for me to
stay, making squeaky little sounds like the language of
mice.

The three young men in my cabin had been sent by
the Soviet government to study American coke processes.
They had bought American clothes, and two of them, at
any rate, looked very much like Americans. They all had
fairly important jobs: one was Chief Engineer at the coke
by-products plant in Magnítogorsk. They seem to try as
much as possible in Russia to put young people at the
head of things.

From these boys I got a favorable impression of the quality of the new Soviet culture. They were natural and
frank like Americans, but, unlike Americans, were very
quiet and behaved toward one another and toward me
with the most extraordinary consideration. One night
when I was going to stay up after the others had gone to
bed, I turned out the light as I left the state-room, but
they protested that I would need it later, and, though I
had left it turned out, I found when I came down that
they had turned on another for me. If they were up earlier than I was in the morning, they would talk almost
in whispers in order not to wake me. It was strange for me
to hear them use quite naturally, with no consciousness of

asserting a point of view, Lenin's phrase "the Imperialist War" where we should say "the World War." It seemed amazing that a single man should have impressed upon the thought of a whole people a conception of society and history which changed the very names of past events.

I was reading in Krúpskaya's memoirs the story, which would be almost unbearable if it were not told so coolly, of the poverty, imprisonment, exile, persecution, insanity and suicide with which Lenin's generation had paid to make these young men possible.

It is pleasant to travel on a Russian boat. There is a general quiet amiability, and everybody does what he likes. The Soviet liquidation of social and racial distinctions comes to affect even the attitude of foreigners, and all classes, nationalities and colors are able to meet and talk together freely. It had a little the atmosphere of a club: the international club of people interested in the Soviet Union. The weather was marvelous: the middle of May.

[There was an American Negro intellectual married to a white woman. They sat off by themselves in a corner, but she, rather ostentatiously, would lean her head on his shoulder, and this seemed a little to embarrass the man. They had long sociological arguments, in which he would explain to her what was what.]

The only passengers who did not seem at ease were three English people who sat at my table. There were two ladies traveling together and a man traveling by himself; and there seemed to exist between them some impassable social gulf—so that, though I, being American, could talk to either of them, they were unable to talk to each other. One of the ladies was a woman doctor, who had seen a good deal of Europe and who had dragged the other off on this trip. She was evidently an old maid and wore her mouse-colored hair in a bun. The other—both were quite elderly—was a married woman with grown-up children. She had still a certain firm Tennysonian blue-eyed English-gentlewoman prettiness. They were the very best upper middle-class and carried a certain kind of thing to a point which, I realized as I talked to them, we in America could only approximate.

The unfamiliar Russian food deeply worried these English people. "I've never seen tea with lemon before!" said the man with something like alarm. The milder and more naïve of the ladies, when confronted the first morning with caviare for breakfast, took it for marmalade, but, imperturbably masking her surprise, remarked that it would be good to make sandwiches. When sliced sausage appeared, she declined the bologna, saying quietly, "It's a little unusual, isn't it?"; but took some salami, murmuring, "It's more like what we have at home." And when I said that the enclosed upper deck was probably intended for drinking, the man, in a low voice and with a look of consternation, as if he were disclosing a horrible secret on which he had long brooded, exclaimed: "There *aren't* any drinks!" I told him that there were vodka, wine and cognac. "There's no beer aboard!" he said. The sturgeon, as to which they couldn't at first be sure whether it were meat or fish, put them all to a severe test: it seemed to be an occasion for as much self-restraint as if it had been a shipwreck.

The milder lady, in her mild way, was uncompromisingly snooty about America: she said that she had understood that there were a great many Presbyterians there. The only thing connected with America in which she seemed to feel an interest was the career of Lady Astor. She inquired about Lady Astor's family and seemed to assume that I must regard her as the highest-ranking living American. She asked also about the Duponts, who, she

understood, had noble French blood. In connection with
Russia, they were much concerned about the fate of the
tsarist nobility, discussed the execution of the royal family with a peculiar combination of horror and relish, and
were inclined to believe in the genuineness of the supposed Grand Duchess Anastasia, because the sister of the
woman doctor had known, or had known someone who
knew, the nurse who had identified her.

It had been the woman doctor's experience that if you
did things for the poor, they were ungrateful; and her
quieter and sweeter companion admitted that no one for
whom she had done anything had ever shown her any
gratitude, and she told a long story about a woman, "a
woman of education, evidently a lady," who had had children and been very poor and had tried to borrow money
from her. She rolled on her tongue, in her gentle way,
this woman's humiliation.

The Englishman never told me what he did and he was
usually silent at table; but by talking to him between
meals I discovered that he was by way of holding radical
views. He had very little idea of Marxism, did not know
what the Comintern was; but he had just read John
Strachey's book *The Coming Struggle for Power* and
seemed very much impressed by it. He didn't know, he
said, what had happened to political life in England:
when he was young, a situation like the present one
would have aroused great public excitement. He supposed people's indifference was due to the fact that the
issues were becoming too complicated, too difficult to understand. It used to be that people just took sides, as they
did over the Oxford, Cambridge boat-race. The Fabians
had died away, and he didn't see anybody to take their
place. The English nowadays, he told me, were paying a

lot of attention to the United States, but very little to the Soviet Union. They didn't even print the news about it. English free speech and justice existed only theoretically: you needed money for the courts, and although you could write what you pleased, there were many things you couldn't get printed. I asked him from what sources the English now derived their opinions: "Many of 'em haven't gottany!" he replied.

He was very funny in his solemn way about English relations with Russia—the complaints of the English embassy that they couldn't get English food in Moscow. He was traveling in his vacation and had only three weeks for his trip. I liked him. He was elderly, bespectacled, long-faced, dry, independent. He represented, I thought, some of the admirable qualities of the English middle class.

————

I woke up to find the porthole divided by a straight line, on the upper side of which were land, grass, people, houses and cows. It was the Kiel canal: Schleswig-Holstein. Flat grass-grown grazing land in a funny bleak-for-all-the-lushness yellow morning light. Men and boys riding bicycles in visored German caps. A barefoot girl in a field; a woman darkly dressed. All the figures of people seemed dark, walking along the straight roads among groves of tall straight trees. Red cattle; farmhouses all alike, with high red corrugated roofs to stand up to the northern winds.

Kiel: a peremptory sign in thick upstanding German characters, which forbade the taking of photographs, "from the bridge, the water or the shore, of the ships in the Kaiser-Wilhelm Canal."

Out into the Baltic, foggy and gray.

————

One day I decided to take a bath. I rang, and there appeared, after an interval, a gray, thin and anxious-looking elderly woman. I asked whether I could have a bath, and she said something in Russian and vanished. Then she came back, looking anxious but saying nothing; then she went away again. At last, after a long long wait, during which I was afraid she had forgotten or was not the proper person, one of the little stewardesses appeared and smilingly unlocked the bathroom door and showed me how the faucets and the shower worked. Then she handed me a towel of the thickness and texture and the non-absorptive properties of a napkin. I called her attention to the fact that there was no plug in the tub, and she went off and got me one. It turned out that there was only one plug for both the men's and the women's baths, and that they carried it back and forth.

None of the things in the bathroom did what she said they would do. A short spurt of hot water from the hot faucet was followed by coldish water. The shower, when I turned it on, trickled a few drops, then ceased. The bathroom, which was under a stairway, had no means of ventilation and was heated like a Turkish bath by the hot-water pipes than ran through it. The door did not have a latch, and as I lay in the cold water and the suffocating heat, people would walk in on me from time to time, then with exclamations withdrew. I was afterwards to learn that latches on bathroom and toilet doors and plugs for wash-basins and bathtubs hardly exist in Russia.

When I reached for the roller towel, it immediately came off the roller, and I fell against the hot-water pipes and burned my elbow severely.

In the smoking-room, I talked to a little boy of nine who had left Russia when he was five and had been living at Sea Gate, Brooklyn. He asked me whether I thought Lenin was a good man, whether I was with the Communists, and whether I believed in God. In the Soviet Union, he told me, they cured children of believing in God by shutting them up in a room and pointing out that if God existed, he would do something to get them out. He asked me how in the world people had ever come to believe in God in the first place.

The last day: a popular song, *The Beautiful Isle of Capri*, which I had left them singing in America, came in over the radio in Lettish. We passed near a low dark coast, some outlying island of Finland: pine-wooded, rugged, lonely.

Dinner was a festive occasion: there was a bottle of wine on every table, and the dining room became quite lively. Not at our table, however. My English table-mates would hardly touch the wine. "Everybody's letting themselves go," said the milder of the two ladies, not even glancing around. "It's going to be rather awful, I'm afraid!" She advised us to keep to ourselves, as there was some sort of cold about.

The man, who sat next to the porthole and who usually looked out and said nothing, called our attention to a little island with a tower and some buildings on it. "Lonely-looking place," said the man. The ladies began to talk about lighthouses.—"People in lighthouses take to drink."—"So that then they're not any good, I suppose." —"Or go mad."—"Perhaps radio helps them: then they can at least hear what other people hear."—The mild lady told a story about a woman left alone in a light-house with three small children. The woman was bitten by a snake, and, knowing that the bite would be fatal and that the children would be helpless without her, she killed them before she died.—"Couldn't she suck the poison out?" asked the doctor.—"It would be in her back or somewhere she couldn't reach," the milder lady replied.—"Couldn't she hope the husband would come back in time?" said the doctor, still trying to find a loop-hole for the unfortunate lighthouse woman.—"He would be somewhere very far off," the other lady replied, with cool firmness—and added, with cool admiration: "Her nerve!"—She followed this up with another story about a woman who was afraid of snakes: she had kept crying, "Wolf! Wolf!" until finally she had really been bitten by a snake and her husband wouldn't go.—"What a dreadful thing!" said the doctor. "I suppose it was too late to do anything."—"Died," said the other lady, with deep quiet satisfaction.—She had another similar story which I have now forgotten but of which the conclusion was, "Government's doing something for her, I believe."

There was a wonderful dessert at this last dinner: a mound of vanilla ice-cream swimming in pink grenadine and surmounted by a small piece of cake with a small lump of sugar set on it. The sugar had been saturated with vodka and was supposed, as the Englishman said, to "come on flaming"; but the waiter succeeded in setting fire to the little paper skirt on one of the flowerpots, which blazed up in quite a conflagration. The English ladies were disturbed by this, but, of course, behaved splendidly. The waiter, with Russian insouciance, hovered around it ineffectively for a while, then carried it off blazing to the kitchen.

On that last night, the ladies, who had been eating with the man four times a day for five days, for the first time addressed a remark to him: they asked him whether he was an Englishman. The Englishman answered "Yes," and the conversation went no further.

The Chaikovsky-Pushkin opera, *Píkovaya Dáma,* began to come in on the radio from Leningrad.

It was still light at ten, and we could see a sloping rocky shore. There were faint strips of pink in the dimming blue sky and above them opaque gray clouds. The North, sheer and clean and awful, the clear bleak top of the world.

When I went down to my cabin, I found that the young men had got hold of my Russian grammar and were reading aloud the extracts from Pushkin which were included as exercises. Hitherto, the only thing I had seen them read was a large work in two volumes on coke processes, translated from the German. They told me in their unemphatic way that Pushkin was a great poet. I got into my bunk and listened. They lay on their backs in their berths full of silent appreciation. I observed for the first time how poetry, like music, is for Russians a natural food.

When I went up on deck again, the big opaque cloud had broken up, and one saw through its fragments the last cold light—hardly distinguishable from moonlight except that it grows constantly less luminous—of the vanished sun of the northern day.

In the morning, I told the English ladies about the boys' reading Pushkin in the cabin. I asked them whether English engineers would read Shakespeare under similar circumstances, and said that it was hardly conceivable that Americans would read Walt Whitman. For a moment, this gave them pause. But they soon rallied: the mild one remarked that Pushkin was very simple. The doctor, who had studied Russian to do something in connection with the war and had read one of Pushkin's stories, but did not know that he had written poems, remarked that it was very much easier to read prose fiction aloud than poetic dramas like Shakespeare's. I told her that Pushkin was the great Russian poet. "Great for *them*," said the mild lady firmly—and added: "Pushkin's poems are very simple little things."

The ladies had been wondering about tips and had finally learned that a collection which had been taken up in the Third Class was to be given to the Comintern. "You don't want your money to go to *that*, do you?" said the doctor shortly and sharply. The Englishman was vague about it, and I said that I didn't mind. The woman doctor contracted in something like a nervous spasm. "Well, *I* do!" she said savagely, narrowing her eyes. "They can have it in their own country, but they needn't try to impose it on other people!"

From the moment they left the boat, these ladies never spoke to or recognized any of their former fellow passengers.

———

An American coming to Russia from England discovers, not without surprise, that in certain fundamental respects he has more in common with the Russians than with the English. The people in Europe who speak his language are in some ways the furthest removed from him. The English, with their antiquated social system, cannot forgive a branch of their own race who have scrapped that system and prospered. On the other hand, the Soviet

Union is certainly the European country which has most in common with ours. When we travel from London to Leningrad, no matter how pessimistic we may have been before we left home in regard to the effects of capitalism in creating class distinctions and antagonisms, we are brought to the realization that American democracy means more than we thought. Our period of pioneering was more like the present period in Russia, which is preoccupied with settling new country, constructing new industrial plants and developing natural resources, than like anything that has recently happened in Europe; and the American and the Russian, who have both left the old system behind, feel a natural sympathy with one another. The Soviet Union stands in relation to the rest of the world today very much as the United States stood for a century after the Revolution.

I felt closer to the young engineers in my cabin, with whom I could hardly exchange a word, than with the English people with whom I ate.

III

LENINGRAD THEATERS

THE FIRST IMPRESSION of Leningrad is absolutely dream-like and dazing.

If one has never seen a really backward country, if one knows only the western European countries, one can form no real idea beforehand of what Russia and the Russians are like; and outside the Soviet Union, one can have had no experience of socialism. It is probably impossible for an American—it was impossible for me, at any rate—to imagine Russia correctly. Before one goes there, one is likely to feel, as I had done with the young engineers, the affinities between Russians and Americans; and if one is an advocate of socialism and a reader of *U.S.S.R. in Construction,* one is likely to have a vision of the Soviet Union as simply the United States plus one's ideal of socialism.

Actually, the Soviet Union is not like that at all. My own first impression of Leningrad was of something completely unfamiliar. It is impossible to realize till one gets there what a shock it is to find a city where there are not, as there are in other countries, well-dressed people on the principal streets. All the people on all the streets seem to be dressed about the same, and they are all very badly dressed—or rather, they are dressed drably. The men are bareheaded or wear caps; the women very rarely wear colors, and the soles of their footwear are invariably flat, shoes or sneakers or slippers. They are not noisy like the crowds in America, and to an American this makes them seem unreal. They move quietly and, compared to Americans, slowly; and the background of old St. Petersburg sets them off in a peculiar fashion. These dingy and mute and monotonous hordes inhabit a town of wide boulevards that were designed as the thoroughfares of an empire, and of enormous public buildings and palaces that give an illusion of going on for miles. (Leningrad is, I suppose, the only city in Europe which does not look small when one comes to it after living in American cities. Though there is nothing like the high buildings of New York, it has inordinate horizontal extension.) From these mansions, the nobility have vanished; and—what is unimaginable to an American—in the offices and the shops there is no more business class. And past the shabby palaces, along the straight interminable streets, the crowds move like slow floods of water—not straining, not anxious like our people, not pitted against an alien environment, but as if the whole city belonged to them, as if they could make use of its facilities and feel at ease in any part of it.

———

I went to the opera the first night and had an impression equally novel and equally powerful. It was Verdi's *Otello*. I could not see that it had been given much Marxist interpretation, though I suppose the black-and-white situation has something to do with its popularity.

The people in the theater were better dressed than the people one saw in the streets, but they were not, as they are at the Metropolitan, a small group of the privileged and rich: they were much the same people in better clothes; and they had come because they wanted to hear the opera. I cannot remember any other audience that gave curtain-calls so prolonged and enthusiastic.

[There was an usher who rather astonished me: a tall old man in an elaborate uniform, who belonged to the period of old Firs in *The Cherry Orchard*. He had a wrinkled cadaverous face and the round protruding eyes of the Baltic, and he made a low bow, when I tipped him, with his hand laid flat on his chest. I had only a dollar, which I gave to him to change, and he brought me back six roubles, which meant, as was later explained to me, that I had tipped him sixty-five or seventy roubles. He brought me, also, however, a pair of opera-glasses, and when I went to the opera a second time, he recognized me, bowed low, and, coming to me in the intermission, again brought me opera-glasses, saying, "You keep, *bitte*." Finding they cost two dollars, I had previously declined to hire them, so that actually I saved money on my original extravagant tip. I enjoyed, though a little guiltily, this museum-piece from the old regime; but when I mentioned him to my Russian friends, I found they were slightly embarrassed.]

During the long intermission, they eat sandwiches and cakes and drink tea in large restaurants inside the theater. A Russian theater is built for social life and is comfortable and agreeable in a way that is entirely unknown to Broadway. The audience at the opera, instead of jostling and squeezing like an American crowd, walk slowly around the lobby, all going in the same direction and all moving in a stream at the same pace. And above them stands a statue of Lenin, one of the most effective in Leningrad, the right arm and hand outstretched and in the eyes a look both piercing and genial, at once as if he were giving back to labor what it had made and inviting it to share in its heritage of culture, and as if he were opening out to humanity as a whole a future of which for the first time in history they were to recognize them-

selves the masters, with the power to create without fear
whatever they had minds to imagine.

————————

Leningrad is dramatic and rather sinister. The Orthodox
Church and the Petersburg Court were monstrosities in
themselves, and their corpses are peculiarly grisly.

St. Isaac's Cathedral, with its hard and dark magnifi-
cence of gold and lapis lazuli and malachite, is in itself
an uncomfortable place; but, turned into an anti-religious
museum, it becomes a Chamber of Horrors. The Russians,
with their wonderful theatrical sense, have staged, in the
interests of Reason, an exhibition arrestingly macabre.
In the middle of the church is a gigantic pendulum illustrating Foucault's experiment to show that the earth re-
volves. It hangs from the remote dizzy dome clear down
to the smooth stone pavement, on which has been painted
a map of the world. The caretaker sets it swinging along
a line that bisects the map, and then points out that in a
few seconds it is seen to be cutting the line on a bias,
deviating more and more as it is tilted by the movement
of the earth. Gradually, silently, relentlessly, to the destruction of the Orthodox astronomy, it marks the revolution of the planet. From this the visitor is led to apply a
scientific criticism to the traditions and mysteries of the
Church. Two hollow-eyed formless corpses which seem
to be molded of earth are exposed side by side in glass
cases. One is the body of a sainted metropolitan who was
supposed to perform miraculous cures, the other the
body of a chieftain of a small Siberian tribe. They are
seen to be equally well preserved, and it is suggested to
the peasant visitor that in both cases the mummification
has been due to climate and soil. All around is a horrify-
ing gallery of the delusions and nightmares and frauds of

religion—from the bugaboo devils of the Buddhists to the unfulfilled millennial prophecies of the American Seventh-Day Adventists.

The Winter Palace is a big low building with what must once have been a very handsome yellow and white eighteenth-century façade; but it covers such an immense extent of ground that it exceeds eighteenth-century measure. It looks disused because the paint is scaling off, and it does not get repainted. In general, the treasures which you are shown inside combine costliness, elaborateness and ornateness with a boorish and Byzantine taste. There is a music-box as big as an organ, with cylinders like thick lengths of log; and there is a great golden cage of mechanical birds, as large as a real aviary, which was given to Potyómkin by Catherine the Great. These toys are set going at regular intervals to the wonder of the sightseeing proletariat—who crowd around the cage in a tight mute mass while, to the tinkle of a little tune of bells, a golden rooster crows and a big golden peacock unfolds his tail and, turning slowly around, displays it. Even the Hermitage seems to me the clumsiest of the great picture galleries of Europe: vast chambers plastered to the ceiling with Rubenses and Frans Snyders and Rembrandts, hung too close together—many of them too high—to be seen.

There is a Museum of the Revolution on the other side of the Winter Palace, with some very effective waxwork tableaux. Going into one of the rooms, you find yourself walking up to an official of the old regime sitting behind a desk, with his pince-nez, his scanty beard, his uniform covered with braid. He is a lifelong denizen of offices, secure behind his doors and his desk, through whose hands the misery and revolt of the people passes in the form of papers; the figure is not caricatured so much that you may not at first take it for real. On the table before

this official lie police records, albums of political suspects, whose faces contrast with his own: fierce, naked
and concentrated. One of the albums is open to the police
photos and red-ink identifications of V. I. Ulyánov and
N. K. Krúpskaya, arrested in 1895 and 1898, respectively,
for their activities in organizing the working-class. Lenin
is slumped down in his coat, he is without either tie or
collar, and his hair is sticking out round his ears; he has
already his high wide dome, but his eyes, though already
stubborn, seem still rather open and wide apart, they
have evidently not yet been brought to their later intense focus. He has the look—a kind of look that we
never find in his later photographs—of a young intellectual, a young idealist, who is recoiling from a collision
with the authorities. Krúpskaya, with her *gamine's* head,
her full mouth, her short hair, her scornful eyes, is like a
dagger of defiant pride. Both are young people forced
from their student days to make decisions and act, to live
out whole arduous lives of intellectual activity, political
organization, prison, before they are out of their twenties.

I got lost in the somber old labyrinth with a pretty little
girl guide from the Caucasus, who had only just come up
to Leningrad and had never been in the museum before.
We wandered through desolate stone corridors full of
formidable-looking closed doors. I had asked to see the
Tsar's apartments, but she did not know where they were.
She asked the way several times of a curious laconic old
woman, whom we kept running into in the guardless halls
and who always seemed to misdirect us. When we would
venture to open a door and find only another darkish
chamber, inhabited by waxwork dummies, the little guide
would cry: "Oh, it is so gloo-my! I am afraid!" [But she
stopped and admired an engraving of the Royalist Ven-
déen leader, Henri de La Rochejacquelein, exclaiming, "I
like such a face: it is so different!"] Once, after leaving

the building and trying it again through another entrance, we looked up and saw a colossus towering over
us, a gigantic effigy of the Worker, made for some celebration but now standing in the empty hallway, with arm
and clenched fist upraised and with staring epileptic eyes.
As we passed by the inside windows, we could see little
children in pink pinafores playing in the vast empty court.
At one point, we became involved in a whole series of waxwork groups which represented revolutionary conspirators working in dark hideouts and convicts in Siberian
camps. The little girl became more and more frightened
and asked if she could take my arm.

At last, through still a third entrance, we penetrated to
the Tsar's apartments. We visited first an enormous bathroom—very queer: it made the little guide laugh. There
was a deep tub sunk in the floor and a great stove to heat
the water. In the tub was a long-handled instrument,
which the girl began to play with, wondering what it was
for; another old woman, who had charge of things here,
arrived on the scene and stopped her. But upstairs we
were very much surprised to find only a small suite of
tiny rooms. There were the desk at which the Tsar had
worked, the army cot on which he slept, some ugly
nineteenth-century furniture, curiously drab and middle-
class, some paintings by one of his daughters of models in
picturesque costumes, and some photographs, now fading to brownish yellow, not interesting, not beautiful in
themselves, but evidently of places they were fond of.
Nicholas had had something like agoraphobia and had
huddled up there in his tight little corner, where he had
tried, as we were told, to make sure that there was nothing that anyone could get under or behind.

In the Peter-Paul Fortress, you see Church and State
side by side: the church with its golden altar, its columns
with golden capitals, its white marble tombs of the tsars

with their heavy gold crosses on top of them, right next door to the deep-walled prison from which nobody had ever escaped, where the guards always wore soft shoes so as not to be heard in the corridors and where men were shut up to go mad in dark rooms; where a woman revolutionist had once killed herself by soaking her hair in the kerosene from her lamp and setting fire to it; where Kropótkin had rapped out for the man in the next cell the history of the Paris Commune; and where, later, the mother of Lenin had come to see her older son, Alexander—sentenced to be hanged for concocting a bomb in a conspiracy to murder the Tsar—and had talked to him through two rows of bars. This was the imperial chapel where the tsars had gone regularly to service. The prisoners had heard the bells.

When I visited this church, a teacher was explaining it to a group of children. She showed them the row of tombs with the big golden crosses on their covers, and told them that the Tsar had been appointed to rule, not because he was a man of ability, but simply because he had happened to be the son of a certain other man.

———

I had a letter to a literary man in Leningrad and went to VOKS (the "All-Union Cultural Society for Relations with Foreign Countries") to find out how to reach him. At VOKS, they had a long consultation, and then, instead of giving me his address, they told me he was to be found at that moment in the room of a visiting German writer, Bert Brecht, who was stopping at my hotel. I immediately went back and called the room, but nobody answered the phone, so I had the porter leave a note. I found considerable difficulty in accomplishing even so much as this, as it happened that the first name of the literary man, whom we will call Mr. S., was the same as the last name of a man whom I did not know at all but who had at first been assigned to the same room as I. The Intourist girls were fatally attracted toward the idea that I wanted to get in touch with this man and would half-close their eyelids trying to grasp what the situation was.

I heard nothing more from this note, so, after the theater, I tried to get the desk to call Bert Brecht's room. A tall well-dressed man with spectacles and a shaved head, who looked as if he might be a German, asked me whether I were looking for Herr Brecht. I answered that this was the case and asked whether he were Herr Brecht. I understood him to say that he was, and a short conversation followed, in which he explained that he had no idea where Comrade S. was at the moment, and presently remarked, "I'm not Herr Brecht. My name is Trétyakov." I said that I had seen his play *Roar, China!*, and he asked me whether I had read one of his books that had been published in the United States; then he disappeared.

I heard nothing further that night from either Comrade S. or Herr Brecht; but in the middle of the next afternoon I had a call from Comrade S. on the telephone. Just as we were about to make an appointment, we were cut off, and, though I waited for some time in my room, I received no further call. The next morning I tried to phone him. His number had been written out for me, but in such a way that one of the digits looked as much like an 8 as a 9. The Intourist girl was sure it was 8; but the 8 number was always busy, so I had her try the number with 9. This number did not answer. I tried again in the afternoon. The 8 number was now out of order. The girl thought it was 8 or nothing, but I made her try the 9 again, and sure enough the 9 was the number, and S. himself answered the phone. He said, "You are a hard man to get!"

We made an appointment for 6 that afternoon, and at

that hour he promptly appeared. He seemed to me energetic and practical and was dressed in square-cut clothes like an American; yet when we tried to make another appointment, we were dissolved in confusion again. I at first understood him to ask me whether I had anything to do for the next evening; but it seemed to turn out a little later that it was that night that he wanted to take me around. I tried to pin him down to one or the other: "Today or tomorrow?" I asked. "Today is tomorrow," he seemed to answer. I attacked the problem again, but found my own steadiness shaken by the strange shifting currents of this unknown world. The base of the conversation had been English, but with a sprinkling of other languages: "Today, *heute, hier!*" I exclaimed. *"Aujourd'hui,"* he suggested. And finally, just when I thought we had it nailed at 8 o'clock that evening, he quickly and recessively added, as if things were getting too definite: "Or 9, if you would like better!"

I tell this story at length because it is typical of a certain aspect of Russia. Americans who have decided, as I had done, that Americans and Russians are much alike, discover that in the ordinary technique of life their habits are antipodally different. It is not merely a question of language difficulties or of bad telephone service. It is the native indisposition of Russians to be punctual, to be final, to be precise. Americans settle on a program, check it up and carry it out. Russians, even when they carry out their programs, do so without the settling and checking that seem indispensable to us. And they never do anything right away. Furthermore, they have an oriental reluctance to say anything disappointing, which is likely to lead to trouble when they promise things they cannot perform—as Trétyakov, whom I met in the lobby, allowed me to think at first he was Bert Brecht.

Americans, when they first arrive here, are likely to become very much exasperated, and consider it an inexplicable miracle that Five-Year-Plans are ever completed.

The Red Flag Textile Factory. It is an old one, and dreary enough; nor do the workers look very much different from textile workers in other countries. But they have things that our workers do not have: radio concerts, for example, and an hour off for lunch. It was lunch-time, and in one of the aisles two girls were practicing ballet; through the window I saw another pair pirouetting and bending in the yard. Almost all the girls had had their hair done in beauty parlors. An old woman was sitting at a table, her head sunk down in her arms.

There is pressure here, but nothing in the least like our fiendish American pressure. They are organized in work brigades, each with a chief, whom they elect. The brigades compete; and the winners get special privileges: theater tickets, longer vacations; their photographs, in the case of the girls, posted up in prominent places. The names of the ones who are not up to scratch are posted for public ignominy. At the end of each of the aisles is a blackboard with the names of the persons working there and the amount of work each has done. This was the system of Robert Owen at New Lanark.

The skilled workers are paid more than the unskilled. They work seven hours a day—except the men in the drying-room, who work only six hours. Disagreeable work earns special privileges. This was one of the ideas of Fourier. It is strange to find these devices of the early nineteenth-century idealists made the ordinary practice of a modern industry.

Here you see them engaged in making the simple and rather inelegant clothes that the people wear on the streets. But they are beginning now to have colored shirts, bright dresses and fancy ties.

———————

I was walking home from the theater with M. D., an American friend. We crossed the Névsky Prospékt at the wrong time and place, and heard voices exclaiming behind us, apparently instructing or rebuking us, from the people lined up waiting on the curb. One man, my companion told me, was calling out that we were "badly educated" and followed us, threatening and scolding. But the other people, seeing that we were foreigners headed for the Europa Hotel, told him he was drunk and called him off. You get fined if the police catch you crossing the street against the regulations; but I suppose that in the attitude of these people there was "proletarian discipline" involved—something we haven't got in America. At home, we will all beat the rules if we can: if the police don't stop us, nothing will.

———————

M. D. had been very eager to see what Meyerhold had done with *Camille;* and having heard of the proletarian interpretation which old plays were given in Russia and especially of Meyerhold's bold innovations, she had not been at all surprised when she was confronted, before the curtain went up, with two sailors who came out to meet one another from opposite sides of the stage, exchanged greetings and heartily shook hands. Nor was she disturbed when, instead of a Paris salon, the curtain revealed the deck of a ship; nor when it turned out that the lady of the gardenias was some sort of woman sailor who had not merely a handful of lovers but literally a whole crew. She told me that she came to the conclusion that there were factions among the lovers; those who loved her because she could talk and those who loved her because she could listen, those who loved her because they thought she was virtuous and those who loved her because they thought she was wanton, etc. At the end, instead of dying of consumption, the Camille of Meyerhold seemed to be shot down on deck with her shoes on. M. D., on her way out, discovered that what she had been seeing was a play called *The Optimistic Tragedy*, presented not by Meyerhold but by Taïrov at his Kámerny Theater, and dealing with the adventures of a woman commissar in the Baltic fleet during the Civil Wars.

One arrives prepared for anything in the theater; but the period of extravagant distortion of the classics seems now to be pretty well over.

————

I met some of the young pupils of Eisenstein, who had been sent on a tour for general culture. One of them, clean-cut and alert, in a faultless double-breasted blue suit, told with a great deal of mirth how he had got into the Winter Palace without paying, on the pretense of being a member of a workers' delegation which was just entering when he came along. When they had found out the truth, they put him out and made him come in again properly. The commissar's wife who had explained this story exclaimed at the end: "And he thinks that's funny!"

————

I was taken to the opening of an historical play made by Alexéy Tolstóy from his novel *Peter the First*. It was done in a magnificent theater, all imperial gold and white and with a box all in gold for the Tsar. The production was the most gorgeous I have ever seen: they evidently believe that the small amount of dye which they can spare the foreign currency to invest in will go further if it is used for scenery and costumes. And in general they try to make up for the meagerness of some aspects of their lives by lavish expenditure on the theater.

It was by way of being an official occasion. The President of the Leningrad Soviet was there, a short man with a formidable black beard; and so, also, was Alexéy Tolstóy, [who was throning, in his floor-level box, with the girth of an overgrown pumpkin and a pale, loose and formless face]. The Leningrad writers attended in a body and had a section especially reserved for them.

The first scene showed Peter in the shipyard, working at the forge himself, despite the gibes of the old-fashioned persons who told him that was no place for a tsar. Even so early as this, I had the feeling that some modern application was intended; and as the scenes of the chronicle unfolded, I became rather uncomfortably certain of it. Finally, my companion whispered: "Here certain historical parallels begin!" Tolstóy had rewritten his play in order to bring it up to date; and every incident seemed to have a counterpart in recent political events. I imagined that Peter's mustache got larger as the play proceeded. There was a scene in the Peter-Paul Fortress in which Peter came to see his reactionary son, whom he had had imprisoned for conspiring against him; he spoke a few words of stern tenderness over the young man limp from the torture: "After all, you were my son—I loved you!" Then, "Let him be executed!" When the curtain went down, there was tense silence. Peter was represented as making the people learn to dance just as the present administration is. In the last scene, betrayed by his wife, he exclaims that all his work has come to nothing from the disloyalty of those in whom he trusted. What is he to do? "Blood and steel!

Blood and steel! I can't execute everybody!" He bids the people be gay, and they strike up a minuet. But the gigantic man with the boots and mustache turns his back on them and folds his arms and stands looking out the French window. Then the lights in the foreground go out, and you see only silhouettes of the dancers, dominated by the towering black figure outlined against the panes. When I later read Griboyédev's classic comedy *Góre ot Umá*, I realized that the author of *Peter the First* had here imitated its famous last scene, in which Chatsky, the young idealist, expresses his disillusionment in a soliloquy directed at the audience, while a ball is going on in the background. Peter is thus left in tragic grandeur; but it was also, one reflected, rather hard on the dancers, who had to be gay by command in the presence of that ominous shadow. One remembered the young men and girls in the dining-room of the Hotel Europa performing so carefully and slowly the dance-steps they had recently learned.

————

[I was unable to do justice to this occasion, when I first published the account of it above. At the time I visited Russia, the old rivalry between Petersburg and Moscow —which figures so importantly in *Anna Karenina*—was still very much in evidence. The Leningraders were still standing up to the Kremlin. I felt it in many small ways —as when one of the women guides said to me: "I wonder—I'm not quite sure whether the Red Square in Moscow is bigger than the square in front of the Winter Palace." The President of the Leningrad Soviet had been Sergéy Kírov, who represented a liberalizing policy characteristic of the Petersburg tradition. He had become immensely popular, had received a tremendous ovation at the 1934 Party Congress. It was obviously time to let up on the rigors of the post-revolutionary period, and Kírov had been working in this direction. He had advocated drawing up a new Soviet constitution which was to be "the most democratic in the world," and he had been allowing Leningrad to become the cultural center of Russia, admitting the members of the intelligentzia who had fallen out of favor in Moscow. The assassination of Kírov in December 1934 is generally believed to have been engineered by Stalin. I did not know this at the time I was there, and was edified with touching stories of the terrible grief of Stalin, of his noble indignation; of his having made a special trip to Leningrad to question the assassin himself, of his sitting up all night, in devotion, on the train, with Kírov's body, when it was being taken to Moscow. It was quite obvious to me, however, that this version of *Peter the First* had been written as an apology for the persecution of such critics of Stalin's regime as Kámenev and Zinóviev—a persecution for which the murder of Kírov had provided him with a pretext. The costly and dazzling production seemed to be directed especially at the art-loving sophisticated elements in what was still the most civilized city in Russia—precisely those elements among whom I was sitting. The lack of applause at the end was due to their obstinate independence. They knew that the fable was meant for them, and the answer to this was silence. In silence they left the theater, giving one another sly looks. "You see," said the literary man who had brought me, "Stalin has sometimes been criticized as not having distinguished himself as a Marxist. He wants to show that he is capable of historical analogies." "But what," I asked, "is the point of the episode in which Peter steals Ménshikov's wife? What is that an analogy for?" There had been a violent curtain, for which Peter, who had come to her house at a time when her husband was at home, had thrown her upon a bed, grunting like a great bear. "Ah," my companion answered—we had touched already on the political issues— "that might be something else!" I do not know whether he had in mind some aspect of Stalin's affair with the sister of Kaganóvich or Yágoda's appropriation of Gorky's niece, whose husband he is supposed to have had murdered.

Alexéy Tolstóy was several times to rewrite his *Peter the First*, which had originally been a novel—twice, at least, as a play and once as a film. Each of these versions marked a new stage in the progress of Stalin's tyranny. The figure of Peter—who, in the version I saw, was at least protesting that it broke his heart to do such awful things to people—became, at each of these stages, coarser and more menacing. Later on, the career of Peter was found to be inadequate in providing parallels, and a shift was made to Iván the Terrible, about whom, in the early forties, Tolstóy composed two plays, in which this partly demented tsar was shown as a far-sighted statesman. To that most unlucky genius Eisenstein was entrusted the official duty of glorifying Iván in a film. This production was in two parts. In the first part, Iván was shown as a constructive statesman and a loving husband, who was embittered by the death of his wife and a boyar conspiracy against him (accompanied by close-up muggings on the part of the conspirators that Eisenstein would never have perpetrated in the days of his relative early freedom). But at the end, he has become neurotic. As a procession makes its way to the palace, he is shown, in perhaps the one fine shot in the film, lurking behind a pillar, morbid and misanthropic, insanely suspicious, afraid of the people. The second part of the film was never publicly shown. Here Iván was allowed to become quite mad and to deserve his epithet. In one scene, I understand, he was made to chew the carpet, like Hitler.

Eisenstein was reprimanded, and sentenced to the usual confession. His way of complying with this was to acknowledge himself at fault, explaining that he had been "misled by historical accuracy." Soon after this, he died.

It ought to be borne in mind, in connection with these Russian notes, written in 1935, that this was, in certain ways, the most liberal period ever known in Soviet Russia. Visitors from abroad were welcomed for the valuta they had to spend, though they were, of course, closely watched; contact with the West was encouraged. The political terror had already begun with the first trials of Stalin's opponents; but the writers were still being urged to avail themselves, from bourgeois culture, of whatever it had to offer them.

The theater, the ballet and the opera still enjoyed perhaps a greater degree of independence than any other institutions in the Soviet Union, and their continuity had been less broken than in the case of any others with the cultural world of old Russia. What I saw was, I suppose, the last of this. Their greatest man of the theater, Meyerhold, of whom I write below, was less than three years later to have his theater closed. When he attempted, in 1939, to defend himself against charges of "formalism" and of obstructing the progress of "socialist realism," and denounced the mediocrity of the Soviet stage, he was arrested and evidently done away with, for he has never been seen since. Even the name of Meyerhold has recently been all but entirely expunged from what is supposed to be the scholarly and definitive edition of the "complete collected works and letters" of Chekhov, the editors of which have suppressed Chekhov's correspondence with him, though Meyerhold acted in Chekhov's plays and Chekhov is known, from a passage not published in the Soviet edition of his letters, to have followed his career with sympathetic interest.]

Leaning against the stone parapet of the Neva, we talked amid the desolate long perspectives—S. and I—in the night that was still white. Dark palace of the Grand Duke Constantine, uncle of the late Tsar. "He was a poet, quite a good poet"—had simply signed himself C. R. He had been executed after the Revolution. I asked S. how they had filled those huge palaces. He smiled, shrugged, said he didn't know—Constantine had had a large family, many servants. "Ain't it beautiful!" he said of the city. The Square of the Victims of the Revolution—"so quiet here you could sleep."

M. D. had an extra ticket for the ballet and invited one of the Intourist interpreters to go with her. The girl said at first that she couldn't, because she didn't have the clothes; then when M. D. had persuaded her and she went, she refused to go out in the intermissions, because she said she wasn't fit to be seen.

I told M. D. one day about the English people on the boat and their troubles with the Russian food. She said that her brother-in-law in England, having heard that there was no cream in Russia, had tried to get her to take a machine for making cream out of melted butter. He wondered how she could go to a country which had executed a whole royal family.

He was tall, slim and pale in his uniform, talked English beautifully and wrote poetry in French, was cultivated in every language on every conceivable subject, as only a Russian intellectual can be. And he manipulated his cigarette with insinuating conscious grace. He was an instructor in Methodology at the Naval Academy and had been reading Donne's poetry to the sailors, who, he said, were crazy about it. He was much interested in a poem by a Russian, written, he said, partly under French, partly under German, influence, which invested the raising of Lazarus with homosexual suggestions. I was surprised when he began to tell us how wonderful the new film *Chapáev* was, how nobody but a Russian could understand it.

Looking dazedly out the window of the electric-lighted director's room, with its gold Empire sphinxes and its classical figures in brown polished wood, I lose myself, having dined well, in the outside day still light at nine— the cobbled street, an old woman sewing in the doorway of a great shabby yellow stucco building. I am actually in the Marínsky Opera House, named for the wife of Paul I and one of the handsomest theaters in the world. In the room behind, among others, are Harold Clurman, a friend from New York, who does not make things seem any more natural; Shostakóvich, a shy little sandy-colored and boyish-looking man, with unobtrusive glasses; a Leningrad woman intellectual who has been trained as a psychologist but is now translating Mark Twain: she has a bad monkey mouth with too prominent teeth, but she curiously compensates for this by nervous energy, high flushed cheek-bones and the intensity of her eyes, and, in spite of her flat shoes, has a distinct, even strong, sex appeal. Yet I ask myself, where am I? This moment is quite unlike anything I have ever experienced before. This *mouvementé* and magical daydream at night is St. Petersburg, Leningrad.

We go down the stairs to a box, from which, on a

queerly tilted stage and framed in the splendor of the great gold-and-white imperial proscenium arch, we watch the Chaikovsky opera *Píkovaya Dáma* (*The Queen of Spades*), produced by Meyerhold.

The fables of Pushkin, when we hear of them abroad, have little significance for us, and the music of Chaikovsky is perhaps never really good except in Russia. Meyerhold has made of *Píkovaya Dáma* a disturbing and fascinating drama. He has had the libretto rewritten and has rearranged the score—many of the old operas ought probably to be rewritten—so as to give it new point and suspense. The old Countess who knows the secret of winning at cards is not, as in the ordinary version, introduced in the first scene: we only hear about her. Nor do we see her even when Hermann goes to her house: we only hear her voice calling. When she finally appears, she is terrifying: an inscrutable and queenly old mummy who sits as mute as Fate while a sort of *commedia del' arte* of pantaloons and harlequins and shepherdesses is performed for her entertainment. When it is finished, she silently rises and goes. The bedroom scene is terrific. She has been sitting in her *négligé* and singing a little song in French about a visit to Versailles in her youth. Hermann suddenly appears from the closet, with his green, sleepless, burning-eyed face and, threatening her with a pistol, tries to force her to tell him her secret; but he frightens her too much: she falls dead. The scene ends with harsh satisfying trumpets. Hermann and the Countess's companion stand by the parapet of the Neva: she discovers that he has never loved her but only used her to gain access to the old lady. The Countess's ghost appears to Hermann and finally tells him the secret. He goes back to the card-table, and once he wins. But, disregarding the old woman's warning, he tries the trick a second time and loses. The Queen of Spades turns into the Countess and winks at him malignly. He ends in an insane asylum, on which the final curtain descends.

What has Pushkin put into this story? the foreigner asks himself. The ironic tragedy of the will that tries to cheat on the rules of life? From where did the old Countess get her secret? From experience, and she knew that she must not abuse it. All this passes behind the façade of the gallantry, the champagne, the card-playing of a smart Petersburg winter. A poor officer has gone mad.

Afterwards we drank vodka in little cut-glass goblets and ate iced caviare. I went to bed full of vodka and Pushkin—outside the high windows, the long curtains, the sky was still pale with unfading day . . . on a table there were a cut-glass decanter with a curious high square stopper and full of water that hadn't been changed for days, and I saw it as if it were standing in the room in which Hermann had lain awake, brooding, desiring, scheming . . . they had always stayed up all night, insatiably talking and drinking, dancing and playing cards . . . and about them the vast sprawling city with the bottomless spaces behind it . . . the palaces full of vistas, like the streets, the broad river, the waterways . . . the bridges, the characters of Dostoevsky, uneasy, unable to relax in sleep, roaming the bridges in the half-day of night: the dissipated, the lonely, the thoughtful, the poor . . . the great unintegrated city which in itself seemed to have no meaning, in which the individual had to make his own meaning, in which he despaired by himself, beating his head against the vistas . . . away there on the outskirts of Europe . . . They had come back as we had done at home to a straggling provincial civilization among prairies and wild rivers and forests, bringing books and manners from Europe, and, like Goncharóv's Oblómov, they had remained in bed in the morning for hours trying to make up their minds whether or not to get up: I had done the same thing myself . . . In these countries we are freer, less certain of what we want, we think the long long thoughts of the poem and they are lost in the quiet of the province . . . unless, all alone in the spaces, we are possessed by some passionate purpose . . . We never know what we have got in the forests and wastes of these countries; we never know what is going to come out of them . . .

IV

ON THE MARGIN OF MOSCOW

I WENT TO THE STATION with the Englishman from the boat, who said that the food was all right, but he couldn't get enough fruit and vegetables.

In the train, they told us to watch out for our suitcases, not to leave them alone a second.

I "traveled hard," which is much more comfortable than the second- and third-class compartments in the western European countries. In those, you have to sit up all night; but in Russia you have a bunk to lie down in, and if there isn't one, you can't buy a ticket. For five rubles, you get a small mattress and a pillow and a blanket.—The man in the berth above me—heavy body, inchoate face and some kind of official-looking cap— flopped in his clothes without a mattress and apparently never moved all night.

I bought beer and slices of bread with pressed caviare, sausage and cheese, from a man who came round with a basket, and I drank the beer with a passenger who knew a few words of English and had helped me to talk to the man. The passenger was a tall stooping fellow, with childlike eyes and a walrus mustache. He told me that he was a Pole and that he had worked eleven years in Detroit, had drawn five dollars a day at Ford's. I asked him why he had come to Russia, and he replied: "I t'ink I'm crazy!" I said that Detroit was in a bad way and that he might not have his job there now. He told me, with some satisfaction, I could see, that he was making two hundred and seventy-five rubles a month, pretty good pay for the Soviets. He spoke with great pride of the new Moscow subway and said that I would see nothing like it in America. One thing he was sure of, he said: he would never go back to Poland.

I ate the slice of bread spread with caviare, leaning on a kind of little shelf and looking out the window, absorbed by a totally new landscape: forests of slim straight pines and birches with fine white stems; this part of Russia is hirsute. Log houses like America and not like Europe. I kept on sitting up, waiting for it to be dark, as you do—till I realized it was getting on toward midnight.

———

I had originally proposed to go from Leningrad to Moscow by day in order to see the country, but everybody told me this was impossible. Their accents seemed to suggest that such a thing had never been imagined. I inquired of a literary man in Leningrad, who knew a good deal about a good many other things, what there was between Leningrad and Moscow, and why people never made the journey by day. He replied that he did not know. "It has never occurred to me," he said, "to wonder who the people are who live between Leningrad and Moscow. I don't know who they are or what they do."

This seemed to me a curious attitude, but when I questioned other people, I could not find anyone else who was able to throw light on the matter. I came at last upon the explanation in my antiquated Russian grammar. "From St. Petersburg to Moscow," says the grammar, in one of its exercises, "the locomotive runs for a distance of 400 miles, almost as the crow flies, turning neither to the right hand nor to the left. For fifteen hours the passenger in the express train looks out on forest and morass, and rarely catches sight of human habitation. Only once he perceives in the distance what may be called a town; it is Tver, which has been thus favored simply because it happened to be near the straight line. And why was the railway constructed in this extraordinary fashion? For the best of all reasons, because the Tsar so ordered it. When the preliminary survey was being made, Nicholas learned that the officers entrusted with the task (and the Minister of Ways and Roads in the number) were being influenced more by personal than by technical considerations, and he determined to cut the Gordian knot in true imperial style. When the Minister laid before him the map with the intention of explaining the proposed route, he took a ruler, drew a straight line from the one terminus to the other, and remarked in a tone that precluded all discussion, 'You will construct the line so.' And the line was so constructed."

For this reason, there are no intermediate stations; for this reason, the trip is always made at night.

It is characteristic of the Russians that the railroad should have been built in this way; and it is also characteristic that people who travel frequently on it should neither know nor wonder about it.

———

I had expected Moscow to be old and musty, but it is modern and energetic. The people are better dressed and more prosperous-appearing, in general, than the people of Leningrad. The main business section, the "Center," is much like an American city. They have set out to rearrange the whole place, and already there are only little patches of the original Moscow of the Muscovite tsars, embedded in drab streets and crowded traffic: the jewel-box of the Kremlin with its needle-pointed gleaming gilt spires (which, as a result of the Kírov shooting, visitors are no longer allowed to see); the shabby domes of St. Basil's in their big ugly bulbous mushroom-clump. St. Basil's, inside, is a labyrinth, lined with faded saints and angels which the authorities have done nothing to freshen, and plastered with aggressively glaring texts from Marx and Engels and Lenin, which declare that religion is a fraud. In the streets, the innumerable stubby little people who have been flocking into the metropolis but who are not used to getting around in a city, are plunging about and bumping into one another. Moscow seems even to a New Yorker a terribly exhausting place. The tram-cars are usually crowded, and the people hang on to the outside and fall off and get under the cars and have their legs and arms run over. And though the pace of Russian life is in general so much slower and less effortful than ours, their new mechanical means of locomotion seem sometimes to have gone to their heads. They rip around the streets in their Russian-made cars, tooting wild defiant horns, like galloping Cossacks; and the escalators in their new little subway rush the passengers up and down at a speed unknown in America. Women and children scream: a first ride is a major adventure. When the subway was opened, Comrade Stalin, who can take it, rode the escalator twice in succession.

This subway, for the foreign visitor, is worth thinking about. They are all very much excited over it, and they eagerly ask every foreigner how it compares with the subways in other countries. The truth is, of course, that, compared to most of them, it is tiny; but it is the only *pretty* subway in the world. Every station is in a different style, so that it is full of delightful surprises, like a superior sort of scenic railway: there are murals, ornamental columns, novel effects of light. Even the trains are done in pleasing combinations of red, light tan and yellow, or red, light tan and green. What it most resembles, on its smaller scale, is the interiors of the Radio City theaters. The moral of the Moscow subway is that it is perfectly natural that a public utility, if built by the people for their own use, should be dignified, handsome and attractive.

I sometimes wake up in the morning with a feeling I have never had before of being obliged to adjust myself to a new set of social dimensions.

———————

They are certainly much pleasanter with each other, for all their jostling and jamming, than New Yorkers. They have arguments on street-cars and in queues, always calling one another "Comrade"—quite different from our crowds in the subway, for example, where the people rarely speak to one another, each penned up in his particular anxieties, each with his particular schedule to make. In Moscow, if anyone behaves hoggishly, there is general remonstrance and protest. In one case I heard of, a man in a street-car was made to feel so cheap that he got off.

It is much easier to establish friendly relations with Russians than with the people of any other country I know. When you smile at them, they always smile back: it is a queer kind of childlike responsiveness. When they are frightened or suspicious, they become, not stiff, but simply shy.

———————

Old women walking along the streets with cigarettes drooping out of their mouths. The Russians have been getting more cigarettes lately.

I was taken to a commissar's home for tea. He and his family were living in what would be for New York a very moderate-sized middle-class apartment. Lots of interesting sweet things to eat: cranberries candied in white sugar, for example. The Russians love these sweets and are only just beginning to get them again. The Commissar had the Communist seriousness, reticence, intentness, severity. Over tea in the bosom of his family, he almost never smiled—though he was evidently not unamiable and, from behind his rather heavy manner, was evidently going to be helpful in the case of some unfortunate person in whose behalf one of the visitors appealed to him.

They tried to tell me the news that Roosevelt's N.R.A. had been declared unconstitutional by the Supreme Court; but, little confidence though I had in the N.R.A., I was so unprepared for this, subconsciously no doubt so loth to admit it, that I thought they said *constitutional*. They had apparently been surprised and had expected that I should be surprised. It was only the next day, when I read about it in the paper, that I grasped it.

It is curious losing track of the days of the week. Their week consists now of six days, with a holiday called "Free Day" on the sixth. Everything is reckoned by the date; and I believe I miss the old Saturdays and Mondays. Each of the traditional days has its own special psychological atmosphere; the week is a moral cycle.

We went up to a traffic-cop, and I was astonished when she turned around and revealed a little, red-cheeked, freckled country girl, very serious, concentrated and cute in her helmet and masculine clothes.

It is unexpected and stimulating for an American, after leaving the writers at home preoccupied with what they imagine to be the Soviet point of view about literature, to find the Russians studying intently everything that reaches them from the States—rather dissatisfied now with their own post-revolutionary literature and seeming to feel that in America we have been able to do the kind of thing that they would like to do themselves. Very amusing to reflect that the three living American writers most popular in the Soviet Union—Upton Sinclair, Dos Passos and Dreiser—are all people who have recently been in wrong with the literary Communists at home.

Hemingway has just been translated and, among the intelligentzia, is attracting a great deal of attention. I come to realize that the young people in Russia are interested in the American writers for certain reasons, among others, which I hadn't been aware of before. I was told by a Russian that the hero and heroine of Dos Passos' *Manhattan Transfer,* both types of the unquiet intellectual, were as well known in Russia as characters in Pushkin; that young men would say, "I am Jimmy Herf," etc. The young Russians of the Jimmy Herf type have this in common with these characters of Dos Passos: that they are up against a social machine to which they have difficulty in adapting themselves. That the Soviet machine has a more rational base and a nobler aim than American business does not always make the situation easier—and, after all, the conditions of a democracy, with their tendency to lower cultural standards, present the same kind of problems to both. And there must be people in Moscow who would sometimes be glad of "a clean bright place," like the man in Hemingway's story—a story which, I note, is included in a Russian selection from his work. I am reminded of a young woman who tells me that she dreams about having a room to herself.

———

An air-meet. It took place on the outskirts of Moscow, and we reached it along a road lined with little old mud-brown log houses, which had fancy peaked cornices over the windows and fringes of wooden lace. Some of them seemed to have sunk into the earth till their windows were almost on a level with it.

It was on this field that the crowds were trampled to death at the coronation of Nicholas II. Today there is a loud-speaker and a band playing the *International* through it. Ballet-patterns by gliders, which would sheer off symmetrically from the plane that had trailed them and wheel slowly over on their sides; a regular rocket-burst of parachute-jumpers, some of the women coming down with two parachutes. The weather was cold and wet: a little group of girls and young men had joined hands and were running around in a ring to keep warm. There were appealing boy and girl couples leaning against their bicycles and looking up at the flyers.

A small policeman in a helmet was trying to make the people get back behind a rope. They argued with him about it, calling him "Comrade." The crowd maintained that so long as there were cars parked in front of the rope, people ought to be able to stand there. The policeman, on his side, pointed out that, so far as seeing airplanes went, it didn't matter where you stood. Somebody said that it wasn't that you couldn't see: it was the psychological effect of having something in front of you. The policeman apparently felt the force of this, but he urged them to get back "a tiny bit." Presently, the cars drove away, and the policeman then returned and showed logically that, now the obstruction was removed, they ought to keep back behind the ropes. Persuaded by this argument, they finally complied.

The relations between the police and the public seem almost ideal. Lenin insisted on having the former called "militia." The role of the old police had become so hateful to him that he had not wanted to preserve even the name. The "militia," like any other militia, were supposed to represent the citizens themselves; and it is true that on an occasion like this air-meet, the Moscow militia are much more like the ushers at a college ball-game than like the police of the capitalist states. I afterwards saw a man arrested, and the same sort of parliamentary methods seemed to regulate the proceedings. Two militiamen had the man by the arms, but he kept stopping and arguing with them. They would unhand him and explain their case. Finally, they led him away.

There are, of course, the secret police, who are apparently a different matter.

I have not been troubled by espionage, as some people complain of being—though I have had one or two mysterious telephone calls which woke me up at early hours of the morning. When I answered, there would be nobody on the line; and I was told that this was the ordinary way of finding out whether you were sleeping at the address you had given. Once when I was taking a Russian lady home from the Metropole café, we were followed very closely by a man who seemed to have a special interest in us.

I always find that Americans who become bitter over espionage in Russia have never had any experience of what may happen in the United States in any industrial center. These people have never been made uncomfortable at home, because they have never been suspected of supporting the interests of labor against the interests of the employing class. So I was not made uncomfortable in Russia, because I was a visiting journalist known to be sympathetic with the Soviet regime. In America, the visiting journalist whose sympathies are not known, though he may be merely reporting strikes or even merely looking at factories, soon finds the police and the officials checking up on his lodgings and his movements; and in the ruder and more remote communities, he is likely to be confronted with gun-thugs who threaten to run him out of town. If he is known to be engaged in pro-labor work, he may be followed on the train by a detective and very likely *will* be run out.

I locked myself out of my room at the hotel. There was no one at the chambermaid's table. The elevator-boy promised to send the porter, but nothing came of this. I went downstairs and told the porter myself, and he immediately turned to a young boy who was standing across from the desk with a box of tools under his arm. I asked the porter whether he didn't have a key: they had opened it that way before. But he insisted that the boy would attend to it. I went upstairs with the boy, who produced from his kit a large wedge and started hammering it, with deafening racket, into the crack between the double doors. Presently he stopped doing this and, taking out another huge tool, began to gouge it into the keyhole. Then he tried the wedge again. He had evidently no equipment for dealing with locks. An old man with a shaved head had turned up at the chambermaid's table. I told him that they had a key there with which they had let me into my room before; but he only opened his drawer and looked at the keys and shook his head. I remonstrated with the boy, who was damaging the door but

who was easily persuaded to stop. And now the old man
and I, seizing two different phones simultaneously, made
efforts to get the porter, but nobody even answered.
The boy and I went downstairs, where we found the
porter behind his desk. He immediately produced a key,
with which I opened the door. His sending the boy in
the first place had apparently been due merely to the
accident that the latter happened to be standing by with
a box of tools for breaking into things, and that it had
seemed to the porter a pleasing idea to have him give
a demonstration on my door. I had been trying to think
that Moscow was much more efficient than Leningrad.

I am continually surprised at finding Russians who are
crazy to go to America. I tell them there is a capitalist
crisis there, with many people out of work; but, though
their own newspapers and official publicity are continually telling them the same thing, many people do not
seem to believe it. I have already been asked several times
whether Roosevelt were not a great man—in spite of
Stalin's admirable analysis of the impossibilities of the
New Deal in his interview with H. G. Wells, which has
been circulated here in Russian. It is partly of course because Roosevelt has recently recognized the Soviets; but
it is also because there is still a tendency in all this part
of the world to regard the United States as the Promised
Land.

I spoke of this to an American Communist, who had
been working in Moscow several years. Yes, he said, it was
hard to explain to them: all the Americans they saw, even
Communists, were a good deal better dressed than most
Russians. When he spoke at meetings, he said, and tried
to tell them about the depression, they would ask him,
"But Communist literature isn't illegal in America?"

"No." "Well, why isn't there a workers' revolution?" "Maybe you think that's an easy one to answer," he concluded. "I thought so at first, till I tried."

I told him, also, I was beginning to wonder whether the privileges and the chances to make money of the popular writers in Russia were really a good thing for their work, whether writers shouldn't always be at odds with society. He said that they had plenty of thorns in their flesh. They had to appear at workers' meetings—every factory has its literary circle—and justify what they were doing. "Very often they're told that they're lousy." I tried to imagine how this would work out: it would be good education for the workers, but would it be good for the work of the writers?

———

I met my Englishman from the boat again on the steps of the Hotel National. When I told him I was hoping to stay several months, "You get along all right, do you?" he said. "I couldn't stand it!" The reason he thought he couldn't stand it was that he didn't get enough fresh fruit and vegetables. I said that you could buy oranges, though they cost a lot. "I had an orange and a bottle of beer the other day," he replied, "so I was all right for a time." I thought of how amusing he had been about the complaints of the Englishmen in the Embassy. "Well, it's interesting to see it," I said, "isn't it?" He made no reply.

———

That same evening I went to *The Pickwick Club,* a dramatization of *Pickwick Papers,* in which the Russians, on their side, were making a (perhaps diplomatic) effort to understand and appreciate the English. It was not the very best I have seen them do in fidelity to the color of a foreign classic; and the English-speaking spectator did

not quite know very often whether to be rubbed the
wrong way or amused. The moment after Mrs. Bardell's
fainting in the arms of Mr. Pickwick, the attorneys Dod-
son and Fogg popped up in grotesque make-ups, which
resembled the wizard Koshchéy the Deathless in Dyági-
lev's *L'Oiseau de Feu* rather than the illustrations of
Phiz; Mr. Pickwick and the other gentlemen were continually kissing each other as Russians do but Englishmen
don't; and Mr. Wardell's great hall was decorated with a
bizarre mirth-provoking picture of a man in red coat and
shooting-cap with a ramshackle Russian grin, holding up
a fox by the tail with the fingers of his hand extended like Ed Pinaud in the hair-tonic ads. Yet it
seemed to me that more study and imagination had gone
into this production to make it English than had gone
into, say, Jed Harris's *Uncle Vanya,* in New York, to reproduce the Russian atmosphere of Chekhov, and with
more successful results.

The "Moscow tic": I hadn't believed it when I had been
told that people always looked over their shoulders before venturing to say anything about politics. But they
do, and I find that I do it, too.

I was taken to *Romeo and Juliet* at the Theater of the
Revolution, the first classic that this theater has put on.
They have been working on the production two years.
It was Shakespeare for the Komsomól. They had
Romeo and Juliet and Mercutio and the Nurse leaping on
and off balconies and running up and down stairs and
hurling themselves into the audience, with the kind of
energy required for parachute-jumping and tractor-
driving; and the actors had been directed to break in,

from time to time, on the spell of the balcony-scene by playing certain lines for laughs. The director explained between the acts that this was "in the mood of Soviet youth": ironic, casual, tender; and really much closer to Shakespeare than the way it was usually played. Shakespeare had already made the love scenes sensual; and sentimentality with sensuality was intolerable. They are trying, it seems, to encourage love, but not too much romance. The whole tragedy, as thus interpreted, seemed to go to show that young people subjected to their families' wills under the arrangements of the feudal system were a good deal less happy and free than Komsomóls under the Soviets.

Yet they did have some extraordinary sets, and Juliet and the Nurse were excellent. When I compared it with the *Romeo and Juliet* I had seen before I left New York, I was doubtful whether it was not really true that the Russians had been closer to Shakespeare than the American production had been. They had certainly much more vitality. I remembered how I had gone to sleep while Katherine Cornell was sitting on the bed and thinking about taking the potion—more moved by the idea of a narcotic than by the passionate tides of young love; and how her deliberate, conscientious and wholly unprepared-for yell at the thought of Tybalt moldering in the tomb had most unpleasantly waked me up.

The Moscow *Romeo and Juliet* lasted from seven-thirty to twelve-twenty—the longest theatrical performance (barring, perhaps, Wagner's operas) I think I have ever sat through. They take the theater seriously in Russia, as no one has for years with us. They do not allow anybody to be seated from the moment the curtain goes up: they will not even let you into a movie once the picture has started. During the long intermissions, the people have tea and discuss the play. Even productions the Russians think inferior seem to me satisfactory in a way that our skimped and hurried comedies and our knocked-together revivals never are any more.

Many things that we apply ourselves to they slight. But a dinner, a play, a ballet, a meeting, a Russian lesson, an after-dinner conversation, are likely to go on for hours and to deal with the matter in hand far more thoroughly than we ordinarily do.

They have dinner, their main meal, sometime between three and six, and do much of their executive work at night, eating supper between eleven and two. Stalin goes to bed every morning at four. This is precisely what I do myself at the present time; but, although it is admirable for writing, I am not sure it is so good for administrative work. I should think their nocturnal projects would tend to become works of the imagination.

An official to whom I applied for a permit promised to expedite matters and told me to come round at eleven the next morning (offices never open before ten). When I arrived the next morning, he wasn't there; and I had to make several visits before I found him in the afternoon. He said that he was sorry to be so late, but that if I knew how the head of the department had sat up working till two!—But, after all, in spite of these vigils, his subordinates had not been in their offices to carry on the business of the department.

This habit of having dinner in the middle of the afternoon is, it seems, an eighteenth-century institution. It is one of the many examples of things which present to Westerners the aspect of anachronisms but that co-exist with other things which we have not caught up to yet.

I found L. in her office, eating large chocolate candies which were done up in colored paper wrappers with pictures of bears climbing trees and labeled in English, "Baby-Bears." With her small thick body, her broad paws, her childlike, round, brown eyes and her protrusive nose with its open nostrils, she looked rather like a little bear herself.

She is the daughter of a scientist of the old society, now in business of some kind in Egypt. She remembers being at school when the classes would be interrupted by the dropping of British bombs—she could see that the teacher was terribly worried; and the strain of trying to do homework when they had so little light. The food was so insufficient that her nails became disfigured from lack of calcium. Her parents left Russia; but L. stayed behind and made a place for herself in the new society. She had mastered English early, and she took a job as technical interpreter for one of the big economic conferences that worked up the Five-Year Plan. She says it was very exciting, but brought her to the verge of a breakdown. Her sister would have to wake her up at night, because she would still be interpreting in her sleep. Then the sister got away to join her parents in Egypt, but L. stuck by the Soviet Union. She has burnt up some of the best years of her youth on work for the Five-Year Plan, and she is sometimes a little wistful about it. But the letters that she gets from her sister abroad seem to shock her sense of propriety—all the more, perhaps, because they make her a little envious: they are all about night-clubs and dances, she says; and all that kind of thing "is not to be compared with what is being done here." She is always impatient with people who are nostalgic about the old regime.

She is so far the Russian I have met whom I find the

most sympathetic and the only really attractive woman whom I have so far seen in Moscow. The only one, also, who knows how to dress. I thought at first that her clothes must have come from abroad, but it seems that she gets them in Moscow, which shows—though she makes more money than most women—that it is not only meager materials and the austerity of the post-revolutionary period which are to blame for the appearance of the Moscow women, but also lack of taste. They will have to be educated in taste as in so many other things.

I took L. to an old play of Ostróvsky's, *Talents and Admirers,* at the Art Theater. She changed in her office, before we went, to tiny little high-heeled shoes—she wears twos—and produced a pair of mother-of-pearl opera-glasses which she said had belonged to her mother. The play was marvelous: the Art Theater has brilliantly succeeded in reproducing the effect of the mid-nineteenth-century *genre* pictures of the Trétyakov Gallery, so that the tableaux on the stage have the color and composition of paintings. At the same time they have invested the characters with so perfect an illusion of life that you quite forget they are actors wearing period costumes and make-ups, and are unable to imagine them out of their roles. L. translated for me with astonishing intelligence and fluency, and seemed deeply to appreciate the play. I don't think I have ever enjoyed theater-going more.

Men in uniforms whom you meet that tell you that you can talk to them freely because they do not represent the government.

Arkhángelskoye, the Yusúpov estate: all sorts of statuary and paintings and furniture and panels and books brought from all over Europe to this remote magnificent house in this immense countryside which it dominated. The foliage of the slim-stemmed trees which seem to surround it for miles, making a screen both porous and dense, is of a peculiar light bright green that I have never seen anywhere else. It is the color and texture of Turgénev.

Today the following announcement appeared in *The Moscow Daily News:*

PLENUM OF THE CENTRAL COMMITTEE OF THE CPSU

INFORMATIONAL STATEMENT

The Plenum of the Central Committee of the CPSU held June 5 to 7, 1935, discussed two questions: 1) on the harvesting campaign and deliveries of agricultural products, and 2) on the personnnel of the Secretariat of the Central Executive Committee of the USSR and on Comrade A. Yenukídze.

ON THE PERSONNEL OF THE SECRETARIAT OF THE CENTRAL EXECUTIVE COMMITTEE OF USSR ON COMRADE A. YENUKÍDZE

RESOLUTION OF THE PLENUM OF THE CENTRAL COMMITTEE OF THE CPSU ON THE REPORT OF YEZHÓV, ADOPTED JUNE 7, 1935

1. To approve the measures of the control organs for checking up and improving the personnel of the Secre-

tariat of the Central Executive Committee of the USSR.

2. For his political and personal dissoluteness, A. Yenukídze, former Secretary of the Central Executive Committee of the USSR, is to be removed from membership in the Central Committee of the CPSU and is to be excluded from the ranks of the CPSU.

This is all. Yenukídze has for seventeen years been secretary of the Central Executive Committee. His political dissoluteness is supposed to consist of leniency to political prisoners; his personal dissoluteness, of ballet-girls. There has been a rumor among the newspaper men around the Metropole Hotel, where he lived, that he was led through the lobby handcuffed. But no definite statements are made, and nobody knows anything for certain. We are likely to think at home that our newspaper publicity is a curse; but the Russians, with their policy of suppression, have gone too far in the other direction. A tourist told me that when she had inquired of a guide whether the Kremlin was where Stalin lived, the guide had replied: "Comrade Stalin is an employee of the government. His private life is none of our business, and we do not think about where he lives." Thus charges against an official never have to be substantiated to the satisfaction of public opinion. The result of this is that the public create their own tabloid journalism. I have never heard more scandalous stories circulated about public figures than those that get whispered in Moscow.

———

Only gradually you come to be aware of all the things that Moscow lacks. There are very few dogs and cats, for example. People haven't had room enough or food enough to keep many pets in the past. At one time they had to get food-cards for dogs. Nor does Moscow, so far as I could notice, have even a special smell of its own, like the European cities. This is partly, I suppose, because it is kept so uniformly clean: they are always playing the hose on the streets, and in all my wanderings through the city, I was never able to find anything like a slum or any quarter that even seemed dirty. But it is also partly due to the absence of so many things that have smells: foliage, for example, and perfumes; restaurants cooking rich foods and bars serving pungent liquor; fruit-stands in the street, incense in the churches, and the fumes of private motor-cars and taxis.

Visit to a small collective farm just outside Moscow. Getting started was no end of trouble. We had a little Komsomól girl guide with blond curly hair and a blue beret on one side of her head. First she thought it would be a good idea to take a bus which left every ten minutes, but then, on second thought, she decided the train would be quicker. When we got to the Warsaw Station, they told us at the Information Bureau that the train was just about to leave, so we hurried to the ticket-window. But then when our tickets had been paid for, they told her that Information was all wrong, because the train did not leave for three-quarters of an hour. We had come an immense distance from the bus terminus, so we decided to take a taxi. We tried to give back the tickets, but the woman wouldn't accept them: she said they had already been stamped, so that she could give us our money back only if somebody else came along who was going to the same station, in which case she could sell him our tickets. A long argument then took place between the guide and the woman at the window, a fresh-cheeked and clear-eyed little girl who kept smiling in the most friendly fashion. But we couldn't do anything with her. Finally I took the change and shoved the tickets through the window, and we set out for the taxi-stand. This put the poor girl in a terrible dilemma, and we heard her calling after us and looked back and saw her leaning down and sticking her head out the ticket-window, trying to call us back and make us take the tickets.

We waited in line for a taxi, but when it finally came our turn and we told the driver where to go, he said that he could not take us out of town because he had to be back in the garage in half an hour to give the taxi to another man. Presently another one came up and said that he would take us out if we didn't stay there too long. "He says that he will wait half an hour," explained the guide. "That means he will wait an hour."

In the taxi, I talked to the young Englishman who was the only other member of the party. He was working in the Ministry of Agriculture and seemed to be pretty far to the Left, but, like the Englishman on the boat, he did not seem to know where to come to roost. The little Komsomólka began to apply herself to an English translation of Engels' pamphlet, *Socialism, Utopian and Scientific,* thus improving her English at the same time as her Dialectical Materialism. I had seen her before: she had taken me to the Women's and Children's Museum and had explained to me the fetuses in various stages and the birth control devices. She had been working hard at English and said that she especially admired—as I discovered all the students did, because it is given them as a reader, I suppose—*A Picture of Dorian Gray.* Now she told me that she had finished her courses in Dialectical Materialism for the summer and was soon going for her vacation to a *dácha* (summer villa). I suppose she was doing this work for VOKS simply in order to be helpful and to have a chance to practice her English.

Rutted roads and mussy country. Old brown wood-lace frills around the windows.

The President of the collective farm came to the door with his napkin in his hand, but insisted, in spite of our remonstrances, on taking us around right away. He had a farmer's red complexion, cropped head, straight and cool blue eyes; the same kind of dignified and simple good manners as the young engineers on the boat. He made us sit down in his office. A pretty little girl brought us sprigs of lilac; then a good-looking woman came and presented us with a bouquet. The President explained, and we asked him questions. Here the farmers all lived in their houses; in some farms, there were dormitories, too. They had chickens and cows of their own. The land was cultivated in common. What was left after the government levy and when they had taken what they needed for themselves, they were permitted to sell in Moscow. They either brought their babies up at home or put them in the crèche, as they wished. They either, as they wished, kept house or ate their meals in the common dining-hall. The young Englishman rashly suggested that the President might like to ask *us* questions; and the farmer politely made some queries about English soils and crops, none of which the boy seemed able to answer. He finally explained that his own special department did not involve knowing much about soil.

The babies in the crèche looked attractive and seemed to be well taken care of. Red-faced women who were working in the fields made us presents of radishes and tomatoes. They laughed at the boy who had driven us and said he could have a radish, because he was a guest, too; and this seemed to embarrass him extremely. They were also raising cucumbers in frames and that herb they chop up and put in soup. I asked the little guide what it was called, but she said that she had never known what it was called in Russian, so she couldn't tell me in English. Nor did she know why the horses wore those great arched collars. I never met any Russian who knew this: it is like the railroad between Leningrad and Moscow. In the cowshed, I asked whether they had milking-machines, but the farmer had never heard of them. I told the guide that in Ireland the machines had upset the cows so badly that they had refused to give any milk; but that in America our cows were quite used to them. "The cows in America are more cultural," she said. The *"Kultúra"* of which one hears so much in Russia is preëminently sanitary and technical. Among the collective services, there was a homely Beauty Parlor. It seems that all the farms now have them, since the women have been encouraged to look attractive.

The collective dining hall was rather like a country tavern. The farmer invited us to sit down, and they brought us beer and bread and sausage. Another party arrived, which included a tall Englishman with a beard, who looked like some faintly shoddy Sir Somebody. "You speak English very well," he said to the girl interpreter with gracious and patronizing blandness. "Have you been in England?" The girl said no, that she had learned all her English in Moscow. He questioned her in the same gentle tone, as if he were addressing a child, but with insistence and latent irony, on the mutiny and expulsion of the kulaks. As we were going out, the young Englishman introduced himself to his compatriot. It turned out, very much to my surprise and to that of the little guide, that the courtly man with the beard had been Minister of Agriculture in the Labor government.

We laughed a good deal on our way back to Moscow over the Minister of Agriculture. I had sympathized with the little interpreter when he had been cross-examining her about the kulaks. "He was putting you on the spot,"

I said. "You don't know that American expression?"
"Yes," she said. "You mean, he thought I lived there."

———

At dinner, from the window of the Nóvo-Moskóvskaya.
The rain is coming up: as the wind blows in at the window, all the crystals on the chandeliers begin to jingle.
The deepening gray of the sky brings out the buildings
of the city so that their colors count a little more: dry
pale gray and pale straw or cream—what can you call
those neutral colors?—with their short rectangular windows in rows, rising to red roofs and a few sharp spires,
above the old wall with its regular slits and its vines
creeping up from the base, and the quiet river below,
rippling gently, not seeming to flow either way, with its
rowing parties, its slow little speedboats.

———

They have been whitewashing everything in Moscow.
The Russians know how to avoid running into it, but the
foreigners get it all over them and are always brushing
one another off. The foreigners call it "culture."

———

The lady from whom I took Russian lessons was the
wife of an old Social Democrat and had lived for many
years in exile; she had spent some time in England at
Cambridge. I remarked that Cambridge was a beautiful
place. "Yes," she answered drily. "I used to say it was a
pity I was not Chekhov—because if I had been Chekhov,
I should have had some excellent subjects at Cambridge."

———

Borodín: big straight-standing man with a fearless,
direct, dark-eyed gaze; square face, square broad shoul-

off, they don't need it so much any more." My attention
was called to the fact that the portrait of Engels has been
dropped from the big public celebrations. He has, in
fact, pretty completely evaporated, and even Marx is beginning to dematerialize.

———

I understand that the Society of Old Bolsheviks has
lately been liquidated by Stalin. Our Ambassador, William C. Bullitt, was telling me of a conversation he had
had with a highly placed Communist. He had asked who
would be Stalin's successor if anything happened to
Stalin: would it be, he suggested, Voroshílov, the popular
Commissar of War? "Voroshílov?" replied the Communist. "Oh, no: Voroshílov is a Bolshevik."

———

The Park of Culture and Rest* is neutral, enormous,
bare, colorless. It is impossible to imagine till you see it
a world without paints or dyes. There are a few indispensable red flags in the Park of Culture and Rest, but,
in general, there is no more color than you find in a
photograph in either clothes, posters, buildings or signs
—nor in faces: the people are pale like all people who
live in cities. Vast expanses of wide dirt walks, recently
scraped out on the shadeless site; only meager sprigs of
trees, dim grass. In the eating pavilion, where the women
in sneakers, the men without neckties, the shaved-headed
children, drift in by the thousand and are gradually
served, there are only heads of purple hortensia among
the bottles of pale yellow wine and the Soviet chocolate
slabs spiral-piled on the bar. To an American, it seems
like limbo—for we, in our amusement parks, have wild

* It would probably be better translated "Park of Recreation and
Training," but this is what everybody calls it.

games and giddy music; we squeal and guffaw and shriek. But these people move very slowly; they neither laugh aloud nor sing, they seem not even to talk to one another, and in their faces there is no expression. Are they afraid of being overheard? are they afraid of being arrested for "hooliganism"?—or have their hardships sobered them so terribly?—or are they still so numb and dumb from their old subhuman life of serfdom that they have not yet been able to discover how human beings enjoy themselves?

Yet at the same time—it is one of the paradoxes of Russia which make it so hard to explain to people who have not been here—one finds here a kind of freedom that one does not feel in other countries. Here nobody is socially self-conscious; nobody is disagreeable or rude. There is no class of petty officials who snap at people and keep them from doing things. If one carelessly throws anything away, one at once picks it up again: one remembers that there is an old woman standing by with a long-handled broom and a long-handled shovel, who is ready to scoop up a cigarette butt the moment that one is dropped, and one's relation to this old woman is already quite different from one's relation to the people who sweep up parks at home. Here the people in the park do own it, and they are careful of what is theirs. A new kind of public conscience has come to lodge in these crowds.

One wanders with the flaccid stream, dazed by the wanness and rawness. The amusements are mostly intended to train people for aviation—for aviation and war. The young people go in for contrivances like metronome pendulums upside down, which swing them over and back, in order to get themselves accustomed to looping the loop in the air; or, to develop their sense of equilibrium, they balance on narrow rails and try to knock each other off by slapping their right hands together; or they jump from a spiral tower in parachutes fastened to strings. Sometimes the parachutes get caught, and they remain dangling half-way down. One tries an exhibition of paintings, and it turns into a revolutionary museum, where little children who have come out for a holiday are looking at photographs of Communists having their penises strung up by Nazis and wax tableaux of women with their breasts cut off.

In the depths of the park, one finds at last a corner of natural trees and grass. To the music of a three-piece orchestra, a little group of young people in a clearing are dancing an old-fashioned Russian dance. It is simple, very quietly cheerful; they dance round and round in a ring, the same figures, the same little tune, again and again and again. A group of girls on a grassy bank—an outing of some sort of girls' club—are singing an interminable and sad-sounding song, an old ballad, I was told by my Russian companion, lamenting the plight of young daughters married off against their wills.

One returns and tries a movie: *The Golden Lake,* a very poor adventure picture, with scarcely a tinge of imagination. It is almost with a shock one realizes that it is possible for a Soviet film to be mediocre and dull.

At last, one decides to leave. The entrance is decorated with flowerbeds, planted on steep banks, that make portraits in pansies of Lenin and Stalin. Outside, the toneless loud-speaker is relaying *Cielito Lindo* and *Oi Mari,* the songs of happier ages, brighter climes.

The whole world is stalled today. Capitalism runs down, ceases to function; Communism makes little progress. The nations and the classes wait. We go neither forward nor back, we hardly know which way we are facing. And in the meantime, while the capitalist New Deal goes through its unreal motions of imitating the Five-Year Plan, even in the Soviet Union the weight of the heavy old society dragging down the world outside, the old fear of the rapacity of one's neighbor, must obstruct the way to health and freedom.

———————

He had refused a cognac at dinner. Later we went to the Artistic Café (this kind of thing is new, too), and he suggested a bottle of wine (hm?), then he decided that, as for himself, he would rather have an ice. He asked me whether I'd have coffee, and I said I'd have an ice—so he ordered an ice for me and coffee for himself. Then he lightly and brightly suggested cognacs. He always gives money to beggars, which one is not supposed to do. [This was Prince D. S. Mirsky, the critic, who had been converted to Marxism and had recently returned to Russia under the protection of Gorky.]

———————

[My enthusiasm for the manners of the Muscovites did not receive very much encouragement from persons who had been living in Moscow. When I spoke of it to an Englishwoman who was married to a Soviet official, she exclaimed, "Why, we're perfectly bloody, aren't we?" I mentioned the behavior of the people on the street-cars. "One reason they behave themselves," she answered, "is that they can be fined for 'hooliganism,' if they don't." When I told Mirsky that I found the people amiable, I was made to feel by his silence that this had not been his own experience. I pled in evidence how sweetly I had been smiled at by a woman who sold tickets in the subway. "She was probably laughing at your Russian," he said. At last, when I had been there longer and got to know my Russian friends better, I commented to one of them on the quietness of the crowds in the Park of Culture and Rest, compared to American crowds. After a moment, she replied in a low voice, *"C'est que tout le monde a très peur."*]

I stood against the wall under the archway beside a sharp-nosed green-eyed girl, together with a lot of other people who had wanted to get out of the rain. The rainstorm had turned into a hailstorm, and now something like a cloudburst occurred. A sudden torrent of water came flooding the arcade from the courtyard, and, like a river, swept through to the street. I had thought that it was all a damned nuisance; but none of the Russians caught there showed any sign of anxiety or irritation, and now that they seemed about to be inundated, they all began to laugh. The moment it was over, they knew, and—where, in any other city, some would uncertainly have lingered—everybody at once slipped away.

There is a green-eyed kind that wouldn't be gentle. I saw a girl in a street-car whose green eyes gave a hard jewel-point to her prettiness and plumpness: a kind of beauty I had never seen; and then, in another street-car, a boy with the same kind of eyes, very thin, at once wolfish and fascinating; he was staring as if he saw something that the rest of us didn't see, as animals do when they hear or smell—or rather, perhaps, as if he saw what we saw with far more intensity than we did.

Bolsháya Ordýnka, where I rented an apartment: named after the Tartar Horde, with a few squat Tartar houses; formerly a section of merchant residences. Old white walls and wide courtyards, with some careless Russian greenery seen through gates. Old churches, closed and dead, faded pink or carnation: if they would only repaint them, the city would be gayer. They are loading some kind of archives into one of them.

One gradually comes to realize that, though the people's clothes are dreary, there is little, if any, destitution; though there are no swell parts of the city, there are no degraded parts either. There are no shocking sights on the streets: no down-and-outers, no horrible diseases, no old people picking in garbage pails. You get to like the little women with their socks and their flat sneakers, with their babies all so nicely wrapped up and delivered to them fresh from the hospital. They are certainly much surer of their babies than the women of the poor with us. One finds, to be sure, in Moscow, among the official and professional groups, a good deal of disquietude and strain, but in an ordinary neighborhood like this, one feels a kind of assurance that doesn't exist with us. The certainty of work means a lot. It is partly on this account, I think, that, in spite of the difficulties involved in getting to and living in Russia, it has, contrary to what I expected, seemed to me a relaxation. At home we are apprehensive because life has grown more precarious, tending to go to pieces as the force which has carried it slackens.

When I am coming home late at night, I like to pass the quiet young people in their pale summer shirts and dresses, as they stand on the pavement talking.

(It is perhaps the Russian temperament, too: see the tranquilizing effect that a visit to tsarist Russia had on Rilke.)

It seems to be peculiarly difficult to write calmly about the Soviet Union. People invariably come here, whether

they think they are for or against, in such an inflamed
state of mind; and even those who are least inflammable
are subject to strange alternations of enthusiasm and dis-
appointment. The trouble is that people can't help feeling that the Soviets have challenged the world, and we,
in turn, challenge them to stand and deliver—with the
result that the traveler is likely to put down everything
that happens to him, good or bad, to the workings of
socialism. When his baggage does not turn up, he decides that the Soviet system is a failure; if he runs into
an amiable official who arranges to have something done
for him, he concludes that the Russian peasants are the
happiest in the world.

From this tendency these notes, I daresay, are not altogether free. I have finally been given a visa which en-
ables me to stay here three months, to spend rubles instead of valuta, and to go and live where I please.

Dinner, and party afterwards. Foreigners and Russians; Americans and English; Negroes and Whites. One
thing which the Soviets have certainly done is simplify
social relations. It is, I suppose, easier for people of all
kinds to get together and enjoy themselves and communicate with one another here than anywhere else in the
world.

After vodka and wine at dinner, I sat bemusedly gazing—through unevenly-divided double panes, old white
rather tasteless lace curtains, and a drooping, pretty, silly
hanging fern—into the light of the late evening sky, a
pale gray and a pale unluminous orange, the loose green
leaves: Russia.

L.'s maid was there to help with the dinner and came to
the party, too. She was older than L. and took care of
her, and they were very fond of one another. At some

point in the evening L. would always come and sit beside her, and they would put their arms around one another. But the maid—from shyness, I imagine—declined invitations to dance, and when L. had gone off with a partner and the maid had sat down in her place, she would get up as soon as L. came back and give her her seat again. I had supposed at first that their affectionate relations were entirely the result of socialism. But it was obvious that the habits of the maid had been more or less conditioned by the old regime; and I daresay that the relations between mistress and maid before the Revolution—especially a mistress as darling as L.—would not have been so very different. Socialism, which had in Russia, from the point of view of industrial development, a very unfavorable field, had, from the point of view of democratic manners, a ground exceptionally well prepared in the natural friendliness of the Russians. It is strange to think that L. and her maid, sitting and watching the dancing with their arms around each other's shoulders, should represent, through a short circuit of history, at once an anticipation of the classless society of the future and a survival of feudal relations.

I took M. D. home in a droshky: transparent night with a bright crescent moon in the sky of almost day—clacking over the cobbles, the droshky shaking from side to side. At a cross street we had to stop while scores of young men on bicycles passed by us as silently and softly as some sort of migration of night-moths. We talked about Lenin and Jesus, Communism and Christianity; the differences in capacity between men; whatever the more "molecular" Marxists may say, this adoring devotion to the memory of Lenin is the measure of his superiority.

———

Dinner in the Sokólniki Gardens: infinitely more attractive than the Park of Culture and Rest—quite entrancing, in fact, in the evening. It was originally the hunting park of Iván the Terrible (*sokólniki* are hunters of falcons); and it was later made a public garden. There are tree-planted walks, secluded benches and a gay little restaurant with an orchestra, tables under the trees and *cabinet particuliers*. It reminded me of old Europe, of Carlsbad; but it is not merely idyllic, it has a wildness which is entirely Russian. The park proper gradually merges with a slender disheveled forest in which people like to lose themselves and lie about among mossy tree-roots. I was told that the "more intelligent people" came here.

As we were standing in the restaurant waiting for a place, a dark man who was eating alone invited us to sit down at his table. My companion [D. S. Mirsky] and I were carrying on in English a long conversation about literature, which it seemed to us the dark man was following. It seemed to me, also, that my Russian friend was laying down, in our discussion of Joyce, a somewhat narrower Marxist line that he might have if we had been alone. The stranger, as he got on with his wine, began smiling and chuckling to himself in such an eerie and disquieting manner that my companion addressed him in Russian. He turned out to be a Turkish businessman.

[The one important aspect of the Soviet Union that I purposely soft-pedalled when, in 1935, I first prepared these notes for publication was a kind of class stratification that was already well advanced. The point about the amenity of the Sokólniki Gardens in contrast to the Park of Culture and Rest was that the Park was intended for the populace while the gardens were frequented exclusively by the privileged and better-paid groups: the Red Army, the secret police, the "technicians" and the government officials. I soon realized that the relatively well-dressed, often uniformed, men strolling with their wives and girls in the dark foliaged alleys of the Gardens would never have deigned to be seen in the wastes of Culture and Rest. They were already a new aristocracy who looked down on the hurrying driven hordes.]

————

There are moments when the evasiveness, the procrastination, the imprecision and the meekness of the Russians bring out the Iván the Terrible in all of us.

————

It is quiet in the Bolsháya Ordýnka. Little naked children play in the courtyard; the radios make an overtone of old waltzes. There is a bookcase full of books about Russia, and I lie on the couch and read them. I can understand how people become fascinated with Russia: the old ambiguous borderland between the West and the East, uncharted, unsurveyed, undelimited, unplowed, unmastered, unaccountable till now to civilization. The people seem to have deep resources, like the minerals of Kúznétsk and the Urals, whose existence has only just been discovered. All about me is the murmur of life—a life immense and amorphous. What is beneath it, still unknown, unimagined?

————

Faces that seemed blank or coarse are suddenly suffused with gentleness or the most sensitive understanding.

————

In no country I have ever been in, even France, has literature such prestige as in Russia; in no country, even in the Germany of the day before yesterday, has science commanded such respect. Books at the present time are hardly less necessary to the Russians than food and clothing themselves. Even the factories have their bookshops.

Abolish the church with its spiritual direction, and put in place of a government based on divine right a government supposed to be derived from a scientific view of history, and you shift to the strictly human sources of order and inspiration a kind of anxious attention which they have rarely enjoyed before. With the passing of the pageantry of church and court, the theater becomes more important. There has been in our own time no parallel— even in the case of Anatole France—to the position of Gorky in the Soviet Union. In the past a close friend of Lenin's, he is at present a kind of Commissar of Literature, and has perhaps come closer at the present time to sharing the glory of Stalin than any other public figure.

The effect on a writer of a visit to Russia is therefore both flattering and sobering. Nowhere else in the world does the writer receive so much honor; nowhere else to the same degree is he made conscious of responsibility. At first, he is likely to find this exhilarating. For from the Marxist point of view, a writer is not guilty of exploitation, and, in consequence (unless he is a Communist and has to give half his earnings to the Party), there is no way, outside the regular taxation, to prevent him from making profits. The result is that Soviet writers, if there is any considerable demand for their work, achieve not only distinction, but a higher standard of living than most of their fellows. Yet when one has looked at things a little more closely, one comes to have certain doubts as to the advantages enjoyed by these writers. There is the same temptation here as elsewhere to cash in on a popular success by playing up to the official point of view; and serious writers whose points of view do not easily fit in with the official one are obliged to take certain losses just as they are in the other kind of society. So that the same sort of antagonisms as elsewhere arise between the writers who have taken the losses and the writers who have cashed in on the market. Alexéy Tolstóy, for example, seems to present the perfect Soviet equivalent to the high-grade *Saturday Evening Post* writer. (I have heard him compared by a Russian to Booth Tarkington and Joseph Hergesheimer.) You find, when you ask people what they think of him, that they either consider him, or pretend to consider him, the best living Russian writer after Gorky or that they do not want to talk about him at all.

There is perhaps a danger in Russia that the writers may become a privileged caste, that they may approximate, even, to a priesthood. In Moscow, there is a special apartment house built by the government for writers, in which most of them seem to be living (though others have obstinately stood out for seclusion from their professional fellows). The government, however, has so far opposed all attempts of organized groups to get the backing of official authority. The official liquidation of RAPP was a blow against literary intolerance (though, characteristically, the government has gone to the length of putting a ban on RAPP that makes it impossible for its leaders to continue to express their opinions, and has prohibited the organization of any literary group whatever). The insistence by Stalin that Pasternák and Bábel be included in the delegation to the Writers' Congress that is to take place in Paris this summer is evidence of a disposition to put a higher value on men of artistic ability, irrespective of their political zeal, than on writers whose only virtue is political correctitude—as Mayakóvsky, who, during his lifetime, was suspected of romantic individualism, seems to have taken his place, since his death, as the sole unquestioned classic of the Revolution. There has certainly prevailed of late a more general respect for art and a freer attitude toward technique.

The new official policy on this was formulated by Rádek and Bukhárin at the All-Union Congress of Soviet Writers in August, 1934. The first period of the Revolution, said Bukhárin, was a period of slogans in literature; the second, the era of the Five-Year Plan, a period of concrete reporting; the third, which was then beginning, was a period in which it would be required that literature should present life more fully and in which it would be necessary for Soviet writers more fully to master technique. While rejecting the ideology of the bourgeois masters, they should study them and learn from them technically: contemporaries as well as classics. To a foreigner there is something a little pedantic in these efforts on the part of officials to prescribe to the writer what and how he shall write: the Communists can no more provide formulas for the masterpieces of "socialist realism" than the Humanists of the school of Irving Babbitt and Paul Elmer More formulas for masterpieces of Humanism (though Bukhárin speaks also of "socialist romanticism" and makes his definitions wide enough to cover hypothetical Soviet works of the type of Goethe's *Faust*). About the only thing you can do is to make the classics accessible and to hope for writers of talent who will be able to profit by reading them.

But this is, in effect, what it comes down to. There are moments, to be sure, in Russia—in a revolutionary museum, for example—when one is still made to feel that the beginning of thought has been dated from the first formulation of Dialectical Materialism. But it is obvious that the Soviets are now working very earnestly to reestablish the continuity of the Russian literary tradition. No longer, as before the Revolution, preoccupied with the literature of the West, they have turned back to find in their own literature a treasure which has come to seem more precious and which they are exercising the utmost diligence to add to and preserve. The first complete edition of Tolstóy is appearing in many volumes, with the excisions of the tsarist censor repaired, and a new edition of Lérmontov, including the bawdy *Sáshka,* which was formerly considered unprintable; they are bringing out the note-books of Dostoevsky and new biographical documents (in spite of his counter-revolutionary *Possessed*), and have announced the publication of new material by Turgénev. They have been celebrating officially this year the seventy-fifth anniversary of Chekhov's birth. As for Pushkin, he has become, under the Soviets, the object of such a cult as Shakespeare has never enjoyed in England. They have even named a kind of sweet cracker after him: there is a picture of him on every box.

They have, also, set out to translate into Russian the classics of the world *in toto*. The latest treasures from the ancient world that had come through to them at the time I was in Moscow were Seneca's tragedies and Lysias' orations. The most popular Soviet dramatist at the present time seems to be William Shakespeare; nor could I see that he was being mistreated. They seem to have got past the stage when they insisted on representing Hamlet as scheming for the crown against Claudius. No new emphasis that I saw in the theater was anything more than the special emphasis which every period and every country has given to its versions of the classics.

The truth is that literature is one of the things for which the Russians have a special genius; and it is probably in the long run impossible to fool them about the quality of writing. They may more easily be satisfied with railroads which, for Americans, are beyond indignation than with the kind of inferior literary goods that they seem to have been getting since the Revolution (due, of course, to the fact that such periods can never encourage the arts; the great writing of the Russian Revolution was done by Lenin and Trotsky).

[I was altogether too optimistic: Gorky's death and the purges of Stalin were soon to put an end to these tendencies.]

The effect of all this upon me was the opposite of the effect I have noted at home, on writers with revolutionary leanings, of repercussions from the Soviet Union. I found in the apartment where I was staying a volume of Elinor Wylie's poems, containing a number of posthumous ones that I had not seen before; and, though I had always had a feeling that her later work was somehow inferior to her early work, an impression that, ingenious though these later poems were and consummate in craftsmanship, they had tended to become more and more like a collection of expensive objects imported by an American connoisseur from abroad, I found that now, in the Soviet Union, they seemed to me more admirable than they had before. I had seen how the new Soviet poets had had to go to school to older writers who, though friendly to the Revolution, were not essentially revolutionary poets—men like Pasternák and Bagrítsky, who seemed to stand to the new generation somewhat in the relation of Eliot and Yeats to us; how they had had to fall back on tools which had been forged for other uses. I had been surprised to be told of the esteem in which even the exile Búnin was now held and of his influence on Soviet fiction. But, after all, in writing as in other things, there is only one kind of excellence. You cannot learn to write well from poor writers, however correct their position may be; and when you are cut loose from supernatural guidance, when money has lost its prestige, when you are thrown into a crude and disorganized world with nothing but the human intellect to organize, to guide, to refine, you realize suddenly how very seldom this intellect is capable of high-grade work. Where literature must take over duties which it has hitherto shared with religion, the genuine masters of literature are seen to bulk larger, stand taller, on an earth that is no longer overhung by the Heavens. As I reread Elinor Wylie, I kept thinking, what a marvelous language! What crystalline colors, what palpable textures! What resource, what felicity, what wit! I had never before felt so vividly the rarity and the value of people who could do something fine very well.

As I was walking one evening in the Tverskáya with a well-known Russian critic [Mirsky], a little stocky man who passed us contemptuously called out my companion's name. The latter explained to me that the man was a poet, whose works he had criticized adversely. We went into a restaurant, and the man came in, too, and sat down at a table with another man and in a loud voice abused the critic.

The next time I saw my friend, he told me that the poet was in jail. He was, it seemed, a Cossack from the Urals, who had been "writing in praise of the old Russia" and making himself obnoxious in various ways. One of the things he admired in the old Russia was its implacable anti-Semitism, and he was attempting to remain true to the tradition. Having some grievance against a Jewish poet, he went and beat him up in his lodgings. As a result of this, a petition to the authorities was signed by most of the principal poets of Moscow, recommending a

jail sentence for the Cossack. He was accordingly sent up
for six months.

———————

Visits to the *dácha*. It had once belonged to a rich
businessman of Moscow, who had been one of the patrons of the Art Theater. Now there were several families
in it, and it was rather like a summer boarding-house. It
is hard to find words for this countryside: loose, level,
untrimmed, running to wilderness. The groves of wild
wispy trees produce a peculiar delight and yet elude the
grasp of the mind, as the landscape is free from cultivation. The crows are cawing among these trees in the late
never-ending afternoon, as I left them doing at home in
New Jersey; but it seems to me that these are Russian
crows and that I don't know what they are saying. There
are glimpses of big light-brown summer cottages built in
the last half of the last century (and now used for rest-
homes and sanitariums) with cupolas and jigsaw woodwork, not unlike such houses on the Jersey coast, and yet
rather unlike them, too. So the life continues to escape
me: there is no emphasis in it, no schedule, everything
flows easily into something else. This *dácha* is like
Chekhov's plays. There are young people playing games;
a "master of the *dácha*" in a white Russian shirt, who
gets up early in the morning and works in a weedy
untidy garden, where he raises great pink and white
peonies; a lady who is always singing and acting out old
snatches of comic songs. Somebody is always sitting
down at the piano, and somebody else may or may not
drift up and begin to sing what he is playing.

———————

The G.'s entertain their many guests and dispense their
generous hospitality in one room of an apartment en-

try in Moscow, where eight families, which include thirty people, are living. They all use the same toilet and kitchen. Around the big table in the crowded room, with the vodka, the cherries and the herring, some of the jolliest evenings I have ever spent. If anyone starts to sing after ten, his companions have to make him be quiet, on account of the other people in the entry.

A girl in a red dress sits reading in the dark hall. She is the daughter of a Communist who lives in the entry, and now that she has finished school, she doesn't know what to do with herself. She is sulky because, unlike her friends, she can't go to a *dácha* for the summer. Stays at home and quarrels with her parents. She reminded me of girls in small towns in the States, in the days before everybody had a car, as I used to see them in summer, stagnating on their porches.

[One day at the G.'s' there appeared a very boisterous and jovial peasant writer. He told a story that had everybody roaring. Afterwards, it was explained to me: but, though G.'s English was usually adequate, he had a certain difficulty here in finding the right name for the animal which was the subject of the story. This was actually a lynx, *rys'*, but *rys'* also means "to trot"; and when, looking it up in the dictionary, he gave a Russian o-sound to "*trot*," I assumed that the creature was a trout, till the course of the story showed plainly that this could not be the case. He then tried the other meaning, but the name given was *leopardus*. The story thus came through to me as follows: "The director of Zoopark [the Moscow zoo] has sent out invitation to provinces to notify if interesting animals are found. In Urál Mountains dey catch kind of interesting deer, and dey notify Moscow. Dey send man from Zoopark—he must travel two weeks. In de mean-

time, dey have put interesting deer in cellar, which is all
dark, and dey don't feed him anyting. When man from
Zoopark arrives, deer is dead—dey have to stuff. Afterwards, dey catch Leopardus, and same man from Zoopark makes trip to Uráls—two weeks he travels. Dey
have put Leopardus in same dark cellar, and dey don't
feed him anyting, but Leopardus is more healthy dan
deer, and he lives. When man from Moscow arrives, he
says, 'Bring me Leopardus.' Dey say, 'We fear dis animal—he has not had anyting to eat.' Dey expect man
from zoo to catch, but he says, 'I do not catch, I only
transport—dat is not my work.' An old man who likes to
boast says he will catch Leopardus: 'I have hunted volks
in Kavkáz, tigers in Seebeér! Why should I fear
Leopardus?' He drinks a litre of vodka—den he drinks
udder litre—den he goes down to dark cellar wit rope.
Leopardus is crouching in corner, and when he sees old
man coming to him, he says, '! ! !' [a hideous spitting
snarl]. De old man runs upstairs—he says, 'Dat not
Leopardus. Dat devil!' Nobody wants to catch, so dey
offer money for who will catch. A bright boy says he will
catch—he is very brave, Young Peeonér. He goes down
into cellar with rope, and he puts it around Leopardus's
neck and pulls him up de stairs. Den he ties him to tree.
Problem is how to transport. De man who has come
from Moscow says dat he will not confine Leopardus, he
will only transport when Leopardus is in cage or box. De
boy has bright idea. He has wagon brought under limb
of tree, and he puts rope over limb, den he pulls up
Leopardus and drops him in de wagon—but de rope
around de neck choke him. He is dead—dey have to
stuff."

On another occasion, the same man appeared and told
another hilarous story, which was relayed to me as
follows: "Zoopark has wanted a peefón [we got this

straightened out as "python"], so dey have bought one from a German zoo. De boy who is bringing it in a car has his sweetheart, and when dey are going back to Moscow, he begins to make love to her in car. Dis make de pyton excited, and he begins to tink about a mate. He escaped from car and went away at rate of fifty kilometers an hour." I asked if they had been able to locate him. "Dey know where he is," said G., "but dey wait till he eats someting solid."

The meagerness of the specimens in the Zoo did not contradict these stories. The only animals I clearly remember were several stuffed bears—as usual, reared on their hind legs.]

———

[In telling the Zoopark stories, G. had been perfectly solemn where the original narrator was bursting with laughter. I much enjoyed his solemn humor. He was a tall shaved-headed middle-aged man of rural Tatar origin and a courageous revolutionary past. He had steely blue-gray eyes and a face that was completely impassive. One day when we had been going through the Historical Museum, I commented on the griffins which were such a frequent motif of the early Scythian art. "I like griffins," he said. "Don't you like griffins, Wilson? I don't know how it is to eat, but I like to see dem!"

One evening he and his wife and I were invited to Louis Fischer's house. G. was a little tight, and his wife was afraid he would make a faux pas. He had already been in trouble, had done time on the White Sea Canal, for having been overheard in a restaurant inveighing against some government policy, and his wife had pledged herself to the authorities that nothing of the kind should occur again. He accepted such submissiveness with difficulty. He had done his Siberian exile be-

fore the Revolution, and he felt that it gave him some
right to criticize the regime he had fought for. "Some
people change," he said to me once, fixing me with his
piercing unblinking eye (the *pristalny vzglyad* of the
Russian novelists that always appears as an exceptional
phenomenon). "But I *never* change!" On this occasion,
however, he was full of deadpan high spirits. He spoke
to a girl on the tram and asked her whether she was
taking those lilacs to her sweetheart, and when she answered, "No: to my mother," he told her that she ought
to be taking them to her sweetheart. "I don't have a
sweetheart," she answered, "so I am taking them to my
mother." When he asked the way of the boys in the
street, they would follow him, impressed by his tall upright figure. At one point, he suddenly left us to escort
an old woman across the street, though she said she could
manage very well by herself. When I asked him why he
had done this, he replied that there had just been an editorial in *Pravda* telling people to be kind to the old
and help them to cross the street.

John Gunther and his wife were in Moscow, and the
Fischers had invited them and me to meet an official
called Umánsky, then in charge of the press relations.
Umánsky was energetic and obviously ambitious, a dark
un-Russian Bessarabian, who spoke German, French and
English perfectly. I disliked him at once—all the more
because I knew I should have to depend on him to get
an extension of my visa, which Fischer was trying to arrange. I later had to go to see him and attempt the distasteful task of convincing him that I had not associated
myself with certain criticisms of the recent trials that had
been made in the United States. At the Fischers', soon
after arriving, this rather domineering visitor gestured
toward a shelf of bottles which he saw on the opposite
wall, and said to Mrs. Fischer, "You will give me some of

that brandy." (He was later the Soviet ambassador to Mexico and was killed making a flight in a plane, which he had commandeered from the Mexican government in, I suppose, the same imperious way.) Gunther asked him some direct questions about what was going on in Russia, and as soon as they began talking politics, the G.'s picked up volumes of Pushkin which happened to be lying around, and became absorbed in this classic. Umánsky soon proceeded, with some arrogance, to denounce, for his attitude toward Russia, the editor of the *Chicago Daily News*, for which Gunther was then correspondent; but Gunther at once put a stop to this by saying firmly that he couldn't listen to anything against his chief, and the conversation now relaxed in anecdotes about a "character," another correspondent of the *News*, who had threatened, in his Moscow hotel, completely to stop all tipping unless the bell was answered in four minutes, and had put a Yale lock on his door, then had locked the key in the room and had to break down the door.

When we had left, G. said—I think, truly—that the conversation had followed a course that was typical of American conversations: we were likely to begin with high politics, then run to seed in funny stories. I expressed a low opinion of Umánsky, and remarked on the contrast between his real caliber and the formidable impression he was able to produce. "Yes," said G., "in another country, he would be simply an ordinary official, but here he has the Soviet power behind him." I realized how proud G. was, in spite of the punishment he had taken, of being a citizen of the Soviet Union. We sat up drinking vodka and cognac till half past three in the morning, in the dining-room of the Nóvo-Moskóvskaya, whose windows give a fine view of Moscow. The G.'s thought the dawn over the Kremlin was wonderful, though it seemed to me uninteresting enough—almost completely gray, with only a little washed-out yellow coming out above the bulbs and the Government buildings. G. said he had no use for anything that left the dawn out of account. Mrs. G. had exclaimed with pleasure, when we were on our way to the Fischers, at a little locust tree in bloom, and G. had invited me to admire the grass between the carline and the Kremlin wall. Now we gazed at the smooth gray and empty streets that went up the Kremlin hill, and this did have its grandeur in the early dawn; but I thought of the people who would soon be out and how dismal they would make it look.]

[They could not understand me as an American, because they thought all Americans were rich. I was wearing a shabby suit, with a hole in it I had not noticed till Mrs. G. called my attention to it and offered to sew it up. Her first way of accounting for this was in terms of Chinese politeness: an intentional dimming of splendor in order not to humiliate the natives. Later, she came to a different conclusion. "I understand: you are very poor," she said to me one day. "You were sent here by a Writers' Union."

A woman lawyer I met, who had seen a good deal of Europe, could not, she said, grasp America. She could not understand what their love-life was like. The only Americans she had hitherto known had been visiting engineers with whom she had had legal business. She had some curious stories about them. One man who had come to her for legal advice had married one of the girls —relatively high-class prostitutes—who pick up foreigners on the terrace of the Metropole Hotel. He had not known that the girl was a prostitute, and had only found it out a year or so after their marriage. She had apparently made him an excellent wife, but he now asserted indignantly that she had married him under false pretenses, and he wanted to bring suit against her to make her return the presents of jewelry and other things he had given her. The lawyer said she could not imagine that anything of the kind could occur with a Russian or a European.]

The Physcultúr Parade, one of the three great demonstrations of the year, the other two being the May Day Parade and the anniversary of the October Revolution. The Arcade Building opposite the Kremlin is hung with great faces of Lenin and Stalin and with pictures of runners and hurdlers so crude that they would disgrace an American billboard. The slogan, "Ready for Labor and Defense!"

The whole thing was quite different and more impressive than any American parade I had seen. For one thing, more people take part: there were a hundred and fifteen thousand men, women and children, and it took them six hours to file by or perform before the reviewing stand. They all wore white shorts and white athletic shoes and socks, and all had short round legs, and at a distance it was almost impossible to tell the women and the men apart. The principal colors were red, white and blue, with occasional variations of yellow and green, and the costumes, which were perfectly simple, had been designed with excellent taste. A band which seemed as big as a regiment played the same simple march from the film *Merry Fellows* over and over again.

They open with a singing of the *International*. Before the little lined-up round legs, a plain black car smoothly passes: in it are the head of Physcultúr, standing up with his arm raised in salute, and Stalin and two other officials, dressed in plain white suits. A cheer like a wave goes around the Square.

The parade now begins to march by. To an American, it seems a little comic to have a sports parade on this scale, or indeed to have a sports parade at all. We take tennis and basketball and bicycling and swimming and shooting for granted. It seems to us we have always been doing these things. But the Russians have only just got them. Before, under the old regime, they were pastimes of the privileged classes. It is only since the Revolution, with the foundation of proletarian athletic clubs, that the people have had sports equipment. What a novelty sport still is may be judged from the proportion of the people parading, the complete personnel of the sports clubs, to the Moscow population of four million. The young people, in all solemnity, have arranged a procession of extraordinary floats glorifying the various sports. There is an example of almost everything going on before your eyes on a float: a tennis-match on a moving court, with the fouls shooting off to the pavement; an imitation mountain-peak being scaled by mountain-climbers; a boxing-match; a football game; battalions of bicycle-riders; tumblers performing stunts inside the rims of great rolling wheels, a diver who dives into a tarpaulin; sharpshooters taking aim under difficulties and hunters bringing down stuffed birds; and, most sensational of all, a miniature inclined track with people running up and down it, as it is slowly wheeled along. There are men and girls posing in niches, or carried by the legs, standing upright, in awkward and unsteady postures. An enormous boxing-glove that marches, which flops to the rhythm of its carriers, like one of the dolls in the Macy's parade. Portrait after portrait of Stalin, with, rarely, one of somebody else: "Long live Comrade Stalin, best friend of Physcultúr!", "Thanks to Comrade Stalin for the good life!"

There passes a detachment of men with shaved heads, bare chests and fixed bayonets. It dawns on me only gradually that this is in reality a preparedness demonstration: "Ready for Labor and Defense!" A fleet of airplanes appear, flying in a formation that spells "Stalin." Black beelike bombing-planes swoop and zoom, menacing, loud and dynamic—then hurtle off, are soon specks in space. A boy goes up in a silver balloon and drops parachutes with wreaths of flowers.

Yet the effect of this is never really comic, as our American parades often are. It is too simple, too sincere —and too powerful. As the minute-hand goes round the Kremlin clock and the clubs keep on marching past with unabated earnestness and vigor, the impression becomes overwhelming. It remained with me the rest of the day. Even while I was dining with friends and when I went out to the *dácha* in the evening, those thick round bare legs in shorts were still marching on through my mind.

I did not stay to the very end. When the parade proper was over, there were Physcultúr mass dances in front of the official stand. I learned afterwards that the great final feature was the emergence from something or other of a gigantic portrait of Stalin.

———————

Everybody had to stand up through the entire afternoon. That was why I left after four hours. There were ramps in the stands that you could sit on; but if anybody attempted to do so, he was smilingly admonished by a militiaman that it was not polite to sit down. I asked several Russians why this was—they did not enjoy it any

more than the tourists—and they said that they didn't
know: it hadn't used to be like that. Finally, a Russian
told me that it was now forbidden to sit while Stalin was
standing up.

The whole thing, from the spectator's point of view,
was a good deal less democratic than any American parade. There were stands on only one side of Red Square,
and these, by American estimates, had room for more
people than were in them. Nobody was admitted to the
Square who did not have a ticket for the stands, and,
since the parade took place entirely inside the Square,
nobody else really saw it. Apparently the only persons
who are privileged to assist at these big demonstrations
are Communists, near-Communists and foreign visitors.
Many people I knew in Moscow, though they had made
repeated applications, had never succeeded in seeing
even a May Day celebration, and envied the fortunate
tourist.

The whole thing is an apotheosis of Stalin on a scale
that makes our poor patient presidents, standing up in
the raw March winds, with their silk hats held in their
hands, while other people sit comfortably with their hats
on their heads, seem the humblest of public servants.

This glorification of Stalin is undoubtedly one of the
things in Russia which affects an American most unpleasantly. The paper comes out almost every day with a
photograph of the "Boss" on the front page, either posing with a distinguished visitor or, if none happens to be
available, paying some sort of official visit; and every
speech and important public document ends with a tribute to Stalin, like the prayer at the end of a sermon.
Stalin is plastered all over the place, and even genuinely
popular figures such as Litvínov and Voroshílov are such

a long way behind him in publicity that they seem to belong to an inferior breed.

When I spoke of this to a Russian, I was told that Stalin himself did not like it. (I have, since returning home, heard the same opinion expressed by an anti-Stalinist Russian: "The situation is so tense," he said, "that they have to have an ikon.") The relation is reciprocal, no doubt, between Stalin and his worshipful public. An American in Russia who has become accustomed to the features which at first aroused his admiration—the natural democratic manners, the throwing-open of everything to the people—is likely, as time goes on, to begin to find himself repelled by what seems to him the cold-blooded manipulation of the people by the governing power. He may have left the United States with a conviction that his countrymen who keep up with the Joneses and believe what they read in the Hearst papers, are a conformist and credulous people; but by the time he has been long enough in Russia to react to the docility and timidity of the Russians, he is likely to come to the conclusion that, compared to them, the citizens of the United States are critical and self-reliant. One's instinct is to resent the brazenness with which the administration seems to direct and dragoon the people while always formulating its policies in some such language as, "The indignant proletariat demand the execution of so-and-so," or, "The victorious proletariat express their gratitude to Comrade Stalin for doing so-and-so." The American is antagonized by this, as he would be if it were done to himself—as indeed, he remembers unpleasantly, it was done, to some extent, at the time of the [first] World War.

Yet a reaction of this kind is misleading. This is not the United States, and the people here are different from us. The Russians, before their revolt, had had a paternalistic government for centuries; they had no democratic institutions: the dumas were the dolls of the Tsar. Remember that before the Revolution, eighty per cent of the Russians were illiterate. Remember that among these masses who march in a Physcultúr parade, there are men who have changed their names from Svinúkhin and Sobákin to Nóvy and Partisánov in order to destroy the memory of the time when their great-grandfathers and their grandfathers were exchanged for pigs and dogs, and to establish the mere human dignity which has been brought them by the Revolution. The dictatorship of so untrained a proletariat inevitably results in a state of things where the "workers and peasants," though the favored class, are dictated to by a governing group. The Soviet workers and peasants are educating themselves with avidity and have now, it is officially said, almost reversed the old illiteracy figures. They are taking with the utmost seriousness their unaccustomed duties of citizenship. But how can people who have just learned to read, who have never seen any other newspapers, be expected to criticize the Soviet press? How can they be expected to develop such political institutions as have taken the Western peoples centuries? In the meantime, for all their efforts at progress, there is always the tendency to lapse back into their earlier relation to the Little Father. Even if Old Bolshevik Stalin had not wanted to be Stalin apotheosized, the people would have tried to invent him. Remember that Lenin, at the present time, is appearing in person like any saint to the more primitive inhabitants of the Union, and that the reason why the visitors to his tomb are kept so rapidly moving is alleged to be a solicitude on the part of the authorities to avert miraculous cures. One has only to attend some great public occasion like the Physcultúr Parade, or even to hear the loud bursts of applause aroused by some popular play that has been written to point up a new policy, in order to be convinced that the relation between Stalin and his proletarian public is very close and strong. They not only fear Stalin: they trust him to see them through. There seems a real identification of will between Stalin and a central element of the people in whose name he speaks.

Admitting this, however, and with all respect for Stalin's abilities: his energy, his positiveness, his shrewdness, his adamantine adherence to his Marxism, with all appreciation of his cardinal importance in Europe at the present moment, is it wise for him to allow this deification to be carried as far as it is? It is true, I discover, in Russia not only that the name of Stalin cannot except furtively be taken in jest—when the radical caricaturist Will Low drew a sketch of him in the dust with his stick, a Russian who was with him smeared it out—but that there seems to be a tendency in some quarters to hesitate to utter it at all, as if it were the unpronounceable name of God. One finds people resorting to circumlocutions, just as in Italy, it seems, they refer to Mussolini as *"Lui."* On one occasion, when I was walking with a Russian in the streets of a country town, he started to make a statement that began, "Our big man—I don't want to say his name." I was prepared for some sinister revelation, but it turned out that he was only going to quote with approval something that Stalin had said in his interview with H. G. Wells. I suppose that the trouble was that he was afraid to be heard talking about Stalin to a foreigner in a foreign language. But, after all, as Van Loon has reminded us, Frederick the Great, that feudal autocrat, when informed that a poster he was trying to read was a satire directed against himself, walked on calmly, merely remarking that they ought to have hung it lower. I got the impression, although no one would admit it, that most intelligent Russians, however loyal to the Soviet state, were a little bit ashamed of all this. I have heard one person groan to another, unaware of a foreign presence, when he looked at the morning paper and was confronted with the inevitable cap and mustache.

This cult has nothing to do with Marxism and is not justified by a socialist dictatorship. Marxism regards the ruler as the human, and hence fallible, representative of the interests of certain human beings. Lenin was irreverent toward himself in the sense that he took himself seriously only as the agent of his cause. He cared nothing about power for its own sake; nothing about admiration. He always confessed and lamented his human errors of judgment. One cannot imagine Lenin, for all the popular devotion he commanded, allowing himself to be cast in a role such as that now assumed by Stalin—a role which gives constant encouragement to the people who want to make it out that the Soviets are the same thing as Fascism, and which invites the fate of Aristides. As the Russians become better educated and more capable of thinking for themselves, how, one wonders, may the more spirited young people eventually react to the ikon?

———————

The relation of the people to the dictatorship is the core of the whole Russian question and must be faced and honestly dealt with by any advocate of socialism in America. It seems to me obviously impossible that a socialist government in the United States should resemble the state of things in Russia; and it is totally unrealistic for either the opponents or the champions of socialism to talk as if socialism would mean for us the *naïvetés* of a Stalin regime. We have, to be sure, in the United States some miserable and illiterate groups; but we do not have a great feudal peasantry or a working class so primitive as Russia's. The farmers and working men and women, the disillusioned middle class and the radicalized executives and experts, who would have to put over socialism in America, would no more, in their political relations, be behaving like the Stalinist Communists and their Stalin-adoring constituents than they would be holding physical culture parades for the purpose of celebrating the bicycle, the basket ball and the tennis racket. In spite of much corruption and many absurdities, we have certainly learned something about self-government, just as we have learned to play outdoor games.

A curious incident illustrated—unconsciously on the part of the persons involved—the attitude of the Russians toward Stalin.

I had gone to the apartment of Russian friends and was talking after dinner with the husband. He was telling me about the tsars. He thought that Iván the Terrible was too pathological to be interesting. "But the people are supposed to have loved him," I said. "Russian-like," he replied, "the ones who survived were grateful because he'd spared their lives. They thought he was an able man —a little bit strong, perhaps!—but an able administrator. And the people he'd imprisoned and tortured and killed of course weren't there to object." Then he went on to Peter the Great, for whom he had a good deal of admiration. He told me how Peter had set out to do away with the old Russian beards. "He would wait for them to come along, and then when he would see one, he would say, 'Ah-ha!', and he would make the man come in and he would shave it off himself. You can imagine an ordinary ruler cutting off *one* beard to make an example; but Peter kept at it for two or three months!

He thought that all the old Russian traditions were nest-
ing in those big beards. — That's a strange thing," he
added, "which could happen only in Russia: that the
word of one man could regulate the habits and thoughts
of a whole people!"

The wife had gone to sleep on the couch, but when he
had finished with this subject, she woke. "I just dreamt,"
she said, "that Stalin and Kaganóvitch came up the stairs
here and came to our apartment. I was terribly frightened, but Stalin patted me on the shoulder—like this—
and smiled."

[One day I met Paul Strand, the photographer, in the
office of the travel agency through which both our trips
had been arranged. I had recently had difficulty in getting in touch with a man named Dynámov at VOKS, who,
like many up-to-date officials, had an ostentatious display
of gold teeth, and I suggested that he was absent at the
dentist's, having his few natural teeth replaced by gold.
There was also a question of some authorization that had
to be procured from the Kremlin and of a run-around
we were getting from a department there. Strand and I,
in our irreverent American way, improvised a little on
this: "Comrade Stalin has just stepped out to the toilet";
"Comrade Stalin is at home with a severe headache."
There was no Russian in the room except L., but the
office personnel were otherwise all English-speaking
pro-Communists who had come to work in the Soviet
Union. A terrible chill descended; the merry andrews
were stopped mid-quip, and since nobody would speak to
us again, we were obliged to slink out of the office. I
never ventured after this to take frivolously the name
of the head of the state. What was more unexpected,
however, I felt something of the same sort of tension

when I criticized Franklin Roosevelt. He was also the head of a state, and it made people nervous to hear me.]

Evening at the *dácha*. We walked to the end of a path while I looked out at the Corot-like birch-trees, flimsy and tall and slim, stringing a loose lacy screen against the sky, still, so late, translucent, the so slowly waning light. We sat down on a bench, and from the *dácha* next door the music of a radio came through to us, and we could see that there were people dancing, but there was shrubbery between us and them. It began to be cold, and we got up to walk.

I had had a dinner already in Moscow, but they insisted on my eating a second. The evening became very gay. The master of the *dácha* sat down at the piano, and the lady who liked comic songs gave us a Caucasian ballad about a woman who went down to the seashore to bathe and there met a dark Trans-Caucasian. When her baby was born, the husband said that he was glad to have a son, but he couldn't see much resemblance. Then they did the old dances, Russian and Gypsy and Ukrainian and Caucasian, with their stiffly held gestures and their stamping steps, and wound up with a touch of ballet. As we were leaving, the Master in the white blouse gave us a handful of his lovely white peonies, wet from the last of the innumerable showers that are a feature of the Russian summer.

When we went to catch the train back to town, it was late, of course, but then, when it did pull in, it immediately made a start as if to pull out again. We rushed aboard without saying good-by to the people who had come to see us off. But then it stopped and backed a little and stopped again. Our friends said good-by

through the window. Then the train seemed to start, and
we waved; but again it began to back. It started and
stopped and backed. Great gaiety: every time the train
returned, the lady who had sung the song would bow as if
acknowledging an encore, and wave her handkerchief in
burlesque farewell, calling out, *"Do svidánya! Do
svidánya!"* My companion said: *"Notre technique
magnifique: illustration pour vous!"*

At one of the stations on the way back to Moscow, two
dwarfish little stocky round girls got in and sat down beside us, opposite one another. They had just been seen
off by two boys, and their talk was all "he said" and "I
said." The prettier one, who was wearing, for the outing,
her best clean scarf tied around her head, bent forward
as she became more earnest and thrust her hands into the
lap of her companion, who, more dignified, cooler and
calmer, sat straight up in her seat and listened. It was a
story about going to a fortune-teller and giving her ten
rubles to read her palm: the woman had said a whole lot
of things but had told her nothing practical; at last, she
had got up indignantly and said that the woman had told
her nothing about whether or how soon she would get
married, and that she wanted her money back, and she
had started to grab it and go; but the woman had hung
on to the money and had said, "You'll get married!
You'll get married!"

Nobody approves more heartily of the more ruthless
policies of the government than P., a young American
living in Moscow. The very thought of the rebellious
kulaks makes him furious: they had "mutinied," he says,
and they "had to be taught a lesson." When Yenukídze
fell out of favor, P. declared that what they ought to do
was "put a little lead poison in his food." For another

young American, the son of an engineer, who has never fitted in in Moscow, he had a ready condemnation: "He always goes around by himself, doesn't talk to anybody, hasn't any friends: he's a regular Trotskyite!" If anyone expresses notions that seem to him out of step, he cries, "Let's have a necktie party!" P.'s family are always kidding him, and are rather troubled about him, because he has never had a girl.

———

A lady of the old bourgeoisie told me that, in earlier years, she had read Dostoevsky's novels as if they were fairytales: they seemed to her to have nothing to do with life. Women like her, she said, had lived pretty closely shut up in their houses. But then, when the Revolution opened everything up, she had seen all the types he describes. "He is very modern," she said. She keeps telling her daughter that she, the daughter, is a character out of Dostoevsky.

———

Opening of a new café in the National Hotel. Very modern and quite pretty bar, with the bottles spaced so far apart that it gives it that flimsy Russian look. Lights too lurid for the dancing. Lots of journalists and poets at the tables. I became aware of a row of dark presences peering in through the windows, over the curtains that half-screened them from the street; and when we left, we saw the people lined up outside with their eyes glued to the glass.

———

We went on to a Gypsy night club, in company with a Jewish columnist, whom we had met in the National café. As we were standing up in the tram-car, a man said

to him: "Don't crowd against me! I've got a sore knee!"
—and repeated an old Russian proverb: "No one can
feel the suffering of others." The columnist had a quick
repartee: "If we felt the sufferings of others, we'd never
be able to live. It's hard enough to bear our own." The
people in the car all laughed.

The Troítsko-Sergéevsky Monastery. It was founded
by a saint of the fourteenth century and, up to the Revolution, had been the principal Mecca of pilgrimage. Also,
I was told, a place, like Fontainebleau, to which lovers on
a holiday used to come. The Bolsheviks have cleaned out
the priests and monks, and now it is as empty as Carcas-
sonne. They have even renamed the railroad station and
have taken out all the seats—I suppose to make it
uninviting.

There was a miry road up the hill, past the dilapidated
droshkies. Then the rainbow delirium of the monastery
appeared, rising out of the irregular green countryside,
under the rain-gray sky, like a mirage of the Arabian
Nights: blue and gold, red and yellow and pink, a grove
of blue phallic spires painted with golden stars. Halfway
to Asia here!

We ate our lunch in a little green hotel, which seemed
to me the oldest and poorest and most primitive place of
the kind in which I had ever been. We had to pay for a
room for a day—it was not, to be sure, very much—in
order to get a place by ourselves to eat the picnic lunch
we had brought with us. There was a little narrow bed
and a colorless dirty couch, full of holes from which
the straw was sticking out. We laughed about it, sent for
a samovar, had vodka, bread and butter, sausage and
hard-boiled eggs, looking out on the monastery walls

and the muddy street of the village. Then just as the samovar arrived, they told us the museum closed at four, so we left the tea and hurried out to see it.

As we walked up the hill, past a booth for beer with a sign that said "American Bar," the little kids in the street, seeing our city clothes, shouted after us: "Moscow! Moscow!"

The monastery made upon me an overpowering and nightmarish impression. All this Byzantine stuff is so new to me that I am drawn out of my sightseer's detachment and lose myself in it completely. Uncomfortable combination of the cruel and the ugly with the pretty and sentimental; Coney Island full of torture chambers and charnel-houses. The Metropolitan's palace: he had a private shrine in his bedroom and little angels painted on the ceiling that look exactly like Renaissance cupids. In another room, there are horrible pictures of floggings and executions by landlords of the old regime, and a model of a peasant's izbá to offset the glamor of the palace. Heavy clumsy gaudy jeweled miters; ikons embroidered on tapestry in amethysts and pearls—including one which had occupied for years one of the wives of Iván the Terrible, when he had sent her into seclusion; a great store-room full of vestments, as varied and gorgeous as women's gowns, carefully put away on hangers and smelling strongly of moth-balls; a gigantic carved wooden wine-boat used by the bibulous prelates, at one end of which a kind of wild dog buries his teeth in the neck of a boar while at the other the handle is formed by the body of a horrid half-insectlike monster. A red and white church in five tiers, given by Catherine the Great, with a long straight stiff square steeple hardly less thick then the church. Frivolous diamonded walls in yellows and browns and blues, with spiral columns twined with painted vine-leaves. A little kiosque for holy water,

as fancy as Russian pastry: pink cream, domy crust, pillars like twisted rolls; and adorned with cupid-cherubim's
faces. Ignoble old tomb of the Godunóv tsars, in terrible
disrepair: somebody has broken a hole under one corner of the big marble lid—in the hope of finding something precious or, perhaps, out of simple curiosity; but
there is nothing to be seen inside except dirt. It seems
that they moved them out here because they were not
true Ruriks, and therefore didn't rate the Kremlin (so I
note that, whereas the Lenin Institute and the Marx and
Engels Institute are right in the heart of Moscow, the
Plekhánov Institute is a separate thing, away off on the
outskirts of the city). The big church behind the tomb
is now used to store cabbages and other vegetables: it
keeps them cool in summer. Church built by Iván the
Terrible to expiate the murder of his son—he had these
alternations of piety with crime: painted all over inside
with pictures of pink angels and saints that cover even
the thimble-cups of the domes. These six-winged angels
give me the willies; and I cannot like the Greek Orthodox
ikons, even the ones, like those of Rublyóv, that are good.
The early ones are so cramped and knotted, their gray
eyes so anguished and so broken to anguish, their souls
so tensely contracted. There is nothing of Fra Angelico
here; they shed forth no human tenderness. And the
later ones are saccharine and sickly. The miracle-breed-
ing bones of St. Sergius, now a museum-exhibit like another: an old woman who has come in behind us shakes
her head and rolls up her eyes, aghast at the desecration.

When we came out, I felt disquieted and rather disgusted. E. said that it had made her sad "to think that
people had believed all that," and that now it was as dead
as the Delphic oracle.

We returned to our room and went on with the tea, the
bread and butter, the sausage, the eggs and the vodka.

We talked about the past and the future. They had cut themselves loose from the past and they didn't yet have the future, for which they had worked so hard. "Come!" said G. "We do have this little room, this vodka, this bread, this sausage, this view of the old monastery— these are *now!*" Full of contentment, I gazed out the window. The sun had unexpectedly come out: the sky was for Russia quite blue, and the smallish white clouds were bright. Against them, an onion-topped spire pierced in the clear air; and below it, a red roof and a red fence set off as vivid white a low building with one row of square windows. A little gray foal with shaky legs came trotting down the sloping cobbled street in front of a horse and cart. Then appeared a queer open carriage, very dirty and rickety-looking, driven by a little boy, and with a lot of other little boys in a long sequence of seats behind him. I asked G. what this vehicle was, and he said it was a charabanc and slipped into a popular song:

> *Ekh, sharabán, da, sharabán,*
> *Ne búdet déneg—tebyá prodám!*
> *Ekh, sharabán,*
> *Da, trógai, trógai!*
> *A ya poidú*
> *Svoéy dorógoi!*

> (Ah, charabanc, yes, charabanc,
> If the money gives out, I must sell you!
> Ah, charabanc,
> Get along with you, giddyap!
> And as for me,
> I'll go my own road!)

They had sung it, he said, during the Civil Wars. It sounded older than that: the tune was like *Fair Evelina*.

How sweet the charabanc, the song, the little foal, the children, the sausage, our company drinking to the present—how welcomely human they seemed, after the miters, the cherubim, the tortured saints!

The train going back was crowded. We thought we were very lucky to get into a little shut-off apartment. But it turned out to belong to the conductor, who appeared and told us to leave. She said she had to have it to herself, for she had been on the train five days. Mrs. G. squeezed in on one of the benches, and presently the old woman sitting next to her fell asleep and toppled over on her shoulder. Later, when there was room on another bench for all of us to sit down together, Mrs. G. couldn't come over to join us because she didn't want to wake up the old woman. She sat there, glancing alternately toward us and down at the head of the woman, which tranquilly reposed on her bosom.

———

A political story brought back by a man who had been traveling in the provinces. In one of the towns he visited, there had been a brilliant theatrical director. This man had composed and put on a chronicle play of the life of Lenin, which had proved such a tremendous success that the town had held a banquet in his honor. It had taken place on the stage of the theater: toasts had been drunk and speeches delivered. The praise of the director was on every tongue. A little while afterwards, however, some political busybody of the town discovered that the play had been based on a little biographical sketch of Lenin written by Zinóviev years ago. This man immediately proclaimed that the production, deriving as it did from a notorious opponent of Stalin, who had just been disgraced and exiled, was corrupted with inaccuracies amounting to heresy. The director was called upon to answer these charges, and, a few weeks after the congratulatory banquet, he was arraigned on the stage of his theater, the same place where the banquet had taken place, and notified that he must leave the town.

The Russians have carried this kind of thing to most absurd and self-destructive lengths. They seem at present engaged in the same sort of effort to outlaw Zinóviev and Kámenev from their histories and their albums of the Revolution as was made, after the expulsion of Trotsky, to strike his name from the rolls of the Revolution. We were working, to be sure, in a similar spirit at home at the time of the War, when we were dropping German studies in the schools and renaming the sauerkraut and Hamburger steaks. But we have never yet, so far as I know, suppressed historical sources. It is one of the paradoxes of the Soviet Union that the country which most reveres science, which has in many fields proved itself most scrupulous in preserving the human record intact, should be capable of these ostrich-like attempts to conceal its own recent history. Certainly one of the very worst features which the Communists under Stalin have contributed to the working-class movement is this practice of systematic falsification.

Nevertheless, it is probably true that it is harder in the Soviet Union to fob people off with pure bunk than anywhere else in the world. The Communists have their own kind of cant, and their pronouncements are not always truthful; but they must always, in the long run, give way to any serious pressure from the people: they have to deliver the goods. When you have made a clean slate of the past, when you have got rid of all the devices for grinding out private profit which have come between the people and the fulfilment of their needs, you make it difficult to satisfy them with words. Think of the reservoirs of delusion and false values which flood our minds at home: the newspapers, the speeches, the sermons, the broadcasts, the sales talks, the advertisements! No matter how much we may think we see through them, we go around partly doped all the time. The Russians are far less free than we are to talk about certain things; but then, on the other hand, they escape a vast amount of pernicious nonsense. In this way, the Soviet Union is bracing.

———

Further visits to the *dácha*. Beneath the fluid surface, I begin to be able to see to the things that are happening below. The inmates are all technical and professional people, some of whom have known each other a long time; and they are living here at very close quarters, each family in a tiny room. There are ancient jealousies among them, dreadful ordeals and anxieties, difficult situations which have for years been mounting up to a crisis. I can see that even the comic songs of the lady who is always asking for music have their relevance to other things. But the texture and pace of their lives are so different from ours in the West.

———

We were waiting at the railroad station. On the platform across the tracks, a group of school-children, on an outing with their teacher, were waiting for the train back to Moscow. They were singing a little song which dealt, as my companion explained to me, with the forests, the fields and the birds. Today they were taught songs of that kind; formerly they had only been allowed to sing songs about the Civil Wars.

A group of soldiers, who were also waiting, presently began to sing. I asked what the song was about, and was told that this was a marching song. I said it seemed sad for a marching song, that most of the songs sounded sad. "*Avant la révolution*," my companion said, "*les Russes étaient très tristes. Maintenant ils sont tristes.*"

———————

"Big Carnival," the first they have had, and a part of their attempt to cheer up the people, but held between rainy days in the dismal Park of Culture and Rest.

This place seemed more awful than ever: it was heartbreaking to see the people strolling so listlessly and dumbly, in their carnival masks and false noses, along those wide naked paths. But what is it that is wrong? I keep asking myself. Where are the gaiety and the fantasy one does find, say, in the popular ballet of *The Three Fat Men* or in the scene of the Capulet's masked ball of the Komsomól *Romeo and Juliet*? I got detached, with two other Americans, from the party with which I had come. One of these was an American-born Russian Jew. He had Communist affiliations and he, too, had just arrived, but, reacting in the opposite direction, was lost in admiration for everything. He remarked, as he looked about him, on the excellence of the Russian taste in decoration, which is certainly one of the fields in which they are weakest; and he exclaimed that "even their names for things showed imagination," because they called a merry-go-round a "gay wheel," though I should have thought that "merry-go-round" was better. We had stopped to watch a typically Russian stunt that *did* show some imagination: a gigantic imitation horse, rigged up between two trees, which at intervals would rear and plunge forward, as if to trample on the crowd. [I had not then read Pushkin's *Bronze Horseman*, based on Falconet's statue of Peter the Great that seems to rear over Russia.] The people would laugh and get out of its way and stand in front of it a long time, watching it, waiting for it to make its next lunge and trying to figure out how it worked.

When we started to walk again, we found we had lost our companions. We looked for them, but it seemed to be hopeless. The Armenian writer and I decided we needed a drink. He had just come from Soviet Armenia, which he had visited for the first time and in which he seemed to have been rather disappointed. He had had, he said, no feeling at all of returning to a fatherland: the only Armenians he had liked were the kind who came to America and they were just like the ones that he knew at home. After struggling and waiting in line, we got hold of some sandwiches and vodka, and consumed them standing up. A man who had been hanging around behind us came forward and spoke to us in English. He said he had worked in America. The Armenian asked him whether he wasn't ever homesick. The man said, Yes, he liked it over there. "And doesn't it mean something to be an American?" the Armenian pressed him eagerly. "Don't you really feel that an American is better than anybody else?" We gave the man some vodka; and he asked us who we were; didn't we want to know about conditions—he could tell us more about things than anybody. He was a Dane and had a Danish self-conceit. He seemed to get very drunk and for some reason made us uncomfortable; we had difficulty in getting rid of him.

Then we stopped outside a movie and considered going in for the next show. Another man who had been standing around came up to us and spoke to us in English. He asked us what we thought of the Soviets—it wasn't up to our expectations, eh? Didn't we find that Intourist overcharged us. The Armenian was innocent and open, and told him that Intourist was terrible; the Russian-American thought it wise to move the Armenian on.

The Communist and I agreed, after we left, that the second fellow, anyway, was phony. In any case, we all decided that we didn't want to go to the movies. The Armenian still didn't understand why the Russian had wanted to get him away. "It's funny," he said, as we were walking toward the gate. "I was just trying to talk to them about their life." It later occurred to me that the Communist and I had probably had different suspicions —I, that the man was a GPU agent trying to provoke us to unfavorable criticism; he, that he was some kind of disloyal character trying to pour poison in our ears. "I'm going to write a story about this," said the Armenian, after a moment. "It's going to be called *A Good Time Was Had by All*."

———

Communoid: This word has been coined, in Russia, for a person who is not a Communist, but who tries to talk and act like one.

———

Free Day: rowing on the river. The little river itself was delightful, as it went curling through the even green countryside, almost level with the grassy banks. On one side of the stream there were meadows, which stretched away to vague farms in the distance. The other side was lined with bushes, and people were swimming there. They wore very few clothes or none. The Russians are queer about this. At the *dácha* from which we had started, it was considered extremely improper to put bathing-suits on in the house and then walk to the river in them. It was evidently some ancient convention that dated back, no doubt, to the era when women wore bathing-stockings. To be seen around the house in a bathing-suit was something, I was told, that was coun-

tenanced only at seaside resorts. What you were supposed
to do here was arrive in your clothes at the river; then
get undressed in full sight of everybody, laying your
clothes on the grass, which was always very wet from the
last shower; then put on a suit if you had one or, if you
didn't, just go in naked. The various parties of bathers
would usually make an effort to maintain a certain distance from one another; but there were so many people
today that this soon became impossible, and the occasional gestures of modesty—the trunks and the brassi-
ères—had a perfunctory look, slightly comic.

The people appeared to much better advantage without their clothes: Moscow clothes at the present time are
so much the same and so dreary that, in order to appreciate the Muscovites, you really have to see them nude:
blond girls with white skin, thick round legs, marvelous
big round breasts, who would flop into the water like
turtles; shaved-headed boys burned brown, with conspic-
uously white behinds that had been protected by trunks
up to the time they had decided not to bother with them.
The Russians in this part of the country have never really
learned to swim—I suppose they are learning now, along
with other kinds of sport; but they were having a very
good time. One man had put up a pup-tent; another had a
shack on a cliff, and the people in passing rowboats were
bantering him; another, with nothing but a jock-strap,
was practicing Physcultúr all by himself in a field. A
fisherman, short and fat, did some heavy and inexpert
casting; an elderly man and woman were sitting on some
kind of box, facing away from each other and both
reading the Moscow papers. A girl in a boat that passed
us suddenly blew a toy-whistle. It startled me: this kind
of thing, which Americans do on all occasions, is so very
rare around Moscow. But she was, after all, a Russian and
tooted only at long intervals—meditatively, as it were. We

watched the Vladivostók Express, very trim for a Russian train, crossing the railroad bridge and tooting away to the East.

We walked on past a beautiful herd of white goats which was grazing on the opposite bank, where there were meadows and no bathers, and came finally to falls and a dam, which prevented us from going further. We landed and pulled up the boat on the bank and stretched out on a fallen tree, taking the sun in our bathing-suits. There were crows and pies in the air; the birch-leaves were light as fuzz. My companion called my attention to some slight almost weedlike trees which were wry and leaning askew. In that landscape, so gentle and level, even such slight distortions as these seemed almost wildly grotesque. It presently began to rain, as it always did at some point every day, and we decided to go in the water. There was a rudimentary landing of planks which had been built by the workers of a textile factory a little way back from the river; and we would plunge off this and climb back and run around in an attempt to keep warm. When the shower was over and the sun came out, we went back to our log like frogs. A militiaman made his patrol in the interests of preventing scandal. But the bushes were extremely thick and served their purpose in concealing the couples, blond as blancmange though they were, who occasionally disappeared among them; and, in the words of a Moscow writer [Mirsky] who had been speaking of the literary censorship, "nobody was incommoded."

Yet this afternoon, so easy, so fresh, had a background of gnawing discomfort. They were beginning not to want me at the *dácha*, where they had at first entertained me so warmly. The other boarders had complained to my friends that they were seeing too much of a foreigner. Who was I? What was I up to? My friends weren't quite sure themselves. I found that they were coming to shy at the most commonplace questions on my part. The companion with whom I was swimming asked me pointblank, at a moment when there was nobody within possible earshot, whether I was not a British agent; and, after our return to the house, I was parked in an arbor on the grounds, so that the other inmates would not see me. I never went to the *dácha* again.

The atmosphere of fear and suspicion does really become oppressive. It has evidently become more tense since the Kírov assassination. A foreigner cannot talk to them about politics at all—least of all, about the Kírov affair. If you venture to ask anybody about it, they either refer you to the official statements, which are certainly extremely implausible, or start to explain and then break down, protesting that it is all very difficult for a foreigner to understand. If Americans discuss these matters at a gathering where there are Russians present, the Russians [as I have noted above] pick up books and begin to read. I came away from the Soviet Union knowing almost as little of its internal politics as I had when I first arrived.

Of course, it is no worse than Hollywood (though the penalties—death and deportation—are greater). Stalin and Kaganóvitch are hardly more sacred names in Moscow than Schulberg and Thalberg on the Coast. Anyone that has ever observed how persons who had been irreverent and full of ideas in the East are reduced to discretion and dullness as soon as they connect with their studios will not be too hard on intelligent Russians who refer you to *Pravda* for politics. Hollywood is full of informers, too; so is Dearborn, Michigan. People are afraid to discuss Communism in Los Angeles and San

Francisco. You cannot talk about organizing labor in Bethlehem, Pennsylvania. I remember that, on a visit to Washington during the happy early days of the New Deal, I noticed that people seemed nervous at pleasantries about the President or General Johnson, and that a radically disposed friend with a Washington job with whom I was walking on the street and discussing the breakdown of capitalism, turned to me and said, with an apologetic smile: "I feel that we oughtn't to be saying such things."

Borís Suvárin, in his book on Stalin, has brought forward a certain amount of evidence to show that denunciation has always been a favorite weapon of Stalin's. It appears that in Tiflís, in his youth, he was suspected by his own Social Democratic Party of having betrayed a political rival to the authorities; in prison, he instigated the killing of prisoners, whom he charged with being stool pigeons but against whom nothing was actually known, etc. He is certainly suspicious and intolerant where Lenin, through his own sincerity and his belief in the good faith of others, created that good faith itself. Was not the young officer who came to kill Lenin so moved by the "kind and simple face; face and eyes smiling at me, warm with tenderness and love," that he could not bring himself to throw his hand grenade?—and did not Lenin laugh over the incident and have the man released? This man worked afterwards for the Soviet government. It has been said of Lenin that he never found it necessary to break any man of ability among his political associates. Did he not induce both Stalin and Trotsky to work for him at the same time?

Again, we must recognize, however, that it is partly the Russian character which is to blame for the current Terror. The Russians, that is, the traditional Russians, habitually evade responsibility: they are only just beginning to learn it, as they are learning motor-driving and swimming. They do not trust one another because they do not yet trust themselves. How, one wonders, is it possible in Russia to be sure whether a given disaster is due to sabotage or incompetence? Do the persons involved always know, themselves? How much of the Ramzín trial was a fairy-tale worked up for propaganda? Was it a fairy-tale in which Ramzín himself was finally persuaded to believe? The official indictments in cases of this kind sometimes sound fantastic to foreigners. A curious example of this Russian incapacity for ascertaining the facts—if not of the Russian weakness for substituting dramatic myths—is the rumor that the crash of the plane *Maxim Gorky* was not the result of a foolish accident, but a terrible piece of sabotage. When anything goes wrong, apparently, there is likely to be an orgy of informing, each accusing his neighbor for fear of being implicated himself. The Kírov shooting was followed by six thousand deportations.

With all this, in spite of their efforts to rationalize and humanize their punishments, they still carry over from the old regime a good share of plain medieval cruelty—like the head-chopping bowl in Red Square, used by the early tsars, which, instead of having been done away with as a symbol of barbaric brutality, has merely been moved to one side in order to make room for the traffic, when the Shrine of the Iberian Virgin has gone the way of all relics.

———

One night I had a curious dream which got to the bottom of this situation. Russian grammar is full of anomalies. For example, the numerals two, three and four take nouns in the genitive singular whereas numerals over four take nouns in the genitive plural. I had asked my Russian teacher why this was so, and she had answered: "What you mean why it is so? That is the way it is!" I had also asked several other Russians, and nobody ever knew: it seemed to be one of those things, like the high wooden collars on the horses and the railroad between Leningrad and Moscow, that everybody so much took for granted that it never occurred to anyone to explain them. I found only one man who would even admit that there was anything illogical about it. Later, I discovered the explanation in Nevill Forbes's Oxford grammar, and the reasons for this anomaly turned out to be such as, it seemed to me, could only have been possible in Russia. (I was forgetting about English spelling, for which, as an American, I do not feel responsible.) It had begun with a dual form, which had been confused with the genitive singular and carried up to five, at which point it had given way to the genitive plural for the reason that—since people used to count on their fingers—five became a critical number, and one hand represented a completed unit. Thus, also, in indicating a number of years, you have not merely to change the ending but to use, beginning with five, an entirely different word.

In my dream, I was questioning a Russian about some such peculiarity as this. I was immediately aware that I had aroused his suspicions. He looked at me coldly and challenged me: "Why do you ask questions like that?"

Unconsciously I had made a connection between the antiquated language forms and the antiquated political methods which have survived the Revolution in such an incongruous way, confused and disguised with the Marxism. The Russians are rather sensitive about their system, which is supposed to be new and advanced, in the same way in which they are sensitive about their illogical language, which is in many ways quite archaic. There is no country where you can wound so easily by the kind of question and criticism which makes up in other countries the ordinary substance of conversation between interested visitors and well informed natives. Nobody else has got socialism yet; and the Russians (unless they are very much imbued with the new Marxist education) can never be quite sure that this, too, isn't something Russian and queer, or that the visitor doesn't think it is. They can never be quite sure which elements of their life are due to the proverbial Russian backwardness and which to sound Marxist doctrine.

This is the great disadvantage of Russia as the first socialist country. The opponents or critics of socialism can always put down to socialism anything they find objectionable in Russia, while socialists are often betrayed into defending ideas and methods that are really distasteful to them and that they have no business defending.

Aristocrats: a play about pickpockets, monks, prostitutes and bourgeois saboteurs, reformed on the White Sea Canal. There is a scene in which the bourgeois engineer, who has been busy on a big piece of construction, asks himself, in a moment of soul-searching, whether he has really been working for the Soviet state or simply because he was interested in engineering. The two Russians with whom I had gone nodded to one another and said that this was very good and very Russian. It would certainly be most unlikely that an American engineer would probe his conscience thus. For us, the practical problem is the thing that primarily matters: a socialist reorganization would unquestionably present itself in terms of practical ends to be accomplished, and I cannot imagine an American, once he was embarked on the project, brooding as to whether he was really sincere, whether his attitude was politically correct, in working on a bridge or a dam. I do not believe that we in the United States shall ever have "the ideology" in anything like the way the Russians have it. To imagine an American engineer in this scene is to reduce the idea to absurdity.

I had heard that Russians liked to break glasses, but I supposed this had ceased with the old regime. One evening one of my guests, however, began throwing wine-glasses against the wall. I did my best to stop her, because they belonged to the family from whom I rented the apartment. When I spoke of it the next time I saw her, she explained: "I don't know why it is, but when I drink I like to hear the sound!" She also likes to drive fast in droshkies—which really is rather exciting, as you always think you are going to tip over. She is, as a matter of fact, the only Russian I know who is reckless enough to ride in them at all. Other people firmly refuse. The trouble is, I have lately found out, that the drivers are all supposed to be GPU agents.

There is a decided hysterical edge to the upper reaches of life in Moscow, just as there is in America. The Soviet world, at the antipodes to ours, reflects our danger and panic. Here, even by the tomb of Lenin, even within sight of the Kremlin walls, the fate of humanity itself must sometimes seem rather precarious. They must sometimes be haunted as we are by a terror lest all we have done and are doing may lose its meaning and value, and slide back to ruin again.

I asked an American doctor who had seen something of psychiatry in Russia whether it was true, as had been asserted, that some of the neuroses common in the West had disappeared in the Soviet Union. He said that he did not think it was true that the sum total of neuroses was less. The new marriage laws were plainly not preventing neuroses based on sexual and marital maladjustment. With us, people marry for money; but in Russia a woman may marry and have children by a man she cares nothing about merely in order to get a room to live in. He found, also, that, though the Russians were not tormented by the fear of losing money, which plays such a role in America, they were equally badly bedeviled by the fear of losing their jobs—not of being out of work, but of being transferred or demoted or sent to a prison camp.

I saw a play called *Platón Kréchet*, which had had its opening in May, the day after Stalin's speech to the graduates of the Red Army Academy, and which was supposed to give a practical illustration of the new directive he had there laid down. Hitherto, the official slogan had been, "Technique decides everything"; but now they were to have a new slogan, "Cadres decide everything." Cadres are the human framework on whom technical efficiency depends; and the idea is to pay more attention to the needs of the individual in his human relations with the group.

Platón Kréchet is a brilliant young surgeon. He and the director of his hospital are in love with the same girl, an architect; and the director, who is a snake, tries to get Platón removed. The President of the city Soviet believes in and protects Platón. A visiting commissar is injured in a motor accident and is brought to the hospital on the point of death. Platón is summoned to operate on him, but he says at first that he cannot go: he is on the

verge of collapse from emotional strain and overwork. He
has just performed an operation on the father of the girl
he loves, but has failed to save his life. He pulls himself
together, however, and in a daze goes off to the hospital.
He asks to be alone in the operating-room, but the director insists on going in with him. "No!" commands the
President of the Soviet, with sudden indignation and an
authority above all directors: "You will stay outside!"
When the young man finally emerges, he announces,
"The Commissar of the People will live," and crashes in-
sensible to the floor. In the last act, the President of the
Soviet appears in the role of Santa Claus. The girl, who
was to marry the director, attempts to run away, but the
President drags her back and hands her over to Platón.
He produces and reads an order which announces that
Platón is to have two months' vacation *with his wife,
Anna Nikoláevna* (or whatever the name was). Dance
music is heard in the next room, and everybody is urged to
enjoy himself.

This play represents in several ways a departure from
previous policies. The Communist, the President of the
Soviet, is supposed to be an excellent fellow with a sympathetic insight into his comrades. In the early part of the
play, he tells Platón that he must not work himself to
death and tries to persuade him to come away with him
for a holiday, on which, he says, they will take along
some vodka. A foolish and senile old doctor— as a member
of the hospital cadre—is depicted in an amiable light: he
refuses to sign the petition which the director is circulating for the removal of Platón Kréchet. The director himself, instead of being condemned, as I was told would have
been the case in a play of any previous period, to hard
labor on the Sólovetsky Islands, is merely transferred to
another hospital and buoyantly comes in at the end to
shake hands with Platón Kréchet, apologize for behav-

ing so badly, and announce that he is leaving the past behind and embarking on a new and nobler life. At one point in the play, unexpectedly, Platón produces a violin and performs a well-worn selection to the surprise and admiration of the girl, who had not known about this side of his nature. This exemplifies the new ideal of all-around human development and the new cultivation of the amenities.

I assisted, in a hotel bedroom, at a long and animated discussion of the Communist policy in the "Black Belt." A highly intelligent Negro professor had presented himself in Moscow in the hope of getting a hearing from the Comintern Congress and persuading the Comintern to change its line on this question, and he was trying out his arguments beforehand on two American Communists from New York, who had only just arrived. It seemed to me that the professor had all the better of it. He was contending that "Self-determination for the Black Belt" (a section of the South mapped out by the Communists, where the population is mostly Negro), based as it was on an analogy with the Ukraine, was totally unrealistic. What was the good of talking about "Negro culture"? The Negroes in the United States had no national language like the Ukrainians. Negro culture was simply a part of the general American culture. And what the Negroes really wanted was, not self-determination, not freedom for a national culture, but simply their rights as Americans. It would be a crime, he insisted, to incite a separatist movement which could only provoke a race war. The Communists, who were upholding the "Black Belt" policy, were white and had never been near the "Black Belt": their knowledge of the Negro question was exclusively derived from Harlem. They would answer: "If so-and-so were here, he'd be able to show you that your criticism is the result of your petty bourgeois background. I am not able to do it myself, but I know that he could do it!" This attempt to refute an argument by asserting that somebody else could refute it, seemed to me about the furthest length to which authoritarian thinking could be carried.

This discussion, my evening with the Armenian in the Park of Culture and Rest, and a number of other incidents, had made me feel as I had never done before that being an American did mean something unique, that Americanism was a solid social entity which stood quite apart from Europe, belonging to a separate category rather than merely differing from it as the characters of the various European peoples differed from one another; something that, in fundamental ways, was just as unlike what one finds in Russia as what one finds in the Western European nations (though the Soviet Union has already succeeded in establishing a category of its own). The prime factor that sets us apart is the fact that we have not got the past on the premises as the Europeans have. And the American attitude, the American character, are more than rhetorical ideals; they are things which actually exist and which political thinking must reckon with. This Armenian of Leftist sympathies showed at once, in the Soviet Union, how proud he was to call himself an American; this Negro, a member of the group which has been most "underprivileged" in America, only wanted to be an American and to enjoy American rights.

I thought of F. in Russia. Her parents were Ukrainians from the neighborhood of Lemberg, and she had grown up among Slavic Americans. I had always attributed the sadness of her voice to the hardships and tragedies of her life, and her quietness and patience and sweetness to the gentleness of her own personality; but now I was able to recognize that her voice was a Russian voice, with older hardships and tragedies behind it, and that what had attracted me in her, what had made her so inexplicably different from most working-girls of her kind in New York, was her having remained profoundly Slavic. Yet I had taken her once to the Soviet film made from Gorky's *Mother,* thinking a Russian picture would interest her, and had found that it had merely embarrassed her. During the scenes of squalor with which it opens, she had said to me with a bitterness that surprised me: "Now you see how my people live!" She had known squalor like that in New York, but she had acquired, along with the new language, the conviction that squalor was not American. Her family and she at that time, fur-workers and textile-workers, were living on relief-jobs or home relief, and had been forced to leave their pleasant little houses in the neighborhood of Coney Island, where they had had front-yards and sea-breezes, radios and kitchens and bathrooms. But I do not think it would ever have occurred to any of them to want to go back to the Ukraine, under either Polish or Soviet administration. America meant to them the kitchens and bathrooms which they had had once and might have again, and, even with the socialism of the Soviets, these conveniences, for people like them, still hardly existed in the Ukraine. The older generation of F.'s family belonged, on the East Side, to Ukrainian social organizations, and they cherished their Ukrainian patriotism. But F. was rather ashamed that her people had come from there.

Of course, terms like "Americanism" are dangerous because they can be exploited to disguise and to justify the most dubious interests and aims. It is true that the citizens of Rome went on being proud of the privilege of calling themselves Roman citizens long after Rome was dead. But certainly the case for socialism, which is the case for a high general standard of living secured by guaranteeing that people shall get the benefit of what they produce, could be made out in the United States on the basis of American tradition and commonly accepted principles. From this point of view, the socialist ideal is more natural to us than to the Russians.

———————

Another torrent of rain in the Málaya Bronnáya just as I was leaving someone's house. You had to wade over cobbles like a river-bed. A girl had taken off her sneakers and socks and was going through the water barefoot. She had pretty feet, smaller than most, and was very cheerful about it: a man in a doorway called after her, and she called something back, laughing.

———————

I get the impression that love-affairs in Russia—and even among the Komsomól?—tend still to have the indeterminate and unpredictable character of the relations, in Pushkin's poem, between Evgéni Onégin and Tatyána.

———————

Stupendous jamboree given by the Journalists' Club for the Proletarian Division of the Red Army. The journalists and the Red Army are both among the privileged groups: they make more money, eat better food, have access to more reading matter and are able to get prettier wives than the majority of the people in Moscow. And they did themselves in wonderful style.

The evening began about nine with tea and enormous fancy pastry. Then there was an entertainment in three long and varied sections by the Proletarian Division and

their families. They put on a very good show. It began
with performances by the children, who, like all Russians
apparently, were born actors: there was a conventional
fairy dance; a nerve-racking stunt by a little girl, who,
while balancing a glass of water, twisted herself like a
rope and gradually lay down on her back on the floor;
and a play in which a boy and girl went to sleep over a
romantic phonograph record and thought they were traveling to Italy, but were waked up by their little comrades
and recalled to the Soviet tasks of the day. There were
operatic selections, peasant songs, recitations of Mayakóvsky, and a whole series of those stamping and leaping
dances, which worked up from relatively simple numbers,
in which only one or two figured, to a finale so huge
and terrific that I thought it would break down the platform.

The officers and men performed together and were
only to be distinguished by the insignia on the officers'
collars. The Commander was a quiet, agreeable and youth-
ful-looking little man, who, if it had not been for his
uniform, his clean-shavedness and his military sunburn,
might have been taken for an artist. Certainly the Red
Army is quite unlike any other which has ever been seen
in our time. Instead of being the least intelligent, they
are among the most intelligent of Soviet groups. They receive a special education, because their role is not merely
to defeat but also to persuade the enemy, and they must
understand their place in history and the Marxist reasons
why wars are fought. They read a special Red Army
bulletin which gives them fuller information about world
affairs than can be got from *Izvestia* or *Pravda*. And they
are the only democratic army in Europe.

During one of the intermissions, I talked to an American girl who had been working for some months in Moscow. She had been highly delighted by one of the songs

which had featured traditional dance figures in old-fashioned peasant costumes. Now, the attitude of the young Red Army men and women, dancing the old dances as village girls and their swains, had been like that of American young people dressing up at an entertainment to sing *Jingle Bells* or *Oh, Susannah!* But the little American comrade, clear-eyed and ardent, said to me: "Wasn't that number fine? It's so like life on the collective farms!" The Russian who had brought me [Trétyakov], a writer whose special subject was collective farms, had just been explaining in apology that the show was aesthetically unsatisfactory, since the folk art had died with the old Russian life and could only be revived self-consciously, while as yet, on the Soviet side, nothing new had been evolved to take its place. I realized that it was possible, in the center of Moscow, to have as weak a sense of Russian realities as anywhere below Fourteenth Street.

When the entertainment was over, we were regaled with a tremendous banquet. First, we had to drink innumerable toasts, accompanied by bugle flourishes and *zakúsky* with wine and beer. The *zakúsky* (very heavy hors d'oeuvres) were the most copious I had ever seen, and I made the mistake of assuming that they constituted the supper. I was staggered, when I had pretty well stuffed myself, to be faced with a succession of further courses. It took several hours to serve them, and all the time a jazz orchestra played. Just before the last course but one, the lights were turned out and a movie commenced: a new German picture with a pretty Hungarian actress. Between reels, the ice-cream and coffee came in. I left about four in the morning, while the party was still going strong.

These superior groups in the Soviet Union are no doubt at the present time among the most attractive people in the world, and they may well be among the happiest.

There is at present a whole hierarchy in Russia, based on various degrees of ability and on different departments of service. The differences of income among them are, from the American point of view, very slight; but for Russia, they are quite considerable.

Many people find this out with surprise and assume that it must be a violation of the ideals of socialist society. This is, of course, not the case. It was one of the prime contentions of Marx and Engels that socialist society could not be equalitarian. It would still have to follow, in important respects, the contours of social organisms that had been shaped by the specializations of capitalism. Differing degrees of ability would be bound to command different incomes. "This equal right [in socialist society]," says Marx in his *Critique of the Gotha Program* "is an unequal right for unequal work. It recognizes no class differences, because every worker ranks as a worker like his fellows, but it tacitly recognizes unequal individual endowment, and thus capacities for production, as natural privileges." (A difficulty, indeed, in the Soviet Union seems to be to make the people in general desire a better standard of living strongly enough to exert themselves to get it. It is the purpose of the "culture" campaign to make people seek self-improvement.) And Lenin, on the eve of October, recapitulated, in his *State and Revolution,* the teaching of Marx and Engels on this point. It is true that, until recently, an attempt was made to maintain a uniform salary for Communists; but now this has been abandoned, and Communists, like other people, are divided into several categories and paid in proportion to their services.

As for Lenin himself, however, he had not only already established his life outside the categories of class society, he had also dissociated himself from the conditions under which inequalities of ability are unequally remunerated. I was told by the wife of a commissar of her calling on Krúpskaya in the Kremlin. There were no comforts in the apartment, she said; no ornaments, except pictures of Lenin. Preoccupied from her student days with workers' education and agitation, after a lifetime of meager and impermanent lodgings in all the countries of Europe, having long ago forfeited with Lenin, in their all-demanding vigilance for the fate of human society, any sense of her own right, as a human being, to beauty or recreation or rest, she now, at sixty-six, after the triumph of her cause, with those who had never had anything and whom she had worked to relieve enjoying their little amenities and herself at last lodged in security under the golden spires of the Kremlin, she seemed never to have noticed her furniture, never to have looked at her walls. There were no pictures, I think the visitor said, except a photograph of Lenin. To such a deliverance from material things the materialist conception of history had led! It was characteristic of Lenin as of Marx—this was the mainspring of the whole Marxist system—that he could not reconcile himself to a world in which the things that men needed were reckoned in terms of money and went always to the highest bidder. And he insisted, in the very act of seizing power, that all he was doing was done in order to arrive at a day when neither capitalist dollars nor socialist rubles would have value. The Soviet Union is still far from that day; the people still work for money, and even the governing groups still work for more money than their neighbors. But they know that their state is not dedicated, as the capitalist governments are, to the mere preservation of the status quo in the interests of a propertied class. It is based on the bare walls and plain furniture of Lenin's and Krúpskaya's lodgings.

———

I had gone to say good-by to an American friend who was staying in a hotel, and I found there a Russian whom I knew. We had some brandy, and I told them about the Red Army party. I had seen there an old-timer with a big black beard who had made a resounding speech, and his image and echo were still with me. Inspired by the brandy and with no explanation, I repeated one of his phrases: *"Íli sotsialízm íli fashízm!"* ("Either socialism or fascism!") "Don't say that!" exclaimed the Russian. "What is there objectionable about it?" I asked. "It's from a speech at the Red Army banquet." "Never talk politics in hotel rooms!" —and he added, "Meekrophón!" I left very soon and did not see him again, so never had a chance to ask him why he should have been so much worried by a phrase which had become a commonplace of Soviet official thought. So much did I take for granted the loyalty of the Russians to their government that it was only a long time afterwards, in connection with a furtive remark about Hitler, that I realized there were people in the Soviet Union who were feeling that, if they had to have a dictatorship, they might do better with a Hitler than a Stalin.

———

[I do not want to leave Moscow without giving some account of my friend Dmitri S. Mirsky, who was such an exceptional figure in the Soviet Union and whose fate was one of the tragedies and crimes of the Stalin dictatorship. I looked him up in Moscow not long after I arrived. I knew that he had seen my work from his having said something about it in an article in some French periodical, and I had just read, on my way to Europe, his books on Pushkin and Lenin. The first of these had made an impression on me, for Mirsky's literary sense was highly developed and he was very sure of his judgment. His discussion of Pushkin's style was the first thing I had ever read that made me realize that a Russian could be a great stylist—such reading of Russian writers as I had hitherto done had been mostly in Constance Garnett's translations, which made them all sound much alike; and I had been stimulated by Mirsky's book seriously to study Russian. His two-volume history of Russian literature, written like the *Pushkin* in the middle twenties, I did not yet know at that time; but I later came to recognize it as a unique and indispensable work. Russians tell me that—in spite of the fact that this book was written in English for foreigners—there is nothing in Russian so good, so perceptive and comprehensive. Though a number of books on Russian literature, both by foreigners and by Russians, have recently been published in English, Mirsky's history and Vogüé's *Le Roman Russe* remain, so far as my experience goes, the only works that make a real liaison between the literature of the West and Russian literature, because they are the only ones whose authors are at home in both worlds and have at the same time a grasp of the literary art.

I also knew something of the circumstances of Mirsky's returning to Russia. Though a member of an ancient princely family and an ex-officer of the tsarist army, who had fought with Dénikin and Wrángel against the Revolution, he had, in exile, while living in London, become converted to Marxism. He was a protégé of Maurice Baring, who had known him in his Petersburg days, and he had been supporting himself in London by various academic and literary jobs. Among these, about 1930, he had undertaken a short book on Lenin. This is not one of his most satisfactory productions, for he was limited to such materials as he could find in the British Museum, which must have been rather meager, since he was not, as I found, aware of such an important fact as that Lenin's maternal family was German; but it is said to have been his researches in connection with this book that first interested him in Communism and enabled him to understand sympathetically the events that had resulted in the Bolshevik revolution. The economic crisis of 1930-31 seemed to confirm for him the Marxist prediction of the inevitable breakdown of capitalism, and the Soviet Union, still at that time identified with its founder Lenin, presented itself to Mirsky as the only modern state not based on decaying foundations. To the horror of his fellow émigrés, he enrolled himself in the British Communist Party, and he decided that the part of a patriot as well as that of a Marxist was to return to his native country. This he managed, in 1932, through the aid of his friend Maxim Gorky, who had gone back in 1929. The price that Mirsky paid for admission was the usual repudiation of non-Communist associations which was always exacted by the Bolsheviks of recruits from other groups, and this took the form of a book called *The Intelligentsia of Great Britain,* first published in Russian in the Soviet Union, then (in 1935) brought out in an English translation. This book was, of course, not calculated to please the English themselves, and it has usually been treated as an abject betrayal of the writers who had befriended Mirsky in England, an exercise in propaganda that marked his extinction as a serious critic. Yet this bold and brisk Marxist summary of the modern intellectual history of Britain and the United States (for he polishes us off at the same sitting) is rather an able and brilliant book. It is today less annoying than pathetic to read a critic who believes that he has just got the key to all the problems of human culture as well as an infallible ferrule with which he can poke into their places the practitioners of bourgeois letters. It is a procedure, a state of mind, that is sure to give rise to absurdities. All the popular pastimes of Eng-

land—from "chapel prayer meetings" to liquor, the
cinema, betting on the races, and "the commercial spectacular development of football, cricket and tennis"—are,
for example, put down by Mirsky to the devious cunning
of the capitalists in procuring "the stupefaction of the
masses" by "canalizing" their emotional energy and divert-
ing them from revolution. And in the cocky exhilaration
that has followed his first whiffs of Marxism, he does not
hesitate to brush off with a flick of the wrist—in a way
that he would never have permitted himself in his earlier
more scholarly days—writers he has hardly read. We are
told, for example, of Henry James that his residence in
England had "given full vent to his minutious analysis
of the most inconceivably petty incidents"—though I
know, from my conversations with Mirsky, that he had
read only one book of James, *The Ambassadors*. Yet there
are very good things in this ill-inspired book. I am not sure
that there is any other in which a foreigner so well-informed has attempted in so unihibited and so unacademic
a way to run through the main currents and figures of
recent English literature and thought. The categories and
conventions of Marxism do, of course, by themselves
impose a constraint, but the book was produced at a time
when the culture-crushing hand of the Kremlin had not
yet put the critic in irons, and it is full of original insights
of the social-economic kind and of descriptions of literary
milieux which do not necessarily depend on these. He is
very good, it seems to me, on Bloomsbury, and on the difference between what constituted being "advanced" in the
Bloomsbury generation and what constituted being "advanced" in the period of Wells and Shaw. Mirsky's delight in, his appetite for good literature is still partially
able to express itself, as when he calls Virginia Woolf "a
great writer" or Conrad "a great psychologist." His comparisons of English philosophy with the systems of Ger-

many and France are illuminating and quite independent of the Communist frame of reference.

The preface to Mirsky's book on Lenin contains his apologia for his shift of allegiance to the Soviet power. It has been pointed out to him, he says, that his book needs some special explanation as "coming from a member of the class that was most effectively eliminated" by the Bolsheviks. The answer is, then, in the first place, that the Russian "squirearchy"—it should not, he says, be called an "aristocracy"—"had reached such a state of cultural degeneracy that the mere fact of possessing a certain amount of intellectual culture 'unclassed' those of its members who possessed any," and that these had had no reason to be prejudiced in favor of the bourgeoisie "by the unsolicited opportunity of seeing European capitalism not as guests, but as subjects, not as more or less moneyed tourists, but as more or less unemployed proletarians." Such people—a minority—could not be content to live on old memories, as many did, or "amalgamate on a basis of inferiority with the middle classes of Europe." This last point, I think, was important. Mirsky's full name was Svyátopolk-Mirsky, and his lineage was that of the earliest rulers, the Svyátopolks and Gedemíns, when Kíev and Nóvgorod were dominant principalities. My impression of him was that—for all his talk of a simple "squirearchy"—he was, at bottom, a terrific snob of the peculiar Russian kind that prides itself on its descent from the Rúriks, regards the Románovs as upstarts, and, still keeping something in its bones of the old barbaric overlordship, is not necessarily revolted by Stalin. I found it quite comprehensible—given Mirsky's force of intellect, his love of Russia and his self-identification with her destiny—that, ignoring Western conventions, he should stride from the arrogance of the prince to that of the commissar: they had in common their contempt for the bourgeoisie, their refusal to accept solidarity with it. It was enough, as he goes on to say, for such a person as him, to recognize, in any case, that, "whatever the Communists might be worth in their international function, as a Russian party they had preserved the independence of the country from foreign intervention, restored under a new name . . . the geographical limits of the empire, and made Russia a cultural and political force of universal significance. Before we became internationalists, we had come to understand that, whatever else they might be, the Communists who had vindicated the independence of a Workers' and Peasants' U.S.S.R. were better patriots than the 'national Russians' who had allied themselves with foreign imperialism in return for help against their class enemy." That he had never accepted the Tsar with anything like conventional loyalty is shown by a pre-revolutionary anecdote. He is supposed to have caused scandal in his regiment by refusing to drink to the sovereign, remarking, according to one version of the story, "I never drink to people that I do not know," and, in another cruder version, "I refuse to drink to that idiot."

In any case, having reached these conclusions, he proceeded to act upon them—as Russian intellectuals did not always do—and he was thus a unique figure, the strangest and one of the most interesting that I met in the Soviet Union. He was the only one of his breed that I have seen on his native ground, and as we dined in the Sokólniki Gardens and he would comment on an expansive and very *soignée* white beard as a relic of the old régime, or point out, as we walked at night behind the Kremlin wall, the scene of one of the episodes of *War and Peace,* or talk about current events outside Russia in a curious Russo-centric way as if they were all peripheral, as if Europe was going to wreck while only the Kremlin remained (he rarely read foreign periodicals, he made a point of telling me, and did not miss them at all), I felt that I had, indeed, come in contact with a permanent Russia, that not merely was *War and Peace* not far behind us there in the background, but that Kíev and Nóvgorod and the Golden Horde (from whom he must have got his Tartar eyes) were not entirely remote. I felt the survival, in Mirsky's mind, of a Russia that continued through all her vicissitudes; but I was not always sure that Moscow, as he had come so positively to hold, was absolutely in advance of the rest of the world. There were moments when I was worried by the medieval aspects of the Soviet power. It was odd, it was uncanny to hear the tune of the *International* played at midnight on the Kremlin bells; if I had not been told about it, I should never have recognized it—so out of our rhythm it seemed, indecisively and haltingly jingled, so out of our scale, in fact—unless it was simply that it was out of tune; and there was perhaps a little of that, for all his knowledge of the Western world, about Mirsky's way of playing it.

I found Mirsky, when I first went to call on him, in antique and rather shabby surroundings at the extreme other end of Moscow from the Nóvo-Moskóvskaya and the other hotels, the main shops and the government buildings. When Moscow was not brand new, it had nothing in common with anything as disciplined and modern as Communism was supposed to be. Almost anything might lurk in those neglected old houses, and a good many queer things did. I heard stories of outlandish religious cults, spiritualistic séances, dens of gangsters and houses of prostitution. This seemed to me the kind of quarter where such things could be expected. The address I had took me, I found, through a dark and narrow passage that was cluttered by a second-hand bookstall. I came out into a cobbled court where the walls had once been painted pink, and had to penetrate beyond that to a second one, in which they had been painted white. I located Mirsky's door on the stairway of one of the entrances. It was covered—I supposed, for warmth—by what I took to be a piece of old carpet. This muted my attempt to knock, so I tried turning the bell, which did not seem to ring. Though he had made an appointment with me, I decided he had not yet come in, so went away to kill time for an hour by visiting the Museum of the Revolution, which was not very far away. When I returned, I worked the bell in the other direction, and this time I heard it ring. The door was opened, and I saw before me, standing immobile and very erect, a tall, bearded, bald and bespectacled man who stared at me without shaking hands. He invited me in, however, and apologized for receiving me in his dressing gown, in which he said he always worked. In appearance, he had something of Kropótkin, something of Edward Lear. His large and glowing brown eyes had a pronounced oriental slant that was particularly noticeable in profile, and he would knit his dark bushy eyebrows, when vexed or perplexed about something, in a way that suggested the frown of a tsar; but his gaze was more often quite friendly and straight. He had a high intellectual forehead, with a large brown mole on one side of the crown. As in the case of many Russian émigrés, his teeth were in hideous condition. He was stiff and seemed rather shy, but I guessed that the constraint of our conversation was due to the difficulty of adapting himself to a visitor from the outside world, and one whom he did not know. He invited me to dinner for the following night, and, this arranged—since our talk seemed so halting and I supposed that he wanted to go back to his work—I got up to take my leave; but he checked me and made me sit down. He said he was in no hurry, inquired whether I was in a hurry, and apologized again for his dressing gown. There was an unmade bed in the background, and a door stood open on a bathtub which was also made to serve as a washstand. When I came there the next evening, he complained that the soap smelt badly. I learned later that, returning to Russia, he had insisted on only one thing: that he should have a room of his own. He told me now that he had been revising an old translation of Milton, and that the speeches of God the Father were "an awful bore." A flat and explicit atheism was a part of his Marxist stand, and when I mentioned T. S. Eliot, whom I knew he had known in London, he made fun of Eliot's play *The Rock*, written to raise funds for the London churches, and of his having said, in some connection, that family prayers were important because they were good for the servants. I tried talking about the Museum of the Revolution, but this brought little response, except for his asking me whether I was able to read "the letterpress"—and we were stalled in one of our silences. I said that I had come by way of Leningrad, and he asked me whom I had seen there. It was always very important in the Soviet Union in those days to know whom people had seen, since everybody had to be identified with something—some movement or milieu or group—other than his own individuality. I mentioned a number of names, but he made, I think, no comment on any of them. I told him about the accomplished young man in Leningrad, who had spoken so highly of a poem in which the raising of Lazarus had been invested with a novel implication, and showed him a list of names which this young man had written down for me when I had asked him who were the best recent Russian poets. Mirsky looked at the list and handed it back, announcing with a certain sternness as he contracted his heavy eyebrows, "Almost every one of those poets is homosexual." I knew that there had just been promulgated an edict against homosexuality, imposing severe penalties, and I resolved to destroy the list; but this again stopped the conversation. I made, however, a last effort to stimulate it by telling him about seeing in Leningrad Alexéy Tolstóy's *Peter the First*. "Ah, you saw that?" he said with some interest. "I suppose it will be done here," I ventured. "I don't think so," he answered laconically, but looked at me with a gravity that seemed just to stop short of the quizzical. He volunteered, however, no explanation; and I still do not know what the point was. Every novel, play and poem in Russia seemed to have some political significance. We were stalled again, and I left.

The next evening, when I went to dinner, I found a professional linguist, who had had his head shaved in the Soviet style, and a Jewish woman, who did translating. We had pressed caviare—cheaper than the regular kind—black bread and the little Russian cucumbers that you peel and dip in salt. (A friend who knew Mirsky in Paris has told me that he was then a gourmet, who delighted in the best restaurants.) A Russian girl who spoke French and was writing an article on *"Poètes de café,"* came in later to take tea. In the course of the conversation, Mirsky, talking of Gorky, said that he had become in the Soviet Union *"une manière de personnage,"* and, turning to the French specialist, quizzed her: "Who said that of whom?" It had been said of Voltaire by Saint-Simon: "Arouet, the son of a notary who was employed by my father and me up to the time of his death, was exiled and sent to Tulle for verses that were satirical and extremely impudent. It would not amuse me to record such a trifle were it not that this same Arouet, today, under the name of Voltaire, a great poet and academician, has become, after many tragic misadventures, a kind of personage in the republic of letters, and has even acquired a certain importance among a certain set." The allusion was characteristic of Mirsky's systematic practice of deprecating the aristocracy

of birth by playing off against them the aristocracy of
talent. The young woman now put a problem. She had
been trying to look up something in connection with the
history of the Communist Party, but the books she had so
far consulted had seemed to her strangely baffling. She
asked Mirsky where she could find something more satisfactory. He replied, *"Vous êtes terrible, ma petite,"* and
diverted the conversation.

I began to be aware of the dislocation in Mirsky's whole
intellectual life that had been caused by his conversion to
Marxism. When he spoke of *The Waste Land* as a document on the decadence of capitalist society, I said that that
did not prevent it from being also a very fine poem. He
surprised me by answering with enthusiasm that Eliot was
the greatest living poet. On another occasion, he was praising Belínsky, the early nineteenth-century critic who had
written of Pushkin and Gogol in terms of their social
content in so relentlessly moralistic a way, and had thus
become the patron saint of the dogmatic Soviet criticism
which made of every work of literature a move in the
game of propaganda and tried to rule on the attitude of
the author as "correct" or "incorrect." I remembered having read in Mirsky's *Pushkin* a characterization of Belínsky's Russian as "long-winded, vulgar and untidy," and
the assertion that "the man who could write such insipid
and vulgar journalese about Pushkin cannot be believed
to have had any real understanding of literary art." When
I reminded him of this, he murmured, "Ah, that was
von einem anderen Standpunkt." I admired his way of
disposing of this by stepping over into another language.
When he spoke to us that evening of Mayakóvsky, I felt
that he was very much pleased at believing himself to
have found a thoroughly Soviet writer who satisfied his
literary taste. "I've just been reading Mayakóvsky," he
said, "and you know he is a really great love poet—I mean,

really great." It was as if he were dealing with our doubts as to whether Mayakóvsky's poems of love might not be mere declamation. I have been told that Mirsky himself was always in love in the most romantic fashion, and that an unwise affair in Moscow supplied one of the pretexts for banishing him.

These people I met at his house—all remnants, it was obvious, of the old intelligentzia—admired him and came to consult him; but my friend G. believed that his life was lonely. His relations with the rest of the Soviet world could not have been at all easy. On the part of the typical intellectual of Moscow, he inspired, I think, a mixture of jealousy, annoyance and awe. His learning and his information were enormous, exact and wide-ranging. He had nothing of the dilettante: his reading had been systematic; nor had he anything, on the other hand, of the academic scholar, who specializes minutely in a single field. He wrote effectively in English and French; and his unusual historical range, when he had once got the hang of the Marxist method, enabled him to make novel interpretations. He was conspicuous, also, in public, not merely, as my friend G. was, by his being so much taller than the people on the street that he towered above them like Gulliver among the Lilliputians, but also by reason of his British clothes: Oxonian gray flannel trousers, a jacket that did not match, and a flat English cap with a visor—all shabby to the point of trampishness. I have told about the Black Hundreds Cossack who pursued and abused him in public—denouncing him as a renegade aristocrat; and on another occasion a man that Mirsky said he had never seen came over and spoke to him in a restaurant. Dining out with him was always liable to queer or uncomfortable incidents.

On the other hand, even people who had something in common with Mirsky could not afford to know him. I had once heard an intelligent Englishwoman married to a commissar make fun of him as "Comrade Prince." He had been famous for his arrogance and his irascibility among his own social world, and I used to shudder to think of the effort of self-restraint that his relations with his Soviet colleagues must cost him, and of the consequences when it inevitably broke down. My relations with him at first were a little uneven, because, not being involved as he was, in spite of my then Soviet sympathies, I would tend to base my conversation on our common love of literature, and he would have to pull himself up by remembering his new orientation. He was not naturally a pedantic or fanatical man, and the wobblings, the abrupt shifts of mood, that were apt to result from this had sometimes their comic side. His wavering over the cognac on the occasion recorded above was characteristic of him, as was his giving money to beggars, which was not considered correct. He usually started out by maintaining his attitude with a certain rigidity and tartness, but I soon found that he would readily relax under the influence of a bottle of Caucasian wine followed by several cognacs, begin quoting favorite poems—he seemed to know yards of poetry in half a dozen languages; and on one occasion, for some reason I cannot remember, he sang the Greek national anthem. He would offset the bristling and slanteyed mask that recalled the Muscovite tsars by a giggle that suggested Edward Lear and was not always the proper accompaniment for the conventional Communist sneer. Or Kropótkin would come to the fore, and, warmed by the good cheer (of which he did not get much: he was not, and made a point of not being, a member of the privileged groups), his dark eyes would melt and glow with an emotional sensibility and idealism that had something quite guileless and touching. On the subject of the United States, at that time much admired in Russia, he

combined the condescension of the official line toward a
bankrupt capitalist society with an anti-Americanism
which had evidently been stimulated by his residence in
England. He had once done a lecture tour in Canada
and the United States, and was equipped with the usual
anecdotes about the impossible people one met there. Once
I described to him my state of mind when I had made a
prolonged sojourn in Italy: my surfeit with the furniture
of the past, my restlessness at feeling that the big parade
was going by in another street; and he told me that he had
never felt like that in the least, that such a reaction was
possible only for an American tourist—an inappropriate
attitude, I thought, for one who was under the impression
that he had just proved the insufficiency of two or three
centuries of Western art, and was ready to kick them
downstairs. In the course of our evening at the Sokólniki
Gardens, I became a little nettled by this attitude. I had
asked him whether I could send him any books when I
was back in the United States, and he replied without
enthusiasm that he would be glad to have the Beards'
The Rise of American Civilization and Vachel Lindsay's
collected poems, adding scrupulously, with an accent of
Soviet disdain, "Those are the only American books that
interest me." A little later, when we were sitting on a
bench and well out of earshot of anyone, he asked me
what the Ford plant in Dearborn was like. I replied that
it was a whole domain in itself, completely walled off
from the rest of Detroit; that one could only gain admit-
tance with difficulty, and that, once one was inside, one
became aware of being checked on at every point; that
the workers could never escape from the demands of industrial discipline, and that they were spied upon every
moment. "In fact," I concluded, "it's rather like here." He
was silent for a little while, then got up from the bench
and said, "Shall we be moving?" In spite of some provoca-

tion, I at once regretted this dig, for, though I was quite free to criticize my country, he was not so to criticize his.

One day I attended a meeting especially held for the enlightenment of a delegation of American schoolteachers. Mirsky, who was usually produced when fluent English was needed, was there on the platform to answer their questions. One woman wanted to know whether modern writers like Joyce didn't have a bad influence. "I'd say," he equivocated, "that a book like *Ulysses* could only have been produced by a perfectly putrid society." He came over to me after the meeting and asked what I had thought of his answer. Feeling that he was rather ashamed of it, I told him, non-committally, that the question had been stupid. "But it had to be answered," he said. I did not know then that *Ulysses* was, for Mirsky, a delicate subject. There was actually a good deal of interest in Joyce—*Ulysses* was being translated (in a curiously literal word-by-word way), and coming out in one of the literary magazines, and there had just been a controversy about it. I learn from Mr. Gleb Struve's book *Soviet Russian Literature* that Mirsky had written, two years before, some articles condemning the influence of Joyce, and that one of the writers he had criticized, a playwright named Vsévolod Vishnévsky (later, in 1949, the winner of a Stalin prize for a drama that glorified Stalin as a hero of the Civil Wars) had vigorously defended himself on the grounds that *Ulysses* constituted "a perfectly outspoken portrayal of men in the capitalistic era," and that Eisenstein had known Joyce in Paris and learned from him some of his methods. The discussion reached such a pitch that it had to be adjudicated by Rádek at the Congress of Soviet Writers which took place the following year. He—so soon to be liquidated himself—declared on this occasion that "Joyce stands on the other side of the barricades ... Our road lies not through Joyce, but along the highway of Socialist realism." This justified Mirsky, no doubt, but at that moment he was taking a beating over his criticism of a novel by Alexander Fadéyev. Though Mirsky, Mr. Struve informs us, had written "from the ultra-left standpoint and shown himself *plus royaliste que le roi même*," he was given an indignant blast by the "proletarian" critics, who declared that an ex-White Guardist had no right to find fault with a Communist writer, and he was henceforth excluded from the *Literary Gazette* till Gorky came to his rescue in January 1935, declaring that "everybody knew" that Fadéyev's novel was bad, and that Mirsky should not be disqualified for having been, through no fault of his, born a prince. The attack on him had been renewed with a certain official sanction, since an article denouncing him was published simultaneously in both *Izvestia* and *Pravda*. This had happened not long before I saw him, but Mirsky still had Gorky's backing.

I did not find him at home one day when I called at his flat to return some books, and did not see him for weeks. At last, just before I left Moscow, he turned up at my own apartment, having walked the whole distance across the city. We dined at the Nóvo-Moskóvskaya. He was quite frank in falling in with a proposal that, rather than sit down for a drink in the new Moskóvskaya bar which was advertising *koktéyli*, where we should have had people close around us, we go up to the outskirts of the dining-room—that this would "perhaps be more to the point" was Mirsky's way of putting it—where we could have our drinks in relative privacy. He explained that he had been out of Moscow: they had sent him out somewhere beyond Tashként, a journey of many days, traveling "hard" all the time, so that he had had to sit up for nights. I had already had the impression that he was purposely given hackwork, and I suspected now that this mission had been meant to humiliate him. But, if so, it had affected him in the opposite way. I had never seen him so stimulated and cheerful. To get away from Moscow on his own must in itself have been a great relief. "You know, there are place-names out there," he told me, with the relish of the traveler discovering unexpected things, "that have no vowels at all—they consist of just three or four consonants!" He had been lecturing to the local officials about Russian literature—"rather elderly men, you know—very much interested, they're very keen to learn." Instead of proving a hardship and bore, the trip was the kind of thing he was ready and glad to do, for it gave him the satisfaction of feeling that he was performing, at the cost of inconvenience, a service to the national culture and a service to the new Russia. After dinner, when I suggested a second cognac, he answered, *"Je ne dis que non."* When he left, I told him I was going away and thanked him for all his kindness. "No kindness on my part!" he answered, with a beaming benevolent glow.

That was the end of July. Struve says that Mirsky was arrested "in the summer of 1935"—if this is true, it must have been in August—and that he was released a few months later, but forced to live outside Moscow. I have been told, however, by Mr. E. H. Carr, the historian and biographer, that he saw Mirsky once on a visit to Russia which took place sometime after my visit. Though he and Mirsky had been formerly on very good terms, he found now, he said, that Mirsky could no longer talk to him when other people were present, and it had been only by stopping in the mens' room together that they had been able to exchange a few words. And a Russian friend of Mirsky's, Mrs. Vera Traill, has written me as follows: "I arrived in Moscow in August, 1936, and saw Dim nearly

every day. He was arrested in the very first days of June,
1937. (I think it was on the third.) He had never been
arrested before. Though he might have been through
some kind of interrogation—I cannot vouch for that."
This final disappearance, then, took place during the
purges of 1937. Gorky, reputedly murdered, had died a
year before, in June, 1936, and Mirsky had been left at the
mercy of the sycophants and jailors of Stalin. The pressure of mediocrity, of avid inferiority, cannot be over-
estimated in any field; but in the department of literature,
it is likely to be particularly rampart. The arts of music
and painting, the discipline of learned subjects, the technical domain of the sciences, require a minimum of training; but anyone who can read and write—and even the
partly illiterate—are at liberty to occupy themselves with
literature. In a dictatorship, this is fatal, for the hacks can
then rule the roost. Maxim Gorky had been doing his
best to prevent the ascendancy of the second-rate, but
when he died, he left the literary world to the type of
vindictive journalist who, elsewhere as well as in Russia,
attached themselves to the Communist movement and beside whom the Salieri who murders Mozart in Pushkin's
terrible little play is a man of respectable talent. The
aristocracy of letters was going by the board as well as
the old nobility. Not, of course, that one needed this
animus to account for the suppression of Mirsky at the
time of Stalin's gigantic purges. In any case, I do not like
to think of Mirsky opening his door in his spectacles and
dressing gown, and being dragged from his pressed caviare
and bad-smelling soap, from those almost Dostoevskian
lodgings, in which he had had momentarily the illusion
that he was serving Russia in lecturing to provincial officials and revising a translation of *Paradise Lost*.

There were at first various rumors as to what had become of him—that he was confined in a monastery and

allowed to do nothing but translating, that he was editing a local paper in a remote Siberian town. Since nothing certain was heard, it was assumed, as time went on, that he was dead; and this supposition has been confirmed by a letter (dated May 1, 1952) written to one of Mirsky's friends by a Russian D.P. in Europe. I here translate this document, which has never been published before. It is obviously not written by a person of very much education, and I have had to straighten out some bad grammar.

Gracious Lady
Much-esteemed ——————— ———————,
  Most willingly and with sorrowful heartfelt pain, I am complying with your request. I had unfortunately few meetings with Prince Svyátopolk-Mirsky—the dates are rather uncertain, since everything then was rather confused—we felt like flies in autumn.
  Like many other political prisoners, I was sent, at the end of September, 1937, from the Ussurískaya Taigá to a transit camp on our way to the city of Vladivostók. Two or three days after my arrival there—on October 3, 1937 —there arrived in that transit camp a detachment of prisoners from Moscow, who had been condemned under the political statutes. In this transit camp were concentrated political prisoners to be sent to Kolymá. About a hundred and fifty had been assigned to our barracks, "brand-new" prisoners from the Moscow detachment. Finding myself in the same barracks with them, I made the acquaintance of Zhénya, the son of Professor Alexander Alexándrovich Florénsky, who in time made me acquainted with the people in his section, among whom was D. Svyátopolk-Mirsky. They were interested, on our first meeting, when they learned that I had already done about a year in the camp, whereas they had only arrived from Gigorkhána. He questioned me about the conditions of life, the food

and the work in the concentration camps. Then Zhénya, the son of Professor Florénsky, told me about each of the people in his section. And from him I learned that Prince Svyátopolk-Mirsky had been in England and that he had been persuaded by Maxim Gorky to return to the U.S.S.R., that the Prince had worked at the Academy of Sciences in the Literary Division. He was arrested in 1937 in I do not remember what month and condemned without a hearing, not in court but at a special council of a special N.K.V.D. troíka, to ten years' imprisonment. We had arrived in Vladivostók by October 27, 1937, and during those three weeks we were in the same barracks. At the time of our conversations, the Prince was not very communicative, but he did not refrain from expressing his opinion on the subject of Maxim Gorky. He said that Maxim Gorky ought to be removed if he had planned to spread such a mass terror through the whole country, and that he could not be an indifferent observer of this bloody despotism.*

On October 27, 1937, four hundred and fifty men, including four hundred women, were loaded on the steamer Kuku, and on November 4, 1937, we arrived at the town of Magadán, four kilometers from the Bay of Nagáev, in the [name illegible] Point No. 1. There I landed in another barracks; we met seldom, and I only rarely dropped in on their barracks. On November 16 or 17, they were sent to the "Five Year Plan" gold field, but I to the "Unexpected" gold field. The winter of 1937-38 was terrible for the prisoners in Kolymá. In some of the camps, up to 75% perished.†

---

* There is clearly something wrong here. The writer must have reported Mirsky incorrectly. The latter can hardly have imagined that Gorky was responsible for the purges.

† Kolymá in northeast Siberia is almost uninhabitable. The rivers are frozen up for eight or nine months of the year, and the polar night lasts from six to ten weeks. In a snow-storm the natives will

In 1938, in the month of December, after getting my feet frozen, I was sent as an invalid to the invalid camp, which was twenty-three kilometers from the town of Magadán, where I met some of the people from the Moscow group, and they told me that Prince Svyátopolk-Mirsky was then in that camp in the hospital barracks. He was violently insane. I several times asked for permission to go to the hospital barracks, but this was always refused. At the end of several weeks, I was notified by the orderly that Prince Svyátopolk-Mirsky was dead. I suppose that this was at the end of January, 1939—the exact date I do not remember.

Out of this group of prisoners only Florénsky's son Zhénya survived. A. A. Florénsky himself had died a long time before D. Svyátopolk-Mirsky's death at the "Five Year Plan" gold field at the beginning of 1938.

This is all, much-esteemed ———— ————, that I know about the sad story of Prince Svyátopolk-Mirsky. Accept the assurances of my perfect respect.]

——————

[I should also give some further account of the L. I have mentioned above, who had worked for the Five Year Plan and who produced, when we went to the theater, the mother-of-pearl opera-glasses. During the summer I spent in Moscow, she was working for the Open Road Travel Agency, through which I had to make my arrangements. She was married to a young American, the son of one of the engineers who had been brought over as advisors on the planning of Soviet industry. The father had been

not venture out without a rope tied to the izbá, since it is possible to be buried in the snow and die a few yards from one's own doorstep. It was the decision of Nicholas II that conditions in Kolymá were too severe for human beings to be made to live there. Stalin had no such scruples.

born in Germany and was a socialist, who had been so
much impressed by what was going on in Russia—he went
there in 1929—that he had brought his whole family
over. The American mother did not care for it and referred to Stalin as "Joe"; but the family, at the time I was
there, enjoyed a position of privilege. The boy, who was a
photographic expert, was employed making microfilm in
the Institute of Experimental Medicine, and he was given
an apartment in a special new building assigned to foreign
"technicians." Thus, L., who belonged to the old bourgeoisie and had never quite adapted herself to Soviet life,
now found an approximation—in her relative security and
comfort—to the pre-Revolutionary standard of living; and
her husband, though he rated, I suppose, as a "worker,"
had as an American a much freer mentality than that of
the peasant Russians. They were expecting a baby at the
time I left, and I thought them in many ways fortunate.

But when the purges got under way in 1937, there
commenced one of those xenophobe periods which have
been a recurrent feature of Russian history. When L.'s
husband applied, at this time, to renew his Russian
visa, though his previous applications had always been
granted, he was given ten days to get out of the country.
He was obliged to leave L. and her baby behind, for he
had to establish a residence and provide himself with a
job at home before he could bring them over. In the meantime, L. discovered that no Russian office would employ
her. She could only get odd jobs translating and working
for the New York *Herald Tribune* correspondent. She
applied for a visa as a Soviet citizen, and when this was
refused, she renounced her Soviet citizenship, and again
applied. The visa did not come through. In 1938 there
was an epidemic of dysentery, and she nearly lost her
little girl. In order to get along, she had to sell her per-

sonal things, and she was so sure of leaving Russia that she disposed of all her winter clothes.

I have spoken above of the readiness with which the people in Moscow responded to a visitor's smile. Harrison Salisbury, the former New York *Times* correspondent, says in his recent book that he had been in Russia three months before he received a smile from any woman whom he casually encountered. L. tells me that by 1938 people did not even look at one another: they would stand with their eyes on your feet, and from your footwear they would recognize you. As the wife of a foreigner, L. herself was by that time completely in Coventry. No one would have anything to do with her, and she hardly dared greet old friends. One day in the September of 1938, a handsome young man in civilian clothes called at L.'s apartment. He handed her an order from the NKVD and made her sign an acknowledgment that she would not reveal anything of the interview to which she was being summoned. This interview was not to take place for three days, and she at once wrote a letter to the American Embassy—dating it in the previous year—saying that in case of an accident or her death the child should be sent to its father in the States.

The day of the interview, L. packed a small bag, left the little girl with the wife of the head of the travel agency, whom she had taken into her confidence, and presented herself at the Lyúbyanka. There her Russian passport was taken away, and an NKVD official explained to her that she had been selected by the NKVD to track down American spies in Moscow and later to be sent to America to work for the Soviet Union. She replied that she had no experience and no qualifications for that kind of work. He lectured her on her duty to the Soviet Union, but she now flatly refused. The official began to threaten;

but she says she was not afraid: she felt only resignation and indifference—for she knew that, if she did not come back, the child would be taken to the American Embassy. "Suddenly," she writes, in an account of this, "I heard an angry voice shouting: 'Read and sign!' A sheet of paper was thrown at me. He made me very angry. I told him his attitude was that of one of the Tsar's gendarmes, who had been abolished, I thought, with the Revolution. He did not reply. I read and signed the paper. I solemnly swore not to disclose this meeting, etc., etc. When I had signed, my passport was returned—this meant I was allowed to go. I did not move; I never expected to be free again. The young man who had served me the paper helped me to get up and escorted me to the gate. I did not know what time it was. The streets were deserted. I started to walk toward Theater Square. The hands of the clock in the square pointed to four o'clock in the morning. I don't remember how I reached the apartment of [the director of the travel agency], I know I walked all the way."

"A week later," she continued, "I had a nervous breakdown. Most of the winter I spent in bed." The maid who had worked for her several years and upon whose affectionate relations with L. I have commented so admiringly above had left her by this time, helping herself to L.'s jewelry, money and clothing. But she had found someone else to take care of the baby when she herself was out: "Olga, a young and attractive girl, not the peasant type," who had become very fond of the little girl. "When Olga learned I was sick, she came almost every day after her work in the factory office and without any pay did all the housework. Sometimes she even spent her own money for food. My neighbor, a wife of a factory manager, was also very kind to us. She, too, shared her food with us. Some of my American friends sent us warm clothes and frequently fruit and canned food. Thus we lived through the winter, and another year passed. In 1939, I gave up all hope of leaving Russia." She sometimes considered suicide.

But her husband was working on the other end; under pressure of the menace of Hitler, the Soviet Union was anxious to preserve friendly relations with the United States; we sent a new ambassador to Moscow. The last straw for L. was a notice of eviction from her room. She wrote letters, she says, "to every Russian official I could think of, including Stalin." She did not dare now to go near our embassy, but she got her friend of the agency to show them there a copy of the eviction notice. At the end of May, at last, she was granted permission to leave. "I had to sign a statement that I would never ask to come back, not even for a visit."

At Riga she encountered an obstacle that was characteristically American. The latest fad in American medicine—like "bursitis" today—was "fungus," which was supposed to account for a variety of ailments. When L. applied for her visa, the American doctor who examined her noted her deteriorated fingernails, which had crumbled from a lack of calcium, and told her that she was suffering from fungus and would have to have them out before she could enter the United States. She was subjected to the painful operation—which had, however, the good result that, when they grew back, her nails were normal.

L.'s husband was living at that time in an Eastern industrial city. He had been brought there by the wife of one of the owners of the company that dominated this city, who grew orchids and had sent photographs of them to be processed and developed by the photographic laboratory in which the young man was working in New York. She had been so much impressed by his prints, one of which had won a prize, that she had set up a studio and laboratory for him. L. at first had found it rather difficult to adjust herself to her new life. "I really think," she writes, "I was a very sick person when I arrived. I was afraid of everything—to answer the doorbell, telephone, to speak to strangers." But she enjoyed the greater freedom and the better food of the United States. When Roosevelt was running for reëlection in 1940, she listened to radio speeches and was astonished that people could criticize the president—and in such an aggressive way!—without being punished for it. But she felt very much an alien. Her little girl "had no playmates. In spite of the fact that she did speak English, the children called her a 'foreigner!' " And L. made no real friends. The lady who grew the orchids, herself from the Middle East, was kind to L. and her husband and often invited them to her house by themselves. She had, among other things, a painting of Pávlova by Sórin, two medieval ikons and some old Russian silver. "These visits and this atmosphere brought memories of my very early childhood. All through my life in Russia I had tried to erase these memories as a shameful past, to find myself now in America longing and yearning for it." But though her husband was a photographic expert, not a factory worker, she found herself living in an industrial community, with whose members she had little in common. The family who virtually ran the city did very little, she noted, for the education or entertainment of their army of employees; and L. had no way of getting to know—except for her husband's wealthy patron—the educated people of the city. They made the acquaintance of a couple who were by way of being "fellow travelers" and were interested in L. and her husband because they had been in Russia. Her relations with them were rather uncomfortable, since they would not believe what L. told them about what had been going on in the Soviet Union, and insisted that she was hopelessly prejudiced and did not really know about the wonderful things that were still being done over there. Except for their evenings with this couple and their contacts with the lady who grew orchids, she was condemned to a double exile—an ex-citizen of the workers' republic, whom her government had tried to eliminate; now the citizen of a bourgeois republic, where the workers owned their own cars but where, among them, she was still out of place. Her father used to tell the family after the Revolution, that they at least had their education: this was something that the Communists could not take away. But now, after two decades of Soviet Moscow and fifteen years of an American industrial town, she is not so sure even of this.]

V

VOLGA IDYLL

TRAIN from Moscow to Gorky. There was a young student who was designing gliders. When I told him that I was an American, he asked at once whether I was an engineer. An Alaskan who spoke Russian in my compartment was able to talk to him about his subject, and the boy leaned over excitedly, holding out a book of diagrams and eager for information about what was being done in the United States. Two younger boys in blue uniforms and blue peaked caps, with round pink sun-baked faces, lay stretched on their stomachs in their bunks with their arms folded under their chins, listening with solemn attention. I had never seen illustrated so vividly their intensity about what they call "technique." Finally, the boys fell asleep; but in the semi-darkness, with its single feeble light, the student still went on talking passionately about glider-designs.

Gorky (Nízhni-Nóvgorod). Slow old sprawling provincial town, dating from the thirteenth century: white fragments of an ancient Kremlin; quiet streets of blinding summer sun; a big white state bank built by the Tsar, bristling and grimly ornate; people better-looking than in Moscow, good color, without the city blight. The girl in the principal book-shop wouldn't sell me a volume of the new edition of Lérmontov, apparently for no better reason than that it was part of their window display.

We bought cherries in a market-place full of people. There was a man sitting out of doors and embroidering tapestry animals on a frame: clumsy swans with very thick necks and a blue oriental-looking tiger, surrounded by orange butterflies and pink roses. I bought the tiger for sixty rubles: the man said it had taken him months, and it was really quite a handsome production. I can still see him looking up from under the visor of his cap when I asked him what he wanted for the tiger, with deep-set limpid brown eyes which were at the same time as piercing as his needle.

Much squalor, large sections of the town gone to seed, as on the street where Gorky was born—the usual wooden fretwork of lace. One steep little cobbled street was scooped out by the rain like a gutter and grass-grown along the trough. An old woman who limped, carrying horizontally before her an acquiescent gray goat; another, younger woman carrying a squealing little pig. A young sorrel horse, with no harness and all alone, had just turned into the drive which runs along and looks down on the river: he was simply out for a walk.

They have a mania for renaming places. This is the naïve side of the Revolution. Surely it is a great mistake to name so many things after Gorky; old names like those of Nízhni-Nóvgorod and the street called the Tvérskaya in Moscow, which have no tsarist connotations, but simply recall the early map of Russia, might better have been left as they were. Even Leningrad is still Peter's city and might better still bear his name. Besides, a whole country of Gorky-villes and Stalin-villes, as Russia seems in a fair way to become, with a Karl Marx street in every town and village, tends to have the effect of making Gorky, Marx and Stalin commonplace. Yet these cities belong to them now and never belonged to them before, and they have a right to name them what they please.

The Volga. Enormous, passive, wide open and smooth, spreading down the whole middle of Russia: a female river. The steamboat, winding its way among shoals, wanders all over the surface. Flat banks—fields of yellow grain —an occasional sharp isolated steeple. Sandy shore, a form-less river.

One of their great phrases is "bourgeois prejudice." When the elderly waitress on the boat was asked as a joke by one of the tourists for lemon to put in the tea (they haven't been importing lemons), she retorted, in the same spirit: "Bourgeois prejudice!"

I stopped over a boat at Ulyánovsk in order to see the Lenin Museum; [but this, I had found out, could not be accomplished without difficulty. The director of the travel agency, who had got me my passage on the Volga boat, had already tried to discourage me from making this un-usual stopover—"Don't do it! don't do it!" he had suddenly cried; and the Intourist woman interpreter on the steamer, who was responsible for the foreign tourists, had also made efforts to dissuade me. At the last moment, just as we were getting in at four o'clock in the morning, she ap-peared to me on deck and made me a dramatic scene in the mist-thickened river-darkness. "Tell me!" she de-manded tensely. "Why you want to go to Ulyánovsk?" I told her what I had told her before: that I was writing

about the Russian Revolution and wanted to see the birth-
place of Lenin. It was almost impossible for her—as it
seemed to be for many Russians—to believe that this could
be true, so she appealed to me now again: "But tell me,
please, why you really want to go to Ulyánovsk?" I could
only repeat my reason—adding, "your great leader, Lenin"
—a line which was likely to stop them, since the greatness of Lenin was a part of their credo which still had
to be treated with respect. "But you will get lost," she
protested, "and I will be blamed for this. How will you
catch the next steamer?" I said that I knew enough Russian to ask my way around. "I am afraid you will disappear. I ask you please not to get off here." I insisted that
I had fixed it up in Moscow, that the travel agency knew
what I was doing, and since there was nobody else to
hinder me, I went off in the dark down the gangplank. I
was sorry to leave her so worried, but all this kind of thing
in the Soviet Union was thoroughly exasperating.]

On the dock, I was directed to a flophouse where travelers were put up between boats, and I plodded with some
effort up the high steep bank. There was mud that was
deep and adhesive, like the slime at the bottom of a pond,
and this made the ground as slippery as if it had been
covered with ice. It was hard even to walk on the steps
that led to the top of the cliff.

When I awoke, after everybody else was up, I lay looking at the girl who was making the beds. She was pretty, a
blondínka, with bobbed fair reddish hair. She was also
extremely nice. She told me that I shouldn't have to walk
up the hill, because there was a man with a horse coming
to take me.

This man was an extraordinarily nice old Bolshevik with
a brown beard and large brown eyes: he was the humane-
eyed rather than the sharp-eyed type. It was raining a fine
dense rain, and he tried to give me a rain-coat, which I

very foolishly declined. So we started up the hill in the old backless droshky, which was shaken by the cobbles so violently that everything I saw seemed flickering and jerking like a bad old-fashioned film.

At the top, the little provincial city, which is said once to have been so beautiful from the river, seemed like a place that had been forgotten and left behind up there. Like many towns which are not centers of industry, Ulyánovsk has been neglected by the recent Soviet programs. It looked to me not merely down-at-heels since the days of the Karamzíns, the Goncharóvs, the Kerénskys and the Ulyánovs; it seemed, on this day of mud and drizzle, actually to be decomposing. I stopped for breakfast at a shabby-looking restaurant on a main business street where everything looked shabby. All I could seem to get was black bread without butter and bad coffee. I asked for an omelet, and, after some demur—they said at first they couldn't make one—they produced a kind of tasteless fried custard. [I believe that this rundown condition of Ulyánovsk was one of the real reasons for the opposition to my going there. Tourists never saw these dead cities.]

I got back into the droshky, and the driver drove me out to the early home of Lenin. I wondered, on the way, whether a big church they were knocking to pieces was the cathedral in which Kerénsky tells us he used to sing in the choir like a little angel while that little fiend Vladímir Ilyích was sitting in the congregation and doubtless making game of the whole thing.

The Ulyánov house,* carefully preserved, with a custodian who showed you around, was a contrast to the rest of Ulyánovsk. With its sobriety and shining cleanness, its fine mahogany furniture, its maps and music and books, it reminded me of the houses of cultivated New Englanders

---

* I have described this house at length in my book *To the Finland Station*.

as I used to see them in my youth. So that was what it
had been like, the life of the educated middle class out of
which Lenin had come—breaking out of the mold himself and leaving the old town, in which he had been
bred, distinguished by its learned names, to disintegrate in
the rain. Now no doubt there were only a few of them
left, lurking in their damp rooms among books and old
pieces of furniture. For today the river of civilization was
running in another channel. To have changed the course
of the Volga would certainly have been less astounding!

The driver took me all over town and back to the
flophouse again. He shook hands with me at parting and
wouldn't accept a kopek—whether by arrangement with
Intourist or because he didn't want to take money for
showing the house of Lenin, I do not know.

I went in. There was nobody there but the *blondinka*.
I prepared to kill time till the next boat and sat down
at a table to write. But the *blondinka* had made all the
beds and now had nothing to do, and she picked up a
guitar from one of the beds and sat down on a bed and
began to strum. I said that the weather was bad, and she
agreed that it was very bad. It was raining harder now,
and the little wooden shacks outside the window looked
peculiarly dismal and raw. I asked her whether the guitar
was hers and she said no, it belonged to one of the tran-
sients. She came over and sat near me and went on strumming. I asked her to sing something, but she wouldn't.

I gave up trying to write. A great liking for this blond
girl began to warm me—the kind of liking that sometimes
arises, without utterance or special occasion, in the presence of the sweet Russian blend of sensitivity with can-
did simplicity. Her hair, as I have said, was fair and
reddish, a deeper shade in some places than in others; and
she had pale rather weak blue-green eyes, eyebrows that
seemed to have been plucked and quite a little yellow

mustache on her upper lip. Her figure was rather thick, and her hands and arms were tanned. She said that she was twenty-one, that she was not married and had no sweetheart. Her name was Clavdia Dmítrievna.

There was a checkerboard, and I suggested playing. She protested that she was terribly bad, but I said that I was, too; and as a matter of fact, it turned out, we were pretty evenly matched. The rules in Russia are different from ours, and this made it disconcerting at first, since Clavdia Dmítrievna and I were acting on different assumptions; but after I had got the hang of the game, I had a peculiar feeling that, with the give and take of the moves, we were getting to understand one another intimately. It would be with a shock that I would realize, when we would stop and begin to talk again, that our verbal communications were still imperfect. It seemed to me that the sympathy I felt for her must actually be pulsing through the pieces. She was so gentle, so amiable, so natural, so immediately responsive to everything. There was something about her that seemed stolidity, yet she would constantly surprise and delight me by the quick coming to life characteristic of a certain type of Russian woman. It was a kind of sudden flurry of animation, volatile, emphatic, smiling, which would be started by so trivial an incident as my moving one of her men by mistake (*"Éto moy!"*) And when she saw that the odds were against her—what seemed to me, also, peculiarly Russian —she would begin throwing away all her pieces. We went on playing game after game; and she, I knew, would have gone on indefinitely, as they always seem willing to do with any kind of intellectual pursuit, if I, with my American restlessness, had not felt it was time to try something else.

I went out into the quagmire-like mud and the rain and, visiting the riverfront booths, where skinny pigs and children were poking about, I bought some black bread, some bad beer, some sour Volga apples, some sausage and some candies in fancy paper wrappings.

Clavdia Dmítrievna and I ate up the food together, though she would not drink any beer. If it had not been for my bringing these things, she would never, so far as I could see, have done anything about getting herself anything to eat during the whole of her twenty-four hour shift. She must have had all her meals at home.

Two men had come into the room: they were working on a "buffet" to adjoin the flophouse; and I offered them some of the food. They smelt the sausage before they ate it, and one of them asked me what I thought about war. He thought war was coming soon. Then they went on with their work and, having finally put up a door in the doorway that led to the buffet, they closed it with themselves on the other side, so that Clavdia Dmítrievna and I were again thrown in on one another. She had been strumming the guitar more or less all the time, without ever quite arriving at a tune—it was an accompaniment to a song that was never sung; and she seemed prepared to go on strumming interminably. Nothing except hours of work ever begins or ends in Russia. Their time behaves so differently from ours. It is of the essence of Russian time that the "imperfective aspect" of their verbs, the form which represents a continuing action, should be the norm from which the "perfective aspect," which represents the action as completed, is usually a variation; and that the perfective in what seems to be the present form, which ought to mean that an action is completed in the present, should have, actually, a future meaning. I had been wondering what I should do to fill the time till the boat left that night, but now I was quite content to let the rainy day slip along with the chords of Clavdia Dmítrievna's guitar. I asked her again to sing, and again she answered

"*Nyet.*" She sat on the edge of the bed, looking very attractive, I thought, with one of her blue-sneakered feet turned under her against the floor.

Presently her sister and brother came in. They were both younger than Clavdia Dmítrievna. The girl was seventeen and was dressed in an old dark dress much too long for her, which had probably been handed down from a whole series of older sisters, and what seemed to be a pair of boy's shoes. This sister was pretty, too, in a less developed way; she had put spots of cold cream on her chapped lips. Clavdia Dmítrievna explained that her sister knew the words of the songs from the film *Merry Fellows* which I had been asking Clavdia Dmítrievna about, and the younger girl immediately sat down and wrote them out, without hesitating a second: five stanzas of one song and two of the other, with the appropriate refrains. Then she wrote her full name at the top of the page, Praskóvaya Dmítrievna Lázareva, and engrossed a fancy monogram at the bottom. One of these songs was called *Sérdtse,* and I asked what that meant. Clavdia Dmítrievna, in one of her gusts of animation, pressed her hand under her left breast; and when I said, "Oh, yes, I understand!" they all exclaimed in a general gust, "He understands! he understands!" Clavdia Dmítrievna's gesture seemed to me natural and lovely, and "*sérdtse,*" with its sound of a muffled beat, a beautiful word for "heart."

An older girl now came in: she looked capable and had strong dark eyes. She was wearing some kind of badge and, unlike Clavdia Dmítrievna and her sister, was evidently the more serious type of young Russian. She asked me where I worked in America—in Russia they always ask you where you work instead of where you live; and whether "life was better in America or here." They wanted to see my foreign money, which excited them very much. They cried, "Silver!" They had never seen any before. They seemed a little abashed when I showed them the head on a florin, and said it was the English tsar. They asked me so many questions and I had so little Russian to answer them that I presently became exhausted. Feeling this with the ready Russian intuition and acting with the Russian lack of explicitness, they all (except Clavdia Dmítrievna) suddenly melted away. I lay down on my cot for a nap.

When I woke up, the day was darkening. It was Clavdia Dmítrievna who had wakened me. All alone with her guitar in the gathering dusk, she had finally begun to sing: one of those strange little old-fashioned songs, apparently simple and gay, which the minors of the old Greek modes in the limitless spaces of Russia have imbued with a wildness and a sadness. I was enchanted: I listened till she stopped, then called out that the song was "wonderful." She answered, "What? what?", as they so often do, and came out of her little office. I told her how much I had liked the song and, as she came near me, stretched out my hand. She gave me her hand and permitted me to hold it, though in a curiously unresponsive way, as if no one had ever taken it before and she did not know what to expect. She simply stood there; I kept it for a moment, and then pressed it and let it go. She did not return my pressure or allow her own hand to linger; but she stood for a moment yet before she went back to her room.

I got up and washed at a tap in the wall, and asked Clavdia Dmítrievna for a towel. She had done nothing about giving me one, after our eating the sausage in the afternoon, when I was drying my hands on my handkerchief, though she had been using one herself. But now that I made the request, she promptly and cheerfully produced a clean one. It never would have occurred to her it was part of her job to give the travelers service. This attitude, in Soviet Russia, is only to be found in Intourist hotels, where it is cultivated artificially or has been taken over from the old regime.

She was reading. I asked her about the book: she immediately shut it up and brought out of a drawer of her desk an old volume of *Crime and Punishment,* which she now began to read instead—either to show me that she was capable of more serious tastes or out of simple native volatility. I asked her to go over the words of *Sérdtse* with me. She did so, and when she had finished, much struck by the complicated monogram which her sister had made at the bottom of the page, she picked up a pencil and became for some minutes absorbed in an attempt to reproduce it. I took her hand in mine and examined it and told her that all Soviet girls were strong. She replied, without any kind of coquetry, that she didn't know about that, but that she herself was strong, because she had done a lot of work. She held up her right arm and clenched her fist and made me feel her muscle, which was certainly very hard. I tried to kiss her other hand, but she took it away and said, *"Nyet!"*

A little dampened by this, I presently left her to read and went in and took another nap. This time it was black night when I was awakened by low voices: a young man and a young woman were getting ready to go to sleep in the beds opposite mine. When they had both got into bed, the young man stretched out his hand across the gap beteen the cots, and the young woman gave him hers, which he held till they went to sleep. I decided to get up and go in and visit Clavdia Dmítrievna again. I found her in her little room, lying down, with a blanket over her, on a hard wooden cot with no mattress. I thought I would sit up and read Lenin till the boat got in at 2:30. Clavdia Dmítrievna went straight to sleep and snored with such shattering violence that I could not keep my mind on the book. It got colder, and I went back to bed.

I slept till 2:15 and then sprang up, much alarmed for fear I had missed the boat. I said, *"Do svidánya"* to Clavdia Dmítrievna, who woke up as I came through the office, and kissed her good-by on the forehead; then made a dash for the dock. I stumbled down the hill through the mud, which was harder now from the cold, but found the gate locked and no one around. I went back to the flop-house, much worried, believing that the steamer had left, and Clavdia Dmítrievna called up the dock. She was told that there would not be a boat that night—there would not be another boat till two o'clock the next morning, twenty-four hours away. I could go back to bed now, she said, as if the news were sure to be welcome—I should not have to worry any more about catching the boat that night. That I might feel impatience at being delayed would obviously not have occurred to her.

So there we were, Clavdia Dmítrievna and I. We sat gazing at one another. After a moment, I began to pet her. I patted and stroked her cheeks and neck, and she sat there looking straight at me with her frank and gentle eyes. This went on for a considerable time but did not seem to lead to anything, and I began to feel as if I were patting a pony. I stopped and said good-night and went to bed.

In the morning, the weather was wonderful. The sun was out and the mud drying up. We leaned on the railing of the porch and looked down on the unrippled Volga, where the mists were now cleared away, so you could see the wooded bank on the other side. I asked her whether she liked to swim, and she replied with her usual vivacity that she did like it very much and that that was why her arms were so brown. Today was her day off, she told me; I asked what she was going to do, and she said that she and her brothers and sisters were going to the kino and to dance. I found that I could resign myself easily to another

day in Ulyánovsk: I would ask Clavdia Dmítrievna to go
swimming with me and take her, perhaps, to the movies.
Was she perfectly sure, I asked, that the boat would not
be in till two the next morning. She told me she had just
called the dock and it was expected at one that afternoon.
I went off to buy something at the booths for her and me
to eat, and when I came back, she was gone.

I wandered down to the dock, and there I found her
younger sister in her men's shoes and long dress. Praskóvaya Dmítrievna told me that the boat would be in at
ten: she was waiting there for the loading. I didn't believe her about the boat, but stayed around the dock myself. After a time, I went up to Praskóvaya again to make
sure that I had not misunderstood. "It's coming now," she
said: it was nowhere near ten yet. I didn't believe this either; but she took me up to the top deck of the floating
boatlike wharf, and there, sure enough, was the steamboat
coming around the bend. We sat there and went through
Sérdtse again, and she asked me to read her some English:
she wanted to hear how it sounded.

The boat came in, and I lost her. When I looked for
her, to say good-by, she wasn't there. But she suddenly appeared at the gangplank just as the steamer was pulling
out. I stretched out my arm and shook hands with her, as
the steamer was moving away from the dock, and called
out what nice girls they were.

———

The Volga again: white clouds which seem painted in
relief on the blue, as in the skies of the American Southwest—or clouds made of gray ink and outlined on a surface of gray. The eternal flat green shores—on the third
day, low pelted hills, reflected dull green in the water—
one little town had thatched roofs, all the towns were
gray and unpainted.

There was a very pretty woman in the second class, small, with lively dark eyes and a way of doing her hair in a pompadour which reminded me of the early nineteen hundreds. She was the type of Russian woman who, though young, is not the Soviet type. There was, also, a man who would sit down at the piano and run on with old popular tunes that brought back the same period as the pompadour. One of the tunes was *Hiawatha,* an American song of my childhood, and he made me extremely nervous by playing it with all the wrong emphasis, so that it sounded tinkly, minor and Russian, instead of two-stepping with the marked American rhythm.

One day we stopped for an hour or more at a dismal manufacturing town called Volsk. Everything was gray with cement dust. Men and boys were plunging into the muddy water from a prodigiously high diving platform, with no form but plenty of nerve. Presently I saw in the water the lady with the vivacious eyes, who was doing a very feminine breast stroke and who shot back at the people on the steamer what would once have been called a gay and flashing glance. Out of the water, she walked along the pier like a bird, on small-boned ankles and feet, her body bending forward from the waist so that her big and shapely hips stuck out behind—like old postcards of bathing girls.

She and the man who played the piano contributed to an impression I had had before: that the isolation of the Soviet Union has had the effect of preserving, within its close-guarded boundaries, old habits, fashions and tastes which have quite disappeared from the rest of the world, as the prehistoric animals in Conan Doyle's *Lost World* survived on their high plateau. The real innovations in Russia have been mainly in the field of mechanical technique; and it is curious and rather charming to observe that in other respects the Russians are sometimes still back in 1914, when they were first cut off from Europe. You may hear any night on any radio in Moscow, or played by any café orchestra, that old sentimental waltz which is given so nostalgic a value in the scene in *The Cherry Orchard* in which the family estate is sold.

In the first class, I met a young couple who represented something altogether different. They were two prize aviation students who were getting a two months' vacation and all the best of everything that a Volga boat could provide. They were both exceedingly handsome: she a very dark Rumanian, he a very blond gray-eyed Russian—"a contrast, light and dark!" he pointed out to me. They were shining, enthusiastic, well-dressed, the young man approximating to something American. They invited me into their cabin and gave me apples, candy and cakes. The cakes she had made herself, and he was very proud of her having made them. They had been "registered"— that is, married—only a year. He told me that he and she were "one," holding up a finger to make this plain. He asked me whether we had love in America—to be sure, with a certain archness, but—influenced, as he evidently was by the recent official policy of encouraging the domestic affections and making it possible for husbands and wives to take their vacations together—not without an implication that genuine love was among the peculiar benefits—possible only in a socialist society—conferred by Comrade Stalin on the inhabitants of the Soviet Union.

We talked about the different classes of cabin on the boat, he calling them "classes" at first, then remembering and calling them "categories." He asked me if I was a friend of the U.S.S.R., and in the conversation that followed, I told him that I had stopped off at Ulyánovsk to see the Lenin Museum. "Lenin," the boy replied, "yes, Lenin was a great leader. He loved the people very much. All the country people have pictures of him up in their houses." I realized that the Revolution was already a long time ago for the young people of their generation. For me, who had been twenty-two in 1917, Lenin was a great contemporary; for them, he was already on his way to becoming an historical hero, as Washington and Lincoln are for us.

I would sometimes go down to the hold and walk through the third-class cabin. The people were not traveling very comfortably; they were carrying their possessions on their backs and sleeping on the cargo or the floor. But they did not look ill-fed or unhappy. On the contrary, they had rosy country faces. There were a great many musical instruments among their baggage; and one little half-naked boy was playing a balalaika—as the children in the first-class saloon were playing the piano: by ear.

The fifth day of the voyage down the Volga gets to be rather boring: it is all so much alike. One moderate variation: a ribbon of liver-colored cliffs, on top of which was scattered a pale wooden village, without human color or shape; then, more liver-colored cliffs, which had been cut into chunks by the rain, and the chunks further cut into slices, above liver-colored water of a deeper brown.

VI

ODESSA: COUNTER-IDYLL

STALINGRAD. A new town, an industrial center, at the opposite pole from places like Ulyánovsk. Life seems attractive in Stalingrad. The big tractor plant is certainly very different from anything to be seen in Detroit. I had wondered in Leningrad and Moscow where were the strapping exuberant Soviet workers of whom one saw photographs and films; but I found them in Stalingrad. These people are another race from the short formless Muscovites (of small stock, I suppose, in the first place, and stunted further by the malnutrition of the years of revolution and war). The Stalingrad tractor workers are peasants just in from the fields, and—though it is true that they have been having a certain amount of difficulty in learning to manipulate the machinery—they are certainly the handsomest lot of people I have ever seen inside a factory. The woman workers are the only women I have ever seen look attractive in working clothes: they wore overalls and sleeveless jerseys, many of them pink or red, which stretched tight over their superb breasts. They would examine the clothes of the women tourists and ask them about the materials and how much they cost in America.

The pace was much more leisurely than Detroit, the aspect of things much less grim. At Ford's, for example, the drop forges, one of the most dangerous departments of the plant, give the effect of an antechamber to Hell; visitors are not taken to see them. At Stalingrad, the drop forges seemed farther apart and were certainly much better ventilated. And the men there work only six hours. When I visited the tractor factory, it was noon, and they had simply stopped the conveyor, and everybody had gone off to lunch—a thing inconceivable at Ford's!

Surely nothing could be more absurd than the objection one sometimes hears that the Soviets are headed for a civilization overmechanized and materialistic like that of the United States—though the Soviets' own propaganda for mechanization and their boasts of their industrial progress have given encouragement to this. The truth is that, in spite of the Russian enthusiasm for emulating American technique, it would take them several decades, even with their Stakhánov version of the American Taylor Plan, to approximate American efficiency; and the whole genius of the Russian people is so different from our practical Anglo-Saxon one that their carrying these tendencies to extremes is impossible for me to imagine. They may surely be pardoned at present for their efforts to provide themselves with the necessities and a few of the comforts of life!

———————

After the spectacle of the conveyor which had stopped for lunch, the American tourists in the party were continually making me feel the difference between Americans and Russians. There was a strong-minded old lady among us who insisted on lecturing the guide for having lost some of the members of the party; and, on our way back to the hotel in the bus, another American woman made the driver stop so that two little boys who had been hanging on might not be carried too far from home—just as I myself, on the Volga boat, had gone to considerable trouble to expel from the saloon a bird which had got in and which was making a most piteous and exasperating plaint, while the Russians, at their interminable card games, were not in the least concerned. No Russian would have thought of doing any of these things. It was the American instinct to control, to check up, to see to it that things were properly attended to, that they were brought to a decisive conclusion.

———————

This old lady who had scolded the guide was probably a little cracked. She had eyeglasses, some rouge on her cheeks and an old-fashioned motoring veil tied around a straw hat and knotted under her chin; and she talked all the time in a loud nasal voice that cut right through everything and everybody. She came, it seemed, from Springfield, Illinois. People at home had opposed her going to Russia, but what had made her do it was a book that she had read about women in the Soviet Union; and now that she was here, she was crazy about it. When you considered that Roosevelt back home had them throwing their hogs into the Mississippi! And she always said that she felt safer in Russia: in Springfield, there was civil war between the Progressive Miners, the U.M.W.A. and the authorities, so that you were afraid to go out on the streets. Why, somebody at the Capital mine had turned a machine-gun right into the crowd, and they never would tell who it was! If Abraham Lincoln could see Springfield now! She predicted a revolution within fifteen years. The only hope was that the Republicans might nominate some good clean man whom the people could really trust!

She was traveling first class and had hired a special guide to go with her. She bossed the Russians around with benevolent condescension and harassed the other tourists with monologues that seemed to be pouring from the neurosis known as "total recall." When I met this old lady again, at a later stage of my journey, I saw in the eyes of

her special guide a look of mute unspeakable suffering.
Yet I rather liked the old lunatic: she could never have
been produced by any other country than ours.

———————

I found myself traveling "soft," with a woman tourist
from Prague, a Turk from the Embassy in Moscow and a
Russian boy who was some sort of engineer and had been
working on the Moscow subway. The Turk was a most
amiable man and had rescued the Czecho-Slovak lady, a
little Germanic woman with spectacles, who spoke very
genteel French, from the discomforts of the "hard" carriage. He answered her questions about Russia with, it
seemed to me, intelligence and sympathy. She said that
things were terribly bad in Czecho-Slovakia, that the people were frightened of fascism and that the result of
Czech nationalism since the depression had been that the
German inhabitants were being turned out of their jobs.
She wondered when the other countries would learn to
straighten out their economy sensibly the way the Russians had. I had met, beginning with the Englishman on
the boat, a number of such middle-class people, dependent on their salaries in jobs that required special training,
who, without any Marxist ideology, had been coming to
have doubts about the capitalist system and were using
their vacations to visit Russia. She confided to me later,
when I was taking her around, that she wanted so much
to hear "the Comintern song." It turned out that she
meant the *International*. I asked whether she had never
heard it in Prague. Oh, no, she said: she was sure they
would never allow it to be sung.

The boy who had worked on the Metro had the same
kind of effervescence as Clavdia Dmítrievna and represented in its most glowing form the Boy Scout side of
young Russia. He had a translation of Upton Sinclair's

King Cole and Mayakóvsky's poems, and he told me that Sinclair was a great writer and Mayakóvsky a very great poet. I saw him later in the conductor's compartment sitting in his undershirt between the conductor and the trainman, and reading Mayakóvsky aloud to them. The conductor, a cunning little butterball of the fair-skinned and green-eyed type, had just taken off her uniform and was engaged in touching up her face; and the trainman, a good-natured old bird with a lantern and a mustache, was sitting and smiling at the humor and doing his best to get it.

————

Rostóv-on-the-Don. The further south you go, the pleasanter the cities seem. The people are taller, easier, freer, better-looking, better-dressed; and they seem to be enjoying themselves as they never do in Moscow. There are gay little European parks in Rostóv, with fountain-spray, shiny white statues, fragrance of large red flowers, secluded walks among the shrubbery with lovers immobile on benches and little bright-lighted restaurants lively with Viennese music. Also, written up over gates and worked out in flowerbeds, the new slogan: "Cadres decide everything."

When, however, the Czecho-Slovak lady and I looked in, with agreeable anticipations, on an advertised ballet performance in one of the public gardens, we did not find what we expected. This turned out to be a Soviet specialty called "Plastic Ballet," which consisted of Physcultúr versions of old chestnuts by Grieg, Brahms and Liszt. The dancers had the muscles of gymnasts and were almost completely naked. Like the production of *Romeo and Juliet* at the Theater of the Revolution, it was an attempt to make love attractive without yielding an inch to romance and without forgetting a moment the need for strenuous effort.

As I was walking back to the hotel one night, I heard wild and thrilling strains of Gypsy singing coming out through the open windows of a restaurant. I stopped and found that other people had gathered and were listening outside. The next moment a man had reached in with a rough uncontrollable gesture and snatched back the heavy red portière that kept the people outside from seeing. Sitting just inside the window was a party dining at a table, who were now exposed to the street; but they could not, as undoubtedly they would have done in any European country, order the headwaiter to close the curtain or even gaze at the intruders angrily. They could not; and I am by no means sure that they even had the impulse to do so.

We visited one of the homes where prostitutes were being reclaimed. There were two of these in Rostóv: one for girls with venereal disease and one for girls who were not infected. They were made to do various kinds of work, and when they were cured, they were given jobs. Some of them seemed depressed. There was one rather pretty little dark one who was standing in the doorway as we left: I smiled at her, and she answered at once with a sweet, pleased and childlike smile, which followed us, as we drove off, till we were out of sight down the street.— Visit to a maternity hospital: they took us through the wards and into the room where the newborn babies were kept. This last they should not have done—it would never have been done in America—since the voices of the tourists woke the babies up. They even brought us into the delivery room, where two women were being delivered. This shocked the Czecho-Slovak lady, and we all of us withdrew at once. But the nurse broadly smiled and asked whether it nauseated the ladies; they have no feeling about anything of that kind.

———

We paid rather a burlesque visit to another collective farm. The cracked old lady from Springfield was in ecstasies about everything she saw, and when the director gave us all ripe red tomatoes, she told him that she was coming right over to live there. The director, when this had been explained to him, bowed gallantly and said, "Please!" In the kitchen, a bright Jewish girl from New York, who had been sitting with the old lady in the car and who had been taking from her a good deal of punishment, pretended to collapse on a table. The annoying old lady at once showed the keenest solicitude and wanted to know what was the matter. The girl's boy-friend, not so rude as the girl, explained that he had hurt the girl's feelings. The old lady, well in the van on the way to the next point of interest, called back to the girl in her piercing Western voice: "Now, let me tell you something, honey love! I'm an old woman, and I can tell you that you'll get a whole lot more out of life if you don't let those things upset you!"

In a vineyard, we met a nice-looking old man, whom an Alaskan in the party questioned in Russian. The old man was extremely dissatisfied and complained that all kinds of things were being done all wrong. He evidently belonged to the class who had suffered from the collectivization; and I suppose that he had been forced by new methods to violate the habits of a lifetime. The Alaskan led him on, and he became more and more voluble. The guide, much embarrassed, took us away.

On the wall of the children's nursery, there was a row of little toothbrushes hung up, over which was a sign that said, "Be sure to go over your teeth three times." How many of those children's parents had ever had a toothbrush at all?

The Don was flowing slow and even between its level banks. We think in America that Kansas is flat, but you have to go to Russia to know how flat the earth can be. The steppe opened out, beyond the Don, as smooth as the top of a table, with not a tree, not a bush, not a mound, not a fence, not a house, not a stream: nothing but the great yellow haystacks. It seemed as vast as the sea.

All this time I had been getting sick. I had noticed that Clavdia Dmítrievna seemed to have a cold in her throat, and immediately after leaving Ulyánovsk, I began to develop a cold. When I got to Kíev, I had a fever and spent most of my time in bed. I only got out late one afternoon long enough to walk up through the park which looks down from the bluffs above the Dnieper. It is a wonderful park; and the people in Kíev gave me the impression of being happier than any others I had seen in Russia. The women were extremely good-looking and of a type I had not encountered; they had immensely big broad bodies, but small well-shaped hands and feet, and faces that were, surprisingly, not fat. Yet the people also seemed quieter than anywhere else. The couples were all talking to one another in a manner much more lively than in the North; yet their voices were so low that I could hardly hear them, and as twilight fell, it all began to seem like some faint but pleasant drift of phantoms that merged with the vagueness of my fever.

I had a very bad trip to Odessa. The Intourist service had been surpassing itself. I had always before thought it

funny when I had found myself assigned with two other
people to a room with only two beds or charged for a
room with a shower when the shower had been removed;
and I had been laughing at the indignation of the lady
from businesslike Prague, who was having her first experience of this. But I was ill now, and I wanted to be comfortable. I had told the Intourist girl at Rostóv that I was
sick and that I wanted to change my "hard" accommodations for "soft." "Come to me tomorrow," she said lan-
guidly. I told her I thought it ought to be done right
away, as otherwise it might not be possible. "Today or tomorrow," she said, "it is all the same thing,"—adding, "It
is *so* hot! and there are *so* many people!" So she let it go
till the next day, and the result was that, just as I was
leaving, she appeared in the bus and told me that she had
not been able to arrange for the soft accommodations. She
had not, as a matter of fact, even arranged about the hard
accommodations, and I was obliged to harass the conductor
for hours to get him to the point of giving me a mattress
and a blanket. He had not been told about me, he said,
and had not brought any bedclothes for me; but he finally,
I am afraid, took some away from someone else.

There was a man in the compartment I grew to dislike. He was like some sort of Jewish traveling salesman.
He spoke Russian very glibly and talked incessantly to the
other two men, two big unshaved, bare-throated, round-
headed louts. He rattled on at length about war and then
got on to the theater and literature, in which I was surprised to see that the hard-boiled-looking Russians took an
interest. But in Russia you found very few people who are
actually hard-boiled, as we understand toughness in America. I became depressed, however, as I listened, for they
seemed to be saying all the expected things about all the
regular productions. When the salesman had become
aware of the deficiencies of his companions' culture, he

proceeded to give them a lecture—which seemed to me more or less incorrect—on the philosophic background of Marxism.

Of course, in spite of the heat, they shut the window tight when they went to bed. This hatred of fresh air had always been one of the things which irritated me most about the Russians. The three boys with whom I had shared the stateroom on the boat from London to Leningrad had insisted on closing the porthole every night, even in the mildest May weather, so that I had always waked up in the morning in a state of partial asphyxiation; and in the apartment I had lived in in Moscow I had found that I had to take down the curtains in order to get the windows open and that, as soon as I would go out, the old woman who was looking after me would at once close them up again and put the curtains back. It made people so unhappy to have the windows open in trains that I had finally given up suggesting it. And in my present feverish state it seemed to me very important that someone should tell the Russians that they could never master American technique unless they learned to get used to fresh air. A great sourness against Russia possessed me. I felt that I was glad to be leaving.

I thought about the glasses they drink tea out of, which are always too hot to pick up in any ordinary convenient way. They have to put their thumb underneath the glass and stretch one finger up to the rim. It seemed to me characteristic that they should have drunk tea in gallons for ages without ever contriving a handle.

I thought about their heavy food. When I had first been invited out to dinner, I had mistaken the *zakúsky* (*hors d'oeuvres*) for a supper, and, what with these and the vegetable soup that followed, would find myself so utterly stuffed before we arrived at the meat course that I would have to skip the main part of the dinner. I brooded on the fact that they had never been able to think up any better hard liquor than vodka, which is simply a form of raw alcohol.

I brooded on their confounded language, of which I had just been getting such a dose in the chatter of the men in the compartment, with its eternal *kak-kak* and *tak-tak,* and its *da da, da da da!* It was encrusted with as many old barnacles and seaweed-strings and scallop-shells as a bottle that had been lying at the bottom of the sea. They had more inflections than Greek or Latin, and the endings were so irregular that a paradigm could teach you little. I thought about their fantastic alphabet, originally designed for Old Bulgarian, from which it had been possible to banish, after the Revolution, five wholly useless letters without leaving it much less cumbrous. I did not know which I disliked more: the prepositions that consist of a single consonant or the words that begin with such spluttering combinations as *vkh* and *vsp.**

I reflected that it might have been an excellent thing for the revolutionary government to have prohibited the use of such phrases as *"Seichás,"* "Right away," which is said by the Russians more often and lived up to less often than by the people of any other nation, and *"Nichevó,"* which means "It doesn't matter" and which passes off many sins. They might also have included *"Bolshóy skandál!",* "Big scandal!", which seems to have come to be used for everything from the arrest of the director of Intourist, for abusing his position of authority by compelling—I think it was—something like eight hundred and fifty of his women employees to sleep with him, to making little

---

* I should hate to have this taken seriously as my opinion of the Russian language, with its rich and poignant music, which makes it so fine a medium for poetry and the theater, and its variety of language elements—a variety only comparable to that of English at the other end of Europe. The alphabet has also advantages, as one can see by looking at Polish.

children eat their suppers. When a Russian says "Bolshóy
Skandál!" a gleam comes into his eye: nobody is really horrified. I wasn't sure, on second thought, that I would be
on the side of the government if they tried to suppress
this phrase.

I thought about their abominable waste-baskets, which
are always made of wire and have meshes so large that almost everything you put into them falls right through
onto the floor. You cannot clean up your business, you
cannot get rid of old manuscripts and letters, because,
when you have thrown them into the basket and the basket has been removed, the papers are still under the table.

It was no credit to the Russians, I brooded, that they
had never made a good job of capitalism. If they had done
so when the Western countries were working on it, they
wouldn't be hampered now by trains like the one I was
on, which made long journeys at twenty miles an hour
and kept you under the constant illusion that they were
only just getting under way—for an American, an intolerable state of suspense.

I thought bitterly about their bedclothes, which are
never tucked in at the bottom or sides but simply laid on
the bed, and are usually not quite large enough to cover
it, so that your feet are always coming out. If the nights
are so cold in winter, why haven't they learned to cover
themselves up? And their pillowslips, which are not bags
like ours, but rather in the nature of loose envelops that
usually work off the pillows.

I thought about the way that, when they clear off the
tables, they always sweep the crumbs on the floor.

I thought about Clavdia Dmítrievna, and she, too,
seemed somewhat repellent. Mustn't there be something
wrong with a good-looking Russian girl who had no husband or lover at twenty-one.

Nevertheless, as I would struggle along the train on my

way to and from the dining-car, through doors with people against them, through groups of men talking together, past women with babies and great bundles of baggage, I had to acknowledge that the Russians were much the nicest people to be sick, while traveling, among. They were considerate, amiable, quiet. I had never fallen in with a Russian who was obnoxious, as the Germans were. Now and then my attention was called, in simple wonder or a spirit of helpfulness, to a saucer-sized gray spot on my shirt, the stain from a bottle of ink that had become uncorked in my suitcase.

All night I had to keep gulping from a bottle of insipid pop, and would get up and go for air to the shut-off end of the car, where the only open window was. I would look out at the white thatched cottages and the hay-ricks and the fields of sunflowers, and breathe in the cool country air. But the Ukraine, enormous and fertile, became monotonous, too; and I was sickened by the eternal sunflowers—plants that have a kind of personality if grown in small groups in gardens but which, raised in great herds for their seeds, seemed somehow unnatural and gruesome: like cattle, yet less than cattle, and at the same time perverted from the role of flowers. How horrible to think of them standing there, huddled and turning their faces to follow the sun in a mass! How disquieting to realize they were cultivated for the purpose of providing such oil as that in which would certainly be fried the unappetizing greasy omelet that I should not be able to eat for breakfast!

The dusty approaches to Odessa seemed to go on for hours.

———————

In Odessa, I stayed in bed and became sicker and sicker, while I waited for the Constantinople boat. At last I had them call a doctor.

The doctor was an extremely genial man, in white trousers and a white Russian shirt, who discussed with me my travels in the Soviet Union and how beautiful Kíev was, and put on, with an old international *femme de chambre,* a wonderful act in French, designed to impress upon me how well I should be taken care of. He asked me what my temperature was, and I said that I hadn't taken it. This did not seem to lead to any action on his part, so I asked him whether he had a thermometer; with cheerful unconcern, he shook his head. He looked at my throat and told me that it would be a matter of two or three days; then suddenly jumped up, shook hands with me, and skipped out, exclaiming with debonaire grace: *"Je vous dis au revoir, monsieur!"*

He gave me several prescriptions for drugs, one of which turned out to be unobtainable. The international *femme de chambre* assured me that she would do something about it, but when I asked for her the following day, I was told she was off duty.

I started to read Gibbon, which somewhat cooled me off and aroused agreeable expectations, since I thought I was going to Constantinople. I was alone for days with the monotonous sobbing of a couple of goofy Russian doves. I didn't then know Krylóv's famous fable about the two pigeons who loved each other so much that "they didn't notice how the time flew by" and, "though they were sometimes sad, were never dull." But if I had, it would only have irritated me.

I got worse, and after two days, I called the doctor again. This time he told me he had traveled in every country in the world except America; he had even taken part in an expedition to the North Pole. The hotel people had found me a thermometer, but I couldn't be sure what my temperature was because the Russian way of calculating is different from ours. When the doctor saw the thermometer, he said the degree indicated was pretty high, but he seemed so unwilling to accept it as correct that I suggested the high figure registered might be due to my having forgotten to shake the thermometer down before I used it. The doctor agreed with alacrity, and I took my temperature again, but it came out the same as before. "That's high," the doctor remarked, but without showing any sign of following the matter up—as if it were all an after-dinner conversation. Then I showed him a spot that had appeared on my arm. He peered at this intently: we found other spots. His whole demeanor changed in an instant to one of acute anxiety and something like aversion. He muttered, "It's scarlet fever! it's scarlet fever!" "What should I do about it?" I asked. He gave a tremendous shrug, and threw out his hands at a total loss. "Go to the hospital, I suppose," he said, finally, as if this were something he had heard of as having been done in such cases. Then, without another word he darted out of the room. I waited for the *femme de chambre*, who had been looking after me up to this moment with the most charming and assiduous solicitude; but she did not reappear, and it was only after I had called the office that she rang me up on the phone and explained that it was impossible for her to come to the room because she was just going off duty; and I never saw her or the doctor again.

After an interval, the manager appeared with a tense little woman in a red-visored cap. She confirmed the diagnosis of the doctor and took me off in an ambulance.

I was received at the Hospital for Contagious Diseases by a doctor of a different kind, a younger man of the modernized generation, not unlike a young American Southerner, and by a competent blond girl, one of the most beautiful I had yet seen. With expedition, I was registered by the blond girl, given a shower and a scrubbing by an old woman, neatly done up like a mummy in a blanket so that only my head stuck out, and laid out on a stretcher on the floor. Rather impressed by the good job that they seemed to have made of this and reassured by the appearance of the doctor, I was beginning to have hopes that the hospital might be one of their more up-to-date institutions. I lay there a long time on the stretcher regarding the blond girl's feet: she had thick ankles and wore no stockings, and she had unbuttoned the straps of her shoes. Then it turned out they had swathed me too soon, that I should have to burst out of my cocoon to count my money and sign receipts for my things. There were two Jewish helpers hanging around, who looked like old Weber-and-Fields comedians; they had whiskers that went all around their chins, reaching from ear to ear. At the time we were counting the money, one of them peered through the door just behind the blond girl's shoulder and, grinning, extended a clawlike hand. With one vigorous push, she slammed the door. I wound myself up in the shroud again, and the two comics carried me out. After taking me a little way, they grew weary and set me down in a courtyard. I lay looking up at the Euxine night, still, blue, starry and clear, while my bearers discussed at some length whether or not I had been given a receipt for my money. Then they carried me into a stale-smelling building with high ceilings and dirty blue-gray walls. Everybody was terribly nice and anxious to meet the emergency. A bed was set up for me in a doctor's room. When I had been put in it, I called attention to a bed-bug that was crawling on the tablecloth of the little table beside the bed. The nurse at once changed the tablecloth, but did nothing about the bug. I asked whether I could have a window open. "Certainly," said the young doctor and told the nurse to open one. "Don't you want them both open?" he asked. It was hot: I said yes. But the nurse seemed to demur. "Open the other one, too," said the doctor. Here was a man who had "culture!"

As soon as the lights were turned out, I was made unmistakably aware of the myriad teeming bed-life. They were swarming out of the pillows and the mattress. I got up and went out into the hall, and there I found two old women. They were two opposite types, but both very Russian; one was always cheerful and the other was always sad, but both had that deep resignation, that incapacity for being surprised. They brought in another bed, put me in it, and proceeded to treat the infested one with a roaring kerosene torch. I suggested that bugs sometimes lurked in the mattress, but they scouted this idea. In arranging the new bed, the sad old woman knocked over a big wine bottle filled with gargle, which inundated the floor and had to be mopped up; and, in mopping, the cheerful one knocked over the medicine glass and broke it.

Then, when everything seemed to be set for the night, I was confronted by two more *klópy*—which was what the old woman called them—reconnoitering on the tablecloth of the night-table and evidently getting ready to drop on me. I pointed them out to the sad old woman, who immediately caught and killed them, making half-stifled grief-stricken sounds, as of one who had seen many little children die and who knew that there was nothing to be done. Then she strapped onto her foot a polisher like the one that the orderly uses in the Soviet film *Chapáev*, and began rubbing it back and forth on the

floor. It was a sort of dolorous dance, evidently hard on
her back. She would stop and rest, and then go on, and
then, after a time, stop and rest again. I felt rather
sorry for her, because she had been so sweet about
everything, and I had noticed that the nurses tended to
pick on her; but I should probably have felt more sorry
if she had not seemed so terribly resigned. Her eyes
looked as if she were always crying, or rather as if she
had cried so much that they had gone dry a long time
ago.

I fell asleep and went into my fever-dreams. I
thought that a play I had written and had titled *A Bit of
the New* was being produced at home by some serious
theater group. But the producers had kept it so long that
it had finally been found necessary to change the
title to *Quite a Lot of the Old*. Seeing a poster in the
lobby of the theater, I was suddenly seized with disgust.
I resolved to go on in the second act—which took place
on an old-fashioned American porch—made up as an unknown stranger with a derby hat, side-whiskers and a
watch-chain, and deliver a long speech bearing vitally
on the plot of the play, but unconnected with what was
to follow. I hoped that this would break up the show. I
woke up—it was morning now. Repressing hysterical
laughter, I said to myself: "I mustn't let Russia get me!
That was a Russian dream!"

A figure now appeared before me, who might have
been part of the dream: a man in a straw cap, spectacles,
a black coat, a white vest and a pair of striped trousers,
who carried an umbrella hooked over one arm. He was a
very old man, as I later found out; but, in spite of the
gray bristles of his shaved scalp, he did not give the
impression of being old. He had broad shoulders and
dark heavy arched eyebrows. As soon as his attention
was directed to me, he was energized into extraordinary

activity. First he made somebody give him a spoon and, after nervously scratching his bristles with the handle, he thrust it down my throat and peered in; then, nervously and heavily coughing down my chest, he applied a stethoscope to my heart.

Then, in a deep loud theatrical voice, he told the attendants to clear out the furniture, addressing them as *"továrishchy,"* but in the magistral peremptory tones of one who has always commanded. They stood, of course, without doing anything, as Russians are likely to do when confronted with a demand for immediate action: the room was the doctor's office, and there was quite a lot of equipment to be removed. He ordered them again to start at once. They reluctantly carried out a few pieces. Then the doctor drove everybody out, and, closing the great, old, high double doors, he first stood for a moment with his back to them, then marched over to me in the manner of an operatic bass about to impart a secret or vow a revenge, and announced in thundering accents that he was putting his office at my disposal in order that I might have a room to myself. He then went on to declare that he would have me well in no time, emphasizing the climax of his solo by clapping his palms together and holding up his right hand with all five fingers extended. Then, unexpectedly, cocking his head, he lapsed into a whimsical smile that had something almost childishly appealing; and ended with a little aria, based upon the phrase "All right!", the only words of English he knew, and its Russian equivalent, *"Khoroshó."* At last he summoned the attendants back and directed them to go on with the dismantling. This took hours: they accomplished it by stages, with long intervals between their appearances. When the old doctor made his rounds the next morning, he brought me a small volume of Tennyson. It had belonged, he said, to his daughter, who knew English and was living in Paris.

———————

I spent six weeks in that Odessa hospital. I recovered very quickly from my original attack, but had to stay on account of the quarantine; then, just as I seemed to be cured and they were going to let me out, I had a relapse and had to spend another week.

The life was pretty monotonous: it was a little like living in a monastery. At the end of a few days, they moved me out of the doctor's room into a ward with other patients; and my world was contracted to that ward, the corridor and the operating room, which they let me use at night for a study. I would read Marx and Engels during the daytime and Gibbon in the evening. An old Jewish doctor who knew some English brought me a volume of Sir Alfred Lyall's poems and a small book of selections from *Little Women,* edited for German readers. The only thing to be seen out the window was the Bacteriological Institute across the street, and one of the events of my stay was when it was repainted.

Yet it was interesting to watch day by day, from inside, the working of a Soviet institution, and I got in some ways a much clearer idea of the processes and relations of Russian life than I had been able to do in Moscow.

The hospital itself was old and dirty. It had been built about 1795—one of the oldest public buildings in Odessa —and it seemed to have remained practically untouched. Those high-ceilinged high-windowed rooms had been harboring contagious diseases since years before the exile of Pushkin, when he had come to live in Odessa, almost ever since the days when the town had been only a Turkish fort. Odessa, which has very few factories and little value now as a port, has been neglected in the Soviet programs. There is, I understand, one fine new hospital, but efforts on the part of the Odessans to get a new contagious hospital have so far been unsuccessful; and what I saw was a bit of old Russia with very few of the cobwebs knocked off. I was subjected, for example, to treatments which I had supposed were entirely obsolete: at one time they "cupped" me daily with a set of twenty heavy brass cups which must have been a part of the original equipment, and they dosed me continually with valerian, an old-fashioned bitter drug, of which, according to the modern pharmacopoeia, the effects are "largely psychic."

There was evidently a scarlatina epidemic: the cases were coming in by the dozen—women, children and men. At one time there were three hundred cases, out of a city of half a million. One woman died while I was there. They would allow them to accumulate in the corridor, in their lazy Russian fashion, putting off as long as possible the necessity of opening another room, which would involve the displacement of furniture. Everybody, as far as I could see, got exactly the same care and the same food, and everybody was treated with kindness. The *besprizórnye*, little homeless tramps, and the children of Communist officials were put to bed just as they came, and all the rooms were crowded—though the little waifs, to be sure, had nobody to bring them toys, fruit and books, as the children of well-to-do parents did.

It was a public service, of course, and nobody paid a kopek. I was not even allowed to pay for telegrams or cables: they told me that there was money set aside for such things. The food, although greasy like all Russian food and tiresome like all hospital diet—I got terribly fed up with potatoes—was good of its kind, and there was plenty of it: the vegetables and fruit of the

Ukraine. Only the milk did not seem to me what it ought to be, and they did not have any real coffee.

The hospital, as I have said, was terribly dirty. I never realized how extremely low the Russian standard of cleanliness had been till I saw the conditions which were tolerated in one of the places where sanitation was most necessary but where the new broom had not yet swept clean. The wash-basin in our room, for example, though it did have running water, was used for face-washing, dish-washing, gargling and emptying urine; and I once saw one of the older doctors spit into it without bothering to turn on the faucet. The toilet had no seat and no way of fastening the door, and, though the hospital people tried to keep it in order, the patients, as is usual in Russia, generally left it in a mess. The glass panes in the door could not have been cleaned up since at least 1915, for that was the earliest date which had been scratched in the paint, or whatever it was, with which they were partly coated. When you went to take a bath, you were likely to find garbage in the bathroom (just as in Chekhov's story of a provincial hospital, *Ward Number Six*, the potatoes are kept in the bath tub). I never understood why they put it there unless they used it for fuel for the stove that heated the water. The flies were frightful, and nothing was done in the way of screening the windows, except for a single piece of netting nailed over one of the windows in the doctor's room, which did not, of course, prevent the flies from entering through the other window. Nor was anything done to prevent them from breeding in the long grass outside, which was allowed to grow rank with weeds.

Periodically there was a bug crisis. The only thing they knew to do about them was to apply the torch to the iron bedsteads, and I never could convince them that bugs also lived in the cracks of the wood. Finally one day, however, a fastidious woman doctor, who always smelled of lavender water, discovered some *klópy* on the old horsehair chair in which I used to read every day, and insisted that action be taken. The sensible thing to do would have been to burn the chair, but it is hard for them to take summary measures in Russia. At first they would go only so far as to peel off the strips of ribbon that were tacked along the back and arms, and then when, a few days later, the doctor was still able to show bugs walking in and out of the cracks, they took to spraying it with something or other.

The nurses were almost entirely untrained. They were generally middle-aged women, with children and no husbands, who had been forced to earn their livings. They would make wrong entries on the temperature charts (I was once given a rise for the following day) and lose the papers out of the dossiers for the cases. One nurse smoked continual cigarettes and made the patients cough. One, whose husband had left her, frankly disliked the whole thing and paid as little attention to it as possible. One got sick at the operations. The ward, to be sure, was understaffed: ten nurses to a hundred patients; and they had to do all the things which in our hospitals are done by orderlies. Visiting mothers and grandmothers were permitted to sleep in the ward and take care of their own children. The nurses had no control over the little boys, who kept climbing in and out of bed, went to sleep at any hour they pleased and engaged in hilarious roughhousing when they were running high temperatures. The way of handling the hospital nightgowns was typical of nurses and patients alike: I used to wonder at first why so many of the nightgowns had the strings about the neck left tied but one of them always torn off. Then I noticed that when they removed them, they would never go to the trouble of untying the knot, but simply rip them apart. What the nurses did best was amuse the children, reading to them, telling them stories and acting out little plays. They had for themselves, the nurses, two principal sources of diversion: a shabby geranium plant, which they would water from time to time but which never flowered; and an old volume of Lérmontov's *A Hero of Our Time*, which they would read in moments of leisure, each one, apparently, taking it up where the last one had left off.

———

The Head Nurse was quite a different matter. She was a much more energetic and positive person, and she was also much bulkier and taller. She looked a little like the Ugly Duchess, but her expression of haughtiness or indignation would melt into tenderness or humor when the slightest appeal was made to her. She had that ready humanity of Russians which, when character backs the generous impulse, may take such heroic forms; and she worked exceedingly hard, wrestling with the hospital arrangements, seeing to it that the nurses gave the treatments on time and did not lose the records, banging the hands of the neophytes when they tried to fool with the surgical instruments, and in the moments when she had nothing else to do, reading to the children herself. One day she showed me her Communist card and told me that she had formerly done more active work, but that her heart was bad and that they had put her here where the work was not so exhausting.

In the hospital, as I gradually came to find out who were and who were not Communists, I got a much clearer notion than I had had before of the relations between the Communists and their followers, on the one hand, and the rest of the Russian community, on the other. The Communists, it was plain to me in Odessa, were the peo-

ple who took all the responsibility. And though I had
sometimes resented in Moscow the constraining and intimidating effect which their presence had on other Russians, I was grateful to them when I got into the hospital, because they seemed to be the only people who
were sensible, efficient and up-to-date. If you really
wanted to get anything done, you had to go to a Communist about it. I came to sympathize with their constant
trials in making the other Russians get things done.

One day, for example, not long after I had come, I
gave some letters to one of the nurses and asked her to
mail them for me. She told me that I would have to ask
the doctor, which puzzled me, as I had had letters
mailed before. When the old man, the one who had received me so dramatically and who was supposed to be
in charge of the ward, came in on his rounds the next
morning, I told him that I wanted to mail some letters.
In his resounding basso profondo, first in Russian and
then in German, he tried to impress upon me, with terrible emphasis on all the grave consequences, that it was
prohibited for scarlet fever patients to send letters out of
the hospital: the letters would transmit the germs and
the recipients would catch the disease. I became indignant at this, for I knew that they had had all my telegrams translated in order to find out what was in them,
and I dreaded their devious methods of censorship. I
demanded to see the director. He was a young man, a
Communist, I suppose, at any rate the new type of
Russian whom, despairing more or less of the older generations, they are training as fast as they can to take
command of Soviet institutions. He and the older doctor
discussed the situation in my presence. The director was
for letting me send the letters. "But," the old man insisted,
drooping but throwing out his hands, "the people who
get them will catch scarlatina! *Bolshóy skandál!*" "Ilyá

Petróvich," replied the director, "that's nothing but *pe-dantízm*. People don't get diseases from letters." And he took my mail, explaining, to save Ilyá Petróvich's face, that he would disinfect them before he mailed them. Afterwards the Head Nurse came in. "All that fuss about a few letters!" she said. "Don't you remember that you gave me some and that I mailed them the other day? You can't give people scarlet fever through your hands."

On another day, the Workers' Inspection came round. The delegation sent to the hospital turned out to be an old man and an elderly woman, who behaved very much like simple workers in any other country. The old man held his hat in his hand and was very respectful toward the nurses. The woman looked around her, eyes shining, deeply gratified that this was their hospital, that she herself had been appointed to approve it. They asked me how things were, and I told them that everything was fine. When they were gone, the Head Nurse said to me, "Why did you tell them that everything was all right? You know that plenty of things are wrong." It was plain that the Workers' Inspection would never have known for themselves whether things were wrong or right.

The children were extremely attractive and extremely badly behaved. They ran wild when the doctors were away. With their shaved heads, they looked like picked chickens.

There were three little boys in my room, two of them the sons of officials. The father of one was a Communist, and a certain amount of fuss had been made over him when he had first been brought in. "We have a little Narcomfin with us!" they would tell me, and the little boy would say "No!", having perhaps been taught

that it was not well-bred to accept distinction for his father's office. He was twelve—the frailest, most sensitive,
most volatile type of Russian, very spoiled by his
mother, I thought. He chattered like a bird, incessantly,
in the curious Russian way that is almost like operatic
singing, and would go on chirping, appealing and whee-
dling even after the person to whom he had been talking had left the room some minutes before. I had a feeling he was likely to grow up to resemble that Leningrad
aesthete who had been reading the sailors Donne—an
impression that was strengthened when his mother arrived and turned out to be a Leningrader. She, too, was
frail and small-featured; but she had not, as I supposed
at first, been molded by the old society: she did not
speak any foreign language, and her ideas were the orthodox Communist ones. She had, for example, named the
little boy Elmar, a name which had been concocted out
of E for Engels, l for Lenin, and m-a-r for Marx. Her
tastes and her habits seemed exactly those of a serious
middle-class woman in the other kind of society; and
I was relieved when she began to tell me how terrible the
hospital was, since I hadn't, up to that time, been certain
whether anybody else was aware. She had cause to be
worried about this, because the boy had developed a
double mastoid and had to be operated on in both ears.
She broke down when they took him into the operating
room and wept in the hall so terribly that the big bustling woman who managed the mess presently emerged
from the kitchen, told her quietly that she mustn't behave like that and led her away to her room.

The second little boy was ten, and his nickname was
Vóva for Vladímir. His mother had a rosy round face
and wore a handkerchief around her head: she looked
like a country woman. His father was quite different, the

new type: he was clean-shaved, and had well-cut features
and sharp clear gun-barrel-colored eyes; he wore a dark-
blue business suit. The boy was extremely bright and a
little demon of energy. He had clear hard eyes like his
father's, but light green, with the oriental slant. His
vitality was indefatigable: from early morning till ten or
eleven at night, he was making airplanes out of paper and
sailing them around the room; acting out one-man
playlets of war, in which he was always getting shot or
shooting; singing songs, of which he had a large repertoire, ranging from the *International* and *Partizány*
through Russian Gypsy songs to selections from Italian
opera, of which he knew all the Italian words; and starting public speeches, which would begin with a ringing
"Továrishchy!" but never get any further: in order to
avert an anticlimax, he would flop with a bang on the
bed. In moments of relaxation, he read, with absorbed
attention, everything he could find in the hospital; and
he drew remarkably well—soldiers, cannon, airplanes,
gunboats and tanks—with little imagination, but considerable technical accuracy. The only thing that could
divert him from reading or drawing was the consciousness—he would know it at once—that somebody had
brought a new toy to little Misha across the room. Vóva's
attention would then be seen to wander from the
drawing-pad or the book, but he would lie silent till the
visitor had left. Then, oblivious of the whinings of Misha,
who was weak and only five years old, he would go over
and take the present away from him and play with it until
it broke; then he would take it to pieces, and, finally,
throw the pieces at Misha. When little Elmar was taken
off to be operated on, Vóva frightened poor Misha into
spasms by acting out the operation; and then went on to
operations on flies.

I liked him, but he got to be a nuisance, and I presently tried to repress him. But whenever I would jump up and grab him and put him back in bed, he would regard it as an invitation to roughhouse and immediately leap out again and make himself more obnoxious than ever. [One day I broke down and spanked him. I was aware that the news of this was getting around—I could see it in the attitude of the nurses; but it was a long time before anyone spoke of it. Then the Head Nurse came to see me. She sat down beside my bed and said in a low voice, "Is it true that you spanked Vóva?" I replied that it was, and that he ought to be disciplined. *"Nelzá, nelzá!"* ("You mustn't!") she warned, shaking her finger at me. The point was that he couldn't be punished because his father was a commissar.] I discovered, however, that I could keep him quiet by playing with him a children's war game, which was something like checkers and chess but in which the pieces were soldiers and had various military ranks. At first, I was winning so often that I thought I ought to let him win. When he saw that the next move was going to expose him, he would turn away to the window, as if absorbed by something outside, and I would have to prompt him to play. But then he put his mind on the problems and worked out so astute a strategy that I was never able to beat him again.

He would fearlessly bedevil the older boys, and then, when they finally retaliated, he would rush back into his own room and throw himself on his bed, not in fits of childish weeping, but with hoarse roars of rage and defeat. Only rarely did he break down and shed tears. He was so pretty and had so much charm that it was difficult for the nurses to be cross with him, but as his health got better, his behavior grew worse, and he made little Misha so miserable, messed up so many treatments, created so much wreckage and got into so many places where he was not supposed to be that he was by way of becoming a *bolshóy skandál,* and there would be nurses or doctors or Elmar's mother coming in every half hour to lecture him or bring him back from some mischief.

The day when his mother, at last, was coming to take him away, he got hold of a rubber ball and played handball against the walls and worked himself into a frenzy of badness. Then he was told that his mother was waiting for him, and they wrapped him in a blanket and took him out, while his face was suffused with a look of bliss. A little later, I heard a voice outside and went to the window: he was calling good-by from the street. He was walking beside his mother, she patient and pink-faced and innocent, with her handkerchief around her head; and, overwhelmed by her ample figure, he looked now so unexpectedly tiny in his knee-breeches and his cap, after the havoc he had raised in the hospital.

During my first days in the hospital, I was mystified to find wet condoms trailing around the room, and, not without some hesitation, I finally inquired about them. I learned that they filled them with water and tied them behind the children's bad ears. Since they never thought of throwing them away but always simply dropped or draped them wherever they happened to have been taken off, little Vóva very soon got hold of them and discovered he could blow them up and explode them like paper-bags. He then went on to turn them into balloons by blowing them up and tying them with thread. The nurse who smoked cigarettes and who was good at putting on little plays, had the further happy idea of painting faces on them with mercurochrome. Everybody was very much pleased.

It was curious to note that even Vóva, the most high-spirited of the children, had in his voice those plaintive cadences which are a part of the language itself.

The children, too, were always acting, and whenever I was stuck over the meaning of a word, I had only to ask a child or a nurse and they would instantly act it out for me with astonishing resourcefulness and vividness. I have spoken of the old doctor's declamations; I used to think when I first heard him talk that he was quoting some play in couplets. And the fastidious woman doctor who discovered the bugs in the chair, would make scenes with the nurses in the mornings, when she came in and found the room in a mess, that were exactly like an old-fashioned comedy. There was one magnificent soliloquy which went on after the incorrigible nurse had scurried out of the room, and ended with rolled-up eyes, supplicating sweeping gestures and a sardonic, *"Krasívy! Krasívy!"* *("Beautiful! Beautiful!")*. She might have been doing it for me, though her tirade was not directed toward me, but I imagine she would have delivered it anyway, whether or not there had been anyone else in the room. So far as I could see, it had no effect.

The street-life was quite different from Moscow: very much more spontaneous and lively. It was a relief to hear the people outside laughing and whistling and singing, and at night having drunken disputes.

The Odessans were good-looking people, mostly with round black eyes. Even ill and in their old hospital nightgowns and inside the dirty hospital walls, they were

unmistakably attractive. There was one young mother
with a fascinating baby, whom I used to hunt up every
day. The baby was a girl with these round black eyes,
who, when admired, would turn away and hide her face
in her mother's shoulder. She seemed to have come into
the world with a fully developed feminine beauty and a
feminine consciousness of it. There was a grandmother
who had moved into the hospital to take care of her little
grandson. She had been run down by a droshky, and her
face was disfigured and flattened; her ears had been
cauliflowered, her cheeks ripped open in such a way that,
when they healed up, her mouth had been pulled awry,
and her nose had been squashed upwards so that there
was little left but two large holes.

The Intourist interpreter who came to see me was a thin
washed-out girl with eyeglasses. I got to like her. She
told me that she was a real Odessínka; that Odessínky
were supposed to be frivolous, but that all were not so,
certainly. When I asked her why the Russians were so
wonderful in the theater, she said, "Because they feel
things more deeply."

She did her best to get me what I needed and to arrange about my transportation; but she vanished for
several weeks, and when she turned up again, explained
that she had herself been ill and had been unable to
persuade anybody at Intourist to run the risk of coming
to see me—though they would have had only to talk to
me through the window as the families of the patients
did. She was loyal, deep-feeling, unpunctual and vague;
but quite different was the handsome brunette Komsomólka who paid us a visit every afternoon. At first I
classed her on the credit side with the Communists; then
I realized that, in spite of her spruce appearance, which

contrasted with that of the other nurses, she was not really making herself very useful but in fact tending to get in the way of such things as were being done. She would come in and talk world-events at moments when the nurses were too busy to be able to deal with such matters; and all her politics came straight out of *Pravda*. She would snatch Vóva out of his crib, kiss him violently and exclaim, "I love children so much!" when the nurses had just been hoping that they had got him quieted down. But she had a kind of edge on everyone else by virtue of her Komsomól standing.

There was another Young Communist who regularly visited me, a very dark Mediterranean-looking girl. She was a bacteriological research-worker engaged in studying typhus and absorbed by her experiments with rabbits and mice. She had learned to speak French very well without ever having been in France, and she used to come around and talk to me and do things for me when the Intourist interpreter had disappeared. She was quite unlike these Intourist women: she always did what she said she would do at the time she had said she would do it; and she had none of the tiresome side of the Girl-Scoutish Komsomólka. She was not cocky and not complacent, but sensible, straightforward and adult, full of vitality and free from attitudes. I liked her extremely. She was not merely interested, but actually deeply happy in the consciousness that she was doing something to get rid of the dirt and disease of old Russia. She did not talk about this, but it was plain in all that she said and did.

One day one of the older nurses asked me slyly: "Should you say I was a Russian or Jewish?" I had always assumed she was Jewish. A little while afterwards, in conversation with a young Komsomól girl, I asked her

whether she was a Ukrainian. "No: I'm Jewish," she replied. I saw then that her features were just as Hebraic
as those of the other Jews in Odessa, yet, although I
had seen her a number of times, I had not thought of
her as being Jewish. It must have been her own lack of
self-consciousness which, in her case, had made the difference. It would never have occurred to her to put to me the
question of the older woman. She had grown up in a
world in which Jews were neither persecuted nor discriminated against. For the younger generation in Odessa,
there was today nothing in particular about being Jewish
any more than being Greek or Rumanian.

———————

I was anxious to get back to the States, and I tried to
induce Ilyá Petróvich to cut down my quarantine a little.
The Russians cannot understand impatience: they are so
used to standing in line for things, waiting for meetings
to begin, traveling on slow trains through endless spaces.
The nurses and hospital workers were always sticking
their heads in at the door and saying to me cheerfully,
"Skúchno právda!" ("It's dull for you, isn't it!") or
"Skóro domói!" ("Home soon!"). This latter used to ir-
ritate me, because it was so far from being true. They
seemed to have no sense of time; and I reflected that
the Five-Year Plan had probably been contrived in an
effort to give them one.

I would lie there and wait for the days to elapse and
listen to the Russian diminutives, which also, I began to
find exasperating. They seemed to give diminutives to
everything. My books were always *knízhky*, instead of
knígy; the nurse was always *sestríchka*, instead of *sestrá;*
even an apple was a *yáblochka*, instead of a *yábloko*. I
kept wanting to say, "Don't be silly!" As soon as they de-

part from the plane of the strictest and most pompous formality, they seem to go all to pieces with diminutives. The opposite pole of this—the result, I suppose, of reaction against the inveterate laxness—is the dehumanized and schoolmasterish political style which is one of the more dubious gifts of the Soviets to the development of international socialism.

———————

One night I was sitting in the operating room, with my book on the white zinc table beneath the all-clarifying naked bulb, reading that noble work, Franz Mehring's *Life of Marx*. There was a preface by somebody else, which told of Mehring's difficulties in getting it published and of his death as a result of his shock over the murder of his closest allies, Karl Liebknecht and Rosa Luxemburg: how he had walked his room for hours, unwilling to believe that such a thing could happen. But if he had lived? I thought about Hitler. The papers were full of the preliminaries of the Italo-Abyssinian War. I thought about Gibbon: the long collapse of Rome, imperceptible to those involved in it; the centuries of rule by clowns and brutes, each sweeping out the one before almost as soon as he had stuck his head up. A doctor came in, a very decent fellow, one of the old race of good Russian giants. He picked up the book and looked at the title-page to see whether it had been printed in Germany since Hitler; and we had a few moments' talk in pidgin Russian and German. That evening I felt very sharply that the existence of the Soviet Union, with all its old slowness and rubbish, such as I was pretty well submerged in in that hospital, was the only guarantee in Europe against another such ebb of civilization. Like the old lady from Springfield, Illinois, I felt it was safer here.

———————

Aside from the Head Nurse, there was only one nurse in the hospital who knew anything about hospital work. Like Vóva, she was the green-eyed kind of Russian to whom, according to my theory, the pale-eyed kind is obliged to yield. One day she sat down beside my bed and began to talk apropos of nothing, but as if in reply to unspoken thoughts that she felt might be in my mind. "You know that under Nicolaí Alexándrovich Románov," she said, "the people were kept in ignorance. We had no science and no technique. Now, since the Revolution, we have science and technique for the first time." She told me that, during the War, she had served in a field hospital in Rumania, and that her husband had been a Communist. He was dead now and had left her with a little girl, very blond and very delicate, who used to come to the hospital and pass things to her mother through the window. I remarked that the girl was pretty. "Yes," she said, "I'm fond of my little daughter." She talked about Odessa at the time of the War, when they would hear the machine-guns in the streets and be frightened to go out of doors. The city had been badly wrecked. "But that's all forgotten now," she said.

Another nurse, the Jewish woman, had been married to a chemical laboratory worker and had five grown daughters. They had been fairly well-to-do: she showed me pictures of their bourgeois interior in the days before the Revolution and of their summer vacations in the Crimea. She was old now and had never worked for a living before, and the hospital routine was hard for her: she had continually to be on her feet, and she could not get anything to wear but canvas shoes and heelless slippers. Yet she gave the job everything she had—not like a trained nurse, but like a woman who has brought up a family. She would entertain the children in the hospital with the little paper-folding tricks with which she had amused her own daughters. She was particularly kind to me and gave me special attention on the nights when my fever was bad, at a time when she was half sick herself and had about a hundred patients to take care of.

When I began going down for the second time, I had to give up Marx and Gibbon, and I tried to divert myself with the children's books. Some of them were intended for political instruction. These were drawn from international sources, and it was strange to see Mike Gold and Harry Potamkin [two American Communist writers] turning up in that Byzantine alphabet. [It gave me an unpleasant shock to find in one of these books a fancy picture of a Negro organizer who had been shot in Harlan, Kentucky, for his part in a miners' strike. I had gone down to Harlan myself on one of those expeditions of protest which had been engineered by the Communists (though the well-meaning liberal protesters were not always aware of this), who had intervened in the strike and were creating publicity about it; and this man had been shot by the authorities, all alone in the woods where he was hiding out, the day that I was there. By the time his name reached me again in Odessa, I was able to see how the Negro had been exploited by the Communists— sent into an inflamed industrial conflict which was half a mountaineers' feud and into which the intrusion of a Negro meant almost certain death. They needed a Negro martyr, one who should be killed as an organizer, not one merely lynched on a charge of rape, and the moment they had got him shot, they turned him over to their propaganda experts; and now Vóva and Elmar and the rest of them were already reading about him and looking at a fancy picture of him. The history books we give to children have inevitably an element of legend, but it is chilling to see legend manufactured, at the cost of a man's life, by a process that is half fanaticism, half cold-blooded calculation.]

But most of these books for children were quite free from Communist doctrine: Pushkin's fairy-tales in verse and S. Marshák's amusing rhymes. One of the latter I succeeded in translating just before they turned me over on my stomach and applied to the small of my back the big heated suction cups that would have been in their proper place in the Historical Museum in Moscow along with the drinking-bowls of the Scythians, while Vóva and the other little boy climbed up on the foots of their cribs and were highly entertained by the spectacle.

Whiskers and Stripes
By S. Marshák

Once upon a time there was a little girl—
You would like to know her name to know it's true?
    It is known, I'm sure you'd find,
    To whoever makes her mind,
But it must remain a mystery to you.
You would like to know her age? I will reveal it.
I am powerless to make it any more.
    Neither forty had she seen
    Nor even twenty or fourteen—
In fact, I must confess she was but four.
She had one thing she liked better than the rest.
It was whiskery and gray and beautifully stripèd.
You ask me what it was? You haven't guessed?
Neither veg'table nor mineral nor biped
    But a kitten.

The little girl took the kitten and she put him in bed to sleep.

There's your little back, she said,
Lying on a nice soft bed.
There, to keep you warm, she said,
Are nice clean sheets and nice clean spread.
Nice white pillows for your head
Make you comfortable in bed.

So the little girl arranged the kitten, and then she went down to get her supper.

But when she came back again, what do you think she found?

His tail upon the pillow lay,
His head reposed the other way.

So she turned the kitten around and made him lie the way he ought to.

That's not the way to sleep! she said.
Your back should be upon the bed;
Across the bed, the sheets and spread;
The pillows underneath your head.

So she went down to finish her supper, and when she came back, what do you think she found?

Nor sheets nor spread
Nor furry head.
Whiskers and stripes was under the bed.

Is that the way to sleep? she said. What a silly, silly kitten!

And the little girl decided that she ought to wash the kitten.

So she went and got a washcloth
And a cake of scented soap
And hot water from the kettle

In a pretty china cup.
But when she put him in the water
And got ready for a rub,
The kitten didn't want to wash:
He bolted from the tub.

Who ever saw such a silly, silly kitten!

So the little girl decided to teach the kitten to talk.

She said to the kitten: Old wo-man.
And the kitten said: Miaow.

She said: Horse.
And the kitten said: Miaow.

She said: Teach-er.
And the kitten said: Miaow.

She said: E-lec-tric-i-ty.
And the kitten said: Miaow, miaow.

Always miaow, only miaow. What a silly, silly kitten.

So the little girl decided to feed the kitten.

In a cup she brought him cereal
Of the very best material.
But the kitten wouldn't eat.

In a bowl she brought him greens:
Lettuce and lima-beans.
But the kitten wouldn't eat.

So then she brought him milk in a little saucer,
    and lo!
The kitten had lapped it up before you could
    utter Bo!

Such a silly, silly kitten!

The little girl went out for a walk, and when she came back home, the kitten was nowhere to be seen. She looked under the table, and he wasn't there. She looked under the bed, and he wasn't there. She looked under the bureau and she looked under the stove, but the kitten was nowhere to be found.

Where in the world was the kitten?

Now, there was neither rat nor mouse, but there were pencils in the house.
On Poppa's desk they quiet lay until the kitten walked that way.
A pencil rolled, the kitten pounced; the pencil slipped aside and bounced.

> The pencil fell; away it sped
> Beneath the wardrobe and the bed—
> From bed to table—what a pace!
> The kitten giving eager chase—
> Along the wall, across the floor,
> Till finally it reached the door.

> Now just that instant, full of worry,
> A man came in to talk to Poppa,
> A man with glasses and a hat.
> The pencil tripped him in his hurry
> And so he came a fearful cropper
> And on the floor astonished sat.

The silly, silly kitten!

So the little girl wrapped the kitten up and took him for an outing in the Summer Gardens.

People would ask: Who's that you've got there?

And the little girl would answer: This is my little daughter.

People would ask: Why has your daughter got such gray cheeks?

And the little girl would answer: She hasn't washed them for a long time.

People would ask: Why has she got fuzzy paws and whiskers like a man?

And the little girl would answer: She hasn't shaved for a long time.

And then suddenly the kitten jumped out and ran away, and everybody could see it was a kitten.

Such a silly kitten!

> And after that,
> After that,
> The kitten grew up a sensible cat.

And the little girl grew up and went to high school.

The Russians have never had rhymes like this before. Marshák got the idea from the English, some of whose nursery rhymes he has imitated, but what he has produced is distinctively Russian. His tales have the terseness and the realism that have always been characteristic of Russian poetry. Observe that there is nothing whimsical in this story, as there is in A. A. Milne, for example. The kitten behaves like a kitten, and the little girl behaves like a little girl with a kitten. I saw a nonsense book, too, called *Confusion* (by K. Chukóvsky), in which the kittens decide to grunt like pigs and the frogs to fly like birds and the foxes get hold of matches and set fire to the sea. This seems to owe something to Edward Lear; but in *Confusion* everything goes back to normal, which is not the case in the *Nonsense Books*.

These children's books are cheap, well printed and admirably illustrated.

———

I became rather interested in Ilyá Petróvich and, after my struggle with him over my mail, got to feel for him affection and sympathy. I was sorry that I had been so cross. He had quite enough trials, I could see, already.

Ilyá Petróvich was a gentleman and—what I had not met before in Russia—he regularly dressed like one. I had noted in him a combination, characteristic of the men of the old upper classes, of great stature and very broad shoulders with very small feet and hands. His voice was a resonant bass and his manner was dictatorial; but his most terrible lectures were likely to end in a winning and rather shy smile. His face was as sensitive as a child's: it always gave him away. When he had to move a woman with a baby to a less desirable bed and was threatening to call the militia to quell her indignant resistance, his expression would betray a deep anguish; and on the occasion of a death or a critical illness, he would hover around in the hallway, as obviously worried and nervous as the family of the patient themselves. At one point when it seemed to him that my heart was lagging, he had me dosed with digitalis and would pop in every few minutes to listen with his stethoscope till he thought it was normal again. (His own heart, I had been told, was in very poor shape, and he would sometimes have to stay away from the hospital.) He was never quite so imposing as his figure warranted, because his head was always sunk forward. I used to think that before the Revolution he must have had a fashionable practice, and that he must now find it rather depressing to be working in the dirty scarlatina ward under a director younger than himself.

With children, he had the genial and threatening jokes

of old-fashioned doctors everywhere. He would appear in the doorway of the big ward into which the *bespizórnye* had been packed and boom out in his deep voice, which he loved to exercise: *"Kak váshe zdoróv'e?"* —to which the little boys would reply in chorus: *"Kak máslo koróv'e!"* ("How is your health?" "Fine as cow's butter!"—it makes a jingle in Russian.) There were three questions and three responses. He did this every morning, and one day I heard him do it twice. He must have been particularly troubled and, forgetful, a little gaga, attempting to relieve his tension by throwing himself into the ritual again.

Ilyá Petróvich and the Communist Head Nurse used to have terrific altercations. There was one that seemed to go on all morning and to surge back and forth like a battle. Suddenly the door of our room flew open and Ilyá Petróvich burst in with the Ugly Duchess in full pursuit. He dropped down in our buggy armchair and went on protesting about something while the big woman stood over him, insisting. Neither paid the slightest attention to the people already in the room. But very soon Ilyá Petróvich sprang up again and rushed out, and the Head Nurse rushed out after him. I laughed about it to the green-eyed nurse. "What's the matter?" I asked. She took my dictionary and showed me a word which was defined as meaning "hurly-burly." "But what's it all about?" I asked. "Old!" she answered, smiling serenely. "He's seventy-five and she's fifty-five."

Not long after my conversation with this nurse in which she had talked about Russia under the Tsar, I was gazing at Ilyá Petróvich, as he stood in the doorway with his back to me. He was evidently brooding about his cases, wondering what he ought to do next or trying to remember something. His enormous shoulders were rounded, his head drooped forward on his chest, so that from behind one saw only his shoulders and the gray bristling stubble of his crown. I had always thought of his slumped-over carriage as being due to his age and his social demotion; but now I reflected that he was one of the men who *had* "had science" at the time when, as the nurse had told me, the Tsar had kept science from the people. He had been a man of science in a feudal country, where the implications of science for society were dangerous to pursue and impossible to apply; he seemed a crippled man. They had all been crippled men, even the greatest of them, the old intellectuals and technicians who had lived and worked in Russia. They had always had to keep their heads down, and their position was always ambiguous. Now, with the new regime, they were still compelled to keep them down, and they were still not always sure which side they were on. A big man with small hands, a sensitive face and an habitually bent spine, Ilyá Petróvich was typical, I suppose, of a class who had lost all and suffered much. Yet today he was devoting to these thin little children, the race of the new Russia, as much gentleness and care and solicitude as he could ever have done for the patients for whom, so many years ago, he had assumed his white vest and striped trousers. His daughter was in Paris, but he was here.

I still had some traces of my complications at the end of the six-weeks quarantine, and he did not want to let me go. I should be there now, I dare say, if I had followed his recommendations. But I put up a determined resistance, and after two or three days he yielded. He took it, however, a little in bad part, and, full of fear lest I should make a scandal by getting seriously sick abroad, he insisted that I sign a document affirming that I was being discharged against the advice of the hospital. He suddenly disappeared with the document before I had a chance to say good-by.

The next day, however, when I went back for a moment, I saw him and started to thank him, but he stopped me. " 'Thank you very much'!" he repeated. "Don't thank me: you're not cured! I didn't sleep all last night, wondering whether you were warm enough!"

———

Getting out of the hospital was very curious—probably something like getting out of jail. I had been in bed for most of six weeks and had been living on a vegetarian diet, and, toward the end, when I had my relapse and the fever had taken my appetite away, I had not eaten much of that. The result was that all my senses had been rendered abnormally acute; and going out into the world again was attended by something of the painfulness of what the psychologists call the birth trauma. Having for so long had nothing to smell but the stale unvaried air of the hospital, the odor of the carpets and upholstery in the lobby of the Hotel London, which I had not even noticed when I had been there before, now tormented me almost unendurably with a blending of pleasure and distress; and when I went into the barber shop for a shave, the perfumes of the shaving-soap and toilet water and the emanations from the various bottles caused me a series of poignant sensations of a kind which I had read about in Huysmans and other *fin de siècle* literature, but had never experienced before. Later, when I went up to my room, I was obliged to steady myself to get accustomed to a new set of odors. I pulled the long curtains aside and looked out on the deserted courtyard, which in August had been an out-of-doors restaurant. The tourists who had been there were gone and the place had been dismantled for winter. The night was coming early now. There were trees that were shaking dark leaves in the darkening autumn light, and their shape and their shuddering movement both fascinated me and compelled me to turn away. Alone in the silence of the room, I suddenly dropped into a depression of a kind that I had never known all the time I was in the hospital. It was loneliness: I was missing the children and the nurses who had bothered me when I was trying to work and from whom I had looked forward to escaping. I walked back and forth across the room a few times, then began declaiming aloud some old poems of my own composition. I found that a need was relieved: my loneliness disappeared. It was the assertion of my own personality against those weeks of collective living.

It had been collective living at very close quarters, which collectivization, of course, does not necessarily involve but of which, nevertheless, the Russians have had to endure a good deal.

Yet Russians, I thought, could accept it more easily than the people of Western nations. It was a hardship they seemed perfectly resigned to. This, and waiting for things forever. One had perhaps to be immersed, as I had just been, in the life of one of their institutions to appreciate the deep feeling and the "imperfective" persistence underneath their immense slowness and patience, which one otherwise tended to chafe at. And also to sympathize fully with the desperate measures of their vanguard, who want them to direct their own lives. Gorky, in his memoir of Tolstóy, written before the Revolution, in speaking of Tolstóy's "misty preaching of 'non-activity,' of 'non-resistance to evil,' the doctrine of passivism," says: "All this is the unhealthy ferment of the old Russian blood, envenomed by Mongolian fatalism and almost chemically hostile to the West, with its untiring creative labor, with its active and indomitable resistance to the evils of life." What wonder if Gorky today sits at the right hand of Stalin!

At the new railroad station in Kíev—which combines the high-ceilinged spaces of the Pennsylvania Station with little rows of potted plants purely Russian—a man spoke to me whom I did not recognize. I nodded and did not shake hands; but he kept smiling, and in a moment I knew who he was. He was the conductor of the train in which, almost two months before, I had traveled from Rostóv to Kíev, and in which I was now going to travel from Kíev to the Polish border. I had treated him then like a dog, because I had had a fever and it had seemed to me that he was always bothering me when I wanted to relax and rest. But he seemed now to be as glad to see me as if our relations had been perfectly friendly.

It was a shock to pass from Russia to Poland. The officials in the Soviet customs were serious but amiable little men in the simplest of khaki uniforms. But on the Polish side you found formidable giants with great ulsters and pushed-in noses. A plain-clothes man hung around on the train that took you from the Russian to the Polish customs, listened in on the conversations and presided at the opening of the baggage. "Now you'll find trains that run a little faster!" he told us. Everybody on the Polish side seemed extremely Soviet-conscious. They ask you what you think of Russia and are not pleased if you think it's all right. I was told that at another point on the border the Poles had put up a sign

which said, "Welcome to the Western frontier," and
that the Russians had then put up one on their side saying, "Communism will abolish all frontiers."

I had been traveling with a German professor who
taught Philosophy of Law at Zurich. He was an elderly
man, very lively and with a good deal of intellectual
curiosity. He had been studying Russian three years but
had just paid his first visit to Russia. He was evidently a
liberal of some sort, because he told me, with more
humorous grief than bitterness, of the horrible things
that the Hitlerites had been doing to the German univer-
sities. He was very much more optimistic than anyone else
I had met about the chances of their soon getting rid
of Hitler and the possibility of genuine socialism in
Germany. He couldn't see, he said, how the learned pro-
fessions, the experts, the artists, the engineers, could
help realizing that under socialism they would be just as
well off and more important; and as for the profiteering
classes, their profits were dwindling all the time, and it
would be easy to dispossess them. There was a great deal
of stifled dissatisfaction with the Nazis, and it was certain
that the fall of Hitler would be followed by socialism; a
pure military dictatorship was possible, but that couldn't
last very long. He had got hold of a volume of Lenin
which somebody had left in the Zurich library, and "I
must say," he said in English, "it's very clever!" He had
never read Lenin before. I learned when I got to Paris
that my professor was a distinguished scholar, who had
been turned out of his chair at Frankfort by the Nazis.

When we boarded the train for Warsaw, it was pleasant
to find oneself again in well-upholstered compartments
where everything worked and was clean. But as soon as
we had come out of the customs, we had been set upon
by undiscouragable boys who wanted to sell us sandwiches and tea and by porters who persisted in perform-

ing for us services we did not want and who complained
that we did not tip them enough. "I don't like this ob-
sequiousness!" the professor said plaintively, as he fished
in his pocket for change. Then we both began to laugh:
back in the old capitalist system! Nobody in the Soviet Union ever tries to sell you anything. When you need
something, you go into a store, and a nice little slow-
moving girl interrupts her reading to get it for you. The
psychology of shopkeeping is something that they do
really seem to have liquidated.

The conductor was a comic-opera official with a green
uniform and lots of silver braid, something like the police in Monaco; and just as we had got settled in the compartment, a bloated Polish military officer with a blond
mustache, a florid face and a chest plastered with medals,
strode in and, disregarding the other occupants, slammed
down an upper berth—it was a second-class compartment, not a *wagon-lit*—slammed up the lid of the seat
underneath, grabbed all the pillows out of it, without in-
quiring whether anybody else would have any, piled
them onto the berth and stretched himself out to sleep.
The compartment, the moment afterwards, seemed to be
filled, even crowded by the entrance of two enormous
Polish bullfrogs, who resembled in the most startling
manner the capitalists in radical cartoons. One of them
had pig-like eyes, a head completely bald, fat rolls of
flesh at the back of his neck and ears that came to points
like a bat's wings—the only time I have ever seen this last
phenomenon outside of satirical drawings. He proceeded at once to bang open the window, though it
was the first of October and cold. I reflected that no such
behavior as this was ever to be seen in Russia, where the
people traveling in trains did not feel they had to fight
for advantages; and although I had been glad to leave,
I felt an unexpected wave of homesickness for everything

in the Soviet Union that was natural, decent and humane at a time when the people of the West were so much at one another's throats that they could hardly even pretend to be civil.

I suggested to the professor next morning as we were eating an excellent breakfast in Warsaw—that the characters we had seen on the train were really actors from the Moscow Art Theater who had been sent to put on these performances for the purpose of impressing upon tourists the contrast between the Soviet Union and the outside capitalist world. "Yes," he replied—he had slept without pillows—"I think it must be so. They are like the villages that Potyómkin had put up for Catherine the Great!" Every time we encountered an importunate guide or a peddler who waylaid us with postcards, he would murmur: "Another Russian agent!"

The train stopped twelve minutes in Berlin, and I got out to buy the papers. I had hoped to find out what was happening, but these papers did not go in for news. One of them turned out to be a Jew-baiting sheet, rejoicing in the recent Nazi law to prevent the intermarriage of Jews with Aryans. In a box on the front page was the following warning: "People will say to you, 'Aren't the Jews Germans? They were born here, they speak our language, they have been German citizens, etc.' If anybody tells you this, just reply to them as follows: 'In the United States, there are men of German race who have been born there, who speak English and who are citizens. Yet have they turned into Red Indians or Negroes?' If anybody tells you this, that is all you need to answer!" —For the rest, there were cartoons of bugaboo Communists brandishing long knives drenched with blood.

When one traveled in the early years of the century, the European countries one visited loomed as immense entities, with impregnable national virtues, luminous and civilizing cultures, sacred traditions, majestic histories. At the time of the War, they seemed like Titans colliding. Today, when one has been in the United States and then in Soviet Russia, they seem a pack of little quarrelsome states, maintaining artificial barriers and suffering from morbid distempers. How the map seems to have changed since our youth!

———————

Rigor mortis has set in in Paris.

VII

FINAL REFLECTIONS

ONE'S FIRST IMPRESSIONS of Russia are likely to be contradictory; but once one begins to get glimpses of what is going on beneath the surface, one becomes aware of an extraordinary heroism.

The effect of this is very sobering. Only idiots gush about the Soviet Union. Only idiots pretend that life there is easy. Whether one runs into a Communist official who is obviously working his head off in an effort to make socialism succeed in the face of inertia at home and hostile pressure abroad; or a professional man or woman of the old bourgeoisie or nobility, who has lost position, property and family, who lives always more or less under suspicion and who may have already done time in a prison or construction camp, yet who still remains loyal to the Revolution; or a member of the Komsomól intoxicating himself with study and work; or a peasant woman applying herself with desperate earnestness to the duties of ticket-taker on a train or a tram; or a doctor or farmer, now old, but deprived of his whole life's achievement, yet still sticking to his former work, in the interests of a future he will never see, of benefits he will never share; or a cultivated and charming young woman grown up amid the anarchy of the Civil Wars and the Spartan early years of the Revolution, with no dancing and no pretty clothes and breaking down her physique

and her nerves under the exactions of the Soviet programs—whomever one sees, wherever one turns, one is
made to feel the terrible seriousness of what is being
done in Russia and the terrible cost it entails.

But it is as foolish, on the other hand, for a foreigner
to make an issue of the bad aspects of the dictatorship:
the lack of democratic procedure, the suppression of political opposition, the constraint of the official terror. The
Russians can always reply that, with all our democratic
machinery, we are unable to feed and clothe our people,
and that our supposed democratic institutions are illu-
sions to divert our attention from observing that the government and the laws in reality work only one way: to
protect the profits of the owning classes. This last is, I
believe, not quite true: I feel convinced, since I have
been in Russia, that American republican institutions, dis-
astrously as they are often abused, have some permanent
and absolute value. I do not believe that they are certain to be destroyed in the course of the transformation of society, any more than our advanced "technique." On the contrary, I think it probable that, like it,
they will make easier the transition to socialism. But we
shall not be in a position to reprove the Russians till we
have put ourselves in a position to show them an American socialism that is free from the Russian defects.

In the meantime, despite these defects, you feel in the
Soviet Union that you are living at the moral top of the
world, where the light never really goes out, just as you
know in the Gulf of Finland, where the summer day
never ends, that you are close to the geographical top.*
The central fact, from which one never can escape, upon
which one is always stumbling under all the fluid surface
of casualness, frivolity, timidity, evasion and apathy,

* For comment on this statement, see the *Postscript*.

that is one of the features of Russian life, is the relationship of the Russian people to the tomb under the Kremlin wall. Day after day, rain or shine, the visitors line up for hours in slowly advancing queues that loop back and forth across Red Square, in order to go into the tomb, to step down past the walls of Ural marble, black and gray and sown with flakes of lapis lazuli like bits of blue butterflies' wings, and to stare for a moment at that face, where the soldier with his bayonet stands staring. It is not the face you may have expected if you have been looking at pictures and statues, and it is different even from the death-mask. But, in shrinking, the flesh reveals qualities, fundamental as the fine grain of wood, which are also apparent in this latter. We are used to seeing Lenin represented, as he must usually have been during his waking life, determined, intent, energetic, arguing, explaining, imposing himself; and even in the death-mask we are struck by the aggressive intellect of the boxlike skull which seems always to be tilted forward; here the nose and lips are still rather thick, the eyebrows sharply bristling. The casts of the hands show tapering yet effective and square-tipped fingers. But the head in the tomb, with its high forehead, its straight nose, its pointed beard (which has grown gray on the dead man's cheeks), its sensitive nostrils and eyelids, gives an impression in some ways strangely similar to that one gets from the supposed death-mask of Shakespeare. It is a beautiful face, of exquisite fineness; and—what surely proves its authenticity—it is profoundly aristocratic. Yet if this is an aristocrat, it is an aristocrat who has not specialized as one; and it is a poet who has not specialized as a poet, a scientist who has not specialized as a scientist. Nor is it in the least the face of a saint. Except for the slightly slanting eyes, it seems today hardly even the face of a Russian. For here has humanity bred, independent of all the old disciplines, the scientist whose study is humanity, the poet whose material is not images but the water and salt of human beings—the superior man who has burst out of the classes and claimed all that is superior which man has done for the refinement of mankind as a whole. And here we have come to gaze down at this shriveling shell of flesh, in its last thinness, its fragility and delicacy, before it falls to pieces and loses the mold—this bone and skin that still keeps the stamp of that intellect, that passion, that will, whose emergence has stunned the world almost with more embarrassment at being made to extend its conception of what man, as man alone, can accomplish, than admiration at the achievements of genius. So these countrymen of his are amazed, with their formless and expressionless faces, when they look down on him and know that he was one of them, that he summoned from their sluggish plasm all those triumphs to which life must rise and to which he thought himself but a guidepost.

[I PRESENT HERE without apology this sympathetic account of the Soviet Union in 1935. The sentiment about Russia in the United States has, in some quarters, been worked up recently to a pitch of hysterical antagonism and panic that makes this an appropriate moment for reminding Americans of the original ideals that inspired the Russian Revolution and of the period when it occupied a position vis-à-vis the rest of the world very similar to that of the United States vis-à-vis Europe in the first half of the nineteenth century. It is also, I think, important to bring out, as I have tried to do above, what the Russians and we have in common: a big country, a mixture of races, manners that are naturally democratic, a relative unencumberment by the past and a consequent flexibility. At the time I visited the Soviet Union, the Russians, though they were told that they must not believe in any capitalist society, were full of admiration for the United States: they talked about the "American tempo," and their dream was—and no doubt still is— to rival us in modern comfort and advanced industrial development. But in those days they knew more about us— and we knew somewhat more about them. The American engineers who, at the end of the twenties, were brought to the Soviet Union to advise on or direct the new projects, were impressed by what was being attempted. I remember how one of these returned engineers, who had certainly no Left bias, described the first Five-Year Plan

378

and ended by saying, "But they're hardly equipped to carry out such projects over there. *Here* is where it ought to be tried." The Plan by the early thirties was constantly on the front pages of the New York papers. Walter Duranty was writing for the *Times* his admirable dispatches from Russia. He has since, of course, been subjected to some very indignant criticism for his slighting the famine and the terror—especially by the kind of people who at that time were going all out for the Soviets and exercising less discrimination than he, and who are now, with an equal wholeheartedness, declaring that nothing good ever came out of the October Revolution. Yet of everything constructive in the Soviet Union, of what the most devoted Russians believed themselves to be doing and hoped to see done, Duranty gave a lucid day-by-day account which appealed to the American imagination. The New Deal would hardly have been possible, would hardly at least have taken the form it did, if it had not been for the example of the Five-Year Plan. It was, of course, most regrettable that Americans who admired the Soviets should have become involved in the Communist Party and hence dupes of the imperialistic and anti-idealist Stalin; and it was an even more serious disaster when the elements who were alarmed by this began to take over the methods—persecution for political opinions, imputation of guilt by association and general disregard of constitutional rights—to which Stalin had resorted to maintain his tyranny.

Today, although a prominent practitioner of these has taken an official beating, this pseudo-Stalinist terror is still more or less raging, and these notes will, by persons caught up in it—if any such ever read them—undoubtedly be thought friendly to Communism to the point of criminality. At the time of their first appearance, they were regarded as badly as possible in the Soviet Union itself. I had enjoyed, during my stay in Russia, much more freedom to move about and to see what was going on than most travelers did at that time. I owed this to the kindness of two friends who were then in high favor in the Soviet Union: John Dos Passos and Walter Duranty. The books of Dos Passos were, of course—up to the moment when, just after my visit, he protested against the purges—enormously popular in Russia, and he had been rolling up a large sum in royalties there. These royalties were held to his credit, since the Soviets would not send such earnings out of the country, but invited foreign writers to come to Russia and spend them. Dos Passos, who had already been there, succeeded, after the usual bureaucratic delays, in arranging to have them put at my disposal, and I repaid him for them in dollars at their actual, not official, value. At that time, the rate of exchange was officially five rubles to the dollar, but the real value was indefinitely more. Once released, therefore, from spending valuta, I found myself relatively rich and was not confined to the Torgsin stores that dealt with foreigners on a valuta basis. Having rubles, I could purchase in shops, buy theater or railroad tickets, do anything a Russian could do. I should otherwise have been run by Intourist, the Soviet travel office, that kept visitors in special hotels and always under the supervision of guides, both agents of the NKVD.

But from the hotels I might never have escaped—since accommodations in Moscow were few—if Duranty had not been leaving to take his family to England for the summer, so that I was able to rent his apartment. This gave me a certain prestige as well as an unusual degree of comfort. The apartment was luxurious for Moscow—it consisted of four or five rooms and included a bathroom and kitchen. I had also the Durantys' maid—a tall and almost skeletal old woman, left behind from the tsarist régime, who, with her pop eyes and hollow cheeks, speaking servants' French, seemed to present a perfect feminine counterpart to the obsequious old usher in the Leningrad theater. She could not play so smooth a role: she was nervous and nagging, poor thing—and occasionally became hysterical. She was out of place in modern Moscow; but one found it reassuring to realize that she could not possibly be a NKVD agent. There were, also, a signed photograph of Stalin on the bookcase and an electric refrigerator. This latter—brought over from America—must have been almost unique in Moscow, and was a great object of interest to my Russian visitors, who when I showed it to them and opened the door, would usually start back in alarm as the hum of the motor began.

I thus partially escaped from surveillance, and, as is indicated by my effect on the *dácha* and the behavior of the guide at Ulyánovsk, must sometimes have excited suspicion. When I was back in New York and preparing these notes, I was asked to an evening party which turned out to have been arranged for the purpose of bringing me together with the American representative of the Soviet news agency, TASS. He did his best to find out in advance what I was going to write, sometimes barking and leaping at my throat in the way that I had come to recognize as one of the tricks for putting pressure on "innocents" who show signs of resistance. When my articles (this diary) came out, I was told that I had been put on the blacklist of persons who would never, under any circumstances, be granted a visa for the Soviet Union. Not long afterwards, Dos Passos received from Moscow, with no explanation or other enclosure, an envelope containing a check for royalties still due him—the implication being, apparently, that he was all paid up now and that he was not to send any more friends to spend his rubles in the Soviet Union. As for Duranty, when I next saw him in New York, he was most affable but made some remark about the slightly unfortunate consequences of my living in his apartment. I at once expressed my regret, as I had already done by letter, for the glassware broken by my spirited friend who liked to smash the goblets after drinking. But, "It wasn't what you broke," he said. "It was what you wrote!"

When I arrived in the Soviet Union, I did not, as has been seen above, take a pessimistic view of Stalin. I was still capable of imagining that the execution of a group of supposed Whites, as a result of the Kírov murder, might have had some real justification, and I was able to conceive Stalin as a tough political boss with crude Marxist principles and considerable practical ability. I had realized before I left Moscow that—unless with the Komsomól element, of whom I did not see much—he was not really very popular among the better-educated Russians. My first intimation of this came in the course of a conversation with L., when she was telling me of some discussion of the relative sex appeal of the Soviet leaders. Voroshílov was apparently considered tops. "More than Stalin?" I asked. "People," she replied, "are afraid of Stalin—I wouldn't say they think he's attractive." On my way down the Volga, I read the translation put out by the Soviet government of the proceedings of the first Zinóviev-Kámenev trials. Though I had tried to suspend judgment on these, I now came to the definite conclusion that the charges and the evidence were frauds. Yet I had also acquired by this time the impression of a strong but unpublicized sentiment in favor of getting rid of Stalin. The criticisms by the club of old Bolsheviks which they had paid for by having it liquidated, the popularity of the

liberal Kírov, the perceptible tension of a tug-of-war between Stalin's authoritarian and the other more liberal
elements, all seemed to indicate this. In the light of later
events, I assumed that there had been a real conspiracy,
or conspiracies, to put the skids under "Lenin's best pupil."
The public trials, of course, were all fakes to cover up
whatever was going on, and to shift the blame to the
exiled Trotsky on the other side of the world; but since
Tukhachévsky and his brother officers were not tried but
simply shot *in camera,* I imagine that the Red Army had
really planned some action against Stalin. (I learned later
from the illuminating book of two purgees who survived,
F. Beck and W. Godin, *Russian Purge and the Extraction
of Confession,* that the story was going around—for which
"excellent authority" was claimed—that "as early as 1934
Stalin had been called on to resign by a majority decision
of the Party central committee," that Kírov had been
selected as his successor to the secretaryship of the Party,
and that Kírov had been murdered at the moment when
he was just about to assume office.) No one then
could foresee, could conceive, that that half-oriental moun-
taineer, by whom cruelty and craft had been learned
among the traditional virtues, and successful revenge on
one's enemies as among the most desirable of attainments,
would undertake to assure his suzerainty by exterminating
the whole revolutionary generation and everybody else in
Russia who was even suspected of adhering to the socialist
ideas of Lenin; that it would be possible, in the twentieth
century, in what had aimed to be a modern society, for
him to execute or imprison from five to ten per cent of
the whole population of the Soviet Union—somewhere
between seven million and fourteen million people. At
the time I was in Russia, I was told that Stalin had just
made his first broadcast, and I felt that a certain sly
animus was expressed in the criticisms of his Russian,

which people told me was more or less illiterate as well as handicapped by a strong Georgian accent. Lenin had criticized his manners, and Lenin was now dead; Trotsky had criticized his intellect, and Trotsky was now an outlaw and would soon be assassinated. Stalin, it was clear to me before I left, had a good many critics in Russia, and by the end of 1938, according to Beck and Godin, "a point had been reached at which denunciations and incriminating statements had been accumulated affecting practically every man and woman in the Soviet Union." Before we say, More fools the Russians!, let us consider how far, with no dictator, we have already gone in the same direction.]

ISRAEL
1954

I

ON FIRST READING GENESIS

I DISCOVERED a few years ago, in going through the attic
of my mother's house, an old Hebrew Bible that had belonged to my grandfather, a Presbyterian minister, as well
as a Hebrew dictionary and a Hebrew grammar. I had
always had a certain curiosity about Hebrew, and I was
perhaps piqued a little at the thought that my grandfather could read something that I couldn't, so, finding
myself one autumn in Princeton, with the prospect of
spending the winter, I enrolled in a Hebrew course at
the Theological Seminary, from which my grandfather
had graduated in 1846. I have thus acquired a smattering
that has enabled me to work through Genesis, with constant reference to the English translation and the notes
of the Westminster Commentaries, and this first acquaintance with the Hebrew text has, in several ways, been to
me a revelation. In the first place, the study of a Semitic
language gives one insights into a whole point of view, a
system of mental habits, that differs radically from those
of the West. But, besides this, I had never read Genesis
before. In college I had taken the second half year of a
course in Old Testament literature, so I did have some
familiarity with the prophets and the later phases of
Biblical history, but the Pentateuch and the earlier historical books were known to me only in patches or
through simplified versions of Bible stories that had been

read to me when I was a child. I came to them in the original for the first time rather late in life, when I had already read many other books, and since such an experience is probably rare—Hebrew being studied mainly by Christian seminarists and orthodox Jews, both of whom come to it early and with definite religious predispositions—I am going to give a report on it. I am myself neither a Jew nor a Christian, and I propose to disregard, in doing so, the little I know of the tons of theological commentary that have been written by the various churches. I do not propose to take for granted—as, from recent conversations on this subject with even well-educated people, I conclude I am warranted in not doing—that the reader is any better acquainted with even the most famous Bible stories than I was when I recently began to explore them.

First of all, the surprises of the language. The Bible in Hebrew is far more a different thing from the Bible in any translation than the original Homer, say, is from the best of the translations of Homer, because the language in which it is written is more different from English than Greek is. To speak merely from the point of view of style, the writing of the earliest books is a good deal tighter and tougher—Renan calls it a twisted cable—than is easy to imitate with the relatively loose weave of English. It is also much more poetic, or, rather, perhaps—since the King James Version does partly take care of this with its seventeenth-century rhythms—poetic in a more primitive way. Certain passages are composed in a kind of verse, and even the prose has a metrical basis. The first verse of Genesis, for instance, almost corresponds to a classical hexameter, and we soon feel we are reading an epic or a saga or something of the sort. The progress of the chronicle is interspersed with old prophecies and fragments of ballads that have evidently been handed down by word of mouth and that stand out from the background of the narrative by reason of their oracular obscurity and their "parallelistic" form. There are many plays on words and jingles that disappear in our solemn translations, and the language itself is extremely expressive, full of onomatopoetic effects. The word for "to laugh" is *tsakháq* ("kh" as in "Chekhov"), and thus Isaac is called Isaac (*Yitskháq*) because Sarah, in her delightful scene with God, cannot refrain from laughing when He tells her she shall yet bear a child; a light rain is called *matár*, a heavier downpour *géshem* (it was a *géshem* that caused the Deluge). The words for the emotions are likely to come from the physical states that accompany them. The verbs for "to love" and "to hate" are both based on heavy breathing: *aháv* and *ayáv*. Patience and impatience are rendered as the taking of long or short breaths.

The Hebrew language is also emphatic to a degree with which our language can hardly compete. The device for affirming something strongly is to repeat the important word, and God's warning to Adam that he will "dying, die," if he disobeys His orders, seems weakened in our version—"thou shalt surely die"—as does Joseph's assertion that "stolen, I was stolen out of the land of the Hebrews" by "indeed I was stolen." Nor can we match the vehement expression of the violent Hebrew emotions. When Jehovah, about to invoke the Flood, has become disgusted with man, it is not adequate to say that the thoughts of man's heart were "only evil continually"; in the *"raq ra kol hayyóm"* of the text, we seem to hear the Creator actually spitting on his unworthy creation. "And Isaac trembled very exceedingly" is the rendering of the King James Version of the passage in which Isaac discovers that Jacob has deceived him, which falls short of "Isaac trembled mightily a great trembling," and in the next verse we read that Esau "cried mightily a great and bitter cry." This violence and vehemence of the Hebrews is implicit in the structure of the language itself. They did not conjugate their verbs for tenses, as the modern Western languages do, since our modern conception of time was something at which they had not yet arrived—a significant feature of the language that I want, in a later section of this essay, to discuss by itself at length. What the Hebrews had instead of tenses were two fundamental conjugations for perfect and imperfect—that is, for action completed and action uncompleted. And both of these two "aspects" theoretically exist in seven variations for every verb (though actually the complete set is rare) that have nothing to do with time. The primary form of the verb is known as the "light" or simple form, and the second is the passive of this. So much seems plain enough sailing, but what follow are three intensive forms—active, passive and reflexive—and two causatives—active and passive.

These verbs, which take little account of time, are the instruments, then, of a people who, at the period when this language was formed, must have been both passionate and energetic. It is not a question of *when* something happens, but whether the thing is completed or certain to be completed. There are special forms, the causatives, for getting things done: "I will multiply your descendants," "They made Joseph take off his coat." The intensives are unexpected to the non-Semitic reader, who has difficulty in getting the hang of them, but feels a dynamic element in the very bone of the language, and soon begins to find them fascinating. The translator of these strange verb forms, which double the middle consonant and vary the pattern of vowels, is obliged to resort to an adverb or a stronger verb. The intensive form of one of the words for "to kill," the paradigm verb that the student learns, is given in the grammars as "kill brutally." So you have "break" and "break to pieces," "grow" and "grow luxuriantly." A curious example, which occurs in Genesis 24:21, illustrates the problems of translators. When the emissary of Abraham meets Rebecca at the well and watches her attentively in silence, to see whether she will behave in the way by which he has proposed to God that the wife appointed for Isaac may be made to reveal herself, a verb that means "to look at" is put in the intensive form. The old Revised Version made it "And the man looked steadfastly on her"; the new Revised Version has it "gazed at her"—the first of these, that is, adds an adverb, the second tries to find an appropriate verb, and the nuances conveyed are different.

These intensives are sometimes baffling. It is not always easy to see what is implied in a given context. The forms may, in certain cases, turn intransitive into transitive verbs; the intensive of "to learn" may mean "to teach," or indicate multiplicity or frequency. The student soon finds himself groping amid modes of being and acting that cannot be accommodated to our Western categories, and of which the simplified descriptions supplied by his beginner's grammar do not really give him much grasp. The intensive reflexive, for example, has uses that are puzzling to render or even to understand. It seems to imply behavior that ranges from what Henry James, borrowing from the French, meant by "abounding in one's own sense" to what we mean by "throwing one's weight around." When Enoch or Noah "walks with God," he does so in this form of the verb "to walk," and nobody has ever known how to render it. Yet one gets from the Hebrew original the impression that the walking of these patriarchs was of a very special kind, that it had the effect of making them both more important and more highly charged. This expression, in the Old Testament, says Dr. John Skinner, the author of the volume on

Genesis in the International Critical Commentary series, in general "signifies intimate companionship, and here denotes a fellowship with God morally and religiously perfect. . . . We shall see, however, that originally it included the idea of initiation into divine mysteries." I have looked Enoch up in a number of translations, and the only attempts I have found to give the verb form its special force are in the independent modern translations by James Moffatt and Monsignor Knox, the former of whom says that Enoch "lived close to God," the latter that he was "the close friend of God." The flaming sword set by God at the gate of the Garden of Eden is made to "turn" in the intensive reflexive, and the English translations, from the King James Version to the Revised Standard Version, render this as "turned every way." I imagine something a little more spectacular. Gesenius's standard lexicon seems to bear me out in suggesting "brandished, glittering." Yet as soon as you are beginning to pride yourself on seizing the force of the intensive reflexive, you are pulled up by finding that this variation of the verb that means "to shave" implies, in the hygienic prescriptions of Leviticus, nothing more interesting than "to shave oneself" or "to get oneself shaved."

When Abraham, foreseeing that the beauty of Sarah will cause Pharaoh to want her for his harem, has passed her off as his sister, in order that Pharaoh may not be impelled to put him out of the way, and when Pharaoh, afflicted by God for a sin he has committed unknowingly, learns at last what is causing the trouble and sends Abraham about his business, he says, "Here is your wife. Take her and go!" We are amused, when we first read this incident, to find "send" in the intensive form and to hear the brusque snap of "qakh valékh!" Yet we later on find that these words are more or less a conventional formula that does not necessarily imply irritation and that "send" in the intensive occurs when the sending is not necessarily ejective. There is something, we become aware, peremptory in the language itself. You have drawn-out "cohortative" forms that express, for the first person, exhortation, strong intention or earnest entreaty, along with clipped jussive forms for other people or things, as when God says, "Let this or that happen." The whole language is intensely purposeful, full of the determination to survive by force or by wit, to accomplish certain objectives, to lay down laws that will stabilize life and ensure its perpetuation, to fix the future by positive prophecies.

As this will of the ancient Hebrew finds expression in the dynamic verb forms, so the perdurability of the people is manifested in what may be called the physical aspects of the language. The prime unit of Hebrew is a group of three consonants. Nearly every verb consists of such a trinity. The values may be modified—the consonant may be doubled or be altered to a kindred sound, as "f" to "p," "v" to "b"—by a dot written inside the letter, and the intervening vowels may be indicated by a system of dots and dashes written above and below, but they were not so originally written and are not—except in poetry and in a single daily paper—so written today in Israel. The Hebrew alphabet thus differs from our alphabet in not including characters for the vowels, or even, in every case, different characters for kindred consonantal sounds. It is a system of twenty-two integers, a set of unsupplantable blocks, and each Hebrew word makes a shell into which a varying content of vowel sounds may be poured. The verbs are modified by prefixes and endings, and some of the conjugations take prefixes, but, to a Westerner, the most striking feature of the Hebrew conjugations is the way in which a shift of meaning (from active to passive, for example) is effected by a vowel change inside this consonantal shell—the kind of thing that we do on a lesser scale in inflecting our so-called strong verbs: e.g., "sing, sang, sung." We may put in an "o" for the noun and get "song," and the Jews, too, can use the same shell, with a different vowel content, for a noun. What impresses is the hardness of this shell.

Our first look at the text of the Bible, when we have mastered the alphabet, is likely to give us the feeling that this sytem is extremely impractical. It requires what must seem to the beginner an annoying and easily avoidable effort to coördinate with the heavy consonants the elusive little dashes and dots that hover about them like midges, especially since two of the former are not consonants in our sense at all but gutturals, no longer pronounced, which have to be regarded as blanks and read with the sounds of the vowels that are indicated above or below them. Even the printing of these signs is difficult, impossible for a linotype machine, since they appear in innumerable combinations. The result is that, even in learned books, the consonants are, if possible, written without "pointings," and what you get is a kind of shorthand. You must already know the words extremely well in order to be able to recognize them. Yet some further acquaintance induces respect, and a perception that this method is appropriate, an inalienable element of the Jewish tradition. The characters themselves are impressive—not so fluent as the Roman and Greek, and retaining even more than these the look of having been once cut in stone.* To write out Hebrew vocabulary, with black ink and a stub pen, affords a satisfaction that may give one a faint idea of the pleasures of Chinese

---

* The movement from right to left is supposed to have been determined by the engraver's having held the chisel in his left hand and the hammer in his right, and thus naturally having worked from the right.

calligraphy, as well as a feeling of vicarious authority as one traces the portentous syllables. One remembers the hand of Jehovah writing on Belshazzar's wall (though He had to write Aramaic in order to be understood by that alien and uninstructed king). These twenty-two signs that Moses was believed to have brought back from Egypt graven on the Tables of the Law, and from which, in their early Phoenician form, all our European alphabets have been derived, have, austere in their vowel-less terseness, been steadily proceeding from right to left, over a period of two thousand years, among people that read from left to right; and in the Bible they take on an aspect exalted and somewhat mysterious: the square letters holding their course, with no capitals for proper names and no punctuation save the firm double diamond that marks the end of a verse, compact in form as in meaning, stamped on the page like a woodcut, solid verse linked to solid verse with the ever recurrent "and," the sound of which is modulated by changes of vowel, while above and below them a dance of accents shows the pattern of the metrical structure and the rise and fall of the chanting, and, above and below, inside and out, the vowel pointings hang like motes, as if they were the molecules the consonants breathed. Difficult for the foreigner to penetrate and completely indifferent to this, they have withstood even the drive toward assimilation—to their Spanish and Germanic neighbors—of the Jews of the Middle Ages; and in the dialect of German that is Yiddish, in newspapers spread in the subway, they still march in the direction opposite to that of all the other subway newspapers, English or Spanish or Italian, Hungarian or Russian or Greek, with only a light sprinkling of points to indicate Germanic vowels. And we have seen them reassemble in Israel, reconstituting their proper language—not embarrassed in the least by the fear that the newspaper reader of our century, even knowing Hebrew perfectly, may have difficulty in distinguishing, in the British reports, a vowelless Bevan from a vowelless Bevin. They march on through our modern events as if they were invulnerable, eternal.

But in the meantime, the Bible confronts us, in the dignity and beauty of its close-packed page.

The opening of Genesis is wonderful: the spirit of God in the darkness that hovers or broods on the waters, the sudden decree of light, the teeming of earth, sea and sky. The story of the Garden of Eden and the episode of Cain and Abel are imperfectly disengaged from some very ancient matrix of folklore, and parts of them are blotted in obscurity. What is the explanation of the phrase that so strangely recurs? "Your desire shall be for your husband," says God to Eve, "and he shall dominate you." "If you do not do well," He tells Cain, "sin is lurking at the door. His desire is for you, but you will dominate him." Is the second the mistake of a copyist, whose eye has slipped back to the earlier passage, or an obsessive idea of the author's? The serpent here is not the Devil, as the Jews later thought him to have been, but simply "the wiliest of all the beasts of the field." The Fall here has not the importance that it was later to take on for the Christians. Except for one reference to Adam in Job, the Old Testament does not mention it again. It was Paul who set up Original Sin, with the dreadful results we know for Catholic and Calvinist doctrine. The Creator here is all too human—we should nowadays say He was manic-depressive or something of the sort. He immediately becomes jealous of the man He has molded, angry at Adam for eating the fruit that has made him "like one of us" by imparting to him the knowledge of good and evil, and fearful lest he eat of the tree of life and so become immortal, too—as He is later, out of jealousy of human success, to frustrate the building of the city in which everyone speaks the same language and to impose the confusion of the Tower of Babel. What we do find in the story of Adam and his family are those living and salient traits—the relations of Adam and Eve, the sullen personality of Cain—that give these fragmentary legends a human truth and have caused them to haunt our imaginations; and you have, also, the earliest examples of that specialty of the Jewish genius—the development of the moral consciousness, of man's relations with God. This dawning of the moral sense brings with it, for Adam and Eve, an immediate awareness of their animal nature and the impulse to clothe themselves.

After Adam, the chronicle is almost lost in a cloudy domain of myth. Methuselah lives nine hundred and sixty-nine years; Enoch walks with God, then vanishes, "for God took him." The formidable race that the Septuagint calls "giants" and the Masoretic Bible "Nephilím" (fallen ones?) are dwelling on the earth. The sons of God interbreed with the daughters of men. Something in all this has gone wrong, though it is not clear precisely what. The Creator, at an earlier stage so nervously suspicious of man, so anxious lest man try to compete with Him, now decides he has gone to the bad and regrets He has ever made him. He decides to wipe mankind out, but relents in favor of the family of Noah. There follows the account of a flood which, according to Sir Leonard Woolley, must actually have occurred locally some three thousand years before Christ, in the region between the Tigris and the Euphrates—an account that seems less poetic as well as less realistic than the similar record preserved in the Babylonian epic *Gilgamesh*. It is curious to compare the two stories. The Babylonian one mentions reed huts, the remnants of which Woolley found below a thick layer of river silt, and the adventures of the Ark are "lived," described here in much more detail than in the Biblical tale of the Flood. One is struck by the behavior of these earlier gods. "The gods were frightened by the deluge, and, shrinking back, they ascended to the heaven of Anu. The gods cowered like dogs crouched against the outer wall." Later, when the waters are going down and a sacrifice is offered, "The gods smelled the savor, the gods smelled the sweet savor, the gods crowded like flies about the sacrificer." * This was not the way of Jehovah, who has absolute authority and absolute power, and could not behave so abjectly.

It should be said at this point that the text of Genesis is regarded as a patching together of texts by two different hands, combined, perhaps, with passages from still older sources. One sees clearly in the Hebrew the reasons that certain points seem confused in translation—though actually they have partially been ironed out—for the original is still more confused. In the two recensions that have been here brought together, it is evident that one of the scribes had referred to God as "Elohím," the other by the name that we call "Jehovah." The first of these words is a plural—most commonly used with a singular, but occasionally with a plural verb—which seems to designate spirits or powers that preside over the phenomena of the universe. It will be noticed that the Creator in the Eden story expresses his displeasure that Adam has "become like one of *us*," and this plurality of Elohím, the indeterminateness of his or their identity, lends mystery to certain incidents—the wrestling of Jacob with the "angel," the destruction of Sodom and Gomorrah—in which a "man" or several "messengers" turn out to be what

* I quote from the translation by E. A. Speiser, so excellent in its literary quality, included in *Ancient Near Eastern Texts,* Princeton University Press, 1950.

we translate as "God," though the names of Elohím and Jehovah, sometimes alternating, sometimes appearing together, make the ancient conception of deity rather difficult, at this early stage, to grasp. Jehovah is a definitely singular God, the pillar of monotheism. He figures in the Bible at first as the national divinity of the Hebrews, competing with neighboring divinities, but He is later, without ever losing His special relation to the Hebrews, to become a universal God; and one of the things that make Genesis interesting is to see how this universal Deity develops out of primitive conceptions, incompletely fused, of a personal Hebrew patron and a host of primeval spirits. The Jehovah who is to figure for the Christian as an omniscient Heavenly Father, brought closer to humanity by sending them a Son, for the Jew as a transcendent principle that cannot be given a name—"Jehovah" is itself a substitute for the unpronounceable name of God, and the Jew, in his religious services, substitutes for this "Adonái" (my Lord)—this soaring and awful conception is only trying here its first brief flights. Nor are there here any Christian angels, with flowing white robes and great wings, only divine "messengers," easily mistaken for human beings. The Hebrew word for "messenger" was translated by the Greek word "ἄγγελος" and this later gave rise to "angel," which has come to connote a being that does not exist in the Hebrew text. Nor is there as yet a Devil; even the Satan who appears in Job but is otherwise scarcely mentioned is merely "the Adversary," an antagonist opposing Jehovah. There are only the men of a nomad tribe groping after some understanding with a superhuman power or powers. The scribe himself is groping for their history, and his narrative is blurred not only by an undetermined conception of God but also by other discrepancies that result from his pious unwillingness to deal boldly with his differing sources. In comparison with this unknown editor, the unknown writer or writers who turned out the Homeric poems did a smooth and harmonious job on the ancient materials that he or they worked with. But that was not the Oriental way. The Semitic peoples, it seems, liked to preserve all the versions, with the result, in the text of Genesis, that the factual elements are rarely consistent: the chronologies do not come out right, the enumerations do not add up correctly. In the case of the episode mentioned above, of the imposture practiced by Abraham on Pharaoh in passing off Sarah as his sister, you are given the same story three times—told the second time of Abraham and Abimelech, the third time of Isaac and Abimelech. The men of the passing caravan to whom Joseph is sold by his brothers are designated first as Midianites, and then, in succession, as Ishmaelites, Midianites and Ishmaelities. The wonder is, with all this untidiness, these absurdities and incongruities, that the dialogue should be so telling, the situations presented with so sure a stroke, that the personalities of the principal characters should remain so convincing and so interesting. Abraham, Jacob and Joseph are created as living figures in a way that makes relatively trifling the imprecisions of the different versions; it is even perhaps true that their outlines are thrown into a kind of relief by the factual uncertainty of the legend. Renan tells us of one of his teachers at the seminary of St. Sulpice that, in expounding this episode of Abraham in Egypt, he had difficulty in explaining how Sarah, who is apparently supposed to be nearly seventy, was capable of exciting the desire of Pharaoh. He "would call our attention," says Renan, "to the fact that, after all, such things had been known, and that 'Mlle. de Lenclos,' at seventy, had inspired passions and precipitated duels." The extraordinary thing is that, in the course of all the centuries during which these stories have been read and pondered, such outrageous anomalies as this have not bothered people more.

With the emergence of the patriarch Abraham, there begins that remarkable narrative which also includes the careers of his descendants, Isaac, Jacob and Joseph. We may wonder that these personages should run so true to familiar Jewish types till we realize that Jewish children, for more than three thousand years, have been brought up with these Biblical figures before them.

The relations of Abraham with Jehovah strike a note that today sounds feudal. He is respectful toward Him, even obsequious, yet their intercourse exhibits at the same time an element of what may almost be called homely intimacy. Abraham may argue with Jehovah, and Jehovah, who has made with him a covenant and chosen him as "father of many nations," never thunders against him as the Jehovahs of the prophets do. It is natural for this Jehovah to visit His earthly agent, in the guise of a human traveler and in the company of two other travelers (throughout this visit called "men," but later described as "messengers"), at noon, by the oaks of Mamre, as Abraham is sitting in front of his tent. The travelers ask him where his wife is, and he tells them that she is inside the tent. The visitor who is Jehovah explains to Abraham that He will come that way again in the spring, and that Sarah shall then have a son. She has been barren, and she and Abraham have already been through the episode, so painful for everyone concerned, of Hagar, the Egyptian maid, to whom Abraham has given a child and whom Sarah has driven away. Sarah has been listening inside the tent door, and when she hears this prediction, she laughs to herself. "Now that I am worn out," she says, "how should I have pleasure, and my husband an old man?" "Why did Sarah laugh?" asks the visitor. "Does she think that God cannot do it?" "I didn't laugh,"

says Sarah, frightened. "No, but you did laugh," says
God.

In the meantime, Jehovah reflects that He had better
take Abraham into His confidence and explain to him
that recent reports as to what is going on in Sodom and
Gomorrah make the situation sound so serious that He
has decided to have it looked into: He may be obliged to
destroy these cities. When He broaches this subject to
Abraham, the latter thinks at once of his nephew Lot,
who at the moment is living in Sodom. There ensues a
significant dialogue, in which Abraham, playing on Jehovah's sense of justice, gradually beats Him down in such
a way as to insure Lot's survival. Is it right that the good
men in Sodom, Abraham puts it up to Him, should be
punished along with the vicious? "The Judge of the
whole earth will surely not commit an injustice! Suppose
there are fifty good men: would it not be unjust that
these should perish?" Jehovah feels the force of this;
very well, He will spare the city if He finds in it fifty good
men. "Behold, I have dared to speak to my Lord," Abraham is quick to add, relapsing into abysmal humility now
that he has won his point—"I who am dust and ashes!"
But he persists: "Suppose five of the fifty are lacking?"
Jehovah is obliged to admit that this would not be fair
either, and gradually, step by step, begging God not to be
annoyed and protesting his own unworthiness, he persuades Him to agree that for ten good men He will refrain from exterminating the Sodomites. (Nothing is said
of Gomorrah, where Abraham has no relations.)

The messengers of Jehovah arrive at the city, where
they find Lot sitting at the gate. He cordially invites them
to his house, where he gives them an excellent dinner,
but before they have gone to bed, the whole male population of Sodom—to a man, the narrator says—gather outside the house and demand that the visitors be sur-

rendered to them. They have seen the divine messengers and found them all too attractive. In this scene, there is a real terror (echoed with less effect in the similar episode of Judges 19, though the latter is more brutal and more gruesome). Lot goes out and shuts the door behind him. He offers the Sodomites his daughters, if they want them (knowing, perhaps, that he is perfectly safe), but he cannot betray the guests whom he has taken under his roof. "You are not one of us!" shout the Sodomites, with the jeer that was so often to be made to the Jew. "You're all by yourself here—you're only a sojourner! You can't tell us what to do! We'll see that you get it worse than they do!" They yell at him to stand aside, mob him, are about to break down the door, but the messengers pull Lot inside, strike the invaders with blindness, and shut the door in their faces. "Now gather all your family together," the messengers order Lot, "and get them away from here. This place has become such a scandal that Jehovah has sent us to wipe it out." But the Sodomite husbands of Lot's two daughters imagine that the visitors are joking, and Lot himself is reluctant to go. When they have not left at dawn the next morning, the messengers drag Lot and his family out—the sons-in-law are left behind—and tell them to flee for their lives before the brimstone begins.

The insistence all through these episodes of the earlier part of Genesis is on family—i.e., race survival, the importance, by measures however extreme, of perpetuating the consecrated seed. One feels in the story of Sodom, coming after the promise that Sarah shall still bear a child in old age, that the horror for the Jews of the Sodomites is the menace of "genocide." When Lot's daughters, deprived of their husbands, are living miserably with their father in a cave, they have no way of saving this seed except by getting him drunk and inducing him to make them pregnant. We are made to feel not that the daughters of Lot have here committed a sin, but rather that their action is justified by the desperateness of the situation. With this fierceness of the will to persist goes a sense, which redeems the sternness of the patriarchal relations, of the pathos of parental feelings. When Hagar is about to bear Abraham's child, she cannot help being insolent to Sarah, and Sarah retaliates by treating her so harshly that she runs away. She is met by a messenger of God, who reassures her and makes her return; but later, after Isaac has been born, when Sarah has fears lest Ishmael, Hagar's child, may come to share with him Abraham's heritage, she drives her away again. Abraham gets up early and gives Hagar some bread and a skin of water. With the child, she goes into the wilderness, and when all her water is gone, she puts Ishmael under a bush and sits down some distance away, saying, "Let me not look on the death of the child!" Then the little boy begins to cry, and God hears him and shows Hagar a well of water. So later, God, testing Abraham, orders him to sacrifice Isaac. When they are going up together to the mountaintop, the boy speaks up: "My father!" "Here am I, my son." "We've got the wood and the fire, but where is the lamb for the offering?" The father is obliged to reply, "God, my son, will provide the lamb." These strokes of human feeling, of insight, are so trenchant and so authentic, and they so surely awake a response in all kinds and conditions of people, that there are moments when the gods and heroes of the so much more expertly handled, the so much more sophisticated Homeric poems seem less real than the nomads of Genesis when the finger of the unknown scribe, tracing the ancient story, flashes across the page the verses that make them live. This finger also makes the contact, momentous in its day and place, between God and the humblest life, and the

God of the patriarchal chronicle is a much more attractive deity than the God of the Garden of Eden, the Flood and the Tower of Babel. The mind that created Hagar, dying of thirst with her baby, had also to create the God who would pity them and allow them their role in the world. The composer of the conversation between Abraham and Isaac on their way to the sacrifice could not admit of a God who would compel His chosen agent to go through with this cruel ordeal. In these fumbling and awkward old stories, we can see man becoming aware of the conscience that begins to dignify him, that seems to tower above him.

The adventures of Abraham's grandson Jacob are distinguished by no such tenor of submissive and patient piety. His life has a strange discontinuity, for his ultimately successful career is characterized, on the one hand, by exploits of outrageous cunning and, on the other, as it were, broken into by visitations of Jehovah that strike a note quite different from Abraham's intercourse with a deity who treats him as a trusted servant. Jacob, described as a quiet boy, is his mother's favorite son, but his father prefers his twin brother, the more virile and active Esau. The young Jacob first induces his brother, who has come back hungry from hunting, to trade his birthright for a supper of lentils, the smell of which is driving him crazy; then later, when their father is dying, incited by his partial mother, he tricks the old half-blind Isaac into mistaking him for his brother, in order to make sure of receiving his father's special blessing that will establish him as the head of the family. Esau, learning of this, swears to kill Jacob, and their mother sends Jacob away to live with his uncle Laban. On his journey, Jacob sleeps out-of-doors, and in a dream sees the messengers of God ascending and descending by a ladder between Heaven and earth. At the top of the ladder is Jehovah, who tells Jacob that He is the God of his grandfather and his father, and that Jacob can count on his backing; that his family shall multiply and that through them the peoples of the earth shall be blessed. When Jacob wakes up, he is frightened: "What a fearful place this is!" he says. "It must be God's house and the gate of Heaven!"

We now have a long account of Jacob's sojourn with his uncle Laban. He falls in love with Laban's daughter Rachel, but Laban will not let him marry her till he has worked for Laban seven years—a period that, so great is Jacob's love for her, seems to pass, the narrator tells us, like only a few days. But at the end of this time, when Jacob has earned her, Laban fails to keep his promise; in the darkness of the marriage night, he succeeds in passing off on Jacob his older daughter Leah, whom he wishes to get married off first, but then offers Jacob Rachel, too—the marriage to take place at once—if the young man will agree to work for him seven years longer. While Jacob is serving this second term, the relations between him and his wives are subjected to a good deal of strain, because Rachel, whom he loves, has no children while Leah is producing four. Because she is not beloved—because she is "hated," the narrative says—God has taken pity on Leah and is trying in this way to console her. But Rachel makes her maid sleep with Jacob and then claims the resulting two sons as her own. Leah, who has now stopped bearing, makes Jacob give *her* maid, too, two sons. During the wheat harvest, an incident occurs. One of Leah's sons finds some mandrakes and brings them to his mother. The Hebrew word for mandrake has the same connotation as our "love apple"; it was supposed to be an aphrodisiac and also to promote conception. Rachel asks Leah for some of these, but the bitter Leah replies that Rachel has taken her husband's love; will she rob her of even her mandrakes? If Leah will give her the mandrakes, says Rachel, she will let her sleep with Jacob. The result is that Leah again conceives, while poor Rachel has no luck with the mandrakes. But at last God remembers Rachel and allows her to give birth to Joseph. Jacob decides, at this point, that he has had enough of working for Laban, but Laban has come to realize that Jacob is under divine protection, that he has prospered because of his nephew's presence. He offers to pay Jacob whatever he asks, and a duel of cunning commences.

This conflict has its comic aspect. Jacob offers to stay on awhile if Laban will allow him to take for his own all the spotted goats and sheep and all the black lambs. Laban agrees, but then removes these from the flocks and has his sons keep them apart from the rest. Jacob, encouraged by God, as he afterwards tells his wives, secures a mixed-colored breed simply by setting up striped sticks at the water troughs where the animals mate. He also sees to it that the spotted breed is produced from the most vigorous specimens. This makes Jacob extremely rich, and he finally decides to leave Laban. Without forewarning his uncle, he goes off with his wives and his children, his camels, his sheep, goats and asses, his male and his female servants. Rachel, without Jacob's knowing it, carries away her father's household gods, the Hebrew equivalents of lares and penates. Laban comes after them and makes a scene. Why has Jacob left his uncle in this furtive way instead of allowing him to kiss his daughters good-by and to send them away with music? He searches the tents for the household gods, which Rachel hides in her camel's saddle. Jacob, not knowing she has them, becomes angry and denounces Laban. "If I hadn't had God with me," he says, "I should never have got away from you with anything to show for my work!" Laban is obliged to back down. They make a covenant, and Laban goes home. Jacob proceeds on his way and encounters divine messengers. "This is God's army," he says.

But the thought of reunion with Esau now begins to worry Jacob. He devises a strategy for propitiating his brother or keeping out of his reach, in case Esau still wants to kill him. First of all, he sends out men to announce his return, and they report that Esau is coming to meet him, accompanied by four hundred followers. Jacob is apprehensive. He divides his company in two in order that, if one part should get massacred, the other should have a chance to escape. He then prays, reminding God that He has promised to stand behind him and to see to it that his children survive. After this, he instructs his servants to go ahead of him with a present for Esau consisting of over five hundred animals. They are to drive them in procession, drove by drove, with intervals between the droves, so as to make the strongest possible impression. They must wait until Esau has seen the first drove and demands to know whose they are, then they will tell him it is a present for him, sent by his servant Jacob, who is following close behind. Each new drove will come as a fresh surprise. Soon Jacob himself will appear, and perhaps this will do the trick. Yet Jacob is evidently anxious and tense. He sends his wives and his children to the farther side of the Jabbok River. Now he is all alone, and he passes through a strange experience, a crisis and test of the spirit that accompanies this critical moment of his meeting his brother again and perhaps predetermines its upshot. This is the episode that has come to be known as the struggle of Jacob with the angel—perhaps out of euphemism, since the editors of the sacred text had a tendency to play down passages that appeared disrespectful to God. Actually, no angel is ever mentioned. Jacob wrestles all night with a "man." That they all but literally went to the mat is shown by the Hebrew verb, found only here, which is made from one of the nouns for "dust" (which is similar in sound to the name of the Jabbok). They are "dusting" one another. The mysterious opponent realizes that he cannot get Jacob down, so he strikes him on the socket of the thigh and puts his thigh out of joint. "Let me go," he bids Jacob, "for the day is breaking." But Jacob is still able to hold his own: "I shall not let you go till you bless me." The being asks Jacob's name, and when Jacob tells him, he says, "Your name shall no longer be Jacob, but Israel"—meaning "striver with God"—"for you have striven with both God and men, and prevailed." Jacob asks his opponent's name; the other refuses to answer, but blesses him before he departs. Jacob knows that he has wrestled with God, that he has seen Him face to face, yet still lives. The sun rises, and he goes away limping. Thereafter, he is sometimes called Israel. It is the first time the name occurs. Is there some implication here of a rivalry of God with His creation? What is striking for us today in this passage is that even the chosen leader, who identifies himself with the spirits that preside over man's destiny and the forces of nature, must pit himself against them, like Prometheus, in order to win something from them; that this name the Jews gave themselves contained, or was afterwards made to contain, the idea that they had conquered, at a maiming cost, some share in the power of God.

The meeting with Esau goes off very well, though Jacob is plainly nervous. There follows a hideous episode of the kind that even devout readers of the Bible have not often cared to remember. Such stories are in themselves far from elevating; they do not provide texts for sermons or suggest subjects for paintings, yet, in the narrative of the Bible, their savagery has the effect of setting off the

strong purposes, the flashes of revelation, that represent
the emergence of the moral sense, of the nobler human
ambitions—those principles and aspirations that seemed
to the ancient Jew so much on a different level from the
ferocity and the duplicity which were also a part of his
history that he regarded them as promises and precepts
handed down to him by a higher being. Jacob now buys
some land in Canaan, and Shechem, the son of the local
prince, seduces Jacob's only daughter, Dinah—"and hum-
bled her," the narrative adds, which seems to imply rape.
But Shechem's "soul was attached to Dinah; he loved
her, and he spoke to the heart of the girl." Schechem goes
to his father and asks him to arrange for him to marry
Dinah. The father takes it up with Jacob and proposes
that his people and Jacob's should live on good terms together, intermarry and trade with one another, that Jacob
should settle among them. Schechem, whose soul longs
for Dinah, offers Jacob and her brothers any gift they
ask, if they will let him make her his wife. But Jacob's
sons have just come in from the cattle, and, still furious at
the wrong done Dinah but not betraying their feelings,
they make the objection to Jacob that they cannot allow
their sister to be married to a man who has not been
circumcised, and insist that if there is to be intermarriage between Shechem's people and theirs, all the
former must undergo this operation. Young Shechem at
once consents, and his father, who has always humored
him, goes to the gate of the city and announces that this
drastic measure is forthwith to be carried out. Every man
who goes out of the gate must be stopped and subjected
to circumcision. When this has been going on three days
and the male inhabitants of the city are all suffering from
the effects of the operation and unprepared to defend
themselves, two of Jacob's sons, Simeon and Levi,
descend on them and slaughter them all, including, of

course, Shechem and his father, and they carry away
Dinah, who has been kept in Shechem's house. They also
plunder the city and devastate the countryside, driving
off all the animals and enslaving the women and children.
When Jacob finds out what has happened, he rebukes his
revengeful sons; he shows them what a mess they have
made, that his name is now a stink to the people there. He
has only a handful of followers, and his neighbors will
combine against him and kill them all. The stupid young
men reply, "Could we let him treat our sister like a
harlot?"

God tells Jacob to go to Bethel, and Jacob makes his
household purify themselves and hand over to him all
their images of the false local gods. He reaches Bethel
without interference, because God has restrained his enemies, and he builds an altar there. God now repeats his
promises, and Jacob moves on to another place. But
Rachel has conceived again, and on the way she falls into
labor. "Don't be afraid," says the midwife, when her
pains become agonizing. "You will bear another son."
But Rachel dies in giving birth to this son, and, dying,
names him Ben-oni, Son of My Suffering. Jacob, however, changes this to Ben-yamin, Son of the Right Hand.
He marks Rachel's grave and journeys on. The last thing
we hear of him in this section is that one of his sons,
Reuben, has gone to bed with Rachel's former maid, his
father's concubine, by whom Jacob has had two sons.
"And Israel," the narrator says, "heard about this"—
Israel, the striver with God.

There follows the story of Joseph, which I shall not
attempt to retell. It is, of course, a success story, the
prototype of all success stories. Joseph is the able Jew
who makes good in a foreign land. In his function as
Pharaoh's governor, he reminds us of Disraeli Prime
Minister and of the powerful Jewish viziers of the tenth

and eleventh centuries in Spain. He scores off his envious brothers, who have sold him into Egypt, first by putting them to a great deal of inconvenience, then by forgiving them and setting them up in Egypt; and he gratifies his father Jacob and arranges for him a serene old age. There are moments when we feel about Joseph that he is a little what is meant by the Yiddish word *allrightnik,* when we are tempted to sympathize with the brothers in their resentment at his reading of dreams that is always to his own advantage. Except for this gift of interpreting dreams, he has little communication with the Deity, and we may easily find Jacob more interesting, with his trickery, his love for Rachel, his victimization by Laban and his finally sending his father-in-law about his business, his difficult domestic relations and his uncontrollable children, his sporadic contacts with God that jolt him into consciousness of his destiny. But Joseph, with his solid character, his career of worldly advancement, makes a necessary intermittence—or, rather, an intermittence that convinces us we are dealing with a human world—in this chronicle of intercourse with the Deity, so that the next advance in this intercourse will come with a peculiar impressiveness: the Moses of Exodus, who will talk to God, face to face, on a loftier level than Abraham, who will derive from Him authority and leadership of a more compelling kind than Jacob's.

All these incidents take place in a world in which the time values are always vague, because Hebrew verbs have no real tenses. This whole question of time is so interesting, the time-sense of a people is so fundamental, so important for understanding its mentality, that I want to discuss it in a more general way, and not merely in connection with the Bible.

"What was perhaps most astonishing to the modern

European," a former governor of Kenya, Sir Philip Mitchell (quoted in the issue of August 1953 of the German magazine *Der Monat*), has reported of the natives of that region, "was their not having any calendar or way of telling time, the fact that they oriented themselves solely by the moon and the seasons, the rising and the setting of the sun. Before the modern Europeans took over, there did not, except for the Swahili spoken on the coast, exist in any language from Abyssinia to the Transvaal any way of saying 'on January 1, 1890,' or 'at two-thirty in the afternoon,' or of expressing any other such idea."

Now, the Jews of the Old Testament were not, of course, quite in this primitive state, but their time-sense was so little developed that they did not even have a word for "hour," and, as we have seen, they took no interest in accurate chronology. The Babylonians evidently had sundials three hundred years before Christ, but the only possible reference in the Bible to any such time-telling device is a dubious one in Isaiah 38:8, where the "grades" that have been interpreted as the degrees of a dial might mean also a flight of steps. We so much take for granted, in our part of the world, our schedules of clock and calendar time that it is difficult to adjust ourselves to the mental habits of peoples who do not share our conventions.

This is certainly one difference that throws us off in our attempts to deal with the Russians. The visitor to Moscow may at first be misled by the fact that he and the Muscovites make use of similar clocks, and that the Russians, since the Revolution, have adjusted their calendar to ours; he may assume that appointments will be kept, that meetings will begin on time, and he is likely to become impatient when he discovers that *seichás* (this hour) is often equivalent to "never." Yet if he studies the language, he should realize that the Russians are liv-

ing in an older, a much less closely scheduled world.*
The tenses of the verbs in any language are the key to a
people's idea of time, and the tenses of the Russians are
different from ours and different from those, I believe,
of any of the Romance or Teutonic languages. The basic
thing to grasp here is that the Slavs lack the Western conception of a definite moment in the present, of the present as a definite moment. You cannot say in Russian, "I
tell you 'No!,'" or, like John Burroughs in his well-
known poem, "Serene, I fold my hands and wait." The
Russians, like the ancient Jews, make their fundamental
distinction between action completed and action going
on. You can only say in Russian, "I am telling you 'No!'"
—that is, put the verb in the "imperfective." In the "perfective," there is no present tense; you can have an action
completed only in the future or in the past. The line from
John Burroughs would have to be rendered in Russian
either "I am folding my hands and shall wait" or "I have
folded my hands and am waiting." The language does
not allow for an action completed in the present, and
the past is also lacking in precisions that our Western
languages make. The Russian past is an old past participle
that is inflected (quite uselessly, from our point of view)
for gender as well as number, but the use of which is
otherwise exactly like the illiterate use of the past participle that is current in the American South: "I taken
her out for a walk." In Russian there is no pluperfect;
you cannot, by a change of the tense, make it clear that
some action or event has taken place before some other.
Nor is there any distinction such as we make between a
perfect and a simple past; though I have written, "I have

---

* Old Slavonic, a literary language, had a fuller equipment of
tenses, but—except for a few survivals among the southern
tongues—these were lost by the Slavic languages when they developed in a colloquial way.

folded my hands" above, for the sake of natural English, the Russians would be simply "I folded." When something is past, it is past, and the antiquated Russian language does not worry about the chronology of past events in relation to one another. Nor does it have any grammatical machinery for adjusting events in the past to the point of view of the present—that is, to the point of view of the moment when the speaker is speaking.* Thus, it could not be said in Russian of Chekhov's three sisters that they thought they would go to Moscow. A neighbor of theirs would have said, "They thought they *will* go to Moscow." The difference between us and the Russians is that, here again, we are equipped with the conception of the present as a definite point. This point, for us, stands as a limit to the past, and the past, as seen from this moment, falls into an ordered perspective. With us, the conditional "would" relegates the intention of the sisters to a moment when it was not yet possible to know whether or not their intention would be carried out; they might or might not have gone. Chekhov knows, of course, that they will never get off, but if he told you about it in Russian, the language would not provide him with any way of even hinting that there was anything problematic about it. It sets no limit and adjusts no perspective. In telling of the sisters' hopes, the language must transport the speaker to the period when these hopes were being entertained, and at that period, as I have earlier pointed out, there was no way in Russian for the sisters to say, "Today we shake the dust of this place from our feet and

* There is a Russian conditional mode, but it is only used for the past in connection with definitely negative ideas, or when, speaking from the point of view of the present, one is quite sure that something has not occurred. It may be mentioned that the same form of the conditional is used for the past and the future. *I should have done something* and *I should do something* are said in the same way.

definitely clear out for Moscow!" It is easier in Russian
than it is for us indefinitely to put things off, as Chekhov
knows his three sisters will do; so far as their grammar
goes, the time of departure may never come, and from
the moment when this ceases to be future, it is bound to
be conceived as continuous: action still uncompleted. It
will take them a long time to prepare, it will take them a
long time to travel.

What cannot be grasped by your Russian friend who
keeps you waiting an hour and a half is that for you a
moment of the present will come when you stand with
your watch in your hand and the hands of the watch at,
say, two-forty-five (the times for which appointments are
made in Russia often seem to us incomprehensible and
soon cease to carry conviction, as when someone says,
"Two, or perhaps half past two, or perhaps better a quarter to three").* If you make sure to arrive at a meeting
a little in advance of the hour set and find that you must
wait some time before the doors will be opened, it is because the time for beginning is understood differently by
the Russians and the hour officially mentioned has nothing whatever to do with it. Eventually they will drift in,
and the moment to start will come; they will feel it, not
check it on their watches. Nor will their watches tell them
when to stop. Once a meeting, a performance at the theater, a banquet, an interview, a lecture, a lesson has got
itself under way, it will go on till the subject has been
covered, till the drama has run its course, till everyone
has had enough. And, as a result of this willingness to
squander time, the theatrical entertainment or the novel
or the serious discussion, with Russians, is likely to flour-
ish more richly and to develop in a way more organic

---

* Turgenev—in other ways, a scrupulous man—used to tax Henry
James's patience and sometimes offend Flaubert by never turning
up at the appointed time.

than enterprises of this kind usually do with us. As the performance will not be cramped, so the preparation will not have been hurried. Rehearsal, rewriting, preliminary study will not have been menaced by a deadline, by the last train to Montclair or Stamford, by an engagement to meet somebody at six o'clock and talk about something else till you dine with somebody else at seven. And this lack of our sense of clock-time is also one reason the Russians—excelling at research and pure science—have proved themselves, since the Revolution, so ill suited for industrial operations, which depend on close timing and deadlines, the kind of thing perfected by our Taylor system. The programs of the Five-Year Plans were attempts to impose on the Russians the conception of clock and calendar time, to stampede them into the Western frame. In our mechanized part of the world, such a device is neither needed nor conceivable. Our industrial time runs on—the seconds clicking by like cogs—as steadily as the conveyor belt that carries the parts of the car that must always be the model of a particular calendar year. If some step in the process jams, it is soon got going again; our factories do not stop for lunch, as the Russian ones do, or as they did when I visited them in 1935. The accurate continuous functioning of the American industrial machine involves, more or less, our whole lives. But the Five-Year Plans of the Russians were like unaccustomed blocks of Western time set down in the Eastern eternity, as their plants were set down on the steppes; and though their front ends were squarely presented, a triumph of theatrical décor, they would tend to melt away on the other side, to succumb to the Russian continuous present. The planners themselves, in the meantime, instead of starting work with the workers and keeping in touch with the plant, would have been coming to their offices late in the morning and escaping from the discipline of

the clock by getting together for interminable conferences that would go on for most of the night. The recent
order that Soviet officials must be at their desks from nine
to six is one of the ever recurring, the almost Sisyphean
attempts on the part of the governing group to synchronize Russia with the schedule of the West.

Now, the Jews of the Old Testament were living in a
world of time that, from our modern Western point of
view, was even less advanced than the Russian. In their
language, as in Russian, the primary distinction was
made between completed and incomplete action, but
there were no definite tenses at all. The beginner is usually told, as the best rule of thumb to start out with, to
translate the perfects as pasts and the imperfects as futures. But he soon finds out that this will not do. It is
true that the ancient Jew usually thought of future action
as uncompleted and completed action as past, but our
categories of future and past can hardly be said to have
existed for him. In my old grammar of 1838, the author,
a Professor Isaac Nordheimer of the University of the City
of New York, begins his discussion of the Hebrew tenses
by explaining that the efforts of Europeans to work out
a system of tenses has been "hitherto attended with very
incomplete success," because of the fact that "Occidental
scholars" cannot help proceeding on assumptions "derived . . . from the manner in which the various points
of time are indicated in the Indo-European languages,
rather than from the nature of the subject itself." He
goes on to try to grapple with the nature of the Hebrew
idea of time, and he presents us with a diagram. Let the
straight line AB, he says, represent the sequence of
time. Let us assume that for the Jews this sequence extended beyond A into an infinite past and beyond B into
an infinite future. Let us take, upon this line, a point
C somewhere between A and B, which will represent the

present, *our* conception of the present. But here the trouble begins. The Jews even more than the Russians lacked our Western conception of the present moment—a feature that, it seems, marks a very advanced state in the history of language development. For them, no point C could exist. When the narrator of a Biblical story tells of something that has happened in the past, he does not keep it in a definite relation to a fixed point of reference in the present, the point at which the story is supposed to be told. He puts himself back into the time of the story, and by a logic not unlike that which is exemplified by the Russian sisters who thought they *will* go to Moscow, he may put in the imperfect ("future")—since the action has not yet been completed at the time of which he is telling—some event which, from our point of view, is already completed and belongs to the past. If we should try to proceed by our rule of thumb in translating Genesis 41:50, we should find ourselves putting it that Joseph "begat two sons before the years of famine will come." Dr. Nordheimer's diagram elucidates this by showing that the moment the storyteller puts himself back to a point D, between A and C, the happenings between D and C will be shifted from the past to the future; but he tries also to make it account for a feature of Hebrew grammar that must be one of the strangest in the history of language—the principle that when a verb-form follows the conjunction "and," the imperfect is written for the perfect and the perfect for the imperfect. That is, if you relied on the rule of thumb, you would find yourself translating, "And God *will say*, 'Let there be light,'" instead of, "And God *said*." It seems to me that this phenomenon eludes Dr. Nordheimer's argument, and that the Hebrew line of eternity ends by slipping away from all his alphabetical points and retaining only the property of extending indefinitely in either direction; nor have I seen any other explanation that appeared to me satisfactory. I shall not discuss this problem except to point out that it illustrates how difficult it is for us today to grasp the old Hebrew idea of time.

The points on Dr. Nordheimer's line cannot even be used to demonstrate other features of the Hebrew verbs more accessible than the *"and* conversive." A striking example of this, and a very significant one, is the so-called "prophetic" use of the perfect. If Jehovah or a prophet declares with the utmost conviction of certainty that something is going to happen, the action or event is put— since its eventual completion is not to be doubted—in the form of the verb that denotes completion. The implication is "It's as good as done." If you translate, as everybody has had to do, these prophetic perfects as futures, you miss an important nuance. When Jehovah says to Moses, "I am what I am," we are faced with the converse problem. Both verbs are in the imperfect, so, if we followed our rule of thumb, it would give us "I shall be what I shall be"—which again would be incorrect, since what the author of Exodus means to say is that God's existence has never ceased, that it is still going on and will never end. (This passage seems to be echoed in John 8:58: "Before Abraham was, I am.") Both these instances of usage are much to the point, for they both imply the conception of a single and eternal God, which was fundamental to Hebrew thought. For this Deity, the point C, the present moment, is a matter of little importance. Hence the carelessness of chronology in the Bible, the long shadows cast by the patriarchs, the habit of feeling that the prophets are still, like Jehovah, in being (the verb that means "to prophesy" has no "light" active but is always in the light passive, which indicates that God is speaking *through* the prophet, or in the intensive reflexive, which indicates raving or exaltation), so that it shocked no one's sense of reality to attribute to them writings that dealt with events occurring years after their deaths or to read back into them predictions of happenings—the coming of the Messiah, for example—that in their lifetimes had not even been imagined. "Instead of narrating, Israel predicts, that is to say, systematizes," says Renan in this connection. "That is why it has prophets, not historians. The invasion of the Scythians, for example, is not narrated anywhere. The episode of Gog, in Ezekiel, is a description of it, transformed into a symbol for the future. In this curious state of mind, everything becomes a type and a general formula. The thing that has actually happened counts for almost nothing." The Book of Daniel, which is written in terms of Belshazzar and Nebuchadnezzar and the Babylonian captivity, was intended to apply to a situation four hundred years later, when the Jews, then returned to Jerusalem, were being persecuted by Antiochus Epiphanes.

Renan believed also that this vagueness of the time-sense, this lack of an equipment of tenses, which is common, it seems, to the Semitic languages, had been one of the factors that contributed to preventing the Semitic peoples from acquiring techniques and "progressing" along the same lines as the European world. They had never been geared into our time-system. Though modern clocks were not used in Europe till some time in the thirteenth century, it seems to have been the Romans who established our clock and our calendar. The Greeks, of course, had water clocks and sundials and an elaborate system of tenses that indicated with precision, as the Semitic languages could not do, the relation of happenings to one another. But the Romans, with their conquests, imposed their system wherever their armies came; they left the construction of their language along with their other constructions. The Romance languages inherited them, and the Teutonic ones took their stamp. We live today in a Roman structure of present, past, pluperfect, future and future perfect. (The current tendency to drop this last tense, to slur the relations of events in the future, is probably due to our desperate rush to pull future events into the present.) And we live not merely, as the Romans did, in a world of years, months, weeks and days, but in a world of minutes, seconds and infinitesimally split seconds.

Does the Westernized modernized Jew not live in this structure, too? He has mastered it; in a practical way, he lives by it. Yet his Bible and the language in which it was written seem never to be quite absent from the background of his mind. The Talmud has kept them alive as immediate inalienable realities that have annihilated time and space through fifteen centuries of exile and dispersion. Most Jews have a dimension of eternity, and this is one thing that sets them off from, and to some extent makes them seem strange to, the people whose view of the world is conditioned by self-limiting historical units: the development of civilizations, the births and the deaths of nations. Our myths are the temporal myths of Caesar and Pericles, of Charlemagne, Washington, Hitler; but the myths of the Jews are timeless—the patriarchs and prophets who never die, the Messiah who never comes. The legend of the Wandering Jew is an attempt by the Gentiles to synchronize the Jewish eternalness with the vicissitudes of their own intensely temporal history. The sense of persistent values that survive and transcend our historical epochs, as it has always been inherent in Jewish religion, is also implied in their language; and some acquaintance with the Hebrew Bible may be useful in making us realize how much our conception of time is an artificial contrivance; that tonight at eight-thirty, when we hope for a new revelation afforded by some popular drama, the night of August 9th, when we did or did not commit the crime, the point C that fixes the moment of the present, have an importance that is purely conventional. I do not mean that we ought to go back to the world of the Hebrew prophets or that the Jews as a people still live in this world, though one sometimes gets the impression that there are rabbis and scholars who do; but today one begins to be dubious of our passion for historicity, which seems at moments to become maniacal. I have lately been typing old notebooks of mine that go back to 1914, and I find that, for every year, I have recorded the current slang and the favorite popular songs. Is this valuable? I thought it was, and I expect to make some use of this data. Like everyone else in our part of the world, I am incurably history-minded. But what about all the issues of all the innumerable newspapers recorded on microfilm, all the minutes of all the meetings carefully filed away? We are shocked and indignant when the Russians, with their less highly developed historical sense, do not hesitate to sponge out the record of a decade or of half a century and to substitute something simpler, which will be more advantageous to the party in power (remember that the Russian verb does not indicate the relations of events in the past; when an action is past, it is simply past). We are amused by the rabbinical mind, which occupies itself with the moral situation of Jonah inside the whale as if it were a permanently important problem. But how long can our civilization go on storing up and stuffing our heads with so much minute historical information?

M. André Malraux, in his novel *The Walnut Trees of Altenburg,* written in the midst of the last World War, presents an international group of thinkers in various departments of knowledge discussing those basic conceptions that underlie the mentality of every civilization

without ever being subjected to criticism, because they
are so taken for granted that people are not aware of
them. And one of these, a great anthropologist, arrives
at the conclusion that, for us, the uncriticized conception
is not "the nation," as somebody else has suggested, but
the historical point of view itself. We live, he insists, in
history "as the religious civilizations lived in God," and
behind our conception of history is our special conception
of time.

Shall we someday come to reckon differently—to
abridge historical processes, to range over longer periods,
to see events in different relations, to have a different
conception of events themselves? Our present conception of time, which has till recently dominated our imaginative writing and is still extremely strong, seems essential to our mechanics, to our science, which has
merged with our study of morals. Now, the critical study
of the Bible that has been one of the features of our
scientific period has shown that the Jewish ideas about
morals, the principles ascribed to Jehovah, were modified from prophet to prophet—and hence, from era to
era, under pressure of varying situations, economic, political, social. And yet there is something there that is less
affected than one might expect by these changes in time
and locale: the principles of rectitude and justice, represented by the permanent Jewish God (as later, with
Christianity, the claims of human fellow-feeling). When
the resolute Western grammarian makes an effort to intro-
duce our time sequence into the timeless Hebrew verbs,
they continue to remain something else. "Many have concluded," says Dr. Kyle M. Yates, the author of an excellent beginner's grammar, *The Essentials of Biblical Hebrew,* "that uniformity in the determination and translation of these points [the nuances of mood and tense] is
impossible," but he insists that they must exist, and he

draws up a table of them. The weakness of such systems is that they are bound to wear the aspect of gratuitous creations, since the meanings assigned by their formulators cannot, except in a very few instances, be shown to have any connection with the actual mechanism of the verb-forms. And so, when the garbled events of the Bible are subjected to an exact rearrangement that satisfies our Western chronology, we see that they still remain something else—something that is scarcely impaired by the extreme improbability that Methuselah lived almost a thousand years, that Sarah was nearly seventy when she proved irresistible to Pharaoh, that Jacob's great love for Rachel kept him working for Laban seven years. It is something that has done a good deal to sustain the morale of the Gentile as well as that of the Jew through the strictly historical happenings—the wars, the persecutions, the conquests, the migrations and the natural disasters of the last three thousand years.

Yet the Biblical "aspect of eternity" has its disadvantages, too. It is the Jews who have given to the Western world all four of its great religions—Judaism, Christianity, Mohammedanism and the half-religion Marxism—and they all of them have in common a compelling and delusive utopianism. The Jew expected the Messiah, who was to lead him out of captivity; the Mohammedan looked forward to his paradise; the medieval Christian expected the Judgment Day and the reign of Christ for infinity. Karl Marx, who liked to bait the utopian socialists and believed himself free from their errors, actually derived his appeal in great part from his vision of a socialist Armageddon and a socialist Judgment Day, when the sheep would be separated from the goats and the reign of Justice begin, as his "History" was also an omnipotent God that guided a chosen group. All these visions were solemn promises that gave people the courage to live, and in which they believed so vividly that it was almost as if the visions were already fulfilled. They belong to the "prophetic perfect," that phase of the Hebrew verb which indicates that something is as good as accomplished. And the escape from historical time—from the compromise, the modification, the incomplete satisfaction, the accepted misunderstanding, the complicated adjustments of every day—may bring with it something obsessive, as all four of these religions have shown, that easily produces intolerance. Now, intolerance is suicidal, for it stimulates intolerance on the other side. To believe in a word of God unchangeable and eternal (as promulgated by any of these prophets) is to stop human self-improvement, human self-creation dead—in the literal, as it always turns out, as well as in the "spiritual" way. This sense of transcendent principle has always had to be corrected by the realistic observation, the practical worldliness, of the Graeco-Roman tradition. It is the reciprocal relation of the two that has made what there is of our civilization.

II

ÉRETZ YISRAÉL

SAMARITAN PASSOVER: A vertiginous trip up the mountain that commands, astoundingly, stage by stage, a more and more immense view of Palestine. This, in the Biblical sense, is a High Place of worship indeed. At the top, we get out of the car and are struck by a prodigious wind that did not reach us in the valley below but that now seems about to sweep us off. A crowd of Arab children, who have come for the show, follow the foreign visitors and laugh noisily as we struggle against the gale and stumble among the rocks. There is nothing to be seen on this summit but a small Mohammedan shrine and the buried foundations of a Byzantine church that makes, in the grass, an octagon.

But farther down, out of range of the wind, the Samaritans are celebrating their Passover. Their High Priest, since early morning, has been reading the Samaritan Pentateuch and has now nearly got through Deuteronomy. This High Priest and two of his elders are garbed in long gowns of green; other elders are gowned in white. All wear hieratic beards and white turbans with red tops. The Samaritans are extremely inbred; there are now only three hundred and four of them—two hundred and seventeen here in Jordan, and the rest over the line in Israel. The elders, in their robes of ceremony, can hardly be told apart. They are tall and well grown, but their bones look frail. Their faces a little lack character, and yet give the impression of exceptional purity. They do not resemble the Arabs, among whom they have now so long lived; they are paler and like Jews of the classical stamp, whose aquiline profiles have been bred away till their noses are almost straight. In a circle about these *Cohaním* (priests) sits an audience partly made up of other Samaritan men, in red tarbooshes and business suits. The women seem all to be lurking in the tents that the Samaritans have put up on the mountain and to which, for the period of the Passover, they have come from the town of Nablús on the plain. There is an outer ring of alien visitors, whose presence reminds one a little of one of those Indian dances of the American Southwest which sightseers are allowed to attend. The American vice-consul from Jerusalem is there to represent the Consulate, to which an invitation has been sent, and the director of the American School of Oriental Research is also present.

The reading of the Pentateuch ended, the High Priest makes a short speech in Arabic, in which the word "Arabia" comes out in a climactic way and is enthusiastically applauded. Then he leads the *Cohaním* in praying, repeating over and over again, "There is only one God," but steadily increasing, step by step, the tempo and the volume. Just below stands another assembly, a group of the younger men, robed in white and with sleeves rolled up for the sacrifice, wearing red tarbooshes and sandals tied with strings. They, too, are determinedly praying. Beside them, in the angle of a stone fence, wait seven fat brown-faced sheep—one for each of the seven Samaritan families—which have been recently purchased with careful selection and scrupulously washed every day. They conform to the prescription of Exodus, on which the Passover service is based, that "your lamb shall be without blemish, a male a year old." And now the sun is just setting; the moment for the sacrifice arrives. The High Priest gets up on a stone and recites the first six verses of Exodus 12, Jehovah's instructions to Moses and Aaron for commemorating their flight from Egypt, which culminate with the words "And the whole assembly of the congregation of Israel shall kill it in the evening." The young men have carried the squirming sheep to a ditch which contains a stone altar, and they now hold the animals' heads over this and saw through their throats with large knives. This releases a demonstration, not an outburst but a reverential acknowledgment. You hear whistles, cries, clapping of hands. The fathers of families now at once smear the blood on the foreheads of their first-born children, and in earlier days they dashed away to smear it on the lintels and posts of their doors. Inquiries as to why this was not being done brought only evasive answers, and it has been only from *Life* magazine that I have learned—there was a *Life* photographer present—that the Samaritans are now so poor that they have to borrow tents from the Arabs, who object to having them bloodied. On the sheep, now mere fat woolly lumps, they pour boiling water from pots, and begin plucking off the wool, to establish that the bodies are unblemished. The High Priest withdraws to his tent to entertain the invited guests.

By this time the sun has disappeared, and an all-but-full bright moon is shining, but suddenly, as we walk through sharp stones in the direction of the High Priest's tent, the whole world is blotted out by a darkness of a kind that I have never seen elsewhere and that summons to my mind impressively that opaque word *"arafél,"* which is supposed to be compounded of "darkness" and "cloud" and which in Exodus is applied to the obscurity out of which the Ten Commandments were uttered: "And

the people stood afar off, and Moses drew near to the
thick darkness where God was." This darkness is not
black, but a sort of dull and dense brown, and seems almost of the consistency of soft-coal smoke. Invisible to
one another and hoping we are not getting lost, we try to
hold our way on the rocky road that hardly differs from
the stony hillside, till at last we see a group of parked
cars, with the lights of the tents behind them. Received
by Amrán Ishák, the High Priest, cordially but rather
remotely, we sit down on benches and beds and are offered arrack and wine, biscuits of unleavened bread and a
dish of a paste called khúmas, that you scoop up with
pieces of matzah. While the ceremony was going on, the
Arabs, it seems, were not idle. One of the ladies has just
managed to rescue a ring which she felt being slipped off
her finger, and a young theological student from Union
Seminary, in New York, has lost his fountain pen and his
watch. The High Priest assures him with dignity that he
will see that these things are restored. Amrán Ishák has
written a book on his people, their history, beliefs and customs, and parts of it, in English translation, are sold to
the visitors in the form of pamphlets. Up to this year, I
am told, they have been given away, and the visitors have
made small contributions, but this year a set price has
been put on them, and one of the white-gowned young
men snatches a pamphlet away when, in consequence of
a misunderstanding, something less than this price has
been offered. Amrán Ishák draws back from the scene
with a look of controlled indignation. One feels that he
is deeply embarrassed, but one cannot tell whether he is
angry at the visitor's trying to cheapen the sale or at the
young Samaritan's bad manners. It is evident, in any case,
that he does not know how to deal with this situation.
Though the members of his community are, many of
them, small businessmen in Nablús, he still lives in the

world of the Bible, and his book is a résumé of history from the minority Samaritan point of view. There is something about his aspect at once austere and anxious.

The Samaritans originally, of course, were as much a part of the Children of Israel as were the ancestors of the Jews. Their kingdom in the north was, in fact, called Israel, in contradistinction to Judah, the kingdom of the south. But in 721 B.C. this northern kingdom of Israel was wiped out by the descent of the Assyrians, and its people never recovered from this. All the more important elements of the population were taken away to Assyria, but the poorer people were left behind, and these interbred with the conquerors and corrupted their Jehovah worship with that of the Assyrian gods. These were the ancestors of the modern Samaritans. Later on, they were to feud with the people of Judah, who, once the northern kingdom had been destroyed, were in a position to make of their own city, Jerusalem, the unchallenged religious center of the Israelite world. Jerusalem fell to Nebuchadnezzar in 586, and the Judahites were carried off to Babylon, but when, fifty years later, the Persian king Cyrus, in his turn, conquered Babylon, he allowed them to return to Jerusalem, where they set about rebuilding their temple. The Samaritans at this point approached them and offered to collaborate with them, but the Judahites regarded them now as a people of doubtful blood, contaminated by heathen religion, and refused to allow them to participate. The breach was made final when a brother of the High Priest, who had been sharing in the priestly functions, married a Samaritan wife, and was exiled by the elders of Jerusalem, where a very strong policy against mixed marriages had been laid down by Nehemiah. This man, with the backing of his father-in-law and reinforced by other Israelites who had been persecuted for similar reasons but backed by the Persian king, well content to see the Jews divided, withdrew to Mount Gerízim and built a temple there; he seems to have been the founder of the present Samaritan sect of independent worshippers of Jehovah. The Samaritans, in any case, possessed their own text of the Pentateuch, and refused to recognize the prophets, whom they treated as the spokesmen of a rival faction. They rejected the whole version of Israelite history composed by the dominant Judahites; they have never regarded themselves as Jews, but always refer to the Jews as a race of successful impostors, very much as the Trotskyites did with the Stalinist regime in Russia. The Samaritan variants from the orthodox text of the five books supposed to have been written by Moses are relatively slight in extent, but the Samaritans consider them of crucial importance, for they indicate firmly and consistently that Mount Gerízim, at the foot of which they live and on which they celebrate their Passover, is the spot designated by Jehovah as the headquarters of his cult; not Jerusalem, which, at the time when the commands of the Pentateuch were given— that is, at the time when the Children of Israel had just arrived at the Promised Land—was not yet in Israelite hands. The Samaritans assert that the Jews, and not they, have doctored the holy writings—that the selection by God of Jerusalem as the center of Israelite religion could hardly have been made before Solomon's Temple was actually in existence. They deny the contention of the Jews that this designation was really a prophecy, and they point out that the form of the verb "to choose" that occurs in the Samaritan version precludes the possibility of this. The truth is, it seems, that the Pentateuch, in the general version accepted by both Orthodox Jews and Samaritans, was put together during the Babylonian exile—so, on the one hand, the Samaritans are perfectly right in insisting that the mention of Jerusalem was made after the building of Solomon's Temple, while, on the other hand, the inference must be that the Samaritans accepted this version from the Judahites, who had composed it, and that they added to it some references to Mount Gerízim.

Yet actually, from the point of view of history, the Samaritans have a pretty good case. Gerízim and its neighbor Ébal are the mountains named in Deuteronomy as the places for proclaiming, respectively, the blessings and the cursings of God. Nablús is certainly the ancient Shechem, the place in which Jacob is supposed to have settled when he came back from serving Laban, and the Samaritans claim that it is also the place where he had previously had his dream of the angels on the heavenly ladder. They are able to adduce the authority of Joshua 24 that the bones of Joseph were eventually brought from Egypt in order to be buried at Shechem, that it was at Shechem that Joshua set up a great stone "in the sanctuary of the Lord." Here, too, according to them, between the two mountains, was Moreh, the meadow where Abraham pitched his tent, and they believe that it was on Mount Gerízim, and not on the rock in Jerusalem which the Mosque of Omar now shelters, that the sacrifice of Isaac was averted. In any case, they built their own temple on Gerízim. This was later destroyed by the Jews in the period of Hasmonean ascendancy, in the second pre-Christian century; rebuilt, under Hadrian, when, at the time of the Jewish revolt of the second post-Christian century, the Samaritans had aided the Romans; then destroyed again by the Romans, in 484, at the instigation of the Christians. A rebellion under Justinian, in the following century, brought down on the Samaritans total suppression.

That is, political suppression. Their cult, as we have seen, still survives, and we visitors, leaving Amrán Ishák's tent, go back to the sacrifices. The directions set forth in Exodus are being exactly followed. There is, to be sure, one modern innovation. A bicycle pump has been used to blow up the dead sheep and facilitate the removal of the skin from the carcass, but this, of course, has not been prohibited, since no such devices were known to Moses. And now, in the red light of fires—the darkness has passed, and the moon is out—the naked remains are hanging, identifiable only by their dangling heads and their hairy legs and hoofs, each from a horizontal pole supported by two uprights, which are held by a pair of young men. These stand before the butcher, who cuts the carcasses open and removes first the slimy intestines, then the complicated mass of the other organs, from which the liver is hanging. There is a warm smell of raw flesh and excrement. These tripes are washed, salted and burned, according to the Biblical prescription. Then the bodies are salted and roasted—since God has forbidden boiling: "Eat not of it . . . sodden at all with water"—in an oven made of plaster and earth that has been heated over a fire built in a pit in the ground. They will be cooked for three hours, then eaten at midnight, the moment when, relenting at last to release the Children of Israel, "The Lord smote all the first-born in the land of Egypt." They will be eaten to the chanting of hymns, with the ordained bitter herbs and unleavened bread, and hastily—it is part of the ceremony that the celebrants must tear the meat apart with their hands—since God has said specifically, "Ye shall eat in haste," as they had eaten when they were leaving Egypt.

We did not wait for this final rite, but the wife of the director of the American School wanted, she said, to stay long enough to see a sheep actually roasted. A very feminine reaction, I thought: her interest had been excited in a culinary operation, and she wanted to see the meat in

the oven. With the director himself I talked of the Samaritans' pious conviction that they are still being punished
by Jehovah for their dalliance with the heathen deities,
and of their touching resignation to the inevitable dying-
out of their clan. They believe themselves to be fulfilling
the prophecy of Deuteronomy 28:62, that "Ye shall be
left few in number, whereas ye were as the stars of heaven
for multitude." "They were guilty of syncretism," the
scholar replied, and reminded me, by this humorously
meant remark, of the distance between their point of
view and ours. What is strange to us in this ceremony is
the performance of a barbaric butchery with restraint
and a complete sobriety; and, coming from the modern
world, it is difficult for us to realize that the problem that
most occupies the minds of the Samaritans is how to avoid
marriages that will involve a too close consanguinity. In
the Samaritan community in Israel, the elders have so far
relaxed their law as to permit a few marriages with Jewish women, and I was told by someone who had visited it
that he had been startled there to hear German spoken;
yet, in general, the Samaritans expect to die out, and, in
the meantime, the High Priest writes, "This nation carries out the ancient customs according to the Mosaic law
as well as they can, and have always offered the proper
prayers to the God of all creation, that He might keep
them from all harm, misfortune and all violence."

While I was standing there in the dark, a long-gowned
and bearded elder came up quietly from behind me and
begged in a low voice, "Baksheesh for the Samaritans!"

The Guardians of the City: It is absurd, no doubt, as
well as pathetic that, from principles of religious purity,
the Samaritans, after living among Arabs for something
like thirteen centuries without intermarrying with them,
should be dooming themselves today to extinction. It is a

reductio ad absurdum of the Hebraic tradition of exclusiveness. But one finds in the Jewish community, on the other side of the line, in the Meá Shearím (Hundred Gates) quarter of the new city of Jerusalem, a minority no less intransigent—the ultra-orthodox group that calls itself N'tureí Kartá, Guardians of the City. Just as the Samaritans exclude the Jews, and the Orthodox Jews exclude the Christians, so the Guardians of the City exclude, by their rigorous Judaism, not merely non-orthodox Jews but also the majority of the orthodox, and, together with other residents of more or less their way of thinking, have actually established in Meá Shearím, in this modern all-Jewish city, a community much like a ghetto.

This group derives from all over Europe—Poland, the Baltic Provinces, Rumania, Hungary, Germany—as well as from the United States. For hundreds of years, special scholars were sent by the Jewish communities of Europe —and, since the later nineteenth century, of America—to study in Old Jerusalem. They were subsidized for life from a fund supplied by free contributions from the congregations of countless synagogues, and they were expected to devote themselves to the study of Torah—that is, of the Pentateuch and its infinitely elaborated commentaries. The families of these students eventually "increased and multiplied" to a community of some five thousand. They had the comfort, in the Old City, of living close to the Wailing Wall, but, at the time of the war with the Arabs of 1948-49, they were driven to take refuge outside the old walls, where they gave themselves their present title of Guardians of the City. The city they guard is not that which the Israelis have made their capital. The Guardians of the City will not recognize the Israeli state, for they believe that it is only the Messiah who can found a state of Israel on earth, and that the profane impostures of the Zionists are preventing the Messiah from coming. Insisting that Hebrew is a sacred tongue that cannot be used for everyday purposes, they refuse to speak this national language and adhere to their native Yiddish. They will not share in the general life; they have managed to remain more or less autonomous; and though they have come from so many countries, they give an impression of all but complete uniformity. As in the case of the Samaritans, they are very inbred, and there is a dominant influence—Polish. They are said to reproduce in their costume the fashions of well-to-do Poles of two hundred years ago. On a Sabbath, when the people are walking out, all in their best clothes, they strike, in the Middle East, a note strangely inappropriate. Even in the hottest weather, when such costumes must be almost intolerable, the men wear large round fur hats (called streimels) and long straight coats (kaftans) of dull or of glossy black that come down just below their calves, under which they have knee breeches as often as trousers and white, black or yellow stockings. In obedience to Leviticus 19:27—"You shall not round off the hair on your temples or mar the edges of your beard"— they have allowed beards and hair to grow, and have cultivated, in front of their ears, the long locks that are the sign of the most literal orthodoxy. The women must walk behind the men. Their heads were shaved when they were married, and they wear unattractive wigs. The men are not allowed to shake hands with the women, and even their husbands, I was told, are not supposed to look them in the face; there is prescribed for sexual intercourse— which cannot take place in the light or unless the parties are dressed—a method that obviates this. Rabbinical law provides that a husband may divorce his wife for letting the dinner burn. The walls of the Meá Shearím quarter are covered with posters that warn the men not to let their women listen to radio—"You will hear a woman sing, but will it be a clean woman?"—and they are rallied to resist the Israeli law that conscripts women for military service.

The lives of these people, their conviction of merit, their prestige in the eyes of their neighbors, are all made up of observances or of casuistical substitutes for observances. Thus they are not supposed to carry handkerchiefs, and they wind them around their belts. The reason for this is as follows. The prohibition against work on the Sabbath occurs in the chapter of Exodus (35) which orders the building of the Tabernacle. This led to the later conclusion that only work connected with this building was meant, and this work was discriminated into thirty-nine classes, of which one was the carrying of an object from one place to another. The significant types of place were specified, in turn, as four, and the most severe prohibition was that against transferring private property to any public place. The Tractate *Sabbath* of the Talmud discusses, in this connection, the problem of clothing and adornment. It becomes a very nice question which articles may be classed under these categories, and how they shall be worn so as not to be carried and not to be subject to the defilement Leviticus warns against. The handkerchief does not appear in the Talmud, but is later dealt with in the *Shulkhán Arúkh,* a code of religious practice completed in the sixteenth century, which explains that it must be worn "below the outer garment," that it must not be knotted on anything (tying knots on the Sabbath is one of the thirty-nine prohibitions), and that it ought to be "wound on the trousers," so that it will not be directly carried. I was told that if they indulge themselves in trimming their beards, they do it with blunt scissors, since the prohibition of Leviticus 19:27 against "marring" the edges of the beard is thought to be limited by 21:5: "They

. . . shall not *shave* off the edges of their beards"—so that, according to a Talmudic interpretation, it is permissible to use anything but a razor, and having the scissors blunt removes them, presumably, as far as possible from the category of razor.

There are children of all ages in the street, the little boys all with skullcaps and sidelocks, which ought to be worn with dignity and do not suit the scrambling young. A crazy man squats by the wall and prophesies or airs his grievances—it may well be the same thing; an old man of solemn aspect, with white beard and black skullcap, sits out on his little porch reading what must be a holy book. A deformed and cross-eyed man—typical idiot of a Central European village—limps along the pavement. I was told by an American Jew that a visit to Meá Shearím reminded him of nothing so much as *The Cabinet of Dr. Caligari*, but I did not find it quite so macabre. The people seem mostly healthy and rather remarkably tall, but—what is not characteristic of Israeli Jerusalem—they do live in a certain squalor.

I persuaded a newspaperman to take me to the synagogue, which, though its actual congregation is not more than four or five hundred, is the N'tureí Kartá headquarters and the core of the orthodox resistance. He warned me that it would be dirty, but the atmosphere of rigorous devotion did much to redeem this. We arrived during Afternoon Prayers, and a pleasant, stout, white-bearded man offered us seats on a bench; a dingy and much-thumbed prayer book lay on the desk before us. The more pious of the members, in flat-brimmed black hats, were praying against the wall, bobbing their heads at the name of God, which provoked an echoed response even from those who were not actively participating. For people were coming and going and walking around the room. Some showed a touch of dandyism in their well-

curled and well-oiled brown earlocks and their long yel-
low-and-brown-striped coats; others, with sallow complexions, who nibbled their fingers and picked at their
beards, had intellectual faces that seemed capable of exaltation. One lean young man, with a thin pointed beard,
looked a little mad. A small boy, with skullcap, cropped
head, red side curls and a torn yellow sweater, was no
doubt filled with dreams of distinction—dreams the realization of which might seem to the outside visitor to be
bounded by this plain, shabby room, at the same time his
school and his field of ambition, yet which actually know
no bounds, since they must occupy themselves entirely
with a realm of divine law that would always and everywhere remain the same. Above, on one side, loomed the
gallery for women, blankly, inexorably boarded off, in
which they cannot be seen and from which they cannot
see anything.

Prayers over, the black-hatted men sat down at long
tables, on benches along the wall, and stuck their noses
in volumes of the Talmud. You have to study Talmud, my
companion explained, by night as well as by day. Yet the
synagogue is also a social center, and people hang around
to gossip. We go to talk to the rabbi, about whom a circle
has gathered. His name, Amrám, is, I take it, the same as
that of the Samaritan priest, and he makes upon me a little the same impression: of a purity that approaches the
insipid yet is backed by an official firmness. He is pale,
and his eyes and his beard are pale. One eye is half-closed,
as if from too much reading. One would say that his face
is a good face if it were not that it so plainly looks out
from a world that is different from ours that we know it
would not be possible for the Rabbi and us to agree as to
what constitutes goodness. The saintliness of Rabbi Amrám is accompanied—as it were, protected—by a quality
that is not perhaps shrewdness but rather a habit of cal-

culating in his dealings with the people of an alien world which it is impossible for him at all to take seriously. From that world he wants no publicity; he has never allowed himself to be photographed. I feel as if I were peering at something that is hardly meant to be seen. The Rabbi Amrám's family have been living in Jerusalem from five generations back. When he is asked what the aims of the Guardians are, he replies that they just want to be simple Jews who live as their forefathers did. They cannot accept Israel, because it is not the true Israel; the Messiah alone can establish that. At this point, the jolly old man, who had offered us seats and who was now standing by, said something with great emphasis that was relayed to me as "They eat pig!" The Rabbi has never sent a letter since the beginning of the present régime: if he should do so, he would have to buy a stamp, and this would imply recognition. He has refused, for the same reason, to acquire a ration card, but his congregation keeps him fed. He does not think it right to contend with the Arabs, and he adduces a Talmudic teaching that one must not revolt against the Goyím, but he denies that a man named Laibala Weissfisch, a fanatical maker of Torah scrolls, who has recently visited the United States, allegedly to make proposals prejudicial to the interests of Israel to the Arabs in the United Nations, is in any sense a spokesman for the Guardians. When, however, we ask Rabbi Amrám whether or not the story is true that, at the time of the Arab war, the Guardians had flouted the nationalists by going to the enemy with a white flag, prepared to make a separate peace, he answers that actually it is not true, but that he has never made a point of denying it, since he regards it as a good idea, perfectly consistent with their principles, which they probably ought to have thought of and carried out. I asked him whether he hoped ever to get back to the Old City, and he replied, "That would be God's blessing!" When we had left, I said to my guide that I was sorry I had not inquired what he thought of the state of the world. "I can give you his answer," my friend replied, "exactly as if you had asked him: he would have told you that he leaves all that to God."

Yet this mild-appearing patriarch—he has seventeen children—so venerable at forty-eight, has made himself a formidable nuisance. If Meá Shearím is a ghetto, it is a ghetto that persecutes its neighbors as much as they persecute it. The Guardians of the City have constantly to be haled into court and are often sent to prison. They and others of their way of thinking bar off public roads on the Sabbath to make them impassable for cars, which, when stopped, are surrounded by children dangling earlocks and shouting, "Shabbas! Shabbas!" The Guardians take down the numbers of cars that are out between Friday and Saturday evenings, watch to find them parked and smash them up. This has made the police apprehensive. Last Purim, a frivolous young man attended a costume party in the costume of a denizen of Meá Shearím, with streimel, kaftan and sidelocks. After arriving, he went back to get something from his car. It had been raining, and he lifted the hood to see whether the engine was wet. It was Friday evening, Sabbath. A policeman immediately seized him. The young man explained his costume, but the policeman refused to believe him. "Pull my sidelocks and see," said the reveller. But the policeman thought this was a ruse, that the fanatic wanted to frame him and would have questions asked in parliament. The masquerader had to take them off himself. On the issue of female conscription, the struggle has reached a point—with the Guardians and their sympathizers flatly refusing to yield—where, in order to avoid the necessity of trying to use force and creating martyrs, the government may have to back down. The power that the Rabbi wields within his own sphere of influence seems to be all but absolute. The movies are strictly forbidden, and if a man is known to have gone to one, he is sure to have his subsidy cut off or find himself put out of his flat. Since the Guardians of the City do not recognize the Chief Rabbinate, anyone who is known to have stood in the presence of the top-hatted Chief Rabbi (let alone have entered his synagogue), even in connection with a funeral, is immediately ostracized. They have several times burned a newsstand, not far from Rabbi Amrám's synagogue, that persisted in selling the novels that the women are forbidden to read, and the illustrated weeklies, which are considered pornographic. To almost everybody else in Jerusalem, the Guardians of the City are a headache, a constant source of embarrassment. The worst of it is that, unlike the Samaritans, they are militant proselytizers, with methods not unlike those of the Communists. They spy on their own people and spy on their own spies; they organize demonstrations and infiltrate Talmudic schools. What the Israelis are to the Arabs—not that they use these methods—the Guardians of the City are to Israel.

The Fiction of S. Y. Agnón: This obsolete Galician world, preserved in Meá Shearím, has been brilliantly presented in literature by a man of unquestionable genius, Shmuél Yoséf Agnón, who today resides in Jerusalem and occupies, at sixty-six, the undisputed position of foremost living Hebrew writer. I do not hesitate to speak of his genius, though I am unable to read him in Hebrew and have had access only to those of his works that have been translated into English—the novel called *The Bridal Canopy,* out of print but obtainable through Behrman House, New York; a long short story called *In the Heart of the Seas,* which is one of the volumes of the Schocken

Library; and a shorter piece called *Chemdat,* in the autumn, 1952, issue of the Jerusalem periodical *Israel Argosy.* (A book called *Days of Awe,* a treasury of legends and traditions connected with the Jewish high holidays, also published by Schocken, is of less interest to non-Jewish readers.) In Israel, people complain that these versions do nothing like justice to Agnón's remarkable style, but the two books, at any rate, that have been translated by I. M. Lask certainly read very well, and even in the alien medium it is evident that the texture of the writing is distinguished, poetic and strongly personal.

Since I know nothing save at second-hand of the very considerable literature in Hebrew that has come out of Central Europe, Russia and Palestine in the course of the last century and this, I cannot speak of Agnón's relation to other Hebrew writers. But one is struck at once, in reading him, by similarities to two other Jewish artists—Marc Chagall and Franz Kafka, both born, like Agnón, in the eighties. The picture of Jewish life in Agnón is, as in their cases, completely different from any kind of "genre" work that is derived from nineteenth-century naturalism. Involved in this picture, to be sure, is a definite local setting of domestic interiors and taverns, poultry yards and village crafts—long journeys in wagons on country roads, with the landlords looming remotely as menaces more often than patrons, the Gentiles, in general ("forgive me for mentioning them"), present only, as it were, offstage, to be shunned when they parade their "images" out-of-doors in religious processions. (The religion of the Gentiles is so little understood even by the masters of Talmudic learning that the symbolic Christian fishes on tombstones are taken as indicating the graves of Jewish descendants of Jonah.) But far more important than any of this are the rituals of the Jewish holidays, the marriage and funeral ceremonies, the devotions of the synagogue and the pursuits of the yeshiva, House of Study, where young and old pore over the Talmud, memorizing pages, disputing in form. It is these that make the frame on which everything rests—a life of the spirit that requires concentration and is always more or less intellectual, a constant solicitude as to the attitude toward one of God, who is usually called the Name and remains rather impersonal as well as invisible, since He does not, as in Christianity, figure as the Heavenly Father of a part-human intercessor, yet is somehow, in His infinite wisdom, arranging and projecting everything.

The humor and the pathos of Agnón—and he is truly a master of both—result from the spectacle of men and women *living* in a homely environment, which has been searchingly observed by the author but is only implied by his delicate art, yet *imagining* in terms of a universe that has no real locale or date except possibly in the hoped-for return to that distant idealized Israel toward which the most pious among them have never ceased to yearn. The whole content of Agnón's work—at least, in those of his stories I know—is the poetry and irony of this situation. It is, I fear, not very impressive merely to read *about* Agnón; the mixture of Galician village life with esoteric rabbinical learning may well not appear enchanting. And yet Agnón makes it so. He has partly the same sort of charm as Chagall, the charm of a peasant world —though these Jews are not really peasants—both enlivened and veiled by folklore, in which the domestic animals become almost the equals of men, and visions of husbands or brides seem, in broad day, to float in the heavens. The dream of the boy in *Chemdat*, in which he sees his unloving stepmother sitting in the top of a tree and whistling like a bee-eater, is very much in the vein of Chagall, as is such an animal parable as that in *The Bridal Canopy* by which one of the wagoner's horses,

Ivory, demonstrates to his companion, Peacock, that it would be wise not to kick at the yelping dogs of the unfriendly Gentile foresters: "There was a cock that lived with a Jew" and who became very much depressed from brooding on the Eve of Atonement, which requires, as he has learned from the prayer book, the taking of a cock by the worshipper and whirling it about his head, with the words "This cock shall go to death," and then handing it over to the slaughterer. He communicates his anxiety to a mouse, and, as the upshot of a conversation in which a good deal of Scripture has been quoted by both, the mouse makes an offer to help him. "Choicest of Poultry," he says, "the days of the Night Prayers of Penitence that precede the New Year do approach, when men arise betimes to the synagogues; I shall go to eat up the prayer book so that not so much as a single letter shall be left." Says the cock, "For thy salvation have I hoped, O Lord!" When the family of his owner have left the house, the mouse is as good as his word and comes out to eat the prayer book, but "thereupon the cat on the watch fell upon him and consumed him." And when Peacock heard this story, "he kept his legs out of the argument and never interfered with what wasn't his own affair."

But in Agnón you have also the moral, the theological element that is characteristic of Kafka. Kafka, born in Prague in the eighties and the son of a wholesale merchant, was one generation removed from the villages to which his father sold his wares, and he did not study Hebrew until late in life, but he derived from his mother's family a tradition of piety and learning. Though five years older than Agnón, he represents a later, more "assimilated" phase of the same Judaic culture, and it is only by reading Agnón that you come to see how deeply Judaic the work of Kafka is. (I am told that the most recent work of Agnón is even closer to Kafka.) Though in Kafka you do not get explicitly the background of Talmud and ghetto, the typical hero of Kafka, like the typical hero of Agnón, is a man who is trying to survive in an alien, often unsympathetic and only partly comprehensible world, and who is bent on maintaining or discovering a technique that will make it possible for him to live in it on good terms with the Name.

The difference between Agnón and Kafka is that Reb Judel of *The Bridal Canopy*, though equally at cross-purposes with the larger social community and even with the common conditions of life, is diverted only momentarily from the path to salvation he has taken, the path of study and prayer, whereas Kafka's all but anonymous "K.," who is never given a Jewish origin, cannot be sure of anything, and confuses, as Reb Judel would never do, his duty to an imperfectly accessible God with his duty to established society. In Kafka, the situation of the Jew in Central Europe makes connections, as Agnón does not, with a more general social situation, and he becomes the moralist and poet—or, better, perhaps the poet of moral uncertainty—of a baffling historical moment. It is difficult to see how Agnón can ever have Kafka's audience. Yet, inside his traditional Jewish world, the human interest of Agnón's fiction is much wider and warmer than Kafka's. You have not only Reb Judel's relation to the Name; you have also the importunate problems of his family and his neighbors—the good-for-nothing and morally callous cantor who gets drunk on the Day of Atonement yet can make the congregation weep; the poor young man who has slept for years on a bench of the synagogue, using his pants for a pillow, and who, finally becoming betrothed to the daughter of a well-to-do tax collector, looks forward with painful longing to the comforts of the bridal bed, but who, lifting his foot to get into it, on a prenuptial visit to his father-in-law's house, hears the crack of the whip of the coach in which his prospective bride is running away with a Gentile. You have the arrogant and choleric official the whole structure of whose life is shaken by losing his pet cat; the sterile wife, loved by her husband, whom the persistent campaign of his relatives compels him at last to divorce; the gentle daughters of the Hassid Reb Judel himself, who, dowryless, pay the price for their father's relentless piety. These personal situations—by which the ideals of Judaism are shown as implicated with human nature, if not quite, perhaps, tied down to earth—are always treated by Agnón with sympathy. In Kafka, the irony of the French Flaubert has tinctured with a certain contempt the abstraction of Jewish analysis. The irony of Agnón is all-pervasive, too; he is never sentimental, still less melodramatic. But—it may be a manifestation of the spirit of the Hassidic sect, who particularly cultivated cheerfulness and whose exploits Agnón loves to celebrate—Agnón never blights his characters, and he cannot resist a miracle. Reb Israel Solomon's cat will be found; the wife whom her husband is divorcing will faint, in the first sign of pregnancy, when he has taken her before the rabbi; the daughters of Reb Judel will discover a buried treasure in the moment when all seems lost. In the story called *In the Heart of the Seas,* in which a group of Hassidím actually sail to Palestine, the element of the miraculous is carried even further, yet it never offends as incongruous, since it passes into the narrative as something it is perfectly natural to add to the memory, the legend—something, indeed, that is necessary in order to justify the Jews and the ways of the most Holy and Blessed to His People. So a precise and poetic notation—"The day gradually faded. The East turned silver and a rising mist chilled the ground"—may merge in the smoothest way with a vision that is apocalyptic, and episodes built up solidly may finish with the suddenness of a folk tale— Agnón is an accomplished storyteller with a technique of his own of suspense and surprise—and slip without transition to something else.

Agnón is a classic; he is taught in schools; he has been mentioned for the Nobel Prize. One is quite ready to accept him as a true representative of that great line of Jewish writers that begins with the authors of Genesis. But one feels that he comes at the end of a culture. He himself is evidently as saturated with the learning of the Bible, the Talmud, the Cabala, and all the rest as one of his own Hassidim, yet—so far as I have read it, again—there is always an element of pastiche in his work. The larding of literature with ancient quotations has long been a feature of Hebrew writing, and the poetry of the eleventh-century Jehúda Halévi seems almost as much put together from the Bible as a medieval cento from Virgil; but isn't there, after all, a great difference between the attitudes toward the passages they quote of Agnón and of Jehúda Halévi? It was said to me in Israel by an admirer of Agnón that he is marvelously noncommittal—that he never gives it away that he does not see his people in their own terms, that he does not believe as they do. And this made me aware that his public must apprehend Agnón somewhat differently from the reader with no Jewish background. It may be possible for such a reader to misunderstand Agnón's humor. These stories seem at first to belong to the category of the false-naïve. One assumes that they could not have been written by a man who took Judaism seriously in the sense that his Hassidic heroes do. Yet even a slight acquaintance with the Talmud will make us realize from how far back the elements of fantasy and irony have been intimately associated, in literature, with the strictest Jewish religion. Mr. Michael L. Rodkinson, the translator of the Talmud into English, speaks of "the vein of satire or humor that runs through" this variegated work, so difficult for the Gentile to get the hang of. And one remembers Renan's theory that the Book of Jonah was a work of humor, a satire on the prophets of the Exile, so much in love with their predicted dooms that they were furious when these were averted. It may be that this Jewish self-mockery, tragic in its implications, this drollery that is also moral, goes back to the first great defeat at the hands of the Babylonians, and the impotence for action, the minority status, that this for a time imposed. It is, in any case, very old, the irony which still gives its accent to Agnón and to the Yiddish humorists. For the Jew, the fundamental irony is that God should have made him promises of special protection and favor, and then have allowed him to suffer a succession of crushing disasters. There is a story of a medieval rabbi who, at a time of savage persecution, made a public confession of sins that he would have been quite incapable of committing, in order to save face for God. Is he a comic or a tragic figure? The non-Jew must be on his guard against failing to appreciate how deep the Jewish irony goes, and not merely in terms, thus, of Jewish tradition, but also—since our ideals at moments, must seem to fail us all—in experience of human life.

Yet, even allowing for this, is not Agnón's work a monument to a culture that has lost much of its reality, that can no longer be accepted as valid? One of his other two long novels, I understand, deals with the Polish-Jewish world in the period after the First World War, when it was already disintegrating, and the other with the second immigration to Palestine, at the beginning of the present century. It all sounds rather elegiac, and I learn from Mr. Simon Halkin's book, *Modern Hebrew Literature*, that a nostalgia for the life of the ghetto has become an important motif in the writing of Agnón's generation. On the other hand, not quite all Israelis share the general taste for Agnón. I met a few who did not approve of him. These were young people, impatient of the synagogue, who desired to get as far away as possible from Reb Judel, with his drug of study, in his closed-in precarious world.

I encountered a postcript to Agnón's world as I was coming from Meá Shearím one Sabbath. I had not been there before, and, although, consulting a map, I had identified the Abyssinian Church House by a colored nun who was gardening, I presently became confused by the convents and churches and schools of the many nationalities and religions, so uglily and grimly entangled in the great barricades of barbed wire that have not been removed since the Arab war. My objective, as a landmark, was Barclay's Bank. Stopping to examine my map, I caught the eye of a black-hatted, black-bearded, bespectacled little man standing all by himself in the sun on the other side of the street. He came over and addressed me in German. I asked him the way in English, and he walked along to show me. I noticed that he omitted the articles in English and asked him whether he was Russian. "Away back, perhaps," he said. "I don't know." He made a remark or two in clumsy Russian, and then explained that he came from Poland. I asked how he had learned English. "I took ten lessons," he said. How long had he been in Israel? "A year and three-quarters," he answered, "but it only seems a few months." I saw that he was happy to be there. He practiced some craft—I don't remember what. As we went on, I got the impression that he was perhaps a bit off his head. At one point, he slipped into Yiddish—"Do you speak a little Yiddish?" he asked. There were stories I did not understand: a tennis match, and then someone fell dead. But I got an impression of a dreadful experience that he had now at last put behind him and from which he had now ascended into a realm of freedom and peace. "I never had a quiet day in Poland," he said, in concluding these memoirs. When he had brought me to Barclay's Bank, we shook hands, and he beamed and went back.

Theocracy: The Guardians of the City are an extreme and fanatical group. But what is the importance in Israel of the Orthodox Synagogue in its normal official form? The word I heard most often when I asked about this—and uttered with apprehension—was "theocracy." All the most intelligent Israelis I talked with were opposed to allowing the Rabbinate to dominate Israeli life. The principal issues here seem to be the observance of the Sabbath, kosher food and the licensing of civil marriage. On Friday afternoon, at sundown, almost everything shuts down in Israel, and remains so till the following sundown. It is just as complete and frustrating as the old-fashioned Puritan Sunday. The buses do not run, and even the non-religious Jew may not care to be seen in a taxi. The prohibition against working on the Sabbath may, in the case of the more scrupulous orthodox, interfere with the public services, and has sometimes given rise to absurdities of casuistical dispensation, as when a wireless operator was authorized by his rabbi to continue sending messages on condition that he use his left hand and write only in the Roman alphabet. In regard to the kosher problem, though most Israeli restaurants are non-kosher—in the Swiss-run King David Hotel, even bacon occasionally turns up—the importation of non-kosher meat is forbidden by the government under pressure from the Rabbinate, and kosher meat is expensive. The problems—to an outsider, so odd—to which the old dietary

laws give rise was illustrated for me one day when I
visited the children's barnyard on one of the communal
farms (*kvutzót*). Here the children themselves took care
of the animals and poultry (which latter included a peacock), and they all were immensely plump and had the
look of beloved pets. I mistook some little turkeys for
guinea fowl and was told by the doctor who showed me
around that they were hoping to eventually raise guinea
fowl, but that, for reasons of which he was not quite
sure—because guinea fowl did not have spurs, he thought
—they had not yet got it cleared by the Rabbinate. He
inquired of a boy who was standing by, but he did not
know either; "There are better rabbis than I," the boy
added. The doctor went on to explain to me that they
had got around the prohibition against rabbits and guinea
pigs by the plea that these animals were bred not for
eating but for laboratory experiments.

The difficulties and incongruities of rabbinical rule in
a modern state were several times brought out for me in
connection with the marriage question. The insistence on
rabbinical marriage makes it impossible for those who,
by conviction, are non-religious or anti-religious to get
legally married at all—with the result that in the communal farms, as one person delicately put it to me, "there
is a good deal of non-marriage." The anachronistic character of these marriage laws was illustrated in a curious
way by a story that was told me in Israel by an American
businessman, himself a Jew, who had been living in New
Hampshire. He made periodical trips to Israel, and had
been asked by a lady, whom he had known in the States
but who had gone to live in Israel, to appear as a witness
for her at some religious formality in connection with her
coming marriage. He was surprised and a little horrified
to find himself taking part in a ceremony based on Deuteronomy 25:7-9, which decrees that if one of two broth-

ers shall die without male issue, his widow must marry his surviving brother unless it is agreed between them that he will publicly repudiate her. If the parties do so agree, the man, in the presence of "the elders of his city," must announce, "I do not wish to take her," and the widow must then "pull his sandal off his foot," spit in her brother-in-law's face, and answer, "So shall it be done to the man who does not build up his brother's house." It was the carrying out of this that startled my friend from the States. In the course of another conversation—this time with scholars and writers of the generation still in its thirties—I inquired about an anti-clerical organization about which I had heard from someone. Two of the people present did not know that this existed, but it turned out that the third belonged to it. He went on to explain, however, that he could not support one of its principal aims: to get civil marriage and civil divorce legalized. His reason for this was based on Deuteronomy 23:2: "No bastard shall enter the assembly of the Lord; even to the tenth generation none of his descendants shall enter the assembly of the Lord." By "bastard," he meant the child of civilly divorced parents or the child of a married woman by a man who is not her husband in rabbinical law; but it had occurred to him that the child of a civil marriage, as well as his descendants to the tenth generation, would suffer from the disability of remaining, for the orthodox, bastards and excluded from divine service. To the other young people present, this point seemed unexpected, as it did to me. They told him he read the Talmud too much.

Yet, as the conversation went on, these dissenters from Talmudic scruples developed a point of view which, to me, was equally unexpected. I had been talking to a man of about their own age, born in the United States, who had been ordained as a rabbi and who at home had moved further and further in the direction of the Reformed Synagogue. He had finally given up the priesthood and come to settle in Israel, where he was now doing secular work. He had told me that he hoped to see there a complete rewriting of the prayer book and a substitution for the orthodox ritual of a kind of Biblical cult along the lines of the ceremonies sometimes performed in the *kibbutzim*, in which the reading of passages from Scripture was accompanied by singing and dances. This idea, when I probed my young friends with it, awakened immediate derision. They guessed at once that it came from an American and declared that, however little orthodox they were, they considered the Reformed Synagogue entirely inappropriate for Israel. They themselves had come, as children, from Poland, Lithuania and Russia, and they regarded the Reformed Synagogue as an essentially non-Judaistic product of the pressure upon the Jews of Protestantism in Germany and the United States. It was a form of adaptation to alien societies that would be quite out of place for them. And, in talking to other Israelis, I found a preponderant loyalty to the Orthodox Jewish faith as against any substitute. It is difficult to get statistics on Orthodoxy or even on synagogue attendance. The sole figure as to which it was possible to get anybody to hazard an estimate was that twenty per cent of the Israelis wore earlocks. But it is plain that the Orthodox Synagogue, even for many who are not very pious, has its importance as a social center; and the holidays seem to be celebrated by practically everybody. They take them perhaps more seriously, enjoy them perhaps more, than Christians do any of their holy days except Christmas. Rosh Ha-Shanah is a religious occasion, as New Year's is not for Christians, and the latter have nothing like the Day of Atonement, which seems always to impose for the Jew the duty of setting himself right with his conscience by repairing, or at least acknowledging, his trespasses against his fellows. These holidays give its structure to the Jewish year; and without an established religion, it would hardly be possible to keep them up. Besides this, it is the Jewish religion that has sustained the Jews in their exile, that has preserved their coherence as a people and that has led them, at the end of centuries, to return to Palestine. Their secular state is quite new; it is, after all, the orthodox "theocracy" that has provided their internal government for the last two thousand years, and it will not be so easy to get rid of it or even to do without it. In the meantime, it becomes a political force, sits in the Knésset, the Israeli parliament, and enters into expedient alliances. Yet, in spite of this intervention, the Israeli Rabbinate seems to tend, as churches are likely to do, to regard its own welfare as inevitably at variance with the purposes of the secular state. "The anti-religious movement," said a government official to me, "has restrained itself in the interests of the national unity; the religious elements haven't."

Tanách: But, aside from rabbinical influence, the Bible—which the Jews call Tanách, putting together the initials of its three main divisions: the Law, the Prophets and the Writings—figures in the life of Israel in a more striking way than one might expect. Every evening, at what is called the "peak listening hour," just before the eight-thirty broadcast, the music for the chanting of the classic announcement from Isaiah 2:3—"For from Zion will go forth the Law, and the word of the Lord from Jerusalem"—is sounded on the Jerusalem radio, and a chapter of the Bible is read. This reading is a remarkable performance. It is done by Mr. Shlómoh Bertónov, the son of a well-known actor and himself formerly an actor. Now, it is natural, in reading the Bible, to reflect that the narrative and poetic parts would lend themselves to such recitation as has long been practiced in Italy by the professional reciters of Dante, and it is something of the kind, on a very high level, that Mr. Bertónov has been giving his audience. In the course of my visit, I was able to hear only parts of Jonah and Zechariah, but these seemed to me among the best readings that I had ever heard of anything. Mr. Bertónov enunciates so clearly that every syllable tells, and by pronouncing the aleph and the ayin, the two Semitic gutturals that have dropped out of use in Hebrew, he adds to the effect of authenticity. He dramatizes his readings just enough, brings to them just enough of the Russian actor's gift of impersonation, to make you feel you are really listening to God admonishing Jonah or Zechariah foretelling the rebirth of Jerusalem. This, you say to yourself, is how the Prophets must have sounded—at the same time august and astringent, with strong rhythms that seem so natural to the language that this might be indeed the language of God. How positive and vibrant that word "Adonái" that is read for the unutterable name of God and that has now become inseparable from the rhythmical context! But it is not merely the high spots of eloquence and drama that Mr. Bertónov has been broadcasting; he has been reading the Bible straight through, and I was told that he was never more impressive than in handling such unpromising passages as the repetitive rites of Leviticus, the enumerations of Numbers and the ever-recurring genealogies—in which last the importance of every name for the conservers of the old chronicle was brought out in such a way as to make one feel a sense of triumph in the persistence of the Twelve Chosen Tribes through the otherwise anonymous ages. When these readings had gone on for over a year, the audience, I was told, began to grow rather restive, since they had just been taken through

these more tedious books, and weren't sure that they
hadn't had enough; but when at last Mr. Bertónov took
a few weeks off and they had to hear a substitute at
eight-twenty, they soon felt that something was lacking
and began writing letters of protest. At the time of my
visit to Israel, Mr. Bertónov was still only a little more
than two-thirds of his way through. (The Hebrew Tanách
is arranged somewhat differently from the Christian Bible.) I was sorry not to hear him do the Psalms, on which
he was beginning the day I left.

Another and more curious evidence of the vigorous
survival of the Bible in the consciousness of this modern
state is a fortnightly newspaper called *Chronicles,* which
puzzled me when it first caught my eye on the newsstand, and which continued to seem to me odd even after
I had bought and read it. The headlines announced,
"JACOB'S SONS ARRESTED IN EGYPT ON SPY CHARGE," and a
story lower down ran as follows:

JACOB PROTESTS:
"MY SONS ARE INNOCENT!"
By Our Correspondent

HEBRON, 21 Nisan—"It's all a terrible mistake!" said Jacob (also known as Israel), when
he heard that his sons had been arrested in
Egypt as spies. . . . Your correspondent found
the venerable old Hebrew (he is getting on
for 130) lying down in his tent, with difficulty holding back the tears that came to his
eyes. . . .

On the inside page, I found a picture of "seven scrawny
cows"—"TWO DOWN, FIVE TO GO. With each crop failure, another cow is rubbed out"—and a department called
"Learn Egyptian," which contained an easy lesson in

hieroglyphics, with the reminder that "Egyptian, like Akkadian, is read from left to right." An editorial brought out the fact that Zaphnat-Paneach (the name given Joseph by Pharaoh) "comes himself of Hebrew stock. But this very fact seems to cause him to bend over backwards in an effort to be 'more Egyptian than the Egyptians themselves.' Not only has he failed to lift a finger to clear the suspects, but, on the contrary, he was the first to accuse them of being spies and of having entered the country with hostile intentions. It is he who is fanning the fires of racial hatred, with his baseless charges against ten innocent men." The next number of *Chronicles* was devoted to the death of Joseph and contained an editorial beginning, "A great Hebrew and a great human being has passed away," a black-bordered mourning notice inserted by "The Bereaved Family," and an ad by a Theban embalmer announcing, "For the Man of Distinction, there is our 40-day de luxe method— Plan 3: Extraction of brain by special new process, via the nostrils. Removal and special embalmment of all internal organs except the heart," etc., etc.

The whole thing was well sustained, and I assumed that it was meant to be humorous till I learned that this singular paper, which is subsidized by a wealthy Dutch lady, is intended to be educational. It is printed in three editions—Hebrew, German and English—and distributed widely for use in schools. There can be no question, however, that an element of satire has got into it—as, for example, when an editorial mentions that Egypt, "the greatest, nay, the only military power on earth today, the nation on whose good will hinges the fate of a starving world, is in a state of high hysteria and deadly fear over the harmless activities of ten brothers who came to Egypt to buy food for their hungry wives and children." But the paper, in this respect, also, furnishes another exam-

ple of the confusion of past with present that has always
been characteristic of the Jewish point of view.

These Biblical analogies, one feels, are often at the
back of Israeli minds. General Yigaél Yadín, the son of
the late Professor Sukénik of the Hebrew University, is a
scholar as well as a soldier. At the time of the Arab war,
when he was acting as Chief of Operations, he concluded, from his knowledge of the Bible, that the Syrians, in their attempt at invasion, would inevitably take the
same route as the ancient armies of Assyria two thousand eight hundred years before. He read his officers the
relevant passages from Kings before the fighting began,
and consulted them in posting his modern troops. The result was entirely successful, and this story, which is often
told, has suggested to me other parallels, which I did not,
in fact, hear mentioned. It was said to me by a humane
Tel-Avivan, not long ago from the States, apropos of the
murderous raids by which the Israelis retaliate for the
murderous raids of the Arabs, that he feared that his
fellow-countrymen were a little losing respect for the Sixth
Commandment, and the justice-loving side of the Biblical
tradition leads this kind of Jew to worry as to whether
the Israelis have a right to their land; they would feel
better if the Arabs got their compensation. Yet whoever
has been responsible for such incidents as Kíbya and
Nahhalín might have cited plenty of texts, such as Exodus 23:28-30—"And I will send hornets before you,
which shall drive out Hivite, Canaanite and Hittite from
before you. I will not drive them out before you in one
year, lest the land become desolate and the wild beasts
multiply against you. Little by little I will drive them out
before you, until you are increased and possess the land"
—and Deuteronomy 6:10-11, in which Jehovah promises
the Israelites to give them "great and goodly cities, which
you did not build, and houses full of all good things,

which you did not fill, and cisterns hewn out, which you did not hew, and vineyards and olive trees, which you did not plant." Do such memories confirm the minds of the occupants of Arab houses, of the cultivators of Arab farms, whose original owners can still see their old homes, just across the frontier, and occasionally give way to the impulse to revisit them and seize a few sheep? The terrorism of modern Israel was the result of the Nazi persecutions and of the policy of the British, who refused to let those who were fleeing from them even land in a country which the British themselves had set aside as a Jewish refuge, and who finally left the Jews to the mercy of seven Arab states ("seven nations mightier than yourselves," Deuteronomy 7:1). It was in those days as justifiable as anything of the kind can be. But, though many people disapprove of it, the terrorist habit has been established, and the element of moral fanaticism that stimulates and sustains it seems something of a reversion to Biblical times, when the Twelve Tribes, returning from Egypt, invaded and conquered Canaan. The terrorist Menáchem Beígin, who has been described by Arthur Koestler as giving the impression of a gentle young schoolmaster, but who once, in an anti-British gesture, blew up a whole wing of the King David Hotel, destroying ninety-one people, British, Arabs, and Jews indiscriminately, is at present a member of the Knésset. The reprisals against the Arabs are evidently carefully planned (I do not mean to imply that Beígin is necessarily involved in them). The day after the Nahhalín incident—I had heard the explosions at midnight, sitting in my hotel room— the telephone boy said to me, "That was a good operation last night!" As I was later to learn from the New York *Times,* but not from the Jerusalem *Post,* six Arab homes had been bombed and a village mosque had been sacked; nine people had been killed, including a woman, and nineteen wounded. True, the Arabs had massacred the passengers in a bus—killing nine men and two women and wounding a couple of children—in the Négev a few weeks before, and had been long making themselves a nuisance with their continual shootings and thefts.

I am, however, not interested here in examining this situation. I want to suggest, simply, that the Israelis, in relation to the Arabs, have shown certain signs of returning to the callous intolerance of the Israelites in relation to the people they dispossessed. I was sometimes reminded of the tone of Jehovah, in His final speech to Jonah, in regard to the hundred and twenty thousand Ninevans, "who do not know their right hand from their left." Jehovah is scolding Jonah for his indifference to the fate of these Ninevans, but His opinion of their cultural level is undisguisedly low. So the position of the Arabs in Israel —especially as one sees them in the country—is rather like that of the Navahos in the American Southwest: a once fierce but still picturesque, pathetically retarded people, cut off from the main community but presenting a recurrent problem. In a large Arab town like Acre, the squalor of the swarming streets inspires in an Israeli the same distaste that it does in the visiting Westerner. For the Jew, who takes family relations so seriously and who, in Israel, has labored so carefully with the orphans from Poland and Germany and the children of the illiterate Yemenites, the spectacle of flocks of urchins, dirty, untaught, diseased, bawling and shrieking and begging, in the narrow and dirty streets, inspires even moral horror. If the restrictions imposed on marriage by the ancient rabbinical law are considered by many too rigid, the facility of divorce for the Arabs, which, together with their nomadic habits, encourages the father of a family simply to abandon his offspring and move on to take a wife in another place, must be felt to be an evil far worse.

It is not that a certain contempt for the Arabs is not natural for anyone trained in the West, nor is it that any ruthlessness of Israel is not matched by the infantile spite of the Arabs and the rather stupid obstinacy of the Arab refugees in Jordan, who have refused the offers of U.N.R.-W.A. to accommodate them in other localities and continue to insist on returning to their villages and farms in Israel. I am occupied here solely with bringing out the operation in Israel of a certain Jewish tendency toward exclusiveness—I shall deal later on with the converse of this, the life-giving elements of the Jewish tradition—as a limiting and sometimes a destructive influence.

One feels this exclusiveness, also, in the attitude toward the literature and the language. If you arrive with the notion that the revival of Hebrew is an artificial chauvinistic absurdity, like the official use in Ireland of Irish, you will realize the difference between them when you find that all Israelis speak Hebrew and hear how natural the language—so quick and staccato, made up mostly of short words—sounds on Israeli lips. But, though many people in Israel speak English, and though the signs on the principal streets are in English as well as in Hebrew, even the foreigner who knows the alphabet will often be baffled or lose his way. The Israeli will tell you with perfect truth that his children, who have been talking Hebrew from birth, read the ordinary vowelless printing more easily than the exceptional "pointed" text, but for the foreigner it is all a shorthand, to decipher which you have to know the language well even to make out the signs on the shops. It is as if you arrived in an English-speaking country and found everything printed in abbreviations like "blvd.," "bldg." and "Ltd."

This impression of cultural exclusiveness is borne out by a reading of the admirable book—indispensable for the understanding of Israel—called *Modern Hebrew Litera-*

ture: Trends and Values, by Mr. Simon Halkin. Mr. Halkin, who teaches this subject in the Hebrew University in Jerusalem, is a man of the great intellectual world and far from indifferent, himself, to the literatures of other traditions and tongues, but the story he has to tell is that of the turning-away of a certain school of Jewish writers from the German-Jewish enlightenment of the early nineteenth century to a rigorous preoccupation with Hebrew language and thought—a movement which was to concentrate more and more on the Zionist return to Palestine, and then, when the country was won, on the building of the state of Israel. One feels the doors shut behind one. Here is a book which discusses at length the literary activity of the Jews in the Germany of the early nineteenth century, yet which never mentions Marx or Heine; that deals with Moses Mendelssohn almost exclusively from the point of view of his failure in pure devotion to the perpetuation of Hebrew letters; a book for which Kafka and Proust—Europeans, though so deeply Jewish—are completely beyond the horizon. One is guided through a narrow corridor at the far-distant end of which the gleam of the sanctum sanctorum only makes one the more aware of an all-enveloping darkness. In this corridor, we cannot catch sight of any of those outstanding Jews who have made themselves places in the modern world, contributed to the general light: Bergson and Einstein, Trotsky and Freud, Disraeli and Brandeis and Brandes—one would almost say Weizmann himself, who was, after all, a great chemist. There is something of this narrowness, also, in the tendency of even the most alert and the best-educated Israelis to be occupied with the problems of Israel at the expense of awareness of or interest in what is happening in the world at large. In the Jerusalem *Post,* certainly, the quarrel of the Israelis with the Arabs throws everything else into the background, till you are almost ready to believe that more serious hostilities between them would amount to or imply a world war, and the Israeli side of the controversy is presented with such mass and vehemence that you can get no idea from the press of what is really going on in the Arab states only a few miles away.

Even the movement against this narrowness has taken on the characteristic accent of intransigence and Biblical reference. The group of young people that calls itself Aleph and that publishes a paper of that name but is usually known as the Canaanite movement has been interestingly accounted for, in terms of the social forces behind it, by Mr. Robert L. Lindsey in the July, 1954, issue of *Commentary*. Mr. Lindsey explains that, for many young Israelis, the various forms of the Jewish faith have ceased to have any validity. The theocracy of Orthodox Judaism is in process of being got rid of. Zionism has lost its force —since the goad of anti-Semitism that stimulated it has never been felt by the new generation and the return to Palestine from exile is, of course, no longer an objective for the young men and women who were born there. The Socialism that blended with Zionism in one of its early phases has lost credit through the anti-Israel policy of the Labour Government in England and the persecution of Zionism by the Soviets. And if one finds oneself neither a Zionist nor a member of an Orthodox congregation, in what sense is one still a Jew? Let the conception, then, of Jewishness be dropped. Why perpetuate unnecessarily the quarrels of the Israelis with their neighbors? Let them cut off their connections with the Diaspora, let them cease to accept money from abroad. Let them make common cause with the Christians, the Moslems, the Kurds, the Circassians, the ancient Syrian Druses (who are supposed still to worship the Golden Calf) and all the other Middle Eastern groups, who are as much ingrown as the

Jews and equally handicapped by being so, but who are all forced to live together and ought really to call themselves Canaanites, since Canaan is what their country was originally called. But the Canaanite movement, it seems, has also a theological aspect, which Mr. Lindsey does not explain. The Canaanites propose to repudiate not merely the whole Diaspora but also that part of Jewish history —a part which is almost the whole—that is based on the worship of Jehovah. For the Canaanites, not only is Moses a foreign heresiarch, who brought the Israelites from Egypt to Canaan and sent them over to sack its cities, to dispossess its inhabitants and to impose on it the cult of an alien God, but Father Abraham himself is an interloper. They have returned to the worship of Astarte "in groves and high places"—which is jollier, certainly, than the synagogue, since Astarte was the goddess of love. (Let us hope they do not revive Moloch.) But, even in trying to establish a solidarity with the other Middle Easterners, they are behaving with a Jehovan exclusiveness in turning the principle of exclusion against all the rest of the Jews.

I read the Hebrew Bible every afternoon with a young teacher from the University, a man who had been born in Jerusalem and had never been in any other country. From the French windows of the King David Hotel, that opened on a little balcony, one looked over, across the valley of Gihon, to the walls of the Old City, and, pointing to the Jaffa Gate, my instructor was able to explain to me how the "inns" at which travellers slept and such lodgings as the "house" of Rahab the harlot were more or less a part of the gate, which was still—as I was later to find when I visited the Old City—a market place and center of gossip, like the square in a Latin town. One turned from the dark heavy text to the bareness of present-day Jerusalem, with its pale buildings, ancient and modern, below the immense bright sky. The Pentateuch, under these circumstances, came to seem to me so purely, so profoundly Jewish that it became for me a matter of wonder that so many non-Jewish peoples had been able to take it over and adapt it to serve their needs. It began to seem quite grotesque that the chapters and chapters of observances—which would seem to be of serious interest only to anthropologists, historians and Orthodox Jews—should have been studied with reverence by the Christian Church, that the incidents of Israelite conquest should for centuries have furnished texts for the sermons of Anglican and Puritan divines. The reading back of Christianity into the books of the Jewish scriptures, the turning to Christian purpose of the "Yet I know that my redeemer liveth" of Job, and of the "man of sorrows" of Isaiah 53—once the "sea of faith" has ebbed, what a curious exploit it seems! My young instructor was in a constant state of astonishment, verging on indignation, at the renderings of the King James Version, the only English text I had with me, which he had never examined before. I had been told by another young Israeli scholar that it had one day occurred to him to wonder how the Christian authorities interpreted that roundly erotic rhapsody called *The Song of Solomon* or *The Song of Songs,* the rabbinical view of which makes Jehovah the bridegroom and Israel the bride. He had been charmed to discover such chapter headings as "The mutual love of Christ and His church," "Christ awaketh the Church with His calling," "A further description of the Church's grace" ("How beautiful are thy feet with shoes, O prince's daughter . . . Thy two breasts are like two young roses that are twins," etc.). Yet if Israel and Jehovah, why not Christ and the Church? It was, after all, the Hebrews themselves who set the example for the Christians of describing the recent in terms of the ancient, of regarding the careers of contemporaries as fulfilments of inspired prophecies, of showing that the new meaning was there all the time in the old text.

Jerusalem the Golden: Waked up every morning early by the bright, firm and even light, looking out on translucent clouds that hung in a pellucid heaven, far below which Mount Zion, a modest mound in the bosom of the high barren hills, just outside the walls of the ancient city, was crowned with the diadem of its monastery, I grew to be fond of Jerusalem, of which much of the attraction resides in its combining luminosity with bareness. This is said to be the best time of the year—late March and early April: the steep and yet rounded hills, studded with little gray boulders, striated with narrow ledges, are now freshened for a brief time with green, and in the country, where the mixed flocks of goats and sheep graze on the fenceless slopes, there is a sprinkling of wild red poppies and little yellow daisies. In a few weeks, they tell me, the landscape becomes parched, with only the deep-green oases created by irrigation. It is a mild and monotonous country, and this is what is unexpected. Did the Prophets, in their gloom of foreboding, flash their lightning of conviction from these quiet hills, where everything is open to the sky? Were the savage wars of Scripture fought here? Did its paeans first sound from these pastures? The prejudice of the Jews against images may be partly explained by these contours which do not suggest shapes, by these colors which do not compose pictures. The little old villages of the Arabs were almost like boulders themselves; Stephen Spender has truly said of them that they fit into the mountainsides like teeth in a jawbone. The new settlements of the Israelis are equally unostentatious—neat groupings of low white houses that give an effect of ease; I saw one with pale pink roofs that was charming. Modern Israel, on the whole, has kept to the old Jewish severity. There are no pictures in orthodox homes, and the pictures in other houses, even where the books are good, are likely to be not well chosen. It is strange to reflect that from here came those legends that inspired so much of the art of the Renaissance, all that blazing of color, that teeming of flesh—Pharaoh's daughter in her gorgeous silks, surrounded by the ladies of an Italian court, as she comes upon Moses in the bulrushes; the rippling and wistful Botticellian Judith, exhaling a delicate charm after cutting off the head of Holofernes; the beautiful blue madonnas, the heaven-cracking crucifixions; Michelangelo's romantic Moses, his full-bodied Adams and Davids; all the coffers of the Roman churches overflowing with jewels and fabrics, all the Florentine miles of paint. How very unlikely it seems that they sprouted from the history of these calm little hills, dotted with stones and flocks, under pale and transparent skies.

The emotion and the drama of the Bible not only no longer seem present in Palestine; they have left no real monuments behind them. The Acropolis and the Forum are still there to see, but Solomon's Temple and Palace are not. It is only that the site of Jerusalem has in itself an arresting grandeur. No great city of Europe stands so high, and it is wonderful and almost terrifying to look out on the valley of Kidron and across at the opposite hillside littered with the tombs attributed to Absalom and other ancients as well as with the stones of a cemetery of modern Jewish graves which the Arabs have thrown on their faces, or to gaze up the precipitous slope at the wall that still circles the city. But of Jewish pre-Christian Jerusalem, little today survives: the fragment of wall to which the Jews used to come to weep for their lost kingdom, the tombs of the Sanhedrin in the hillside, with their high and imposing façades and their narrow rectangular doors, designed to make looting difficult, that give glimpses of large square chambers, plundered long ago and empty now. The foundations of the present old wall are supposed to have been laid by Herod, but the rest of it was probably built by the Byzantines and Suleiman the Magnificent. If the wide paved expanse of the sanctuary in which the Mosque of Omar stands on what has always been accepted as the site of the Temple was actually laid out by Herod, it was done under the influence of the Romans. Below it lies the only construction that impresses like those of Rome: the great pillared subterranean vaults that are known as Solomon's Stables. Here the Jews took refuge from Titus, come to destroy their Temple; here, more than a thousand years later, come to rescue the Holy Sepulcher, the Knights Templar put up their horses. One can see their hitching holes in the columns. These grim and enormous piers that stretch away in endless long rows, lit only by one set of windows, on the side that forms part of the precipice, make a kind of gray underground forest that is dreadful and troubling today, with its air of an abode of power that no power has permanently possessed or has stamped with its peculiar identity, neither Herod nor Rome nor Christendom. But, for the rest, what could be less suggestive than those dreary grottoes and caves and rocks, sheltered mostly by rubbishy churches, that are shown you as Calvary, the Sepulcher, the place of the Annunciation, the house of Jesus at Nazareth, the Fountain of the Virgin, the Tomb of the Virgin, the place where the Virgin died. They are none of them considered authentic, and would not be any better if they were. Only Galilee, the Lake of Tiberias, as you come down to it from the mountains above —softly misted, with its blues and greens, the far bank a wall of wrinkled yellow rock, and its waters blue, still and dull—has something of idyllic mystery. At Capernaum, on the far bank, is a synagogue in which Jesus is supposed to have taught, and one passes a church on a little hill that is said to mark the setting of the Sermon on the Mount. Yet, even discounting the miracles, it is hard to imagine what happened here in any very lively or concrete way. I found it easier, when I was traveling through Italy and passing the Lago di Garda, on which I could see from the train the little peninsula of Sirmio, to imagine the poet Catullus coming back from his Bithynian exile and, as he puts off the cares of his journey, finding peace in his longed-for bed. For Garda was concrete to Catullus, it was solidly and pleasantly a part of his life. He has left a description of it, by which we can recognize it. But the Gospels do not describe Galilee. Sirmio is still there in Italy, but in a sense the Holy Places are not there.

What you find in Palestine instead is a kind of debris of the three great religions that have sprung from and flourished there. Side by side and mutually exclusive, you have the synagogue, the church and the mosque, as well as the many varieties of the Christian church in both its Eastern and Western, its Catholic and its Protestant forms. They have for so long been practicing dissension in the name of the single God whom they all derive from the ancient Jews that one has almost forgotten the irony of their bitterness or contempt for one another. But the non-religious visitor, in entering these places of worship, bewildered by the constant necessity of remembering whether to keep on his hat, take off his hat or take off his shoes at the door, may become a little impatient with the outward forms of religion. On Mount Zion—which has given its name to Heaven—he discovers a state of affairs, a squalor, confusion and strife, at the same time disgusting and comic. I climbed up there with a guide, by a long flight of steps, to inspect the

so-called tomb of David. You see, first, inscribed on a
wall in bold and clear Hebrew lettering, the familiar quo-
tation from Isaiah—"For from Zion will go forth the
Law, and the word of the Lord from Jerusalem." But
Mount Zion, just outside the old wall, is a corner of the
Old City that has remained in Jewish hands. The frontier,
with its barbed-wire spite-fence, runs right between it and
the wall, and you are obliged to enter the tomb by a narrow path lined with barbed wire and hung with signs in
Hebrew and English that warn you, "Danger Mines."
Beyond the barbed wire are an empty Arab house and
little fields that must once have been lawns but are all
grown up now with long grass. The red poppies and yellow
daisies remind you of that passage from Edgar Quinet
that Joyce likes to play with in *Finnegans Wake*: the wild
flowers that go on blooming through the wreckage of
civilizations and come down to us through the ages,
"fraîches et riantes comme aux jours des batailles."

Inside the supposed tomb, you find a Jewish house of
prayer, dedicated to David, with a display of silver ves-
sels and sacred red cloths, presided over by pale bearded
custodians. This a few years ago was a Moslem house
of prayer, before the Jews captured it from the Arabs. Up
against it is a Benedictine monastery, the Church and
Convent of the Dormition, which is supposed to mark the
spot where the Virgin died, or rather, where she fell
asleep just before her ascension to Heaven. I succeeded
in persuading this man to come with me to see the
monastery, though he showed a certain reluctance—I do
not know whether because he was hesitant about getting
too close to the Arabs or because he was afraid that the
monks might not want him in their Christian cathedral;
and another Jewish visitor, who heard us talking, hooked
on to us and decided to go with us. He said that he ought
not to go—an Orthodox Jew, it seems, is forbidden to

enter a Christian church—but that he didn't want to miss
the opportunity. Most of the monks had been withdrawn
since the war, but we found a German brother who took
us around. It was not a very beautiful place; it had been
built fifty years before, under the patronage of the late
Kaiser, on the foundations of a Crusaders' church.
There was an altar contributed by German Catholics for
somebody murdered by the Nazis, and Hungarian chapels
with frescoes in horned-toad Hungarian style. The monk
took us down to the crypt and lit candles to show us
the monument over the spot where the Virgin is supposed,
not to have died, but to have made her departure from
earth: she lies rigid, with an ivory face and mantled in
dried-blood marble. The two Jews were quiet, a little shy.
Emerging, we explored apprehensively the deserted stone
paths of the monastery that led us between high walls and
ended in barbed-wire cul-de-sacs. There is no neutral
ground here, and where the two sides are close together,
the inhabitants of the two cities like sometimes to take pot-
shots at one another. We returned to the valley, keeping
carefully to the path that makes the right-of-way to Zion
and crosses the neutral strip which separates Israel from
Jordan. This is mined and fenced off with barbed wire.
Occasionally a dog or a child strays over and steps on a
mine. Not far off, an extension of this valley was the ill-
famed ancient Gehenna, where the Hebrews relapsed into
the primitive cult of sacrificing their children to Moloch.
On your way to and from Zion, you pass the Jerusalem
Animal Hospital, which is just over the line on the Israeli
side. The barking of the dogs in this hospital had been
keeping me awake at night, and, before I found out what
it was, I had almost imagined that the dogs on both sides
took up at night the quarrel of their masters and yapped
at each other till morning. (At the time of certain shootings in this part of the city that have taken place since

I left, the veterinary hospital, I learn from the *Times,*
was isolated from food supplies, but the "matron" stood
by her charges and has received a citation from the
S.P.C.A., with a bronze medal of the kind "usually
awarded to an animal for bravery," as well as one from the
American Feline Society.)

The presence of this valley of hatred, though rarely
referred to in Israel, is constantly felt and inflicts constraint. For the Eastertide pilgrims who cross the line on
their way to the Mount of Olives and the other places associated with Jesus, it should heighten their respect for
his teaching. The passage from Israeli to Jordanian Jerusalem has been made by the Arabs, in their fear of the
Israelis and their somewhat childish desire to behave as
unpleasantly as possible, to seem almost as difficult and
perilous as gaining admission to Lhasa. If you come with
an Israeli passport, they do their best to make it impossible, and travelers are driven to such farcical devices as
double passports and detachable visas. One visitor who
had been in Israel and who, just as he was leaving Jordan,
inadvertently thanked the authorities in Hebrew was held
up for several hours. I had found this same atmosphere
of suspicion when I applied for a visa in London: the
doorman at the Jordan Legation had held the door open
on a crack and directed me to the rear of the building,
where I climbed up a kind of fire-escape to some rooms
on the top floor, apparently closed off from the rest, in
which an anxious official, alarmed at my having written
"None" after the question about my "Religion"—I had
previously been questioned as to whether I was Jewish
—suggested in a feeble way that he might forward my request to his capital and convinced me that my case was
hopeless. When I did succeed finally, through the efforts
of our consul—who functions in both the Jerusalems—
in crossing the inflamed frontier, I happened to arrive in

Old Jerusalem at the moment when the Israelis were changing the guard at the Hebrew University on Mount Scopus. This institution was founded by Weizmann in 1925 and has a library of a million volumes, but it is an enclave now in Arab territory, under the protection of the United Nations and not available for use by the Israelis, who have thus lost their scholarly equipment and are obliged to house their college where they can. There is also a Mount Scopus hospital which the Israelis had also to abandon when the Arabs, shooting into their convoys, killed several doctors and nurses. The Israeli guard on these buildings is changed every two weeks, and there at the Mandelbaum Gate, in front of the gashed and gutted houses that have been left as they were at the armistice, with their gaping arched Arab windows that so much suggest a life of ease, stood a squad of Arab soldiers at attention, while the gray Israeli trucks, which were blinded so that the inmates could not see out, had their oil drums and food supplies searched.

The medley of sects and religions is seen at its most fantastic in the shrines of the Old City. The so-called Mosque of Omar is a pretty little Moslem rotunda, gracefully arched and domed, and covered with charming blue tiles contributed by Suleiman the Magnificent, that shelters a large yellowish old bumpy rock believed by the Jews to have been, first, the rude altar to which Abraham came with Isaac, then the threshing floor of Araunah the Jebusite, on which David was ordered by God to build the altar that later became that of the Temple. It is surrounded by an iron grille contributed by the Crusaders. This monument is now in the hands of the Arabs, and it is the Moslems who worship there at the consecrated rock of the Jews. The Church of the Holy Sepulcher, which shelters two other rocks, supposedly Calvary and Jesus' Tomb, is guarded by a Mohammedan

doorman, who always has charge of the keys, but it is
otherwise occupied by Christians. This confused and un-
comforting building—on the site of which, according to
legend, Hadrian erected a Temple of Venus, in order to
keep Christians away from it—now houses five Christian
churches, cathedrals within a cathedral: the Greek Orthodox, the Roman Catholic, the Syrian, the Armenian and
the Coptic, the services of which overlap, interrupting
and blurring one another.

The Church of the Holy Sepulcher is badly in need of
repairs—is, in fact, on the point of collapse and only
propped by a precarious scaffolding—but the five cults
responsible for it can never agree as to what is to be
done. When I inquired what was going to happen to it,
I was given the cynical answer that the very next earthquake would shake it down and that no one then would
have to worry. It is a macabre claustrophobic place, and
probably contains more bad taste, certainly more kinds
of bad taste, than any other church in the world. You
enter the imprisoned parvis through the wall of the Arab
street by apertures inconveniently narrow, and are confronted by a great cage of braces that almost conceals
the façade: a metal structure trimmed with barbed wire,
which makes it resemble a station of the old New York ele-
vated railway. Going in, you see first, on your left, an
Oriental bed in an alcove, on which, when he is not on
his feet, the Mohammedan caretaker reclines. (There
are services that take place at night, when visitors are
locked in the church.) Before you, flanked by monstrous
candles that almost reach to the ceiling, that look as if
they were made of celluloid and are painted like postcards or greeting cards with miniature views of Jerusalem
and little bows of blue ribbon, lies the smooth flat red
Unction Stone, where the body of Jesus is supposed to
have lain and which the pilgrims get down on their

knees to kiss, the more fastidious ladies wiping it first with a handkerchief. Exploring the cramped and cluttered, the labyrinthine and closetlike interior, among blue and red balls, tinsel stars and bulbous brass lamps and thuribles that hang from the ceiling like Christmas-tree ornaments, you come upon the Sepulcher itself, which stands like a kind of tower in the center of a gloomy rotunda, the paint of whose dome was peeled off by a fire in 1808 (caused by a drunken Greek monk) and whose paintings are masked by the scaffolds that hold the pillars erect. On the bases of these pillars are fixed strips of glass that will break if a crack occurs. In your efforts to get the hang of this dark and disorganized interior, you may look in on a kind of exhibition room where reliquaries of gold and silver are lit up in a long glass showcase, and where little old women in black are circulating and kissing the part of the glass that is opposite each of the relics. In a chamber of the Russian Church, hung with embroidered pictures that are heavy with Byzantine gold, and portraits of the prelates of the Orthodox Church, half fancy, half photographic, you come upon a bearded old priest, sitting behind a table and competently answering in various languages the questions of a crowd of visitors, who are writing their names in a book. Climbing narrow and high stone stairs, you arrive at a giddying gallery, one corner of which is scribbled with names and addresses from all over the world, among the scrawled scripts of which the word "DUBLIN" stands out, printed. Here you find dreadful modern mosaics—of Abraham and Isaac, and other Old Testament subjects—the gift of the presiding Franciscans. Descending to the crypt by a broad flight of steps, you are handed a candle and penetrate, in the darkness, to the spot where the True Cross is supposed to have been found, in Constantine's time, by the Empress Helena. Above it looms a faceless statue, bulky and spooky in the darkness, that the flame of the candle falls short of.

At the Tenebræ services of Holy Week, the Church of the Holy Sepulcher is jammed by what is, I suppose, one of the most international congregations and one of the most variegated to be seen anywhere in the world. There are excursions of nuns from all over Europe, accompanied by shepherding and ciceroning priests. The white-gowned choristers, the brown-robed Franciscans, the Greek priests in their flat-topped black hats are all in their best clothes. The Latin Patriarch, in a little red cap and a richly embroidered coat, is conducting the Tenebræ office from a throne that faces the Sepulcher. Christianized Arab women, with white headdresses and Arab robes, kneel on the floor with their children. A black nun in a big starched white cap with corners that stick out like wings is praying by herself in a niche so dark that only the bonnet is visible above the huddled figure. Catholic priests and Anglican clergymen stand about in black clothes and British boots. There are whiffs of urine and incense. What if the whole stale and rickety place, fissured by some piercing note, should come down on our heads and bury us! There is also a claustrophobia brought on by the vulgarity and the scrambled cults. One recalls that, at the ceremony of the Holy Fire in 1834, the tension, the heat, and the crowding produced a terrible panic. When the moment has come for this yearly miracle, a specialty of the Eastern rite, the Greek Patriarch passes into the Sepulcher, in which, the day before, Good Friday, the holy flame has been extinguished, and hands out a bunch of candles, bound together in a cage-topped torch, which are supposed to have been ignited without human intervention. The pilgrims and other worshippers, who have often been standing there all night, now press forward to light their own candles—for the fire, rekindled by a miracle, is supposed to ensure salvation. This results in a mad and remorseless scramble.

At the ceremony on Holy Saturday, 1834, the candle smoke became so stifling that three people fell out of the galleries and were killed on the heads of the crowd below. "One poor Armenian lady, seventeen years of age," writes the Honorable Robert Curzon,* who was present, "died where she sat, of heat, thirst and fatigue." On his way out of the church, he continues, "I got as far as the place where the Virgin is said to have stood during the crucifixion, when I saw a number of people one on another . . . [stretching] as far as I could see towards the door. I made my way between them as well as I could, till they were so thick that there was actually a great heap of bodies on which I trod. It then suddenly struck me they were all dead! . . . I . . . saw that sharp hard appearance of the face that is never to be mistaken. Many of them were quite black with suffocation, and further on were others all bloody and covered with the brains and entrails of those who had been trodden to pieces by the crowd." Farther on, he found the crowd trying to get out the great door. "The guards outside [Mohammedans], frightened at the rush from within, thought that the Christians wished to attack them, and the confusion soon grew into a battle. The soldiers with their bayonets killed numbers of fainting wretches, and the walls were spattered with blood and brains of men who had been felled, like oxen, with the butt-ends of the soldiers' muskets. Everyone struggled to defend himself or to get away, and in the mêlée all who fell were immediately trampled to death by the rest. So desperate and savage did the fight become that even the panic-struck and frightened pilgrims appeared at last to have been more intent upon the destruction of each other than

* Visits to the Monasteries of the Levant, London, 1849.

desirous to save themselves." Curzon himself escaped
only by fighting his way back into the body of the church
across the dead and dying. He noticed that the Unction
Stone was piled with corpses. At least five hundred people were killed. And even in 1918, Sir Ronald Storrs was
forced, at this ceremony, to protect from the blows of
the jealous Armenians a visiting Greek archbishop, "as
he passed in glittering tiara from the Tomb to the 'Gol-
gotha Chamber.' " * Not many years before, the Franciscans and Greeks had come to blows over the right to
sweep certain stairs, and bystanders were hurt by the flying stones.

It is a relief to get out of the place and catch a glimpse
of a courtly kaváss—one of those red-fezzed and bright-
jacketed attendants who walk before important personages, pounding the pave with their staffs—engaged in
exchanging amenities with a lady who had just left the
church.

Yet the lasting significance of Jerusalem is not in the
least diminished by the scandal and grotesquerie of the
Holy Sepulcher, by the fact that the Temple has been destroyed and that its site is in the hands of the Moslems,
who will not let a Jew come near it, that the city is now
split across by the quarrel of the Israelis and Arabs. It
has been always of the essence of the Jewish genius that it
works through the spirit and the intellect, that, in spite
of the importance to the Jews of such names as Jerusalem and Zion, it does not need a habitation other than
the souls of men. It is a paradox of Jewish history that
a moral force, an inspiration, which has leapt geographical boundaries and been felt by so many minds, regard-
less of race or class, should have been generated and
transmitted by a people who have carried exclusiveness
to fantastic lengths, who have manifested the extremes of

* *Orientations,* London, 1937.

intolerance and who have suffered from equal intolerance on the part of the champions of other religions which
have taken their cue from the Scriptures. (It is strange to
think that even the Feeneyites, shrieking against the Jews
on Boston Common—the disciples of a heretic priest,
who has taught them that only Catholics can be saved—
should be doing it in the name of a God whom they owe
to the Jewish Bible.) One cannot, of course, blame the
Jews for all the horrors of Mohammedan and Christian
history; bigotry and cruelty are universal. Yet the Bible,
on one of its sides, does tend to encourage both. Julius
Caesar, who dispassionately and ruthlessly cut off the
hands of the Gauls, who slaughtered them and sold them
into slavery, did not do so in the name of God; and the
Greeks, who looked down on the "barbarians" and who
fought them when the necessity arose, did not preach
their extermination on account of their worship of alien
gods. This has been the regrettable side of the influence
of the religious ideas of the Jews: the impulse to fanaticism. The life-giving positive side—often involved with
the other, though certain of the great Jewish teachers
have embodied it in its purest form—is the faith in, the
affirmation of, the power of the human spirit, in touch
with its divine source and independent of place or condition. This paradox, this contradiction, is illustrated in a
striking way by Jesus' conversation with the woman of
Samaria. On my trip to Mount Gerízim to attend the Samaritan Passover, I stopped off at Jacob's Well, at which
this conversation is supposed to have taken place and
which is apparently one of the very few Holy Places that
have any chance of being real, and I reread the scene in
John 4. The purely sectarian issue between the Samaritans and the Jews is brought up in the most typical way.
(Jesus himself—to the Jews a heretic—was accused by
them of being a Samaritan.) "Our fathers," says

the woman to Jesus, "worshipped on this mountain
[Gerízim], and you say that in Jerusalem is the place
where men ought to worship." The reply that Jesus is reported to have made is a curious combination of the old
point of view of the Jews, and the claim to an exclusive
and literal correctness, with the intense religious instinct
that accompanies this and transcends it. "Woman, believe me," He answers, "the hour is coming when neither
on this mountain nor in Jerusalem will you worship the
Father. You worship what you do not know; we worship
what we know, for salvation is from the Jews. But the
hour is coming, and now is, when the true worshippers
will worship the Father in spirit and truth, for such the
Father seeks to worship Him. God is spirit, and those who
worship Him must worship in spirit and truth."

For the Christian, the center of worship was no longer
to be Jerusalem, and the second destruction of the Temple was to compel even the most orthodox Jews (if not
the Samaritans) to dissociate the spirit of God from any
particular place. Even the later Zionists, returning to the
earthly Jerusalem, were loyal to a vision that was hardly
of earth. How implausible it seems that Protestants in
Britain and the United States should be singing their
hymns about Israel, Zion and Jerusalem the Golden, without—for the most part, certainly—attaching to them very
much meaning of an historical or geographical kind! How
implausible that English poets should have written of the
"Traffic of Jacob's ladder/Pitched betwixt Heaven and
Charing Cross," and of fighting to "build Jerusalem/In
England's green and pleasant land"!

I thought, when I returned to the modern Jerusalem,
that the bright light, the high bare hills, were more surely
the Jerusalem of the Psalms and the Prophets than even
the best-documented relics of the Temple and the ancient
wall. This was the Jerusalem of which Jesus said that not

one stone should be left upon another, that it was destined
to be "trodden down of the Gentiles." The substantial
tomb built by Herod for the family that he murdered and
for whose murder he tried thus to atone is still standing,
just behind my hotel. It was right on the firing line during the war and is still snarled about with barbed wire.
During the period of hardship that followed the war, it
was lived in by a destitute family and is full of tin cans
and turds; it has never been cleaned out for tourists.
Nation has risen against nation, as Jesus predicted they
would, and kingdom against kingdom; there is little now
to be read of in the papers save "wars and rumors of
wars." Through this city, among these mountains, have
passed, in the course of some twenty-five centuries, the
Hebrews, the Babylonians, the Greeks, the Persians, the
Romans, the Byzantines, the Arabs, the Turkomans,
the Franks, the Moslems, the Crusaders, the Mongolians,
the Mamelukes, the Turks, the British, the Israelis. Jerusalem has been ruled or governed by—to name only a few,
the most notable—David, Solomon, Nebuchadnezzar,
Nehemiah, Antiochus Epiphanes, the Maccabees, Pom-
pey, the Herods, Pontius Pilate, Bar Kochba, Chosroes
II, Godefroy de Bouillon, Saladin, Suleiman the Magnificent, El-Jazzar, Sir Ronald Storrs and Ben-Gurion. One
can hardly grasp all these vicissitudes—the peoples and
nations and causes, the policies and personalities. Their
history becomes unimaginable, and they all seem to re-
compose, like the sequence of colors of the spectrum, in
this tranquil luminous sky. The Jews made Jerusalem the
high place of God and thus gave it to the whole human
race.

Degániya: Something of this strange disparity between Palestine's baldness and meagerness and the visions it has always evoked was felt even by the Zionist

leader Aaron David Gordon, when he first came in 1904
to what he called, what was called in the Bible, and what
is still called today Éretz Yisraél, the Land of Israel.
"There was born in me a curious emotion," he writes in
one of his letters, "or, rather, a mingling of two conflict-
ing emotions, which is difficult to explain. On the one
hand, it seemed as if this great wide expanse frightened
me and shocked me. It stood naked in the powerful light
that flooded it, revealing all things with cruel brilliancy
as far as the eye could reach and seeming to say, 'Nothing
is hidden from my eyes.' " And he could not look into the
distance, for the mountains shut off his view, "barriers
against my sight." "Many days passed in this frame of
mind before I began to struggle against myself and to
think deeply of the characteristics of Éretz Yisraél: small
and narrow is the land; just back of those mountains it
all but ends—'For the bed is too short for a man to
stretch himself.' . . . What the mind, however, cannot
succeed in doing, life, nature and work achieve. While
the hands learn to work, the ears to hear, the eyes to see,
the heart to feel and to realize what is here, the soul
learns to soar over mountains, to skip over hills, to exalt
itself, to stretch itself to infinite distance, to embrace the
land around, the world and its inhabitants, and to see itself embraced in the arms of the whole world."

He goes on to speak of Russia, with its pogroms and its
trumped-up ritual-murder case, and of the persecution of
the Jews in Poland—in the lofty Biblical manner, never
naming any country or person: "A great and mighty nation storms against you in an outburst of rage, hurls itself
against you like a ravenous beast. . . . I see a different
nation. This nation, too, is unable to stand on its own feet,
and it, too, wishes to swallow you." He goes on, in the
same high prophetic strain, to the problem of assimilation, of the Jews that want other Jews to build a home "in

a land that neither you nor your ancestors have known. You are ready to go wherever they lead you. They teach you to talk the language that their captors have taught them. You say it is your language, and you repeat all that they say; you sing the songs they sing. There is nothing too difficult for you to do; there is no road too narrow for you to follow, no life too insignificant for you to desire. All is small, poor, weak, wretched, wretched—all is in ruins. . . . Desolate, bewildered, I stand and observe you, my people! I observe you with glazed eyes; I do not understand you, and I do not understand myself." Then, "suddenly a spirit touched and wakened me: 'Son of Man!,' and I was among the mountains, high on the summit of a mountain peak. . . . 'Son of Man!' There will yet come a day . . . when your sons and daughters will dream a dream," and they "will come to seek the interpretation of the dream in the land of their fathers. They will seek it with all the power of their hands, with all the strength of their hearts. They will dig it out of hidden places; they will carry on every kind of work in the field and in the vineyard in seeking for it. They will renew the earth and their lives in the search. . . . In the end, they will become great, greater than the mountain peaks on the face of the earth; they will see what no man saw before them, and they will become mighty on the earth. Then will the Jewish people blossom again; then will they stand upright and live; then will they become a nation."

Gordon, who had spent most of his adult life as an official on a baronial estate in Podolia, in southern Russia, came to Palestine in 1904 and died there in 1922. He did not live to see his prophecy fulfilled. But he spent the last ten years of his life in the pioneer community of Degániya (the name means Corn of the Lord), founded in 1909. He had in Poland been rather well off, and he now had the prestige of a sage and saint, but he worked on the land with the rest and shared a room with three other men. Degániya was the first of the movement of self-supporting Jewish collectives, the *kvutzót* and *kibbutzím*. The members of these in the early days must have been all more or less intellectuals, but Tolstóy as well as Zionism had led them to manual labor.

I had been given a letter by a friend at home to a married couple in Degániya, and when I was visiting Galilee, I looked them up. The wife had been a schoolteacher in Prague, who, as a young woman, had interested herself in the refugee Jewish children from Galicia that had been brought to Prague by their parents when their country, at the time of the First World War, had been overrun by the Russian Army. She had told them little stories that proved such a success that she finally published them in a book, which became the first of a popular series. After the war, she emigrated to Palestine. At the time, 1920, the Degániya community had produced a daughter *kvutzáh*, Degániya B, of which she became one of the charter members. She learned Hebrew, taught in the school. Degániya was still more or less a desert, and they endured a good deal of hardship. She is proud of having been one of the pioneers in what was then a daring experiment. The old group had been quite conservative, but the new one set out to practise socialism. "They said we were subversive and crazy, and now the communities are an institution. It was we who launched the whole movement: *Achtung!*" She is a small brown woman with spectacles, who has injured her foot and has to limp but gets along briskly. She is lively, energetic, enthusiastic. Her apartment—by right of seniority, she and her husband are allowed two rooms instead of the usual one—is full of German literature and books on child psychology, and there is a shelf of prehistoric artifacts, picked up in the neighborhood, for she is an amateur archeologist; but I found her in the mending room, where the clothing of the *kvutzáh* is put to rights, busy at the sewing machine. She showed me the school, which the teachers and children were getting ready for Passover, and the building where those children were housed who were not the sons and daughters of community members. A number of these young boys and girls had been among the victims of Hitler. They were orphaned and neurotic and hard to handle. Some of them had had the experience of seeing their parents murdered and finding themselves totally abandoned. The community had taken them in. We visited the chicken house, with its perspective of caged compartments, all full of snow-white fowls, and its enormous mechanical incubators that turned thousands of eggs around. On the grounds stood an old army tank. At the time of the Arab war, the Syrians attacked Degániya, and a battle was fought on the grounds themselves. The enemy was finally driven out, but not before many members had been killed, including several children. There is a monument now to the dead, but the tank has been left as a souvenir, as well as a bit of the trench from which they had fired on the enemy.

These grounds of the collectives, with their flowers and paths, their oases of shady trees, seemed to me peaceful and pleasant, and though I had heard that the communities were sometimes rent by factional disagreements, I did not get an impression of strain. On the contrary, it seemed to me that things were done in a quiet and leisurely way. Everybody is very soft-spoken. The *kvutzáh* is completely self-governing, and every member is responsible for something. They do not pay for food or clothes, schooling or medical service—they even get an allowance of cigarettes. They also accumulate credits, which they draw in money and spend as they please. One thinks at first of the Russian collectives, but the *kvutzáh* is something quite distinct from those. It is voluntary; the members are well educated; they do not hesitate to say what they think. This is rather the old Russian idealism of the beginning of the present century. Tolstóy is mingled with Zionism—one of the principal buildings is named for him—and Socialism of the old, still innocent brand has been made easily to blend with Tolstóy. And there is also a psychology of pioneers that sometimes recalls America. These Zionists, in earlier days, had to contend with malarial swamps, which they have now filled in and made fertile, and with murderous bands of Bedouins, who now would not dare to come near them. When I mentioned that I felt the atmosphere to be one of security and ease, I was reminded at once that all this had been won only by decades of labor, anxious effort and austere living.

The Zionists, I came to realize, have constituted a kind of élite. I have never seen anyone else quite like some of the children of Zionists, who have been born in or come young to Palestine. The wonder is that, growing up there and sometimes having never traveled, they should be so well bred and so well-informed. They reminded me of young modern Greeks. But to have emigrated to Palestine at all, to have made for oneself a life there, implies, of course, on the parents' part, self-confidence and dedicated purpose, a high level of thinking and feeling; and the children have not known at first-hand the humiliations and horrors from which the parents escaped.

Éretz Yisraél: And now what about the Israel that you read about in the papers? If the reader has expected a survey, this chapter is likely to have sounded like one of those tales of Agnón's in which the narrator, in recounting an anecdote of something that happened to his uncle, finds it necessary not only to explain how his grandparents came to get married but also to involve in his story Moses, Aaron and Jeremiah, Akiba, Rashi, Maimonides and the Rabbi Baal Shem Tov. But, as in Agnón's case, so in this—that is, I think, the right way to tell the story. I have already tried to suggest the perspective of three thousand years in which Israel ought to be seen—though the happenings of these millennia, which to the Western mind present a perspective, are somehow, apparently, for the Jewish mind, all contemporary and real at once, and easily identified with one another.

But what about immediate problems? What about the balance of trade, which seems so overwhelmingly against the Israelis? What about the guaranteed profits, the artificially kept-up wages, that are subsidized by foreign philanthropy? The unemployment, the inadequate housing? The obstructions to arranging with their neighbors for the development of the water power of the Jordan River? What of compensating the Arabs for their losses and eliminating border incidents? What about the danger of war? What about Histadrút, that unique yet typical product of twentieth-century industry—a labor organization which is also itself in business and the biggest employer of labor in Israel, and which is sometimes a little ambiguous on the subject of the right to strike—whose imposing new headquarters, outside Tel Aviv, are sometimes referred to as the Kremlin? What about the color problem, since in Israel the black Jews and the white Jews are obliged now to live together, and the two do not care to mix? What of the problem of educating the Yemenites, who have been transported en masse from the south of Arabia—in what was called Operation Magic Carpet—by planes, which did not surprise them, since they took them for the giant birds that an old tradition had promised would rescue them and carry them back to Palestine, but who found themselves, once disembarked, in a terrifying modern world of which they could not make head or tail? How about the Moroccans and Algerians who had to be brought to Israel to save them from the reprisals of the vanquished Arabs, but who seem to have turned out to be riffraff, the only Jews in the world who are not willing to work? I have suggested, I believe, the one answer to this tangle of questions, too. It is the faith that keeps Israel going and that has allowed her to take all these problems on, the faith of the Jewish prophets from Moses to Aaron David Gordon, and the loyalty of contemporary Israelis to this. "When I first came here from Germany," said the doctor from Berlin I have already mentioned, the physician for a large *kvutzáh,* "I didn't feel at all at home—I could easily have gone to America. But after three years I wanted to stay." The visitor soon comes to see why. The Jerusalem that Israelis adore is not the group of mainly modern buildings, the truncated system of streets, neither colorful nor very bustling, on the bristling edge of hostile territory, but the Jerusalem that lives in their hearts.

It is a relief to come here from Europe, from the European discouragement and cultural staleness, the running down and falling apart. Here the people have something to hope for, a survival that is not yet all achieved; and, though bitterly at odds with their neighbors, they are occupied within their own borders with a work of reintegration among their own so diverse elements. One feels at moments that they have even got used to their nasty feud with the Arabs, and do not think much about it. I felt far less tension in Israel when these incidents were going on—though, of course, I was not so much involved —than I did when I returned to the States, to the atmosphere of the McCarthy hearings, Indo-China and the hydrogen bomb, and, as soon as I stepped on the dock, found the task of getting out my baggage through a

porter system stupidly organized—with passengers exasperated and apprehensive, and porters and officials
surly—so much more difficult than in any other country.
I found no such confusion in Israel, no such ordeal for
the nerves (the whole official side of Israeli life has bene-
fited by British training)—not even in Tel Aviv, which
Jerusalem regards as a beehive but which seemed to me,
so far as I saw it, with its cafés, its coffeehouses, its
entertainments and its boulevard along the sea, to have
something of both Athens and Vienna. Fanaticism you
find, yes. Fanaticism, as was said to me by one Israeli, is
always at home in this land. It grows there like cactus
and citrus fruit, fed by the divine light. And yet the Children of Israel are genuinely at ease in Zion. It is remarkable how soon you forget, as they seem almost to have
forgotten, from how far and from how many places they
have come back to live in Palestine.

The Jews, in the nineteenth century, began for the first
time, systematically, to try to explain themselves—their
literature, their history, their customs—to an "enlight-
ened" outside world that was prepared for the first time
to study them—their language, their religion, their morality—in a serious and sympathetic way. Jewish scholars, for example, wrote popular essays—such as those of
Darmesteter and Deutsch, published in France in the sixties—describing the Talmud to Gentiles, and the Christian scholar Calvin Stowe tried to perform the same service, from the Gentile side, for this hitherto mysterious
work—though the first full translation of the Talmud
into English only appeared in the first years of this century. Instead of Marlowe's Barabas and Shakespeare's
Shylock, you had Lessing's Nathan the Wise and George
Eliot's Daniel Deronda. The process of "assimilation"
was rapidly going on, and in some cases went so far that
the Teutonized or Gallicized or Anglicized Jew quite lost

touch with his own tradition; yet there were always re-
crudescences on the part of the "Christians" of the super-
stitious barbarism of the Middle Ages, and the relations
between Gentiles and Jews were always liable to a certain
amount of strain. Now, the return of the Jews to their
country of origin, the reversion to their ancient language
and, with these, a certain relaxation—in the sense that
a steel spring may be said to relax from bending—into
their habits of self-sufficiency, has made it possible for
them to stand alone and not to worry about pleasing some
dominant "race"; digging themselves in has set them free,
with the result—but superficially a paradox—that the
Jews seem in Israel less different instead of more different from other people. This has had its moral effect on
Jews all over the world, and it is the great thing to grasp
about Israel.

POSTSCRIPT

THESE FOUR UNITS were written at intervals of years and without thinking much about them in relation to one another. Rereading them all together, I have been struck by certain features that recur but of which, when I wrote them, I was not aware. In each case, I visited a country for a few weeks or months, read it up, saw as much as I could of it, then came back home and wrote about it. There is revived for me, returning to these pieces, the delightful exhilaration of the kind of foreign travel which has as its main motive simple curiosity. If one has no practical business abroad and no personal responsibilities, one is free to occupy oneself only with the things that interest one—to generalize, to criticize, to idealize. One can meet people and hear what is going on or move about alone as a comfortably detached observer; one can nourish an imaginative picture of national genius or destiny, one can indulge oneself in historical perspectives. If one stays too long in a country, gets to the point of sharing the common life, one is likely to forfeit this—though we know how Americans in France seem sometimes to remain there for years in an ecstasy of admiration for French tolerance and "gracious living" without ever having any idea of the harsh and sordid elements of French life or even making any real contact with the French. I did not spend more than a month in either Zuñi, Haiti or Israel; but I was five months in Soviet Russia, and my journal above has shown how my first impulsive efforts to accommodate my impressions to the ideal of a dream come true gave way to a cannier perception of the actualities of Moscow, and how later, quarantined in Odessa, I was reduced to experiencing Soviet life in more or less the same terms as anyone else.

In the cases of Zuñi, Haiti and Israel, I have paid a good deal of attention to their respective national religions, which, even when no longer believed in, have continued to influence the ideas and habits of those among whom they are rooted. I have tried to understand their myths, to get the hang of their rituals and to appreciate the value of their symbols for the social groups that accept them. In visiting the Soviet Union, however, I supposed that I was seeing a society which had dispensed with myths, rituals and symbols. My respect for the leaders of the October Revolution was based on their championship of logic as against tradition, of social engineering as against reckless competition, of human brains and will as against submission to "God." I had not yet gone far enough into Marxism to have noticed the religious element that Marx and Engels had smuggled into their system, under the illusion that they were rejecting religion and had stripped Hegel's dialectic of its idealistic associations. I had not recognized yet in the Marxist's apotheosis of "History" the Providence of Protestantism or in the working of the "Dialectic" the Calvinist's doctrine of Election. My own Protestant training had given me a special susceptibility to the assertion of moral authority, the affirmation of the power of the spirit, in indifference to, if not in defiance of, what may be called the worldly situation—that is, of the *mise en scène*, the conditions of life, the amenities, even of the people themselves at whom the reformer is directing his message. Hence the title of my book *To the Finland Station*, a study of the modern conception of history, which cul-

minates in Lenin's arrival in Petrograd in April, 1917.
I wanted to contrast this quite commonplace and, when
I saw it, very shabby little railroad station, at which
Lenin, returning from exile, had got off the train and first
spoken to the men of the Revolution, telling them that
they must sweep aside the bourgeoisie and proceed at
once to build socialism, with the confidence of one who
believed that man could control his own destiny—I
wanted to contrast this uninteresting place, accidentally
the scene of a climax in man's moral and political life,
with the imaginary medieval castle of Villers de L'Isle
Adam's *Axël*, which had given its name to an earlier
book. In this classic of the *fin de siècle*, the hero, who tells
his love that, as for living, "our servants can do that for
us," has insulated himself in his vast château, and his
moral triumph consists in his killing himself and his
sweetheart, in his rejection of life itself, which can never
be so satisfactory as his exquisite and intense imaginings;
his ideal is the private enjoyment by the privileged and
exceptional individual of his own nobility and rarity.
The moral triumph of Lenin was to make himself part of
the people, to identify his interest with theirs, to ener-
gize them with his own drive and to guide them to construct, not an aristocratic dream, but a workable human
society. Or so I thought at the time—it was, in any case,
Lenin's intention. That an element of religious faith
might have entered into my attitude toward the Soviet
Union did not at that time occur to me. Yet it seems to
me, rereading my journal, that a yearning for "Holy
Places" is to be seen in my pages on the tomb of Lenin,
even while I am praising him as the prophet of human
self-dependence and competence, as well as in my
feeling that Moscow was "the moral top of the world,"
where "the light never really goes out," at the moment
when the Soviet Union was just about to be enveloped in

a darkness for which "Cimmerian"—since the Cimmerii inhabited the Caucasus—is perhaps the appropriate word. Like so many other inheritors of the eighteenth-century tradition, I was led by the aspect of Marxism that continues and develops that tradition—the acute analysis of social forces and the belief in human progress—into accepting its disguised utopianism and into failing to recognize that the Marxist's conviction of rightness was the result of having swallowed a dogma and gone to live in a myth. It may be, too, that an atavistic Protestantism pre-disposed me toward the Marxist morality.

When I discovered the myth and the dogma, I rejected them as I had the Christian ones; and, in view of the vogue of religion in the literary world at the present time, I want to make it clear, if it is not so already from what I have written above, that for me Sáyatasha and Hútutu, Baron Samedi and Grandmother Erzilie, Jehovah-Elohím and the persons of the Trinity, as well as the Marxist "History" that does duty as a demiurge and the processes of the Dialectic that differ little from the Will of God—that all these are human projections which have to be taken seriously on account of what they have meant—for social cohesion, for dynamic purpose, for moral discipline or contemplative ecstasy—to those who have believed them actuality; but myths, none the less, which, as myths, ought in the long run to be discouraged, since, when carried beyond their special validity for a period or a people, they must come into competition with other such myths and inevitably prove misleading and dangerous. I hope soon to return to this subject in connection with the American Civil War—so much obscured, then and now, by the semi-religious political myths in terms of which we have liked to conceive it.

In the meantime, however, you next find me in Palestine, and you there find me rhapsodizing over Zion and

Jacob's Well very much as I did in Moscow. Again I am announcing the supremacy of moral force and human will over the adventitious aspects of life, the material encumberments of earth. The Holy Places of Leningrad and Moscow have failed to preserve their sanctity with the lapsing of the gospel they consecrated (though this gospel and Lenin's name still keep their prestige for millions, and will eventually, I do not doubt, be admitted, the one among the great revelations, the other among the great statesmen, of the history of human achievement). But in Palestine the failure of gospels was already an ancient story, and most of the Holy Places had been long ago quite effaced by innumerable migrations and wars. Yet undoubtedly the high inspiration that had sprouted in those hills still lived. And, again, for the visiting American, individualistic and Protestant-trained, the moral of Jerusalem, like that of Moscow, was that spiritual power resided, not in temples or altars or tombs, but in the person of the man who possessed it.

And this brings me home again, where it is always so much more difficult to idealize, to generalize. The foreigner may be aware of national conditions or tendencies of which the native is hardly conscious because he takes them for granted; but his success as a critic—as I sometimes feel in connection with my own reports as well as with those of visitors who write books on the United States—is relatively easy and cheap. It is more difficult to make a picture of the people and things among which we live, because we are involved in the picture yet can never dispose of ourselves as a datum for generalization. We have then to try to know what we are and what we are doing on earth. I have found it a good deal harder to understand the history and the meaning of the little town of eighty-odd souls from which, in upstate New York, my mother's family came and to which I still return—

and my own relation to it—than to explain in a plausible way the situation of the one hundred and seventy million people who compose the Soviet Union—and to present my relation to them. So I do not believe I shall publish any more such records of foreign travel. I shall try in the years still before me to deal in a more searching way than I have yet succeeded in doing with the life that I ought to know best.